Through Alternative Lenses
Current Debates in International Relations

FIFTH EDITION

Daniel J. Kaufman

Jay M. Parker

Patrick V. Howell

Kimberly C. Field

UNITED STATES MILITARY ACADEMY

 **Custom Publishing**

Boston   Burr Ridge, IL   Dubuque, IA   Madison, WI   New York
San Francisco   St. Louis   Bangkok   Bogotá   Caracas   Kuala Lumpur
Lisbon   London   Madrid   Mexico City   Milan   Montreal   New Delhi
Santiago   Seoul   Singapore   Sydney   Taipei   Toronto

Through Alternative Lenses
Current Debates in International Relations

1 2 3 4 5 6 7 8 9 0   QSR QSR   0 9 8 7 6 5 4

ISBN 0-07-305392-9

Editor: Ann Jenson
Production Editor: Nina Meyer
Cover Design: Maggie Lytle
Printer/Binder: Quebecor World

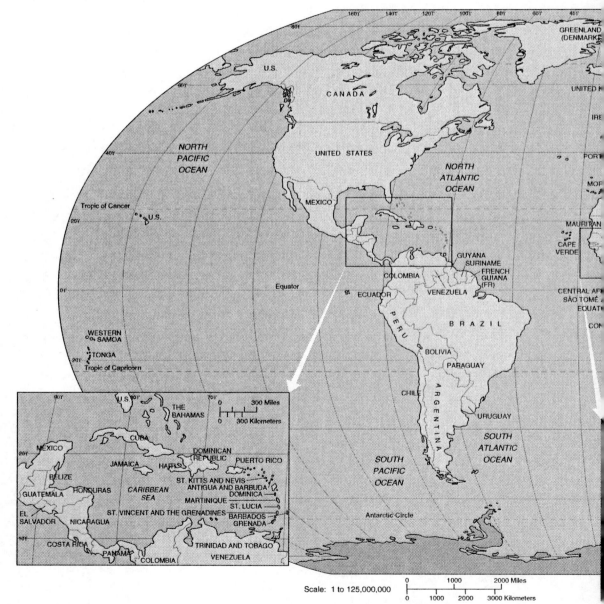

Scale: 1 to 125,000,000

Note: All world maps are Robinson projection.

Table of Contents

Preface

This book was designed as companion to the theoretical text: *Understanding International Relations: The Value of Alternative Lenses (UIR)*. UIR is primarily anchored on the concept of intellectual pluralism—the use of multiple and competing lenses (perspectives) in explaining a single event. It is the purpose of this companion reader to further encourage the development of that skill. You, the student, should be able to explain an international event or an inter-state relationship using more than one set of ideas, ideas from the realist tradition or the idealist, ideas from the security, international political economy, or sub-systemic lens. At the end of this course, you should also be able to evaluate and critique the writing and ideas of others using the lessons you have learned this semester as tools for your analysis.

In this course you will read a great deal of theory. It would be impossible to learn all the facts necessary to equip you to explain events in this ever-changing world; hence, theory. Theory simplifies reality and gives you structures over which to hang individual events. Therefore, we ask you to learn some enduring theoretical works. But simply studying the key concepts of Balance of Power theory, for example, does not mean that you are immediately able to *use* Balance of Power to explain, describe, predict and even prescribe state action. This is where this book comes in. The practice afforded here will help you to learn to handily wield the theoretical tools.

Specifically, you will be asked to read about a particular event or state and to support one of two opposing positions. Neither position is completely right, neither is completely wrong. Often, both sides have merit and, in fact, taken together comprise a big piece of the story. Use theories to provide the foundation and focus for your argument. You will see for yourself that no single theory provides all the answers all of the time. Consider the analogy of the building of a bridge. Is there one single model that comprehensively tells you how to safely and efficiently build the bridge? Of course not. Each technician involved in the design of the bridge views it from a different perspective. To the architect, aesthetics are paramount. The structural engineer is chiefly interested in load-bearing specifications, while the transportation engineer desires the bridge to carry as much traffic as possible. Taken together, the best bridge for the area is designed. There were competing explanations and prescriptions and the bridge builder was not free to guess or build the bridge on a whim. So it is with policymaking as well.

In using theory, you should keep the scientific method in mind. Theory itself is a blunt instrument in accomplishing a task; a hypothesis, however, is a precision tool. Let us look at our construction analogy again to illustrate this point. If the steel erector must bolt a plate to a girder, he may use a standard industrial wrench. He will get the job done, but ponderously. However, and particularly if he is newer at his trade, he would be much better off using a power torque wrench, a precision instrument. The same goes for you, the international relations apprentice, in using the hypotheses derived from theory. A hypothesis will focus your argument and identify readily the variables that need to be supported.

This book combines both supplemental material to be used in debating various issues as well as providing additional theoretical material.

About the Editors

Daniel J. Kaufman, Brigadier General, United States Army—Dean of the Academic Board and Professor of Social Sciences, United States Military Academy. B.S., USMA; M.P.A., Harvard University; Ph.D., Massachusetts Institute of Technology

Jay M. Parker, Colonel, United States Army—Director of International Relations and National Security Studies, Professor of Political and International Affairs, Department of Social Sciences, United States Military Academy. B.A., University of Arizona; M.A., M.P.A., Arizona State University; M.A.I.R., University of Southern California; M.A., Naval War College; Ph.D., Columbia University

Patrick Howell, Major, United States Army—Course Director: International Relations, Assistant Professor, Department of Social Sciences, United States Military Academy. B.S., USMA; M.A.L.D., Fletcher School of Law and Diplomacy—Tufts University

Kimberly C. Field, Major, United States Army—Former Assistant Professor, Department of Social Sciences, United States Military Academy. B.S., USMA; M.A.L.D., Fletcher School of Law and Diplomacy—Tufts University

Part I
Contrasting World Views in Major Policy Statements

In his "Declaration of War Against America", Osama Bin Laden lays out his rationale for confronting the world's sole super-power as well as his policy-strategy in how he intends to lead *al Queda,* a Non-Governmental Organization, to do so.

President Bush's 2002 USMA Graduation Speech outlines his rationale for his highly controversial policy of "Pre-Emption".

Declaration of War against the Americans Occupying the Land of the Two Holy Places

Osama Bin Laden

The following text is a fatwa, or declaration of war, by Osama bin Laden first published in Al Quds Al Arabi, a London-based newspaper, in August, 1996. The fatwa is entitled "Declaration of War against the Americans Occupying the Land of the Two Holy Places."

Praise be to Allah, we seek His help and ask for his pardon. we take refuge in Allah from our wrongs and bad deeds. Who ever been guided by Allah will not be misled, and who ever has been misled, he will never be guided. I bear witness that there is no God except Allah-no associates with Him—and I bear witness that Muhammad is His slave and messenger.

{O you who believe! be careful of—your duty to—Allah with the proper care which is due to Him, and do not die unless you are Muslim} (Imraan; 3:102), {O people be careful of—your duty to—your Lord, Who created you from a single being and created its mate of the same—kind—and spread from these two, many men and women; and be careful of—your duty to—Allah , by whom you demand one of another—your rights-, and (be careful) to the ties of kinship; surely Allah ever watches over you} (An-Nisa; 4:1), {O you who believe! be careful—of your duty—to Allah and speak the right word; He will put your deeds into a right state for you, and forgive you your faults; and who ever obeys Allah and his Apostle, he indeed achieve a mighty success} (Al-Ahzab; 33:70-71).

Praise be to Allah, reporting the saying of the prophet Shu'aib: {I desire nothing but reform so far as I am able, and with non but Allah is the direction of my affair to the right and successful path; on him do I rely and to him do I turn} (Hud; 11:88).

Praise be to Allah, saying: {You are the best of the nations raised up for—the benefit of—men; you enjoin what is right and forbid the wrong and believe in Allah} (Aal-Imraan; 3:110). Allah's blessing and salutations on His slave and messenger who said: (The people are close to an all encompassing punishment from Allah if they see the oppressor and fail to restrain him.)

It should not be hidden from you that the people of Islam had suffered from aggression, iniquity and injustice imposed on them by the Zionist-Crusaders alliance and their collaborators; to the extent that the Muslims blood became the cheapest and their wealth as loot in the hands of the enemies. Their blood was spilled in Palestine and Iraq. The horrifying pictures of the massacre of Qana, in Lebanon are still fresh in our memory. Massacres in Tajakestan, Burma, Cashmere, Assam, Philippine, Fatani, Ogadin, Somalia, Erithria, Chechnia and in Bosnia-Herzegovina took place, massacres that send shivers in the body and shake the conscience. All of this and the world watch and hear, and not only didn't respond to these atrocities, but also with a clear conspiracy between the USA and its' allies and under the cover of the iniquitous United Nations, the dispossessed people were even prevented from obtaining arms to defend themselves.

The people of Islam awakened and realised that they are the main target for the aggression of the Zionist-Crusaders alliance. All false claims and propaganda about "Human Rights" were hammered down and exposed by the massacres that took place against the Muslims in every part of the world.

The latest and the greatest of these aggressions, incurred by the Muslims since the death of the Prophet (ALLAH'S BLESSING AND SALUTATIONS ON HIM) is the occupation of the land of the two Holy Places—the foundation of the house of Islam, the place of the revelation, the source of the message and the place of the noble Ka'ba, the Qiblah of all Muslims—by the armies of the American Crusaders and their allies. (We bemoan this and can only say: "No power and power acquiring except through Allah").

Under the present circumstances, and under the banner of the blessed awakening which is sweeping the world in general and the Islamic world in particular, I meet with you today. And after a long absence, imposed on the scholars (Ulama) and callers (Da'ees) of Islam by the iniquitous crusaders movement under the leadership of the USA; who fears that they, the scholars and callers of Islam, will instigate the Ummah of Islam against its' enemies as their ancestor scholars—may Allah be pleased with them—like Ibn Taymiyyah and Al'iz Ibn Abdes-Salaam did. And therefore the Zionist-Crusader alliance resorted to killing and arresting the truthful Ulama and the working Da'ees (We are not praising or sanctifying them; Allah sanctify whom He pleased). They killed the Mujahid Sheikh Abdullah Azzaam, and they arrested the Mujahid Sheikh Ahmad Yaseen and the Mujahid Sheikh Omar Abdur Rahman (in America).

By orders from the USA they also arrested a large number of scholars, Da'ees and young people—in the land of the two Holy Places—among them the prominent Sheikh Salman Al-Oud'a and Sheikh Safar Al-Hawali and their brothers; (We bemoan this and can only say: "No power and power acquiring except through Allah"). We, myself and my group, have suffered some of this injustice ourselves; we have been prevented from addressing the Muslims. We have been pursued in Pakistan, Sudan and Afghanistan, hence this long absence on my part. But by the Grace of Allah, a safe base is now available in the high Hindukush mountains in Khurasan ; where—by the Grace of Allah—the largest infidel military force of the world was destroyed. And the myth of the super power was withered in front of the Mujahideen cries of Allahu Akbar (God is greater). Today we work from the same mountains to lift the iniquity that had been imposed on the Ummah by the Zionist-Crusader alliance, particularly after they have occupied the blessed land around Jerusalem, route of the journey of the Prophet (ALLAH'S BLESSING AND SALUTATIONS ON HIM) and the land of the two Holy Places. We ask Allah to bestow us with victory, He is our Patron and He is the Most Capable.

From here, today we begin the work, talking and discussing the ways of correcting what had happened to the Islamic world in general, and the Land of the two Holy Places in particular. We wish to study the means that we could follow to return the situation to its' normal path. And to return to the people their own rights, particularly after the large damages and the great aggression on the life and the religion of the people. An injustice that had affected every section and group of the people; the civilians, military and security men, government officials and merchants, the young and the old people as well as schools and university students. Hundred of thousands of the unemployed graduates, who became the widest section of the society, were also affected.

Injustice had affected the people of the industry and agriculture. It affected the people of the rural and urban areas. And almost every body complain about something. The situation at the land of the two Holy places became like a huge volcano at the verge of eruption that would destroy the Kufr and the corruption and its' sources. The explosion at Riyadh and Al-Khobar is a warning of this volcanic eruption emerging as a result of the sever oppression, suffering, excessive iniquity, humiliation and poverty.

People are fully concerned about their every day livings; every body talks about the deterioration of the economy, inflation, ever increasing debts and jails full of prisoners. Government employees with limited income talk about debts of ten thousands and hundred thousands of Saudi Riyals . They complain that the value of the Riyal is greatly and continuously deteriorating among most of the main currencies. Great merchants and contractors speak about hundreds and thousands of million Riyals owed to them by the government. More than three hundred forty billions of Riyal owed by the government to the people in addition to the daily accumulated interest, let alone the foreign debt. People wonder whether we are the largest oil exporting country?! They even believe that this situation is a curse put on them by Allah for not objecting to the oppressive and illegitimate behaviour and measures of the ruling regime: Ignoring the divine Shari'ah law; depriving people of their legitimate rights; allowing the American to occupy the land of the two Holy Places; imprisonment, unjustly, of the sincere scholars. The honourable Ulamah and scholars as well as merchants, economists and eminent people of the country were all alerted by this disastrous situation.

Quick efforts were made by each group to contain and to correct the situation. All agreed that the country is heading toward a great catastrophe, the depth of which is not known except by Allah. One big merchant commented : '' the king is leading the state into 'sixty-six' folded disaster'', (We bemoan this and can only say: "No power and power acquiring except through Allah"). Numerous princes share with the people their feelings, privately expressing their concerns and objecting to the corruption, repression and the intimidation taking place in the country. But the competition between influential princes for personal gains and interest had destroyed the country. Through its course of actions the regime has torn off its legitimacy:

1. Suspension of the Islamic Shari'ah law and exchanging it with man made civil law. The regime entered into a bloody confrontation with the truthful Ulamah and the righteous youths (we sanctify nobody; Allah sanctify Whom He pleaseth).
2. The inability of the regime to protect the country, and allowing the enemy of the Ummah— the American crusader forces—to occupy the land for the longest of years. The crusader forces became the main cause of our disastrous condition, particularly in the economical aspect of it due to the unjustified heavy spending on these forces. As a result of the policy imposed on the country, especially in the field of oil industry where production is restricted or expanded and prices are fixed to suit the American economy ignoring the economy of the country. Expensive deals were imposed on the country to purchase arms. People asking what is the justification for the very existence of the regime then?

Quick efforts were made by individuals and by different groups of the society to contain the situation and to prevent the danger. They advised the government both privately and openly; they send letters and poems, reports after reports, reminders after reminders, they explored every avenue and enlist every influential man in their movement of reform and correction. They wrote with style of passion, diplomacy and wisdom asking for corrective measures and repentance from the "great wrong doings and corruption " that had engulfed even the basic principles of the religion and the legitimate rights of the people.

But—to our deepest regret—the regime refused to listen to the people accusing them of being ridiculous and imbecile. The matter got worse as previous wrong doings were followed by mischief's of greater magnitudes. All of this taking place in the land of the two Holy Places! It is no longer possible to be quiet. It is not acceptable to give a blind eye to this matter.

As the extent of these infringements reached the highest of levels and turned into demolishing forces threatening the very existence of the Islamic principles, a group of scholars—who can take no more—supported by hundreds of retired officials, merchants, prominent and educated people wrote to the King asking for implementation of the corrective measures. In 1411 A.H. (May 1991), at the time of the gulf war, a letter, the famous letter of Shawwaal, with over four hundred signatures was send to the king demanding the lift of oppression and the implementation of corrective actions. The king humiliated those people and choose to ignore the content of their letter; and the very bad situation of the country became even worse.

People, however, tried again and send more letters and petitions. One particular report, the glorious Memorandum Of Advice, was handed over to the king on Muharram, 1413 A.H (July 1992), which tackled the problem pointed out the illness and prescribed the medicine in an original, righteous and scientific style. It described the gaps and the shortcoming in the philosophy of the regime and suggested the required course of action and remedy. The report gave a description of:

1. The intimidation and harassment suffered by the leaders of the society, the scholars, heads of tribes, merchants, academic teachers and other eminent individuals;
2. The situation of the law within the country and the arbitrary declaration of what is Halal and Haram (lawful and unlawful) regardless of the Shari'ah as instituted by Allah;
3. The state of the press and the media which became a tool of truth—hiding and misinformation; the media carried out the plan of the enemy of idolising cult of certain personalities and spreading scandals among the believers to repel the people away from their religion, as Allah, the Exalted said: {surely—as for—those who love that scandal should circulate between the believers, they shall have a grievous chastisement in this world and in the here after} (An-Noor, 24:19).
4. Abuse and confiscation of human rights;
5. The financial and the economical situation of the country and the frightening future in the view of the enormous amount of debts and interest owed by the government; this is at the time when the wealth of the Ummah being wasted to satisfy personal desires of certain individuals!! while imposing more custom duties and taxes on the nation. (the prophet said about the woman who committed adultery: "She repented in such a way sufficient to bring forgiveness to a custom collector!!").,
6. The miserable situation of the social services and infra-structure especially the water service and supply , the basic requirement of life.,
7. The state of the ill-trained and ill-prepared army and the impotence of its commander in chief despite the incredible amount of money that has been spent on the army. The gulf war clearly exposed the situation.,
8. Shari'a law was suspended and man made law was used instead.,
9. And as far as the foreign policy is concerned the report exposed not only how this policy has disregarded the Islamic issues and ignored the Muslims, but also how help and support were provided to the enemy against the Muslims; the cases of Gaza-Ariha and the communist in the south of Yemen are still fresh in the memory, and more can be said.

As stated by the people of knowledge, it is not a secret that to use man made law instead of the Shari'a and to support the infidels against the Muslims is one of the ten "voiders" that would strip a person from his Islamic status (turn a Muslim into a Mushrik, non believer status). The All Mighty said: {and whoever did not judge by what Allah revealed, those are the unbelievers} (Al-Ma'ida; 5:44), and {but no! by your Lord! they do not believe (in reality) until they make you a judge of that which has become a matter of disagreement among them, and then do not find the slightest misgiving in their hearts as to what you have decided and submit with entire submission} (An-Nissa; 4:65).

In spite of the fact that the report was written with soft words and very diplomatic style, reminding of Allah, giving truthful sincere advice, and despite of the importance of advice in Islam—being absolutely essential for those in charge of the people—and the large number who signed this document as well as their supporters, all of that was not an intercession for the Memorandum . Its' content was rejected and those who signed it and their sympathisers were ridiculed, prevented from travel, punished and even jailed.

Therefore it is very clear that the advocates of correction and reform movement were very keen on using peaceful means in order to protect the unity of the country and to prevent blood shed. Why is it then the regime closed all peaceful routes and pushed the people toward armed actions?!! which is the only choice left for them to implement righteousness and justice. To whose benefit does prince Sultan and prince Nayeff push the country into a civil war that will destroy everything? and why consulting those who ignites internal feuds, playing the people against each other and instigate the policemen, the sons of the nation, to abort the reform movement. While leaving in peace and security such traitors who implement the policy of the enemy in order to bleed the financial and the human resources of the Ummah, and leaving the main enemy in the area—the American Zionist alliance enjoy peace and security?!

The advisor (Zaki Badr, the Egyptian ex-minister of the interior) to prince Nayeff—minister of interior—was not acceptable even to his own country; he was sacked from his position there due to the filthy attitude and the aggression he exercised on his own people, yet he was warmly welcomed by prince Nayeff to assist in sins and aggressions. He unjustly filled the prisons with the best sons of this Ummah and caused miseries to their mothers. Does the regime want to play the civilians against their military personnel and vice versa, like what had happened in some of the neighbouring countries?!! No doubts this is the policy of the American-Israeli alliance as they are the first to benefit from this situation.

But with the grace of Allah, the majority of the nation, both civilians and military individuals are aware of the wicked plan. They refused to be played against each others and to be used by the regime as a tool to carry out the policy of the American-Israeli alliance through their agent in our country: the Saudi regime.

Therefore every one agreed that the situation can not be rectified (the shadow cannot be straighten when its' source, the rod, is not straight either) unless the root of the problem is tackled. Hence it is essential to hit the main enemy who divided the Ummah into small and little countries and pushed it, for the last few decades, into a state of confusion. The Zionist-Crusader alliance moves quickly to contain and abort any "corrective movement" appearing in the Islamic countries. Different means and methods are used to achieve their target; on occasion the "movement" is dragged into an armed struggle at a predetermined unfavourable time and place. Sometime officials from the Ministry of Interior, who are also graduates of the colleges of the Shari'ah, are leashed out to mislead and confuse the nation and the Ummah (by wrong Fatwas) and to circulate false information about the movement. At other occasions some righteous people were tricked into a war of words against the Ulama and the leaders of the movement, wasting the energy of the nation in discussing minor issues and ignoring the main one that is the unification of the people under the divine law of Allah.

In the shadow of these discussions and arguments truthfulness is covered by the falsehood, and personal feuds and partisanship created among the people increasing the division and the weakness of the Ummah; priorities of the Islamic work are lost while the blasphemy and polytheism continue its grip and control over the Ummah. We should be alert to these atrocious plans carried out by the Ministry of Interior. The right answer is to follow what have been decided by the people of knowledge, as was said by Ibn Taymiyyah (Allah's mercy upon him): "people of Islam should join forces and support each other to get rid of the main "Kufr" who is controlling the countries of the Islamic world, even to bear the lesser damage to get rid of the major one, that is the great Kufr".

If there are more than one duty to be carried out, then the most important one should receive priority. Clearly after Belief (Imaan) there is no more important duty than pushing the American enemy out of the holy land. No other priority, except Belief, could be considered before it; the people of knowledge, Ibn Taymiyyah, stated: "to fight in defence of religion and Belief is a collective duty; there is no other duty after Belief than fighting the enemy who is corrupting the life and the religion. There is no preconditions for this duty and the enemy should be fought with one best abilities. (ref: supplement of Fatawa). If it is not possible to push back the enemy except by the collective movement of the Muslim people, then there is a duty on the Muslims to ignore the minor differences among themselves; the ill effect of ignoring these differences, at a given period of time, is much less than the ill effect of the occupation of the Muslims' land by the main Kufr. Ibn Taymiyyah had explained this issue and emphasised the importance of dealing with the major threat on the expense of the minor one. He described the situation of the Muslims and the Mujahideen and stated that even the military personnel who are not practising Islam are not exempted from the duty of Jihad against the enemy.

Ibn Taymiyyah , after mentioning the Moguls (Tatar) and their behaviour in changing the law of Allah, stated that: the ultimate aim of pleasing Allah, raising His word, instituting His religion and obeying His messenger (ALLAH'S BLESSING AND SALUTATIONS ON HIM) is to fight the enemy, in every aspects and in a complete manner; if the danger to the religion from not fighting is greater than that of fighting, then it is a duty to fight them even if the intention of some of the fighter is not pure i.e . fighting for the sake of leadership (personal gain) or if they do not observe some of the rules and commandments of Islam. To repel the greatest of the two dangers on the expense of the lesser one is an Islamic principle which should be observed. It was the tradition of the people of the Sunnah (Ahlul-Sunnah) to join and invade—fight—with the righteous and non righteous men. Allah may support this religion by righteous and non righteous people as told by the prophet (ALLAH'S BLESSING AND SALU-TATIONS ON HIM). If it is not possible to fight except with the help of non righteous military person-nel and commanders, then there are two possibilities: either fighting will be ignored and the others, who are the great danger to this life and religion, will take control; or to fight with the help of non righteous rulers and therefore repelling the greatest of the two dangers and implementing most, though not all, of the Islamic laws. The latter option is the right duty to be carried out in these cir-cumstances and in many other similar situation. In fact many of the fights and conquests that took place after the time of Rashidoon, the guided Imams, were of this type. (majmoo' al Fatawa, 26/506).

No one, not even a blind or a deaf person , can deny the presence of the widely spread mischief's or the prevalence of the great sins that had reached the grievous iniquity of polytheism and to share with Allah in His sole right of sovereignty and making of the law. The All Mighty stated: {And when Luqman said to his son while he admonish him: O my son! do not associate ought with Allah; most surely polytheism is a grievous iniquity} (Luqman; 31:13). Man fabricated laws were put forward per-mitting what has been forbidden by Allah such as usury (Riba) and other matters. Banks dealing in usury are competing, for lands, with the two Holy Places and declaring war against Allah by disobey-ing His order {Allah has allowed trading and forbidden usury} (Baqarah; 2:275). All this taking place at the vicinity of the Holy Mosque in the Holy Land! Allah (SWT) stated in His Holy Book a unique promise (that had not been promised to any other sinner) to the Muslims who deals in usury: {O you who believe! Be careful of your duty to Allah and relinquish what remains (due) from usury, if you are believers * But if you do (it) not, then be appraised of WAR from Allah and His Apostle} (Baqarah; 2:278-279). This is for the "Muslim" who deals in usury (believing that it is a sin), what is it then to the person who make himself a partner and equal to Allah, legalising (usury and other sins) what has been forbidden by Allah. Despite of all of the above we see the government misled and dragged some of the righteous Ulamah and Da'ees away from the issue of objecting to the greatest of sins and Kufr. (We bemoan this and can only say: "No power and power acquiring except through Allah").

Under such circumstances, to push the enemy—the greatest Kufr—out of the country is a prime duty. No other duty after Belief is more important than the duty of had . Utmost effort should be made to prepare and instigate the Ummah against the enemy, the American-Israeli alliance—occupy-ing the country of the two Holy Places and the route of the Apostle (Allah's Blessings and Salutations may be on him) to the Furthest Mosque (Al-Aqsa Mosque). Also to remind the Muslims not to be engaged in an internal war among themselves, as that will have grieve consequences namely:

1. consumption of the Muslims human resources as most casualties and fatalities will be among the Muslims people.
2. Exhaustion of the economic and financial resources.

3. Destruction of the country infrastructures
4. Dissociation of the society
5. Destruction of the oil industries. The presence of the USA Crusader military forces on land, sea and air of the states of the Islamic Gulf is the greatest danger threatening the largest oil reserve in the world. The existence of these forces in the area will provoke the people of the country and induces aggression on their religion, feelings and prides and push them to take up armed struggle against the invaders occupying the land; therefore spread of the fighting in the region will expose the oil wealth to the danger of being burned up. The economic interests of the States of the Gulf and the land of the two Holy Places will be damaged and even a greater damage will be caused to the economy of the world. I would like here to alert my brothers, the Mujahideen, the sons of the nation, to protect this (oil) wealth and not to include it in the battle as it is a great Islamic wealth and a large economical power essential for the soon to be established Islamic state, by Allah's Permission and Grace. We also warn the aggressors, the USA, against burning this Islamic wealth (a crime which they may commit in order to prevent it, at the end of the war, from falling in the hands of its legitimate owners and to cause economic damages to the competitors of the USA in Europe or the Far East, particularly Japan which is the major consumer of the oil of the region).
6. Division of the land of the two Holy Places, and annexing of the northerly part of it by Israel. Dividing the land of the two Holy Places is an essential demand of the Zionist-Crusader alliance. The existence of such a large country with its huge resources under the leadership of the forthcoming Islamic State, by Allah's Grace, represent a serious danger to the very existence of the Zionist state in Palestine. The Nobel Ka'ba,—the Qiblah of all Muslims—makes the land of the two Holy Places a symbol for the unity of the Islamic world. Moreover, the presence of the world largest oil reserve makes the land of the two Holy Places an important economical power in the Islamic world. The sons of the two Holy Places are directly related to the life style (Seerah) of their forefathers, the companions, may Allah be pleased with them. They consider the Seerah of their forefathers as a source and an example for re-establishing the greatness of this Ummah and to raise the word of Allah again. Furthermore the presence of a population of fighters in the south of Yemen, fighting in the cause of Allah, is a strategic threat to the Zionist-Crusader alliance in the area. The Prophet (ALLAH'S BLESSING AND SALUTATIONS ON HIM) said: (around twelve thousands will emerge from Aden/Abian helping—the cause of—Allah and His messenger, they are the best, in the time, between me and them) narrated by Ahmad with a correct trustworthy reference.
7. An internal war is a great mistake, no matter what reasons are there for it. the presence of the occupier—the USA—forces will control the outcome of the battle for the benefit of the international Kufr.

I address now my brothers of the security and military forces and the national guards may Allah preserve you hoard for Islam and the Muslims people:

O you protectors of unity and guardians of Faith; O you descendent of the ancestors who carried the light (torch) of guidance and spread it all over the world. O you grandsons of Sa'd Ibn Abi Waqqaas , Almothanna Ibn Haritha Ash-Shaybani , Alga'ga' Ibn Amroo Al-Tameemi and those pious companions who fought Jihad alongside them; you competed to join the army and the guard forces with the intention to carry out Jihad in the cause of Allah—raising His word—and to defend the faith of Islam and the land of the two Holy Places against the invaders and the occupying forces. That is the ultimate level of believing in this religion "Deen". But the regime had reversed these principles and their understanding, humiliating the Ummah and disobeying Allah. Half a century ago the rulers promised the Ummah to regain the first Qiblah, but fifty years later new generation arrived and the promises have been changed; Al-Aqsa Mosque handed over to the Zionists and the wounds of the

Ummah still bleeding there. At the time when the Ummah has not regained the first Qiblah and the rout of the journey of the Prophet (Allah's Blessings and Salutations may be on him), and despite of all of the above, the Saudi regime had stunt the Ummah in the remaining sanctities, the Holy city of Makka and the mosque of the Prophet (Al-Masjid An-Nabawy), by calling the Christians army to defend the regime. The crusaders were permitted to be in the land of the two Holy Places. Not surprisingly though, the King himself wore the cross on his chest. The country was widely opened from the north-to-the south and from east-to-the west for the crusaders. The land was filled with the military bases of the USA and the allies. The regime became unable to keep control without the help of these bases. You know more than any body else about the size, intention and the danger of the presence of the USA military bases in the area. The regime betrayed the Ummah and joined the Kufr, assisting and helping them against the Muslims. It is well known that this is one of the ten "voiders" of Islam, deeds of de-Islamisation. By opening the Arab peninsula to the crusaders the regime disobeyed and acted against what has been enjoined by the messenger of Allah (Allah's Blessings and Salutations may be on him), while he was at the bed of his death: (Expel the polytheists out of the Arab Peninsula); (narrated by Al-Bukhari) and: (If I survive, Allah willing, I'll expel the Jews and the Christians out of the Arab Peninsula); saheeh Aljame' As-Sagheer.

It is out of date and no longer acceptable to claim that the presence of the crusaders is necessity and only a temporary measures to protect the land of the two Holy Places. Especially when the civil and the military infrastructures of Iraq were savagely destroyed showing the depth of the Zionist-Crusaders hatred to the Muslims and their children, and the rejection of the idea of replacing the crusaders forces by an Islamic force composed of the sons of the country and other Muslim people. moreover the foundations of the claim and the claim it self were demolished and wiped out by the sequence of speeches given by the leaders of the Kuffar in America. The latest of these speeches was the one given by William Perry, the Defense Secretary, after the explosion in Al-Khobar saying that: the presence of the American solders there is to protect the interest of the USA. The imprisoned Sheikh Safar Al-Hawali, may Allah hasten his release, wrote a book of seventy pages; in it he presented evidence and proof that the presence of the Americans in the Arab Peninsula is a pre-planed military occupation. The regime want to deceive the Muslim people in the same manner when the Palestinian fighters, Mujahideen, were deceived causing the loss of Al-Aqsa Mosque. In 1304 A.H (1936 AD) the awakened Muslims nation of Palestine started their great struggle, Jihad, against the British occupying forces. Britain was impotent to stop the Mujahideen and their Jihad, but their devil inspired that there is no way to stop the armed struggle in Palestine unless through their agent King Abdul Azeez, who managed to deceives the Mujahideen. King Abdul Azeez carried out his duty to his British masters. He sent his two sons to meet the Mujahideen leaders and to inform them that King Abdul Azeez would guarantee the promises made by the British government in leaving the area and responding positively to the demands of the Mujahideen if the latter stop their Jihad. And so King Abdul Azeez caused the loss of the first Qiblah of the Muslims people. The King joined the crusaders against the Muslims and instead of supporting the Mujahideen in the cause of Allah, to liberate the Al-Aqsa Mosque, he disappointed and humiliated them.

Today, his son, king Fahd, trying to deceive the Muslims for the second time so as to loose what is left of the sanctities. When the Islamic world resented the arrival of the crusader forces to the land of the two Holy Places, the king told lies to the Ulamah (who issued Fatwas about the arrival of the Americans) and to the gathering of the Islamic leaders at the conference of Rabitah which was held in the Holy City of Makka. The King said that: "the issue is simple, the American and the alliance forces will leave the area in few months". Today it is seven years since their arrival and the regime is not able to move them out of the country. The regime made no confession about its inability and carried on lying to the people claiming that the American will leave. But never-never again ; a believer will not be bitten twice from the same hole or snake! Happy is the one who takes note of the sad experience of the others!!

Instead of motivating the army, the guards, and the security men to oppose the occupiers, the regime used these men to protect the invaders, and further deepening the humiliation and the betrayal. (We bemoan this and can only say: "No power and power acquiring except through Allah"). To those little group of men within the army, police and security forces, who have been tricked and pressured by the regime to attack the Muslims and spill their blood, we would like to remind them of the narration: (I promise war against those who take my friends as their enemy) narrated by Al—Bukhari. And his saying (Allah's Blessings and Salutations may be on him) saying of: (In the day of judgement a man comes holding another and complaining being slain by him. Allah, blessed be His Names, asks: Why did you slay him?! The accused replies: I did so that all exaltation may be Yours. Allah, blessed be His Names, says: All exaltation is indeed mine! Another man comes holding a fourth with a similar complaint. Allah, blessed be His Names, asks: Why did you kill him?! The accused replies: I did so that exaltation may be for Mr. X! Allah, blessed be His Names, says: exaltation is mine, not for Mr. X, carry all the slain man's sins (and proceed to the Hell fire)!). In another wording of An-Nasa'i: "The accused says: for strengthening the rule or kingdom of Mr. X"

Today your brothers and sons, the sons of the two Holy Places, have started their Jihad in the cause of Allah, to expel the occupying enemy from of the country of the two Holy places. And there is no doubt you would like to carry out this mission too, in order to re-establish the greatness of this Ummah and to liberate its' occupied sanctities. Nevertheless, it must be obvious to you that, due to the imbalance of power between our armed forces and the enemy forces, a suitable means of fighting must be adopted i.e using fast moving light forces that work under complete secrecy. In other word to initiate a guerrilla warfare, were the sons of the nation, and not the military forces, take part in it. And as you know, it is wise, in the present circumstances, for the armed military forces not to be engaged in a conventional fighting with the forces of the crusader enemy (the exceptions are the bold and the forceful operations carried out by the members of the armed forces individually, that is without the movement of the formal forces in its conventional shape and hence the responses will not be directed, strongly, against the army) unless a big advantage is likely to be achieved; and great losses induced on the enemy side (that would shaken and destroy its foundations and infrastructures) that will help to expel the defeated enemy from the country.

The Mujahideen, your brothers and sons, requesting that you support them in every possible way by supplying them with the necessary information, materials and arms. Security men are especially asked to cover up for the Mujahideen and to assist them as much as possible against the occupying enemy; and to spread rumours, fear and discouragement among the members of the enemy forces.

We bring to your attention that the regime, in order to create a friction and feud between the Mujahideen and yourselves, might resort to take a deliberate action against personnel of the security, guards and military forces and blame the Mujahideen for these actions. The regime should not be allowed to have such opportunity.

The regime is fully responsible for what had been incurred by the country and the nation; however the occupying American enemy is the principle and the main cause of the situation . Therefore efforts should be concentrated on destroying, fighting and killing the enemy until, by the Grace of Allah, it is completely defeated. The time will come—by the Permission of Allah—when you'll perform your decisive role so that the word of Allah will be supreme and the word of the infidels (Kaferoon) will be the inferior. You will hit with iron fist against the aggressors. You'll re-establish the normal course and give the people their rights and carry out your truly Islamic duty. Allah willing, I'll have a separate talk about these issues.

My Muslim Brothers (particularly those of the Arab Peninsula): The money you pay to buy American goods will be transformed into bullets and used against our brothers in Palestine and tomorrow (future) against our sons in the land of the two Holy places. By buying these goods we are strengthening their economy while our dispossession and poverty increases.

Muslims Brothers of land of the two Holy Places:

It is incredible that our country is the world largest buyer of arms from the USA and the area biggest commercial partners of the Americans who are assisting their Zionist brothers in occupying Palestine and in evicting and killing the Muslims there, by providing arms, men and financial supports.

To deny these occupiers from the enormous revenues of their trading with our country is a very important help for our Jihad against them. To express our anger and hate to them is a very important moral gesture. By doing so we would have taken part in (the process of) cleansing our sanctities from the crusaders and the Zionists and forcing them, by the Permission of Allah, to leave disappointed and defeated.

We expect the woman of the land of the two Holy Places and other countries to carry out their role in boycotting the American goods.

If economical boycotting is intertwined with the military operations of the Mujahideen, then defeating the enemy will be even nearer, by the Permission of Allah. However if Muslims don't co-operate and support their Mujahideen brothers then , in effect, they are supplying the army of the enemy with financial help and extending the war and increasing the suffering of the Muslims.

The security and the intelligence services of the entire world can not force a single citizen to buy the goods of his/her enemy. Economical boycotting of the American goods is a very effective weapon of hitting and weakening the enemy, and it is not under the control of the security forces of the regime.

Before closing my talk, I have a very important message to the youths of Islam, men of the brilliant future of the Ummah of Muhammad (ALLAH'S BLESSING AND SALUTATIONS ON HIM). Our talk with the youths about their duty in this difficult period in the history of our Ummah. A period in which the youths and no one else came forward to carry out the variable and different duties. While some of the well known individuals had hesitated in their duty of defending Islam and saving themselves and their wealth from the injustice, aggression and terror—exercised by the government— the youths (may Allah protect them) were forthcoming and raised the banner of Jihad against the American-Zionist alliance occupying the sanctities of Islam. Others who have been tricked into loving this materialistic world, and those who have been terrorised by the government choose to give legitimacy to the greatest betrayal , the occupation of the land of the two Holy Places (We bemoan this and can only say: "No power and power acquiring except through Allah"). We are not surprised from the action of our youths. The youths were the companions of Muhammad (Allah's Blessings and Salutations may be on him), and was it not the youths themselves who killed Aba-Jahl, the Pharaoh of this Ummah?. Our youths are the best descendent of the best ancestors.

Abdul-Rahman Ibn Awf—may Allah be pleased with him—said: (I was at Badr where I noticed two youths one to my right and the other to my left. One of them asked me quietly (so not to be heard by the other) : O uncle point out Aba-Jahl to me. What do you want him for? , said Abdul Rahman. The boy answered: I have been informed that he—Aba-Jahl—abused the Messenger of Allah (), I swear by Allah, who have my soul in His hand, that if I see Aba-Jahl I'll not let my shadow departs his shadow till one of us is dead. I was astonished, said Abdul Rahman; then the other youth said the same thing as the first one. Subsequently I saw Aba-Jahl among the people; I said to the boys do you see? this is the man you are asking me about. The two youths hit Aba-Jahl with their swords till he was dead. Allah is the greatest, Praise be to Him: Two youths of young age but with great perseverance, enthusiasm, courage and pride for the religion of Allah's, each one of them asking about the most important act of killing that should be induced on the enemy. That is the killing of the pharaoh of this Ummah—Aba Jahl-, the leader of the unbelievers (Mushrikeen) at the battle of Badr. The role of Abdul Rahman Ibn Awf , may Allah be pleased with him, was to direct the two youths toward Aba-Jahl. That was the perseverance and the enthusiasm of the youths of that time and that was the perseverance and the enthusiasm of their fathers. It is this role that is now required from the people who have the expertise and knowledge in fighting the enemy. They should guide their brothers and sons in this matter; once that has been done, then our youths will repeat what their forefathers had said before: "I swear by Allah if I see him I'll not let my shadow to departs from his shadow till one of us is dead".

And the story of Abdur-Rahman Ibn Awf about Ummayyah Ibn Khalaf shows the extent of Bilal's (may Allah be pleased with him) persistence in killing the head of the Kufr: "the head of Kufr is Ummayyah Ibn Khalaf.... I shall live not if he survives" said Bilal.

Few days ago the news agencies had reported that the Defence Secretary of the Crusading Americans had said that "the explosion at Riyadh and Al-Khobar had taught him one lesson: that is not to withdraw when attacked by coward terrorists".

We say to the Defence Secretary that his talk can induce a grieving mother to laughter! and shows the fears that had enshrined you all. Where was this false courage of yours when the explosion in Beirut took place on 1983 AD (1403 A.H). You were turned into scattered pits and pieces at that time; 241 mainly marines solders were killed. And where was this courage of yours when two explosions made you to leave Aden in lees than twenty four hours!

But your most disgraceful case was in Somalia; where—after vigorous propaganda about the power of the USA and its post cold war leadership of the new world order—you moved tens of thousands of international force, including twenty eight thousands American solders into Somalia. However, when tens of your solders were killed in minor battles and one American Pilot was dragged in the streets of Mogadishu you left the area carrying disappointment, humiliation, defeat and your dead with you. Clinton appeared in front of the whole world threatening and promising revenge , but these threats were merely a preparation for withdrawal. You have been disgraced by Allah and you withdrew; the extent of your impotence and weaknesses became very clear. It was a pleasure for the "heart" of every Muslim and a remedy to the "chests" of believing nations to see you defeated in the three Islamic cities of Beirut , Aden and Mogadishu.

I say to Secretary of Defence: The sons of the land of the two Holy Places had come out to fight against the Russian in Afghanistan, the Serb in Bosnia-Herzegovina and today they are fighting in Chechenia and—by the Permission of Allah—they have been made victorious over your partner, the Russians. By the command of Allah, they are also fighting in Tajakistan.

I say: Since the sons of the land of the two Holy Places feel and strongly believe that fighting (Jihad) against the Kuffar in every part of the world, is absolutely essential; then they would be even more enthusiastic, more powerful and larger in number upon fighting on their own land—the place of their births—defending the greatest of their sanctities, the noble Ka'ba (the Qiblah of all Muslims). They know that the Muslims of the world will assist and help them to victory. To liberate their sanctities is the greatest of issues concerning all Muslims; It is the duty of every Muslims in this world.

I say to you William (Defence Secretary) that: These youths love death as you loves life. They inherit dignity, pride, courage, generosity, truthfulness and sacrifice from father to father. They are most delivering and steadfast at war. They inherit these values from their ancestors (even from the time of the Jaheliyyah, before Islam). These values were approved and completed by the arriving Islam as stated by the messenger of Allah (Allah's Blessings and Salutations may be on him): "I have been send to perfecting the good values". (Saheeh Al-Jame' As-Sagheer).

When the pagan King Amroo Ibn Hind tried to humiliate the pagan Amroo Ibn Kulthoom, the latter cut the head of the King with his sword rejecting aggression, humiliation and indignation.

If the king oppresses the people excessively, we reject submitting to humiliation.

By which legitimacy (or command) O Amroo bin Hind you want us to be degraded?!

By which legitimacy (or command) O Amroo bin Hind you listen to our foes and disrespect us?!

Our toughness has, O Amroo, tired the enemies before you, never giving in!

Our youths believe in paradise after death. They believe that taking part in fighting will not bring their day nearer; and staying behind will not postpone their day either. Exalted be to Allah who said: {And a soul will not die but with the permission of Allah, the term is fixed} (Aal Imraan; 3:145). Our youths believe in the saying of the messenger of Allah (Allah's Blessings and Salutations may be on him): "O boy, I teach a few words; guard (guard the cause of, keep the commandments of) Allah, then He guards you, guard (the cause of) Allah, then He will be with you; if you ask (for your need) ask Allah, if you seek assistance, seek Allah's; and know definitely that if the Whole World gathered to (bestow) profit on you they will not profit you except with what was determined for you by Allah, and if they gathered to harm you they will not harm you except with what has been determined for you by Allah; Pen lifted, papers dried, it is fixed nothing in these truths can be changed" Saheeh Al-Jame' As-Sagheer. Our youths took note of the meaning of the poetic verse:

"If death is a predetermined must, then it is a shame to die cowardly."

and the other poet saying:

"Who do not die by the sword will die by other reason;
many causes are there but one death".

These youths believe in what has been told by Allah and His messenger (Allah's Blessings and Salutations may be on him) about the greatness of the reward for the Mujahideen and Martyrs; Allah, the most exalted said: {and—so far—those who are slain in the way of Allah, He will by no means allow their deeds to perish. He will guide them and improve their condition. and cause them to enter the garden—paradise—which He has made known to them}. (Muhammad; 47:4-6). Allah the Exalted also said: {and do not speak of those who are slain in Allah's way as dead; nay—they are—alive, but you do not perceive} (Bagarah; 2:154). His messenger (Allah's Blessings and Salutations may be on him) said: "for those who strive in His cause Allah prepared hundred degrees (levels) in paradise; in-between two degrees as the in-between heaven and earth". Saheeh Al-Jame' As-Sagheer. He (Allah's Blessings and Salutations may be on him) also said: "the best of the martyrs are those who do NOT turn their faces away from the battle till they are killed. They are in the high level of Jannah (paradise). Their Lord laughs to them (in pleasure) and when your Lord laughs to a slave of His, He will not hold him to an account". narrated by Ahmad with correct and trustworthy reference. And : "a martyr will not feel the pain of death except like how you feel when you are pinched". Saheeh Al-Jame' As-Sagheer. He also said: "a martyr privileges are guaranteed by Allah; forgiveness with the first gush of his blood, he will be shown his seat in paradise, he will be decorated with the jewels of belief (Imaan), married off to the beautiful ones, protected from the test in the grave, assured security in the day of judgement, crowned with the crown of dignity, a ruby of which is better than this whole world (Duniah) and its' entire content, wedded to seventy two of the pure Houries (beautiful ones of Paradise) and his intercession on the behalf of seventy of his relatives will be accepted". Narrated by Ahmad and At-Tirmithi (with the correct and trustworthy reference).

Those youths know that their rewards in fighting you, the USA, is double than their rewards in fighting some one else not from the people of the book. They have no intention except to enter paradise by killing you. An infidel, and enemy of God like you, cannot be in the same hell with his righteous executioner.

Our youths chanting and reciting the word of Allah, the most exalted: {fight them; Allah will punish them by your hands and bring them to disgrace, and assist you against them and heal the heart of a believing people} (At-Taubah; 9:14) and the words of the prophet (ALLAH'S BLESSING AND SALUTATIONS ON HIM): "I swear by Him, who has my soul in His hand, that no man get killed fighting them today, patiently attacking and not retreating ,surely Allah will let him into paradise". And his (Allah's Blessings and Salutations may be on him) saying to them: "get up to a paradise as wide as heaven and earth".

The youths also reciting the All Mighty words of: "so when you meat in battle those who disbelieve, then smite the necks..." (Muhammad; 47:19). Those youths will not ask you (William Perry) for explanations, they will tell you singing there is nothing between us need to be explained, there is only killing and neck smiting.

And they will say to you what their grand father, Haroon Ar-Rasheed, Ameer-ul-Mu'meneen, replied to your grandfather, Nagfoor, the Byzantine emperor, when he threatened the Muslims: "from

Haroon Ar-Rasheed, Ameer-ul-Mu'meneen, to Nagfoor, the dog of the Romans; the answer is what you will see not what you hear". Haroon El-Rasheed led the armies of Islam to the battle and handed Nagfoor a devastating defeat.

The youths you called cowards are competing among themselves for fighting and killing you. reciting what one of them said:

> The crusader army became dust when we detonated al-Khobar.
> With courageous youth of Islam fearing no danger.
> If (they are) threatened: The tyrants will kill you, they reply my death is a victory.
> I did not betray that king, he did betray our Qiblah.
> And he permitted in the holy country the most filthy sort of humans.
> I have made an oath by Allah, the Great, to fight who ever rejected the faith.

For more than a decade, they carried arms on their shoulders in Afghanistan and they have made vows to Allah that as long as they are alive, they will continue to carry arms against you until you are— Allah willing—expelled, defeated and humiliated, they will carry on as long as they live saying:

> O William, tomorrow you will know which young man is confronting your misguided brethren!
> A youth fighting in smile, returning with the spear coloured red.
> May Allah keep me close to knights, humans in peace, demons in war.
> Lions in Jungle but their teeth are spears and Indian swords.
> The horses witness that I push them hard forwarded in the fire of battle.
> The dust of the battle bears witnesses for me, so also the fighting itself, the pens and the books!

So to abuse the grandsons of the companions, may Allah be pleased with them, by calling them cowards and challenging them by refusing to leave the land of the two Holy Places shows the insanity and the imbalance you are suffering from. Its appropriate "remedy," however, is in the hands of the youths of Islam, as the poet said:

> I am willing to sacrifice self and wealth for knights who never disappointed me.
> Knights who are never fed up or deterred by death, even if the mill of war turns.

In the heat of battle they do not care, and cure the insanity of the enemy by their 'insane' courage.

Terrorising you, while you are carrying arms on our land, is a legitimate and morally demanded duty. It is a legitimate right well known to all humans and other creatures. Your example and our example is like a snake which entered into a house of a man and got killed by him. The coward is the one who lets you walk, while carrying arms, freely on his land and provides you with peace and security.

Those youths are different from your soldiers. Your problem will be how to convince your troops to fight, while our problem will be how to restrain our youths to wait for their turn in fighting and in operations. These youths are commendation and praiseworthy.

They stood up tall to defend the religion; at the time when the government misled the prominent scholars and tricked them into issuing Fatwas (that have no basis neither in the book of Allah, nor in the Sunnah of His prophet (Allah's Blessings and Salutations may be on him)) of opening the land of the two Holy Places for the Christians armies and handing the Al-Aqsa Mosque to the Zionists. Twisting the meanings of the holy text will not change this fact at all. They deserve the praise of the poet:

> I rejected all the critics, who chose the wrong way;
> I rejected those who enjoy fireplaces in clubs discussing eternally;
> I rejected those, who inspite being lost, think they are at the goal;

I respect those who carried on not asking or bothering about the difficulties;
Never letting up from their goals, inspite all hardships of the road;
Whose blood is the oil for the flame guiding in the darkness of confusion;
I feel still the pain of (the loss) Al-Quds in my internal organs;
That loss is like a burning fire in my intestines;

I did not betray my covenant with God, when even states did betray it! As their grandfather Assim Bin Thabit said rejecting a surrender offer of the pagans:

What for an excuse I had to surrender, while I am still able, having arrows and my bow having a tough string?!

Death is truth and ultimate destiny, and life will end any way. If I do not fight you, then my mother must be insane!

The youths hold you responsible for all of the killings and evictions of the Muslims and the violation of the sanctities, carried out by your Zionist brothers in Lebanon; you openly supplied them with arms and finance. More than 600,000 Iraqi children have died due to lack of food and medicine and as a result of the unjustifiable aggression (sanction) imposed on Iraq and its nation. The children of Iraq are our children. You, the USA, together with the Saudi regime are responsible for the shedding of the blood of these innocent children. Due to all of that, what ever treaty you have with our country is now null and void.

The treaty of Hudaybiyyah was cancelled by the messenger of Allah (Allah's Blessings and Salutations may be on him) once Quraysh had assisted Bani Bakr against Khusa'ah, the allies of the prophet (Allah's Blessings and Salutations may be on him). The prophet (Allah's Blessings and Salutations may be on him) fought Quraysh and concurred Makka. He (Allah's Blessings and Salutations may be on him) considered the treaty with Bani Qainuqa' void because one of their Jews publicly hurt one Muslim woman, one single woman, at the market. Let alone then, the killing you caused to hundred of thousands Muslims and occupying their sanctities. It is now clear that those who claim that the blood of the American solders (the enemy occupying the land of the Muslims) should be protected are merely repeating what is imposed on them by the regime; fearing the aggression and interested in saving themselves. It is a duty now on every tribe in the Arab Peninsula to fight, Jihad, in the cause of Allah and to cleanse the land from those occupiers. Allah knows that there blood is permitted (to be spilled) and their wealth is a booty; their wealth is a booty to those who kill them. The most Exalted said in the verse of As-Sayef, The Sword: "so when the sacred months have passed away, then slay the idolaters where ever you find them, and take them captives and besiege them and lie in wait for them in every ambush" (At-Tauba; 9:5). Our youths knew that the humiliation suffered by the Muslims as a result of the occupation of their sanctities can not be kicked and removed except by explosions and Jihad. As the poet said:

The walls of oppression and humiliation cannot be demolished except in a rain of bullets.
The freeman does not surrender leadership to infidels and sinners.
Without shedding blood no degradation and branding can be removed from the forehead.

I remind the youths of the Islamic world, who fought in Afghanistan and Bosnia-Herzegovina with their wealth, pens, tongues and themselves that the battle had not finished yet. I remind them about the talk between Jibreel (Gabriel) and the messenger of Allah (Allah's Blessings and Salutations may be on both of them) after the battle of Ahzab when the messenger of Allah (Allah's Blessings and Salutations may be on him) returned to Medina and before putting his sword aside; when Jibreel (Allah's Blessings and Salutations may be on him) descend saying: "are you putting your sword aside? by Allah the angels haven't dropped their arms yet; march with your companions to Bani Quraydah, I am (going) ahead of you to throw fears in their hearts and to shake their fortresses on them". Jibreel marched with the angels (Allah's Blessings and Salutations may be on them all), followed by the messenger of Allah (Allah's Blessings and Salutations may be on him) marching with the immigrants, Muhajeroon, and supporters, Ansar. (narrated by Al-Bukhary).

These youths know that: if one is not to be killed one will die (any way) and the most honourable death is to be killed in the way of Allah. They are even more determined after the martyrdom of the four heroes who bombed the Americans in Riyadh. Those youths who raised high the head of the Ummah and humiliated the Americans—the occupier—by their operation in Riyadh. They remember the poetry of Ja'far, the second commander in the battle of Mu'tah, in which three thousand Muslims faced over a hundred thousand Romans:

> How good is the Paradise and its nearness, good with cool drink But the Romans are promised punishment (in Hell), if I meet them.
> I will fight them.

And the poetry of Abdullah Bin Rawaha, the third commander in the battle of Mu'tah, after the martyrdom of Ja'far, when he felt some hesitation:

> O my soul if you do not get killed, you are going to die, anyway.
> This is death pool in front of you!
> You are getting what you have wished for (martyrdom) before, and you follow the example of the two previous commanders you are rightly guided!

As for our daughters, wives, sisters and mothers they should take prime example from the prophet (Allah's Blessings and Salutations may be on him) pious female companions, may Allah be pleased with them; they should adopt the life style (Seerah) of the female companions of courage, sacrifice and generosity in the cause of the supremacy of Allah's religion.

They should remember the courage and the personality of Fatima, daughter of Khatab, when she accepted Islam and stood up in front of her brother, Omar Ibn Al-Khatab and challenged him (before he became a Muslim) saying: "O Omar , what will you do if the truth is not in your religion?!" And to remember the stand of Asma', daughter of Abu Bakr, on the day of Hijra, when she attended the Messenger and his companion in the cave and split her belt in two pieces for them. And to remember the stand of Naseeba Bent Ka'b striving to defend the messenger of Allah (Allah's Blessings and Salutations may be on him) on the day of Uhud, in which she suffered twelve injuries, one of which was so deep leaving a deep lifelong scar! They should remember the generosity of the early woman of Islam who raised finance for the Muslims army by selling their jewelery.

Our women had set a tremendous example of generosity in the cause of Allah; they motivated and encouraged their sons, brothers and husbands to fight—in the cause of Allah—in Afghanistan, Bosnia-Herzegovina, Chechenia and in other countries. We ask Allah to accept from them these deeds, and may He help their fathers, brothers, husbands and sons. May Allah strengthen the belief—Imaan—of our women in the way of generosity and sacrifice for the supremacy of the word of Allah. Our women weep not, except over men who fight in the cause of Allah; our women instigate their brothers to fight in the cause of Allah.

Our women bemoan only fighters in the cause of Allah, as said:

> Do not moan on any one except a lion in the woods, courageous in the burning wars.
> Let me die dignified in wars, honourable death is better than my current life.
> Our women encourage Jihad saying:
> Prepare yourself like a struggler, the matter is bigger than words!
> Are you going to leave us else for the wolves of Kufr eating our wings?!
> The wolves of Kufr are mobilising all evil persons from every where!
> Where are the freemen defending free women by the arms?!
> Death is better than life in humiliation! Some scandals and shames will never be otherwise eradicated.

My Muslim Brothers of The World:

Your brothers in Palestine and in the land of the two Holy Places are calling upon your help and asking you to take part in fighting against the enemy—your enemy and their enemy—the Americans and the Israelis. they are asking you to do whatever you can, with one own means and ability, to expel the enemy, humiliated and defeated, out of the sanctities of Islam. Exalted be to Allah said in His book: { and if they ask your support, because they are oppressed in their faith, then support them!} (Anfaal; 8:72)

O you horses (soldiers) of Allah ride and march on. This is the time of hardship so be tough. And know that your gathering and co-operation in order to liberate the sanctities of Islam is the right step toward unifying the word of the Ummah under the banner of "No God but Allah").

From our place we raise our palms humbly to Allah asking Him to bestow on us His guide in every aspects of this issue.

Our Lord, we ask you to secure the release of the truthful scholars, Ulama, of Islam and pious youths of the Ummah from their imprisonment. O Allah, strengthen them and help their families.

Our Lord, the people of the cross had come with their horses (soldiers) and occupied the land of the two Holy places. And the Zionist Jews fiddling as they wish with the Al-Aqsa Mosque, the route of the ascendance of the messenger of Allah (ALLAH'S BLESSING AND SALUTATIONS ON HIM). Our Lord, shatter their gathering, divide them among themselves, shaken the earth under their feet and give us control over them; Our Lord, we take refuge in you from their deeds and take you as a shield between us and them

Our Lord, show us a black day in them!

Our Lord, show us the wonderment of your ability in them!

Our Lord, You are the Revealer of the book, Director of the clouds, You defeated the allies (Ahzab); defeat them and make us victorious over them.

Our Lord, You are the one who help us and You are the one who assist us, with Your Power we move and by Your Power we fight. On You we rely and You are our cause.

Our Lord, those youths got together to make Your religion victorious and raise Your banner. Our Lord, send them Your help and strengthen their hearts.

Our Lord, make the youths of Islam steadfast and descend patience on them and guide their shots!

Our Lord, unify the Muslims and bestow love among their hearts!

O Lord pour down upon us patience, and make our steps firm and assist us against the unbelieving people!

Our Lord, do not lay on us a burden as Thou didst lay on those before us; Our Lord, do not impose upon us that which we have no strength to bear; and pardon us and grant us protection and have mercy on us, Thou art our patron, so help us against the unbelieving people.

Our Lord, guide this Ummah, and make the right conditions (by which) the people of your obedience will be in dignity and the people of disobedience in humiliation, and by which the good deeds are enjoined and the bad deeds are forebode.

Our Lord, bless Muhammad, Your slave and messenger, his family and descendants, and companions and salute him with a (becoming) salutation.

And our last supplication is: All praise is due to Allah .

Graduation Speech at West Point

President George W. Bush

Remarks by the President at 2002 Graduation Exercise of the United States Military Academy, West Point, New York

9:13 A.M. EDT

The President: Thank you very much, General Lennox. Mr. Secretary, Governor Pataki, members of the United States Congress, Academy staff and faculty, distinguished guests, proud family members, and graduates: I want to thank you for your welcome. Laura and I are especially honored to visit this great institution in your bicentennial year.

In every corner of America, the words "West Point" command immediate respect. This place where the Hudson River bends is more than a fine institution of learning. The United States Military Academy is the guardian of values that have shaped the soldiers who have shaped the history of the world.

A few of you have followed in the path of the perfect West Point graduate, Robert E. Lee, who never received a single demerit in four years. Some of you followed in the path of the imperfect graduate, Ulysses S. Grant, who had his fair share of demerits, and said the happiest day of his life was "the day I left West Point." (Laughter.) During my college years I guess you could say I was—(laughter.) During my college years I guess you could say I was a Grant man. (Laughter.)

You walk in the tradition of Eisenhower and MacArthur, Patton and Bradley—the commanders who saved a civilization. And you walk in the tradition of second lieutenants who did the same, by fighting and dying on distant battlefields.

Graduates of this academy have brought creativity and courage to every field of endeavor. West Point produced the chief engineer of the Panama Canal, the mind behind the Manhattan Project, the first American to walk in space. This fine institution gave us the man they say invented baseball, and other young men over the years who perfected the game of football.

You know this, but many in America don't—George C. Marshall, a VMI graduate, is said to have given this order: "I want an officer for a secret and dangerous mission. I want a West Point football player." (Applause.)

As you leave here today, I know there's one thing you'll never miss about this place: Being a plebe. (Applause.) But even a plebe at West Point is made to feel he or she has some standing in the world. (Laughter.) I'm told that plebes, when asked whom they outrank, are required to answer this: "Sir, the Superintendent's dog—(laughter)—the Commandant's cat, and all the admirals in the whole damn Navy." (Applause.) I probably won't be sharing that with the Secretary of the Navy. (Laughter.)

http://www.whitehouse.gov/news/releases/2002/06/images/20020601-3_westpointgradp18166-515h.html

West Point is guided by tradition, and in honor of the "Golden Children of the Corps,"—(applause)—I will observe one of the traditions you cherish most. As the Commander-in-Chief, I hereby grant amnesty to all cadets who are on restriction for minor conduct offenses. (Applause.) Those of you in the end zone might have cheered a little early. (Laughter.) Because, you see, I'm going to let General Lennox define exactly what "minor" means. (Laughter.)

Every West Point class is commissioned to the Armed Forces. Some West Point classes are also commissioned by history, to take part in a great new calling for their country. Speaking here to the class of 1942—six months after Pearl Harbor—General Marshall said, "We're determined that before the sun sets on this terrible struggle, our flag will be recognized throughout the world as a symbol of freedom on the one hand, and of overwhelming power on the other." (Applause.)

Officers graduating that year helped fulfill that mission, defeating Japan and Germany, and then reconstructing those nations as allies. West Point graduates of the 1940s saw the rise of a deadly new challenge—the challenge of imperial communism—and opposed it from Korea to Berlin, to Vietnam, and in the Cold War, from beginning to end. And as the sun set on their struggle, many of those West Point officers lived to see a world transformed.

History has also issued its call to your generation. In your last year, America was attacked by a ruthless and resourceful enemy. You graduate from this Academy in a time of war, taking your place in an American military that is powerful and is honorable. Our war on terror is only begun, but in Afghanistan it was begun well. (Applause.)

I am proud of the men and women who have fought on my orders. America is profoundly grateful for all who serve the cause of freedom, and for all who have given their lives in its defense. This nation respects and trusts our military, and we are confident in your victories to come. (Applause.)

This war will take many turns we cannot predict. Yet I am certain of this: Wherever we carry it, the American flag will stand not only for our power, but for freedom. (Applause.) Our nation's cause has always been larger than our nation's defense. We fight, as we always fight, for a just peace—a peace that favors human liberty. We will defend the peace against threats from terrorists and tyrants. We will preserve the peace by building good relations among the great powers. And we will extend the peace by encouraging free and open societies on every continent.

Building this just peace is America's opportunity, and America's duty. From this day forward, it is your challenge, as well, and we will meet this challenge together. (Applause.) You will wear the uniform of a great and unique country. America has no empire to extend or utopia to establish. We wish for others only what we wish for ourselves—safety from violence, the rewards of liberty, and the hope for a better life.

In defending the peace, we face a threat with no precedent. Enemies in the past needed great armies and great industrial capabilities to endanger the American people and our nation. The attacks of September the 11th required a few hundred thousand dollars in the hands of a few dozen evil and deluded men. All of the chaos and suffering they caused came at much less than the cost of a single tank. The dangers have not passed. This government and the American people are on watch, we are ready, because we know the terrorists have more money and more men and more plans.

The gravest danger to freedom lies at the perilous crossroads of radicalism and technology. When the spread of chemical and biological and nuclear weapons, along with ballistic missile technology—when that occurs, even weak states and small groups could attain a catastrophic power to strike great nations. Our enemies have declared this very intention, and have been caught seeking these terrible weapons. They want the capability to blackmail us, or to harm us, or to harm our friends—and we will oppose them with all our power. (Applause.)

For much of the last century, America's defense relied on the Cold War doctrines of deterrence and containment. In some cases, those strategies still apply. But new threats also require new thinking. Deterrence—the promise of massive retaliation against nations—means nothing against shadowy terrorist networks with no nation or citizens to defend. Containment is not possible when unbalanced dictators with weapons of mass destruction can deliver those weapons on missiles or secretly provide them to terrorist allies.

We cannot defend America and our friends by hoping for the best. We cannot put our faith in the word of tyrants, who solemnly sign non-proliferation treaties, and then systemically break them. If we wait for threats to fully materialize, we will have waited too long. (Applause.)

Homeland defense and missile defense are part of stronger security, and they're essential priorities for America. Yet the war on terror will not be won on the defensive. We must take the battle to the enemy, disrupt his plans, and confront the worst threats before they emerge. (Applause.) In the world we have entered, the only path to safety is the path of action. And this nation will act. (Applause.)

Our security will require the best intelligence, to reveal threats hidden in caves and growing in laboratories. Our security will require modernizing domestic agencies such as the FBI, so they're prepared to act, and act quickly, against danger. Our security will require transforming the military you will lead—a military that must be ready to strike at a moment's notice in any dark corner of the world. And our security will require all Americans to be forward-looking and resolute, to be ready for pre-emptive action when necessary to defend our liberty and to defend our lives. (Applause.)

The work ahead is difficult. The choices we will face are complex. We must uncover terror cells in 60 or more countries, using every tool of finance, intelligence and law enforcement. Along with our friends and allies, we must oppose proliferation and confront regimes that sponsor terror, as each case requires. Some nations need military training to fight terror, and we'll provide it. Other nations oppose terror, but tolerate the hatred that leads to terror—and that must change. (Applause.) We will send diplomats where they are needed, and we will send you, our soldiers, where you're needed. (Applause.)

All nations that decide for aggression and terror will pay a price. We will not leave the safety of America and the peace of the planet at the mercy of a few mad terrorists and tyrants. (Applause.) We will lift this dark threat from our country and from the world.

Because the war on terror will require resolve and patience, it will also require firm moral purpose. In this way our struggle is similar to the Cold War. Now, as then, our enemies are totalitarians, holding a creed of power with no place for human dignity. Now, as then, they seek to impose a joyless conformity, to control every life and all of life.

America confronted imperial communism in many different ways—diplomatic, economic, and military. Yet moral clarity was essential to our victory in the Cold War. When leaders like John F. Kennedy and Ronald Reagan refused to gloss over the brutality of tyrants, they gave hope to prisoners and dissidents and exiles, and rallied free nations to a great cause.

Some worry that it is somehow undiplomatic or impolite to speak the language of right and wrong. I disagree. (Applause.) Different circumstances require different methods, but not different moralities. (Applause.) Moral truth is the same in every culture, in every time, and in every place. Targeting innocent civilians for murder is always and everywhere wrong. (Applause.) Brutality against women is always and everywhere wrong. (Applause.) There can be no neutrality between justice and cruelty, between the innocent and the guilty. We are in a conflict between good and evil, and America will call evil by its name. (Applause.) By confronting evil and lawless regimes, we do not create a problem, we reveal a problem. And we will lead the world in opposing it. (Applause.)

As we defend the peace, we also have an historic opportunity to preserve the peace. We have our best chance since the rise of the nation state in the 17th century to build a world where the great powers compete in peace instead of prepare for war. The history of the last century, in particular, was dominated by a series of destructive national rivalries that left battlefields and graveyards across the Earth. Germany fought France, the Axis fought the Allies, and then the East fought the West, in proxy wars and tense standoffs, against a backdrop of nuclear Armageddon.

Competition between great nations is inevitable, but armed conflict in our world is not. More and more, civilized nations find ourselves on the same side—united by common dangers of terrorist violence and chaos. America has, and intends to keep, military strengths beyond challenge—(applause)—thereby, making the destabilizing arms races of other eras pointless, and limiting rivalries to trade and other pursuits of peace.

Today the great powers are also increasingly united by common values, instead of divided by conflicting ideologies. The United States, Japan and our Pacific friends, and now all of Europe, share a deep commitment to human freedom, embodied in strong alliances such as NATO. And the tide of liberty is rising in many other nations.

Generations of West Point officers planned and practiced for battles with Soviet Russia. I've just returned from a new Russia, now a country reaching toward democracy, and our partner in the war against terror. (Applause.) Even in China, leaders are discovering that economic freedom is the only lasting source of national wealth. In time, they will find that social and political freedom is the only true source of national greatness. (Applause.)

When the great powers share common values, we are better able to confront serious regional conflicts together, better able to cooperate in preventing the spread of violence or economic chaos. In the past, great power rivals took sides in difficult regional problems, making divisions deeper and more complicated. Today, from the Middle East to South Asia, we are gathering broad international coalitions to increase the pressure for peace. We must build strong and great power relations when times are good; to help manage crisis when times are bad. America needs partners to preserve the peace, and we will work with every nation that shares this noble goal. (Applause.)

And finally, America stands for more than the absence of war. We have a great opportunity to extend a just peace, by replacing poverty, repression, and resentment around the world with hope of a better day. Through most of history, poverty was persistent, inescapable, and almost universal. In the last few decades, we've seen nations from Chile to South Korea build modern economies and freer societies, lifting millions of people out of despair and want. And there's no mystery to this achievement.

The 20th century ended with a single surviving model of human progress, based on non-negotiable demands of human dignity, the rule of law, limits on the power of the state, respect for women and private property and free speech and equal justice and religious tolerance. America cannot impose this vision—yet we can support and reward governments that make the right choices for their own people. In our development aid, in our diplomatic efforts, in our international broadcasting, and in our educational assistance, the United States will promote moderation and tolerance and human rights. And we will defend the peace that makes all progress possible.

When it comes to the common rights and needs of men and women, there is no clash of civilizations. The requirements of freedom apply fully to Africa and Latin America and the entire Islamic world. The peoples of the Islamic nations want and deserve the same freedoms and opportunities as people in every nation. And their governments should listen to their hopes. (Applause.)

A truly strong nation will permit legal avenues of dissent for all groups that pursue their aspirations without violence. An advancing nation will pursue economic reform, to unleash the great entrepreneurial energy of its people. A thriving nation will respect the rights of women, because no society can prosper while denying opportunity to half its citizens. Mothers and fathers and children across the Islamic world, and all the world, share the same fears and aspirations. In poverty, they struggle. In tyranny, they suffer. And as we saw in Afghanistan, in liberation they celebrate. (Applause.)

America has a greater objective than controlling threats and containing resentment. We will work for a just and peaceful world beyond the war on terror.

The bicentennial class of West Point now enters this drama. With all in the United States Army, you will stand between your fellow citizens and grave danger. You will help establish a peace that allows millions around the world to live in liberty and to grow in prosperity. You will face times of calm, and times of crisis. And every test will find you prepared—because you're the men and women of West Point. (Applause.) You leave here marked by the character of this Academy, carrying with you the highest ideals of our nation.

Toward the end of his life, Dwight Eisenhower recalled the first day he stood on the plain at West Point. "The feeling came over me," he said, "that the expression 'the United States of America' would now and henceforth mean something different than it had ever before. From here on, it would be the nation I would be serving, not myself."

Today, your last day at West Point, you begin a life of service in a career unlike any other. You've answered a calling to hardship and purpose, to risk and honor. At the end of every day you will know that you have faithfully done your duty. May you always bring to that duty the high standards of this great American institution. May you always be worthy of the long gray line that stretches two centuries behind you.

On behalf of the nation, I congratulate each one of you for the commission you've earned and for the credit you bring to the United States of America. May God bless you all. (Applause.)

END 10:05 A.M. EDT

Part II
Theory

David Plotz's *Greens Peace: A Controversial new Theory about the true causes of War—in 18 Holes or less* is a very humorous piece that explains peace as a function of golfing. Though it is humorous, read this article to see how the scientific method is applied in the field of social sciences.

As you read it, identify the independent & dependent variables as well as the causal factors—you will use the same process for your papers. *Green's Peace* actually illustrates the concept of correlation, not causation.

The Way We Live Now: Greens Peace

David Plotz

Since the rise of the nation-state, scholars and politicians have been struggling to answer the critical question of geopolitics: Why do some countries fight wars and others remain at peace? Yet to date, they have made little progress. Some contemporary thinkers, alarmed by Kosovo and Rwanda, predict that ethnic conflict will be the prime cause of war in the 21st century. Environmental scholars argue that scarce water and land will drive nations to battle. Students of the theory of inter-democratic peace contend that the structure of national government will be the driving factor. But policy makers should discard these dry, unsatisfying academic formulations and start paying attention to a much more powerful explanatory tool: golf.

Countries where golf is popular never fight other golfing nations—and don't fight much at all—while countries without golf are strikingly belligerent. Have you ever met an Afghan who golfs? Are there any Serbs on the P. G.A. tour?

I can hear the skeptical tennis fans out there asking, Where's the proof? Years of rigorous data collection and analysis—or at least days of casual data massaging—confirm the theory of greens peace. I consulted experts at the National Golf Foundation and Golf Digest and scoured the records of PlayGolfNow.com to determine which countries take their golf seriously and which are mere duffers. Because the only remotely reliable international golf statistic is the number of courses, I estimated golf's popularity in each country by calculating the ratio of golf courses to people. Using well-established scientific and astrological methods, I determined that a country needs one course per million people to count as a golf nation. (Fewer than one course per million suggests that golf is confined to rich folks and tourists.)

About 50 countries meet the one-per-million standard. Golf-mad New Zealand leads the world with 136 courses per million. The United States has about 60; France, 11; and Singapore, 6. Sri Lanka, by contrast, has 0.1; Peru 0.08; China 0.05.

I compared the golf stats with a list of the 300-odd major conflicts since World War II, and the evidence is irrefutable. Golfing nations haven't fought one another in 50-odd years, and they aren't very likely to fight one another today. Of the 27 current major armed conflicts, none match golfing nations. Take a quick spin around the globe. Every peaceful European country loves golf. But Russia, at war in Chechnya, doesn't hit the links. Non-golf Greece and non-golf Turkey have long warred over non-golf Cyprus. The former Yugoslavia has fragmented into five states. Only peaceful Slovenia swings the sticks.

Do India or Pakistan golf? Of course not. Algerians shoot one another; Moroccans next door shoot par. Peaceful Thailand is a regular at the range, but belligerent Myanmar isn't. Golf is sadly absent from Sierra Leone, Congo and Eritrea. The Middle East has hardly any courses; Iraqis still think a bunker is something you want to be in. Colombia and Peru have guerrilla wars but little golf.

Magazine Desk, June 4, 2000, Sunday. Copyright 2002 The New York Times Company.

Venezuela has lots of golf but no war. Malaysia is crazy about the game, but Indonesia has been too busy brutalizing East Timor to pick it up. Taiwan loves golf; China doesn't—which one of them invaded Tibet and India? Germany and Japan have become golf junkies since the Second World War ended; South Korea took up the game after the Korean War. Is it any accident they've remained at peace?

And the more golf you play, the more peaceful you are. Sweet-tempered nations like Sweden, Finland, Norway, Denmark, Iceland and Canada play the most golf. Of the 10 countries where golf is most popular, only the United States and Great Britain have a recent history of autonomous belligerence. But the United States has dispatched troops only against anti-golf tyrants: Iraq's Saddam Hussein, Yugoslavia's Slobodan Milosevic, Panama's Manuel Noriega, Somalia's Mohammed Aideed.

Two British conflicts do mar the record. The U.K. and Argentina warred over the Falkland Islands in 1982. (Argentina barely meets the one-per-million cutoff today, and I suspect that it wouldn't have had enough courses to qualify in 1982.) And Northern Ireland's Troubles set the golfing Irish against the golfing English. Apartheid-era South Africa also tarnishes the theory, with the white golfing minority violently oppressing the black, non-golfing majority.

Philosophers and social scientists will undoubtedly puzzle for decades over the association of golf and peace, but I have a few preliminary theories. Golf teaches players to be gentlemen. It relies on an honor system in which golfers police themselves. Golf has no physical violence, unlike basketball, soccer, football, rugby and so on. (Soccer fans riot, and at least one soccer match ignited a war. Have you ever heard of a golf riot?) Golf is not zero-sum. Your performance is independent of your opponent's, and nothing you can do to your opponent can improve your score. War, which is founded on violence, cheating and crushing your rival, is golf's antithesis.

Some cynics may complain that I have it backward: golf doesn't cause peace, peace causes golf. Golf, they may say, presumes a stable economic and political system. Golfers have to be relatively prosperous people with leisure time. They live in countries that can afford to set aside valuable land and water for golf courses. People who have the time and peace of mind to play golf aren't worrying about whether rioters are looting their stores or barbarians are swarming across the borders. (This argument parallels Thomas L. Friedman's "golden arches theory of conflict prevention," which holds that countries with McDonald's are too prosperous and complacent to wage war with one another.)

But the far-sighted people of South Korea, who know firsthand the benefits of golf, are conducting a perfect experiment to prove that it can pacify even the most benighted nation. According to recent news reports, South Korea's first significant capital investment in North Korea will include a multimillion-dollar resort with several golf courses to be built by the Hyundai Group. These will be North Korea's first courses, and they may be the best investment South Korea ever makes. What better way to end 50 years of strife than to teach North Koreans to make par, not war?

Part III
Debating the Future of NATO

Two Realists. One military alliance. Two completely different prescriptions on whether or not NATO should be relegated to the history books or "stay alive".

The concept of intellectual pluralism is not limited to looking at one event from competing points of view *from different* Traditions. Using the same Tradition, two people can arrive at two different, and well-argued, conclusions.

In these two articles, though both use the Realist's arguments and focus on national survival and security, Steven Meyer and Michael Ruhle offer up differing opinions on the adaptability or worthlessness of NATO in the post-9/11 world.

Carcass of Dead Policies:
The Irrelevance of NATO

Steven E. Meyer

In 1877, Lord Salisbury, commenting on Great Britain's policy on the Eastern Question, noted that "the commonest error in politics is sticking to the carcass of dead policies."[1] Salisbury was bemoaning the fact that many influential members of the British ruling class could not recognize that history had moved on; they continued to cling to policies and institutions that were relics of another era. Salisbury went on to note that the cost was enormous because this preoccupation with anachronism damaged Britain's real interests. Despite Salisbury's clever words, his observation is nothing new. Throughout Western history policymakers often have tended to rely on past realities, policies, and institutions to assess and deal with contemporary and future situations.

Post-Cold War American policymakers have not been immune from falling into this trap. Indeed, this inertial approach, characterized by Washington's unbending support for NATO and its expansion, has defined American foreign and security policy since the collapse of the Soviet Union and the bipolar world. During the Cold War, NATO provided the proper linchpin of American—and West European—security policy, and served as a useful, even fundamental deterrent to Soviet military might and expansionism. However, NATO's time has come and gone, and today there is no legitimate reason for it to exist. Although the strong differences exhibited in the Alliance over the war against Iraq have accelerated NATO's irrelevancy, the root causes of its problems go much deeper. Consequently, for both the United States and Europe,NATO is at best an irrelevant distraction and at worst toxic to their respective contemporary security needs.

THE INERTIAL IMPERATIVE

The end of the Cold War presented a problem similar to the one faced by post-World War II American leaders. A tectonic shift had occurred that required innovation, creativity, and a real understanding of the evolving world. For some experts—both in government and academia, as well as on both sides of the Atlantic—the collapse of the Soviet Union and the Warsaw Pact called into question the need for NATO. They recognized that an era had ended and the time was ripe for a basic debate about the future of NATO and Western security policies and structures.

© 2003 Steven E. Meyer

Dr. Steven E. Meyer is Professor of Political Science at the Industrial College of the Armed Forces, National Defense University, in Washington, D.C. He is a graduate of the University of Wisconsin and holds an M.S. in political science from Fordham University and a Ph.D. from Georgetown University. His most recent writings include "U.S. Policy Toward the Former Yugoslavia," a Woodrow Wilson Center publication.

Unfortunately, the policymakers in Washington who established the priorities for the post-Cold War era reacted quite differently from their predecessors. A small, influential coterie of policymakers in the elder Bush and then the Clinton administrations reacted reflexively and inertially, cutting off what should have been useful debate on the future. Moreover, virtually all of the officials who helped define the foreign and security policy in the Bush "41" Administration have resurfaced in the current Bush Administration. According to them, the existence and viability of NATO was not to be questioned. It was to remain basically the same successful alliance of American and European foreign and security policy that it had been since 1949. But a fundamental change was taking place in the post-Cold War security environment. In 1949, a genuine, measurable security threat justified NATO for all its members. Now, with the end of the Cold War, the inertial attachment to NATO meant that the alliance had to seek or invent reasons to justify its existence and relevance.

American officials recognized the threats to the alliance. NATO needed props. Expansion into the former Warsaw Pact was one. Not only did expansion provide a whole new raison d'etre for the alliance, but—perhaps more important—it spawned a large new bureaucracy and the accompanying "busyness" that provide the lifeblood of institutions trying to justify their existence. At the same time, the theological mantra changed. Since there was no longer an enemy, NATO could not be described as a defensive alliance, it now was to be a combination of a wide-ranging political and collective security alliance. There were only two avenues the countries of Central and Eastern Europe could take if they wanted to join the West: NATO for security interests, and the European Union for economic interests. No other avenues were acceptable. Consequently, in 1999 Poland, Hungary, and the Czech Republic joined NATO, and in November 2002 the Baltic countries, Slovakia, Slovenia, Bulgaria, and Romania accepted invitations to join the alliance.

In addition to expansion, the crisis in the Balkans also came to NATO's rescue. For the Clinton Administration, the former Yugoslavia was never really the most important point.NATO credibility was. This distinction is fundamental because policies that were designed to justify NATO were not necessarily the same as those that would deal successfully with issues in the former Yugoslavia. Clinton Administration spokesmen often pointed out that our vital interest was in preserving the alliance and vindicating our leadership of it.

In February 1996, for example, the *Congressional Digest* observed that a primary motivation for the Clinton Administration's engagement in the former Yugoslavia was because it constituted a "test case of NATO's ability to deal with post-Cold War security threats." Three years later, in April 1999, Secretary of State Madeleine Albright noted that "Belgrade's actions [in Kosovo] constitute a critical test of NATO" and that "we were responding to a post-Cold War threat to alliance interests and values."[2] Another former Clinton Administration official sums up the point by noting that a primary "factor contributing to the US decision to engage in Bosnia was the need to defend NATO's credibility."[3] The Balkans became the indispensable vehicle to respond to the perceived challenges to NATO's credibility and viability. For Washington, using the existence and proximity of NATO to justify intervention in the Balkans was less important than using the existence and proximity of the Balkans to justify NATO.

Although the current Bush Administration's focus has been riveted on the post-9/11 war on terrorism and Iraq, it has remained staunchly committed to NATO and its expansion. In its approach to the NATO Summit in Prague in November 2002, the alliance's serious problems were ignored, downplayed, or glossed over. For example, in congressional testimony in February 2002, a high-level Administration official said that NATO expansion was an exercise in "how much we can do to advance the cause of freedom," and that we must strengthen NATO's military capability and political solidarity.[4] In October 2002, in an address to the NATO Parliamentary Assembly, another Administration official noted that NATO"remains the essential link between Europe and North America—the place for free nations to secure peace, security, and liberty."[5]

But no one explains what all of this means—whose freedom, peace, security, and liberty are endangered? Who, after all, is the enemy? How is it possible to argue that there is any sense of political solidarity in the wake of the alliance's deep split over Iraq? NATO enthusiasts repeat their mantra by rote, but none of it justifies supporting a failing alliance.

INEVITABLE DECLINE

There are five interrelated reasons why post-Cold War rhetoric and inertial symbolism no longer conform to reality.

First, the legitimate threat that justified NATO really is gone. All three US administrations since the collapse of the Soviet Union have paid lip service to this aphorism. For more than a decade, US security has advocated cooperation with Russia, but the structural and functional reality is quite different. Essentially, we are following a modified version of the post-World War I model, which excluded the defeated Germany from European and Western councils, rather than the more positive post-1815 and post-1945 models of including former enemies as quickly and completely as possible into the new security system. Consequently, the NATO-Russia Founding Act, the old Permanent Joint Council, and the new NATO-Russia Council speak more to separation and isolation than they do to cooperation and inclusion. They reinforce the fault line in Europe, unnecessarily dividing the continent into "ins" and "outs," with Russia clearly still "out."[6]

The fundamental problem has been the inability of the post-Cold War American—and European—leadership to move beyond old organizations, policies, and philosophies to build organizations, policies, and philosophies that are more appropriate to the current age. Ever since the end of the Cold War and the ascendancy of the United States as the world's only superpower, American foreign policy has been formulated and controlled by a very small coterie of elites from both the Democratic and Republican parties who share a remarkable synonymy of interests, values, and outlooks, differing only at the margins.

Second, the whole nature of contemporary European politics has changed so fundamentally that it has outgrown NATO-type alliances. For the first time in about 1,800 years, there is no world-class threat to or from any European state or combination of European states that requires a wide-ranging, comprehensive alliance such as NATO.[7] For the most part, borders are set, uncontested, and peaceful. Aggressive nationalism (although not nationalism itself) and the race for arms and empire that so dominated the politics of every major power from the 16th through the early 20th centuries are gone.

In Western Europe, the political struggle has replaced many of the characteristics of Westphalian sovereignty with a more intricate system of regions, states, and supra-national organizations. The "constitutional conference" launched in March 2002 ultimately may determine what happens to the residue of traditional sovereignty in Western Europe. The situation is different in Central Europe, where states are trying to reestablish democracy and civil society after years of Nazi and communist tyranny, while at the same time struggling to meet the requirements to join the European Union. And the collapse of the Stalinist system has resolved the "Soviet Question" that dominated much of the second half of the 20th century. Although we can't predict Russia's future exactly, it is highly unlikely that the Stalinist system will be reestablished, and by including Russia as an equal we greatly enhance her prospects for a stable political order and a more traditional, non-antagonistic relationship with the United States and the rest of the West.

The modern sense of security in Europe not only is broader than what even the new form of NATO is built for, it is different in *kind*, and it is best summarized in the (Maastricht) Treaty on European Union (1990-92) and the follow-up Treaty of Amsterdam (1997). These treaties speak to an understanding of security that includes issues of justice, environment, ethnicity, economic development, crime, and terrorism, in addition to references to more narrowly military definitions of security. In those sections of the Maastricht and Amsterdam treaties that deal with a "common foreign and security policy," NATO is not mentioned, but several references are made to the Western European Union. Neither treaty envisions NATO as an integral part of Europe's security future, and a major reason it has been so difficult to implement the "common foreign and security policy" parts of these treaties is because NATO stands as both an impediment and an intimidation to Europe's future.

Of course, the United States does have interests in common with the Europe that is emerging, but without the kind of overall mutual threat we faced in the past, they are much more issue-specific. For example, economic ties now provide America's single most important relationship with Europe—both as partner and competitor. However, we are doing much less than we should do to prepare for the future of this relationship, in part because we are distracted by an anachronistic security relationship. We also have other common interests in such areas as the environment, terrorism, and others, none of which are particularly well suited to resolution by NATO or any other like alliance. Occasionally, the United States and specific European countries or groups of countries may need to engage in joint military activities—the Gulf War in the early 1990s and the more recent war in Afghanistan provide two excellent examples. In both cases coalitions were put together to deal with specific issues and, during both, NATO was little more than a "truck stop." But these conflicts were unique. It was impossible to recreate the Gulf War alliance to confront Iraq in 2003, and within a year or two we probably will be saying the same thing about multilateral cooperation in Afghanistan. At the same time, there also are strong differences between the United States and much of Western Europe on a growing number of issues—such as how to deal with Iraq, the Israeli- Palestinian horror, abrogation of the ABM Treaty, disagreement over the Kyoto Treaty, and accusations in the European press and among European officials about "American hegemony" or "American hyperpower."

As Robert Kagan argues, the differences between the United States and Europe go to much deeper philosophical and anthropological levels.[8] As the US view of engaging the world has become increasingly ideological, that of the Europeans has become increasingly pragmatic. Both sides retain a sense of superiority and arrogance when dealing with the third world. For the Europeans, however, this tends to be more cultural, while for the United States it is a divine mission. Consequently, the United States takes more seriously what Anthony Padgen describes as the "vision of a single 'orbis terrarum'"—the notion "of a presumed right of lordship over the entire world," which, ironically, had been a hallmark of the European empire in America.[9]

In an environment of shifting interests and philosophies between Europe and the United States, Americans and Europeans still share—at least in theory—a respect for democratic values. But that is not enough to hold NATO together. There also is a growing transatlantic split over a range of primary issues: the size, sophistication, and use of military power; environmental issues; budget priorities, including welfare expenditures; the role of state sovereignty, involving especially the evolution of the European Union; and more.[10]

Third, as NATO's relevance has declined as a security organization in the West, it also has become less important for Russian security interests. For a while after the Cold War, NATO enlargement was a top Russian foreign policy concern, and Russia's leaders almost uniformly opposed enlargement as a direct threat to their country's vital interests.

But while opposition to NATO remains strong in the Russian military, for President Putin and his primary leadership circle, the salience of NATO for Russia's security interests has declined dramatically since the 9/11 terrorist attacks. For example, the opposition of Putin and other Russian officials to the inclusion of the Baltic states in NATO—a crisis in Russian-Western relations just a few years ago—has become virtually a non-issue. The Putin government supported the establishment of US military bases in Central Asia after 9/11, an area still considered part of the Russian "near abroad," which was unthinkable before the terrorist attacks. In addition, there has been only mild opposition to the Bush Administration's decision to abrogate the 1972 ABM Treaty. Finally, the serious bickering between the United States and NATO partners in "Old Europe" over Iraq apparently has convinced Putin that Russian interests are best served by holding the alliance at arm's length.

Putin's new, more benign attitude on NATO does not mean that he is becoming "pro-Western." He remains as pro-Russian as ever, but Russia's interests and patterns of engagement in international politics have changed fundamentally. Today, Russia has four major security interests under Putin: (1) reversing the centrifugal pressures on the Russian state; (2) economic development, established especially through ties to the West and a secure position in the oil market; (3) combating terrorism; and (4) China. Although rebuilding the Russian state and economic development are the most important long-term goals, the battle against terrorism is the most important contemporary security issue driving Moscow's overtures to the West. Especially since 9/11, Moscow sees a convergence of interests between the US struggle against al Qaeda and the Russian struggle against Muslim separatists in the Caucus region, accusing "Osama bin Laden and al Qaeda of being behind the problems in Chechnya."[11] Washington's guarded public recognition that Moscow is facing a "terrorism" issue in Chechnya was welcomed by Putin, even as he looks for more support.

For most Russian leaders—more so than for their American counterparts —the events of 11 September 2001 finally brought the Cold War to an end. Concern about terrorism has prompted Putin to seek a new strategic relationship with the West that preferably would replace NATO and end the artificial divide between east and west. Shortly after 9/11, Putin observed that "all nations are to blame for the terrorist attacks on the United States because they trust outdated security systems. . . . [W]e have failed to recognize the changes of the last 10 years."[12] Putin knows that dismantling NATO and constructing a new security arrangement is not yet in the cards. Consequently, he is willing to settle for a new relationship between the alliance and Russia that concentrates on terrorism.[13] In exchange, Russia will "rethink opposition to NATO enlargement" and establish regular, structured meetings between Russia and the European Union focusing on terror.[14] This is intended to draw Moscow and the alliance closer together. However, it is a hollow victory. The new Russia NATO Council will be "strictly limited [and] the 19 members of the alliance would reserve the right to once again take up any topic [considered] strictly as an alliance issue."[15] Russia is back at the table, but as a guest, not as a member of the family, and the tension continues between real-world security interests and an organization caught in a world that exists only in the minds of a handful of inertia-guided policymakers. Putin clearly understands the difference.

Fourth, expansion to the east actually damages the legitimate interests of the new NATO members. NATO membership does not protect the countries of Central and Eastern Europe from any recognizable security threat. The usual argument advanced by NATO enthusiasts is that the new members will become "consumers" of security rather than "providers" of security. But, again, security against or from what? What, for example, is the security threat to Hungary, or Slovenia, or the Czech Republic, or even Poland that requires NATO membership? There is no traditional security threat to these countries that could not be handled by the Europeans themselves—if they have the political will to do so.

The companion argument for those advocating NATO expansion is that the alliance will advance democracy and even "civil society." The 1995 "Study on NATO Enlargement" argued that a primary rationale behind expansion was "to [protect] the further democratic development of new members."[16] It is legitimate to argue that NATO protected the democracies of Western Europe from the threat of the Soviet Union and the Warsaw Pact. But the alliance did not bring democracy and civil society to Western Europe when it was established in 1949, because Western Europe already had a long democratic tradition. In like manner, NATO has not and will not carry democracy and civil society east. As Dan Reiter concludes after a study of democracy in Central Europe, "NATO membership was not necessary for democratization because each [new NATO country] already has a strong national commitment to democracy."[17] There also is a theoretical and practical problem with this rationale. NATO requires that aspirant countries have a working democratic system in place before they are accepted as members. So, by definition, NATO can't carry democracy to countries that already must have it established as a prerequisite for membership.

Enlargement puts the Central and East European members in an unnecessary and rapidly debilitating political and financial position. In particular, the countries of Central and Eastern Europe are becoming increasingly enmeshed in a conflict of loyalty between NATO and the European Union. Despite the propaganda that NATO and the EU are two legitimate, complementary avenues of development, in fact they are becoming increasingly competitive—for attention, loyalty, and resources. Although this problem is gaining momentum in Western Europe, it is becoming especially acute in Central and Eastern Europe, where the resource base is considerably smaller and political affiliations more fragile.

As a result, "since their accession on March 12, 1999, Poland, Hungary, and the Czech Republic have all experienced integration difficulties,"[18] because the real demands of economic and social issues lead to "economic constraints" and "a failure of political will."[19] And still, NATO and EU authorities continue to press these strapped economies to live up to difficult and at times mutually exclusive commitments that undermine pressing economic and social programs. A prime example for the Poles, Czechs, and Hungarians has been the multi-billion dollar competition for the sale of Lockheed Martin F-16 fighter jets[20] and the Grippen JAS-39, produced by Saab and BAE Systems. These three countries neither can afford nor need either the F-16 or the Grippen, a position borne out by the fact that the cost of repairing the damage caused by the floods in the Czech Republic during the spring of 2002 has scuttled the Czech government's decision to buy the Grippen.[21] Hungary faces similar restraints, and even larger Poland is so strapped that it agreed in early 2003 to buy 48 Lockheed Martin Block 52 F-16 C/D aircraft for $3.5 to $4.0 billion, but only if Warsaw was granted a 100-percent offset.[22] Ironically, if anything undermines the budding democracies of Central and Eastern Europe, it will be the inability to fund critical economic and social programs because of NATO's demands.

Romania provides an early example of what is likely to become commonplace as Central Europe's newest invitees prepare to actually join the alliance, probably in 2004. Just a year ago Romania's chances of being invited to join seemed bleak because it did not meet many of the criteria laid out in the Membership Action Plan. But then, in an attempt to improve its chances, Bucharest actively courted Washington by backing much of the Bush Administration's anti-terrorism strategy and by signing a bilateral agreement "not to turn over American soldiers to the new International Criminal Court."[23] Although this gambit worked, it annoyed European leaders and reportedly "will hurt [Romania's] chances for a place within the EU."[24] In like fashion, the Chairman of the European Parliament's Foreign Affairs Committee noted that support by some Central and East European countries for US policy on Iraq "might ultimately endanger those candidates' accession" to the EU. Former French President Valery Giscard d'Estaing, the current Chairman of the Convention on the Future of Europe, followed up by warning candidate countries that the Maastricht Treaty requires all members to support "without reservation the EU's foreign policy positions."[25]

In addition, NATO membership—including vulnerability to Western arms merchants—damages the ability of these countries to deal with genuine emerging security issues. Issues of social and economic justice, crime and corruption, environmental degradation, and ethnic reconciliation bear more directly on the security futures of these countries than does their struggle to satisfy NATO's arcane demands for membership. Consequently, instead of pressing these countries to spend scarce resources on NATO, Washington should encourage them to focus exclusively on European and regional organizations that are better geared to help address the real, pressing interests of the countries of Central and Eastern Europe.[26]

Fifth, since the end of the Cold War, NATO's programs and instruments have expanded seemingly exponentially, and its organizing rationale has changed. Virtually every summit—especially since the fall of communism —has been concerned with attempts to "redefine" or "reinvent" NATO in an effort to ignore history and make NATO relevant to the new reality. The following post-Cold War programs, instruments, and rationales are illustrative.

Combined Joint Task Forces (CJTF). The CJTF program was established in 1993-94 to provide the "flexibility needed to deploy at short notice forces specifically tailored to a particular contingency. CJTFs can also be made available for WEU[Western European Union] operations undertaken by European Allies."[27] In sum, the CJTF program allows NATO assets to be siphoned off for predominantly short-term operations that interest only some (two or more) of NATO's members (although, in fact, CJTFs have been used mostly by the United States and United Kingdom). Although CJTFs certainly do enhance flexibility with respect to the use of people and resources, it is a flexibility that is driven by the centrifugal reality of an increasingly fragmented alliance, which in turn reflects the growing divergence of interests and values. Consequently, almost any deployment, by definition, could be described as a CJTF. Ironically, CJTFs, which were instituted as a mechanism to preserve a degree of NATO purpose and unity, have become quite the opposite.

The Membership Action Plan (MAP). The MAP was established at NATO's Washington Summit in 1999 to provide a "tailored program for aspirants, designed to help build a road map to future membership."[28] The MAP laid out five broad areas that were designed to provide a detailed guide for prospective members to join NATO under Article 10 of the Washington Treaty.[29] But the MAP has been essentially a sham. First, prior to 9/11, NATO headquarters promised that the MAP process would hold aspirant countries to very high standards if they wanted to become NATO members, but that changed after 9/11. Virtually all of the countries invited to join the alliance at the Prague Summit in November 2002 had not satisfied the rigorous requirements of the MAP. The test for membership now became how willingly and quickly an aspirant country would follow the US lead in the "war on terrorism."

Second, the MAP became unnecessarily duplicative. Virtually every part of the five chapters, especially in the political and economic sections, is addressed in the Acquis Communautaire, which lays out requirements for membership in the European Union—and arguably EU membership is much more important for the future of Central and Eastern Europe than membership in NATO.

Third, once the new members have bought into the military, defense, and resource requirements of the alliance, they will be pressured to commit to programs, instruments, and equipment they cannot afford and do not need. We already have seen the deleterious effect of these pressures in Poland, Hungary, and the Czech Republic, and they are likely to have an even greater negative effect on the relatively poorer new inductees.

The Defense Capabilities Initiative (DCI). The DCI, also launched at NATO's summit in Washington in 1999, was intended to prepare the alliance for "the security challenges of the 21st century" by updating military capabilities in five overlapping areas (58 specific areas of shortfall): mobility and deployability, sustainability, effective engagement, survivability, and interoperable communications.[30] It was designed to be a far-reaching, ambitious plan aimed not only at security challenges within Europe, but especially enabling NATO to "deploy forces in distant crises."

The DCI was perhaps the most important program adopted by the 1999 summit because it was designed to reverse the widening technological and materiel gap between the United States and Europe. It was to lead to a tighter, more equal, more interoperable military alliance that could deploy major forces anywhere in the world for long periods of time. Despite the optimistic hopes of the High Level Steering Group assigned to oversee the DCI, it has proven to be an almost complete failure. With most European defense budgets either flat or declining, and with the US defense budget proposed to reach in excess of $500 billion by 2009, the gap will grow even greater.[31] But even more important than indicating a divergence in raw capability, this gap reflects diverging values and interests. The Europeans have sufficient technological capability, economic prowess, and talent to narrow the "capabilities gap" significantly—if they want to. What they do not have is the desire or the perceived security need to do so.

The "Transformation" Summit. The new Prague Capabilities Committee (PCC), formed at the Prague Summit to focus on 12 areas (in four major "baskets") needing improvement, was an attempt to recover the failed DCI. This time, however, the new NATO Defense Transformation Initiative (NDTI) "has a narrower focus on new missions and . . . a small, but select number of forces for them."[32] As the logic goes, each country will take on "capabilities tasks" in advance as one or more of their responsibilities, leading to so-called "niche" responsibilities for even the smallest member, depending on each member's perceived areas of "comparative advantage."[33] Sadly, but eminently predictably, the PCC will be no more successful than its predecessor. Nothing important has changed since 1999 to make success any more likely this time. As in the past, the new—as well as the old—members will find no compelling reason to proceed, will find it too costly to do so, or, driven by more pressing concerns, simply will ignore the program. Just like the DCI, the new PCC/ NDTI is likely simply to fade into insignificance and die in indifference.

The Prague Summit participants also approved the joint NATO Reaction Force (NRF) under CJTF headquarters, to consist "of a technologically advanced, flexible, deployable, interoperable, and sustainable force including land, sea, and air elements ready to move quickly to wherever needed."[34] The NRF also is intended to promote and improve "the alliance's military capabilities." In other words, the NRF is conceived to become a vehicle for the NDTI, nee DCI. The summit also approved a "leaner, more efficient, effective, and deployable command structure," and moved to "strengthen" the CJTF program. But why will any of these initiatives be more successful than the ones that came out of the Washington Summit? The same problems exist and, indeed, have been exacerbated, especially as a result of the disagreements between Washington and several European NATO countries over Iraq. Substantial improvement and interoperability of technical capabilities will give way to diverging interests and values, and the smaller members will succumb to financial pressures and conflicting and mutually exclusive security demands. The NRF, which is merely a concept at this point, also is threatened by the same pressures—in part because maintaining such a unit at a high level of readiness for deployment is extremely expensive, but more importantly because its development will suffer from the tugs and pulls of different political interests.

Finally, the new CJTF is likely to be the most successful of NATO's initiatives. CJTFs—old or new—exist and are used only because NATO's cohesiveness and purpose are so porous and weak. If NATO was the kind of security organization its protagonists wanted it to be, not only would CJTFs be unnecessary, they would be an anathema.

A Collective Security Alliance, not a Defensive Alliance. As the Cold War faded into history, NATO enthusiasts began to argue that the very nature of the alliance had to change if it was to continue to exist. Consequently, as Henry Kissinger noted, NATO "has become more akin to a collective security organization, like the United Nations, than to a traditional alliance."[35] If the alliance was to survive, it had to find a rationale that did not depend on a clearly defined enemy, or even a potential enemy. A loosely formed "collective security organization" was the answer.

In reality, these two types of alliances represent a distinction without a difference. Even in a collective "security alliance," there must be at least some overriding common security bond that holds the participants together. As noted before, quite the opposite is happening—not only on security issues, but in the political realm as well. The NATO that has emerged since the end of the Cold War does not satisfy even the most rudimentary tests of what an alliance is supposed to do. For example, it fails both Stephen Walt's "five . . . explanations for international alliances" and Glenn Snyder's theory of alliance formation and management.[36] And, the further we get from the Cold War, the more serious those frictions will become as the nexus of values and interests between the United States and Europe continues to widen. Two recent examples illustrate the point.

First, after 9/11, NATO's European members declared "Article 5" support for the United States in its war against terrorism generally and the military action in Afghanistan. This was the first time in NATO's history that Article 5 had been formally invoked—and it is likely to be the last, despite the argument that "modern-day terrorism and WMD proliferation are 'Article 5 threats.'"[37] The United States spurned the European action, and in doing so Washington signaled that it did not need NATO and that the European allies counted for little in the greatest threat to US vital interests since perhaps the attack on Pearl Harbor.

Second, differences over Iraq illustrate the widening gap in interests and values between the United States and several important European countries, especially France and Germany. These differences are not superficial; they are rooted in a basic philosophical divergence that will not be explained away by the normal admonition that "there have always been differences among NATO countries." This time, the political survival of the German—and perhaps the French—government depends on it. In both cases, political success depends increasingly on disagreeing with Washington on many of the most important international issues. At the same time, US policy—either by design or by accident—is dividing Europe and thereby damaging the Europeans' efforts to find common ground on the future of Europe and underscoring Europe's irrelevancy for US security interests.

GETTING PAST THE PAST

The Europeans will have to take the initiative to move beyond security anachronisms such as NATO, because it will not happen as a result of US leadership. Washington will cling to NATO even more desperately and continue to manufacture complicated, ineffective, even deleterious mechanisms to "prove" NATO's importance and viability. For Washington, NATO is the security institution that best exemplifies the static world it prefers—it makes no difference that the alliance no longer serves any useful security function. The American political class will not be voluntarily shaken from that perspective, no matter how much the world changes.

The Europeans, on the other hand, have been more ready to recognize and embrace the changes that are taking place in the structure of the international system. They are struggling with the transition and are more fully engaged in the transformation than is the United States. The Europeans have reached a critical juncture in the construction of the "European space." Certainly, questions of "widening versus deepening," problems of a multiple speed Europe, the lasting soundness of the Euro, the equity of the Common Agricultural Policy, and even issues of consensus versus majority rule are very important, and they will be handled one way or another in time. But the critical issue that will ultimately define the nature and character of European cooperation is the whole arena of foreign and security policy—an issue that the Europeans currently are not handling very well.

If the United States is blinded by its own self-righteousness, the Europeans are crippled emotionally by their timidity. For different reasons, then, both sides are unable to shed NATO's Cold War grip, despite the Europeans' greater potential to break this inertia. To do so, they will have to recognize that the conduct of foreign and security policy is perhaps the most fundamental arena that defines any polity. The Europeans are now "a de facto military protectorate of the United States,"[38] unable to fully provide for their own relations with other states and other political organizations on the international stage. To have one's security and foreign policy agenda set by another is the height of servitude.

The Europeans have made a halting start by trying to construct the Common Foreign and Security Policy (CFSP) and the European Security and Defense Policy (ESDP). Efforts in both areas have a long history, beginning in the 1960s and 1970s when the "member states of the European community cooperated and endeavored to consult with one another on major international problems."[39] These efforts progressed through the Single European Act in 1986, received a major boost in the Maastricht Treaty of 1993 and the Amsterdam Treaty of 1999, the Nice Treaty in 2001, and, in security specifically, at the 1999 Cologne Council meeting (including the Petersburg tasks), and the Helsinki Headline Goals (HHG), which are supposed to be achieved by 2003.[40]

But the effort has stalled, and it is likely to remain stalled as long as the Europeans are tied to the myth that NATO and its lore is the appropriate linchpin for the future. Although discussion under the current European Constitutional Convention does not presently provide a major role for foreign and security policy, there is no reason it cannot be extended to do so.[41] The platform and the precedent are available; only the political will is lacking. The Europeans should begin to chart their own course now by exercising their option under Article 13 of the NATO Treaty and announcing their intention to withdraw from the alliance. Ironically, the bitter transatlantic dispute over Iraq may already have started the process.

NOTES

1. David Steele, *Lord Salisbury—A Political Biography* (New York: Routledge, 1999), p. 121.

2. See *Congressional Digest*, 75 (February 1996), 33; "Summary of U.S. Government Policy on Bosnia," released by the Bureau of European and Canadian Affairs, US Department of State, 16 July 1998; press briefing on the NATO Summit and Kosovo, the White House, Washington, D.C., 20 April 1999; statement by Secretary of State Albright before the Senate Foreign Relations Committee, Washington, D.C., 20 April 1999.

3. Ivo Daalder, *Getting to Dayton—The Making of America's Bosnia Policy* (Washington: Brookings Institution, 2000), p. 164.

4. Comments by Undersecretary of Defense for Policy, Douglas Feith; see the Armed Forces Press Service, 28 February 2002.

5. Statement by Undersecretary of State for Political Affairs, Marc Grossman; see *Department of State Bulletin*, 9 October 2001.

6. *The Financial Times*, 15 May 2002.

7. Terrorism does not fit the bill because it is diffuse, sporadic, and of much less salience in Europe than in the United States. All of this requires a different kind of response than NATO can provide. In short, NATO does not have the tools to fight terrorism.

8. Robert Kagan, "Power and Weakness," *Policy Review*, No. 113 (June & July, 2002).

9. Anthony Padgen, *Lords of All the World—Ideologies of Empire in Spain, Britain, and France (1500-1800)* (New Haven, Conn.: Yale Univ. Press, 1995), pp. 5, 8.

10. Clearly, as disagreements within Europe over Washington's Iraq policy demonstrate, European countries are not always of one mind on all transatlantic issues. But intra-European divisions do not undermine the basic point, and once the immediate crisis over Iraq fades, the centrifugal issues separating the United States from the Europeans will accelerate.

11. "New Dawn for Russia," *European Defence*, no date, http://www.European-defence.co.uk/article14.html.

12. BBC World News Report, 25 September 2001.

13. *Der Spiegel*, 3 October 2001.

14. "Russia Ready to Rethink Stand on NATO: Putin," *Dawn*, 4 October 2001, http://www.dawn.com/2001/10/04/int5.htm.

15. http://64.69.109.103/mic/eaabstract.cfm?

16. NATO Basic Texts, *Study on NATO Enlargement*, ch. 1, "Purposes and Principles of Enlargement," http://www.nato.int/docu/basictxt/enl-9502.htm.

17. Dan Reiter, "Why NATO Enlargement Does Not Spread Democracy," *International Security*, 25 (Spring 2001), 60.

18. Jeffrey Simon, "NATO's Membership Action Plan and Defense Planning," *Problems of Post-Communism*, 48 (May-June 2001), 28.

19. Ibid., p. 30.

20. Dipankar De Sarkar, "EUROPE: Arms Trade Launches All-Out Sales Blitz on New NATO Members," *World News*, 18 July 2001, http://www.oneworld.org/ips2/jul/nato.html.

21. *Aerospace Daily*, 28 August 2002.

22. *Fort Worth Business News*, 13 February 2003.

23. Institute for War and Peace Reporting, "Romania: Courting NATO Harms EU Hopes," 21 August 2002.

24. Ibid.

25. Radio Free Europe/Radio Liberty news line, 10 February 2003.

26. Although the EU is the most important organization for the future of Central and Eastern Europe, other organizations, such as the Southeast Europe Brigade (SEEBRIG) and the Southeastern Europe Defense Ministerial (SEEDM) process are potentially more important to the specific security issues of these countries than is NATO.

27. Anthony Cragg, "The Combined Joint Task Force Concept: A Key Component of the Alliance's Adaptation," *NATO Review*, 44 (July 1996), http://www.nato.int/docu/review/1996/9604-2.htm. See also, NATO Fact Sheets, "The Combined Joint Task Forces Concept," http://www.nato.int/docu/facts/2000/cjtfcon.htm.

28. NATO Fact Sheets, "NATO's Membership Action Plan," http://www.nato.int/docu/facts/2000/ natomap.htm. Also see Membership Action Plan, Press Release NAC-S(99)66, 24 April 1999, http://www.nato.int/docu/pr/1999/p99-066e.htm.

29. The five areas or chapters in the MAP program are: (1) political/economic issues, (2) defense/military issues, (3) resource issues, (4) security issues, and (5) legal issues.

30. NATO Fact Sheets, "NATO's Defence Capabilities Initiative," http://www.nato.int/docu/facts/2000/nato-dci.htm.

31. *The Washington Post*, 31 January 2003.

32. Jeffrey Simon, "NATO at a Crossroads: Can it Cope with Post-September 11th and Enlargement Challenges?" unpublished paper, Institute For Security Studies, National Defense University, p. 3.

33. Testimony by Thomas Szayna (RAND Corporation) before the Committee on NATO Enlargement of the US House of Representatives' Committee on International Relations, Sub-Committee on Europe, 17 April 2002.

34. Prague Summit Declaration, issued 21 November 2002.

35. "A Dangerous Divergence," *The Washington Post*, 10 December 2002, op-ed.

36. Stephen M. Walt, *The Origins of Alliances* (Ithaca, N.Y.: Cornell Univ. Press, 1987), ch. 2; Glenn H. Snyder, *Alliance Politics* (Ithaca, N.Y.: Cornell Univ. Press, 1997), chs. 2, 6.

37. Richard L. Kugler, "Preparing NATO to Meet New Threats: Challenge and Opportunity," US Department of State, International Information Programs, 27 March 2002, http://usinfo.state.gov/topical/pol/nato/02032800.htm.

38. Zbigniew Brzezinski et al., "Living With the New Europe," *The National Interest*, No. 60 (Summer 2000).

39. Council of the European Union, "Common Foreign and Security Policy/European Security and Defense Policy," http://ue.eu.int/pesc/pres.asp?lang=en.

40. Some scholars argue that European efforts to find common ground in foreign and security policy can be traced back to the European Defense Community idea (Pleven Plan) of 1966-67.

41. Title III, Article 13, of the preliminary draft Constitutional Treaty provides ample justification for bold moves in the area of foreign and security policy.

NATO after Prague: Learning the Lessons of 9/11

Michael Rühle

It would be an understatement to note that the last months have not been kind to the transatlantic relationship. When Iraq moved to the front burner, the transatlantic community was forced to tackle an issue that threatened to overwhelm it. As a result, the spirit of transatlantic solidarity, which was so impressively displayed after the terrorist attacks on 9/11, has faded rapidly. The United States is disappointed with what it sees as only qualified European support for the war on terror, and it scoffs at European military weakness. Many Europeans, in turn, are disappointed about what they perceive as a US fixation on military responses, and they resent the US approach of casually lumping together the war on terror with issues such as weapons of mass destruction or regime change in Iraq.

NATO, the manifestation of the transatlantic security relationship, could never have remained unaffected by such discord. Although the real debate on Iraq was played out in the halls of the United Nations, and although NATO was not expected to play a direct role in a war on Iraq, sooner or later the Atlantic Alliance was bound to be hit by this debate. In February 2003, a short but agonizing disagreement erupted over the timing of planning for the defense of Turkey in case of war on Iraq. Only a few Allies held the view that the initiation of NATO's planning should be made contingent on further developments in the United Nations, yet for almost two weeks, NATO appeared to be blocked. That the disagreement was indeed one over timing, and not over substance, helped to bring the crisis to an end before any permanent damage was done. As NATO's Secretary General, Lord Robertson, put it in his personal account of the crisis, the Alliance had taken a hit above, not below, the waterline.

The short crisis within NATO, as well as the protracted crisis over Iraq, demonstrated that the Atlantic community has not yet fully adjusted to the post- 9/11 security environment—in either political or institutional terms. However, one ought to resist the temptation to judge a long-term, strategic Alliance by short-term tactical tests. The current focus on Iraq and its discontents obscures the fact that NATO has embarked on a process of post-9/11 adaptation that will help bridge the enormous divides within Europe and across the Atlantic that the Iraq crisis has exposed.

THE NEW TRANSATLANTIC DEBATE: 1990 REVISITED

Today's transatlantic security debate is, in essence, the debate that did not take place a little over a decade ago, when the Cold War ended. Back then, a fundamental discussion about the future shape

Michael Rühle is Head of the Policy Planning and Speechwriting Section, NATO Political Affairs Division, in Brussels. As with all *Parameters* articles, the views expressed are those of the author and should not be construed as representing the views of the North Atlantic Treaty Organization, the US Army War College, or any other official agency. The author is indebted to James Appathurai and Rad van den Akker for comments and suggestions.

of the transatlantic relationship seemed inevitable. But it was put off. There was simply too much unfinished business left over from the Cold War. The transatlantic community could not afford to divert its attention away from the task it still faced together: the task of cleaning up the mess left by the Cold War. That entailed significant challenges:

- To embrace the new democracies in Central and Eastern Europe, who were craving their share of Europe, including its Atlantic dimension in NATO.
- To associate a Russia that, in a sense, was both an old empire and a new state, still unsure of its European vocation.
- And to address the conflicts in the Balkans, which were making a mockery of the idea of Europe as a zone of peace and shared values.

Meeting these challenges required Europe and North America to work together. Accordingly, NATO reached out to Central and Eastern Europe, through its policy of partnership and through NATO enlargement. The Alliance also played a major role in associating Russia to NATO and, thus, to the emerging new Europe. And NATO played a key role in pacifying the Balkans through its military engagement.

However, this impressive display of transatlantic unity could not hide the fact that eventually the relationship between the two sides of the Atlantic was bound to change in the longer run. As early as 1991, the Gulf War raised the question of whether NATO was still in line with the US security agenda after the Cold War. In that conflict, which was taking place "out of area" and fought by a "coalition of the willing," NATO played only a supporting role. Also in the early 1990s, the European Union (EU) started to articulate an ambition to become a military actor in its own right, raising the question of NATO's future. And the initial ambiguity by the United States regarding humanitarian intervention in the Balkans signaled a profound uncertainty about how the United States viewed its own future role on the European continent. And still, despite these changes, a major debate about the future of transatlantic relations did not occur. Those on both sides of the Atlantic did not want it to occur. And they did well by dodging it—and by keeping their eye on the European ball.

THE NEW SECURITY ENVIRONMENT: PUSHING NATO TO THE FRINGES?

After 11 September 2001, however, a fundamental debate about the future transatlantic security relationship could not be dodged any longer. The changes in the international security environment had become too fundamental to allow for business as usual. Both the transatlantic relationship in general and NATO in particular have had to adapt to the realization that the immediate post-Cold War period has ended and a new, still undefined era has begun. Three changes, in particular, stand out:

- The first change concerns the new threats of terrorism and weapons of mass destruction. These threats emerge from outside of Europe. Naturally, they draw US attention away from the Old Continent, toward Central Asia and the Middle East. A focus away from Europe, however, also means a focus away from NATO, an institution that is critically dependent on US leadership.
- The second change concerns the strategies with which to respond to the new threats. Simply put, an effective response might require a different team and a different approach than NATO is able to provide. Afghanistan was the first glimpse of that option. Also, NATO might be sidelined by ad hoc coalitions of states more able and perhaps even more willing

than the old NATO fogies. Furthermore, NATO might also be sidetracked because of the perception that its consensual decisionmaking culture is too slow and cumbersome to deliver results in time.

- The third change concerns the military capabilities required to respond to the new threats. Rapid response, force projection, and protection against weapons of mass destruction are at a premium—precisely the areas in which the United States is increasingly strong and where Europe's Cold War legacy forces are weak. As a result, US unilateralist impulses are strengthened, and Europeans see whatever influence they hoped to exert on Washington drifting away down the Potomac.

In short, by 12 September 2001, a new debate about the future of the transatlantic security relationship had become inevitable. Dodging it again, as was done in the early 1990s, would not work, not least since Europe today appears "settled." NATO had to face the debate head-on, even if this meant, to use John Foster Dulles's term, an "agonizing reappraisal" of the value of this 54-year Alliance.

CONTINUITIES: THE ENDURING TRANSATLANTIC CONNECTION

Despite the fundamental need for change, NATO could take on this reexamination of its internal relationships with considerable self-confidence. After all, 9/11 did not change everything. Despite some American claims that Europe was "fading slowly in the US rearview mirror," there is a transatlantic connection that has become too firmly entrenched to be easily jettisoned.

First, European stability remains a key US strategic interest. The consolidation of Europe as an undivided, democratic, and market-oriented space remains a major objective of US security policy. Only in NATO, the central legitimizing framework for US power in Europe, can the United States play an undisputed leadership role in advancing this strategic objective. Thus, the United States is not likely to surrender this role. Indeed, many US critics of Europe have yet to grasp the fact that both NATO enlargement and the war on terrorism have actually increased the United States' immersion in European security affairs. Consequently, there is no serious political force in the United States advocating a withdrawal from Europe.

Second, Europeans remain the key strategic allies for the United States. This statement does not exclude a stronger US focus on other regions, nor is it contradicted by the emergence of much wider "coalitions of the willing" along the model provided by the Afghanistan campaign. Europe's military capabilities lag behind the United States, yet on a global scale, Europe ranks No. 2 militarily. Moreover, although the debate preceding the war against Iraq may have suggested otherwise, it is only in Europe where the United States finds a milieu of countries predisposed to working with the United States. In Asia, by contrast, the United States will have to continue to rely on bilateral relationships with politically and culturally very different countries. In short, if the United States wants to remain the world's predominant power, it will have to remain a "European power" as well.

Third, the United States remains Europe's most important ally. The United States continues to play a unique role within the transatlantic relationship, as a political crisis manager as well as a military coalition-builder, both within Europe (e.g., the Balkans) and beyond (e.g., the Persian Gulf). This unique US role is widely accepted by the Europeans, notwithstanding ritualistic European criticism of US arrogance or heavy-handedness. As in the United States, there is currently no serious political force in Europe that would advocate a US withdrawal from the continent. On the contrary, with Central and Eastern Europe rejoining the Atlantic community of nations through the enlargement of NATO, the number of countries arguing for a strong US role in Europe has only increased.

MARRYING CONTINUITY WITH CHANGE: THREE DIRECTIONS OF NATO'S REFORM

If the above changes and continuities are taken into account, a fairly clear picture emerges of three major directions for NATO's reform. First, NATO must find a new balance between addressing its traditional, Eurocentric missions and tackling the new global threats, such as terrorism and weapons of mass destruction. Second, it must acquire the military capabilities to fulfill its new missions. And, finally, it must learn to react quickly and flexibly to new challenges.

The Prague Summit, scheduled for November 2002, was becoming NATO's key opportunity to deliver on all three counts. Initially billed as an "Enlargement Summit," the idea of making the admission of new members the sole focus of the meeting was dropped after 9/11. All the Allies agreed that NATO enlargement would be a historic step, consolidating Europe as a single security space from the Atlantic to the Black Sea, and from the Baltics to the Balkans. There were widespread fears, however, that the United States might lose interest in the Alliance if the Prague meeting did no more than issue membership invitations. Accordingly, the Prague Summit was relabeled a "Transformation Summit."

NATO's New Missions and the End of the "Out-of-Area" Syndrome

The first fundamental change alluded to above is for NATO to adopt new roles in countering terrorism and dealing with weapons of mass destruction. This is an imperative driven as much by NATO's survival instincts as by the changing strategic environment. If NATO were unable or unwilling to play such a role, it would become completely detached from the US security agenda. This would not only seal NATO's fate as a vibrant institution, it also would deprive the transatlantic community of a major "transmission belt" for ironing out differences on other issues. And, above all, it would condemn to the fringes what is still the world's most effective facilitator of military coalitions.

Even before the Prague Summit, a NATO role in combating terrorism was being defined by two unprecedented events. The first was the invocation of Article 5 on 12 September 2001. By agreeing that a terrorist attack by a non-state actor should trigger NATO's collective self-defense obligation, the Alliance in effect mandated itself to make combating terrorism an enduring NATO mission. This broadening of the meaning of collective self-defense was complemented by a second precedent: the deployment of forces from many NATO nations to Afghanistan. This marked the de facto end of NATO's out-of-area debate, which, as the French NATO Ambassador put it cogently, had collapsed with the Twin Towers.

The Prague Summit further defined NATO's role in combating terrorism with the development of a military concept against terrorism, specific military capabilities to implement this new mission, agreement on a Partnership Action Plan against terrorism, and a stated willingness to act in support of the international community. Prague's definition of NATO as a focal point of any multinational military response to terrorism was given considerable credibility with the agreement to provide Germany and the Netherlands with NATO planning and support as they assumed command of the International Security Assistance Force (ISAF) III in Afghanistan. The emerging discussion on whether NATO itself should take command of ISAF indicates that this evolution has significant potential to move NATO into a new role outside the traditional Euro-Atlantic area.

A similar approach was taken with respect to the threat posed by the proliferation of weapons of mass destruction and their means of delivery. Before 9/11, NATO's efforts to counter this threat appeared to be something of an afterthought. Non-US Allies had had reservations about giving prominence to this issue, but accepted it as an agenda item in part to accommodate the United States. The Prague Summit presented an entirely different picture. The various initiatives on nuclear, biological, and chemical (NBC) weapon defenses signaled a much stronger transatlantic consensus on the need to cope with this challenge. Technically, these initiatives, which range from enhanced detection capabilities to developing a Prototype Deployable NBC Analytical Laboratory, may not look spectacular. But their immediate significance lies in the political realm. They indicate a heightened awareness of a common threat, and a determination to not let the issue of weapons of mass destruction become a major transatlantic fault line. This was underscored further with the agreement to begin a new NATO Missile Defense feasibility study to examine options for protecting Alliance territory, forces, and population centers against the full range of missile threats.

These decisions taken preceding and at the Prague Summit put NATO firmly back on track. By claiming a distinct role in combating terrorism, and by giving much more prominence to issues related to weapons of mass destruction, NATO has recalibrated its agenda in line with both the emerging strategic environment post-9/11, and with the two dominant US security concerns.

NATO's Military Reform: Bridging the Capabilities Gap

The second major element of NATO's reform is in its overall military capabilities. For the past several years, the priority within the Alliance has been to improve the "European pillar." This process was based on the need to give Europe more military clout to look after its own backyard. Implicitly, it was also based on the eventual diminishing of the US role in future European crisis management scenarios. As 9/11 and the Afghanistan campaign demonstrated, however, "Europeanization" is not enough to ensure transatlantic security. The events since 9/11 demonstrate beyond a doubt that a European priority must remain the ability to cooperate militarily with the United States.

This does not diminish the strategic rationale for a European Security and Defense Policy (ESDP) within the European Union. Yet for the EU countries to concentrate solely on acquiring autonomous capabilities means necessarily to concentrate on acquiring capabilities for low- and medium-intensity conflicts. This would lead to a division of labor which neither side of the Atlantic wants, whereby the United States does the fighting and the Europeans "do the dishes," as a French observer once put it. This would be politically unsustainable, both across the Atlantic as well as within the European Union. Some EU nations will always want to fight alongside the United States, thereby exerting more influence on US strategy (and perhaps sparing themselves the "dishes" part, too). In short, Europe must look beyond ESDP and try to keep apace with the United States.

The Prague Summit made it very clear that this rationale has been understood. In line with the requirement to enhance NATO's ability for power projection, the Alliance set in train a reform of its command structure, which will result in more functionally oriented commands. Another significant summit decision was the adoption of the US proposal to create a NATO Response Force. Not only did it signal NATO's willingness to adapt in line with the requirement for more rapid military action, it is also a catalyst to help Europeans accelerate their force transformation, and a sign of a continued US willingness to view the Alliance as an important military tool.

The key summit achievement in this respect, however, may well have been the Prague Capabilities Commitment. Individual Allies made specific political commitments to improve their capabilities in areas key to modern military operations. Once fully implemented, these commitments would quadruple the number of outsize aircraft in Europe; establish a pool of air-to-air refueling aircraft until additional new tankers will be available; ensure that most of NATO's deployable high-readiness forces will have chemical, radiological, biological, and nuclear defense equipment; and significantly increase the non-US stocks of air-delivered, precision-guided munitions.

These commitments mark a turning point in transforming the defense capabilities of the non-US Allies. If nations stick to these commitments, both NATO and the EU will have made a major step forward toward meeting 21st century requirements. Failure to implement these decisions, however, would deal a major blow to the transatlantic relationship, as it would confirm lingering American doubts about the seriousness of their European Allies. It also would represent a serious setback for Europe itself, by casting a dark shadow over the future of the European Security and Defense Policy. For all these reasons, the Prague Capabilities Commitment must succeed.

NATO's Internal Reform: Toward a More Streamlined Organization

The third area of Alliance reform concerns the organization itself. NATO's working methods must reflect the requirements imposed by the new strategic environment. Although the Alliance will soon have 26 members, the organization's working methods have remained largely unchanged from those developed in the early 1950s for an Alliance of 12. Even if American charges that the Kosovo campaign was "war by committee" were an urban myth, the need for change is still clear. As NATO is enlarging both its membership and its mandate, its working methods cannot be left unaffected. In a nutshell, NATO needs to be less bureaucratic and more flexible.

Almost unnoticed by the broader public, the Prague Summit made a strong start in this direction. Heads of state and government agreed to reduce the numbers of NATO committees (currently 467) by 30 percent. More decisions will be pushed toward subordinate committees, leaving the North Atlantic Council room to discuss strategic issues. The procedures for ministerial meetings have been streamlined as well, sacrificing formality in order to gain time for more substantive exchanges. Over time, these changes should lead to a different working culture within the Alliance.

But more changes may be waiting further down the road. For example, one could foresee arrangements whereby troop contributing nations run an operation and decide on the targeting, while the North Atlantic Council confines itself to providing overall strategic guidance. This model, which resembles the EU's "committee of contributors," may be seen by some as an assault on the cherished rule of consensus. But it need not be. Clearly, a shift to "majority voting" in NATO remains out of the question. The requirement for consensus not only generates pressure to seek compromise, it also provides countries with the emergency brake of a veto—an option that reassures particularly smaller countries that they cannot be steamrolled into submission by the bigger Allies. However, a modification of NATO's working culture that includes the possibility of setting up flexible coalitions, or that includes the possibility of "constructive abstention" appears not only feasible, but indispensable.

In a similar vein, the idea of NATO acting on occasion as a toolbox, i.e. as a pool from which to provide coalitions of the willing with specific capabilities, is here to stay. Even if the notion of a toolbox-Alliance does indeed run counter to NATO's self-perception as a cohesive, all-for-one and one-for-all organization, resisting it may turn out to be futile. Rather than fighting against this concept, the time may have come to look at how a toolbox approach can be reconciled with the continuing need for political cohesion. NATO's long-stated willingness to support the European Union in crisis management is an illustration of how well this can work—because an EU drawing on NATO assets is little else but a coalition of the willing drawing on the NATO toolbox.

A NATO thus streamlined could deliver a range of capabilities to deal with a range of challenges. Even on the issue of preemption, which requires rapid decision-taking on a potentially controversial case, one should not assume *a priori* that NATO would be too clumsy to deliver. The more the Allies absorb the full implications of the new strategic environment, the more they may see a need for quick responses. This is not to belittle the legal difficulties surrounding any strategy that might involve preemption. But these difficulties largely stem from the fact that the current international legal system was not built to deal with scenarios of terrorists using weapons of mass destruction. Over time, this may change. Moreover, as the Allies have demonstrated in their Kosovo campaign, they are perfectly able to act in a legal gray area—and take the heat for it—if the alternatives to action appear worse.

CONCLUSION: UNFINISHED BUSINESS, BUT . . .

NATO's role in the aftermath of 9/11 was hampered by three interrelated dilemmas. First, there was no full-fledged consensus on how to tackle the new threats. Second, the United States felt that the Europeans simply did not possess enough useful capabilities to warrant going through NATO in order to round them up. And, finally, some in Washington saw NATO as an organization much too tedious and cumbersome to subject American policy to it.

A little more than a year after 9/11, the Prague Summit in November 2002 demonstrated that NATO was assimilating the lessons of the attacks and their aftermath. The Alliance demonstrated an emerging transatlantic consensus on how to tackle the new threats; it set in train a process that should result in more relevant European capabilities; and it initiated a wide-ranging reform of NATO's working methods. The organization had displayed that it could handle a steep learning curve.

As with any summit, the meeting in Prague could never be expected to resolve all the Alliance's problems. The subsequent crisis over Iraq has demonstrated that the transatlantic relationship suffers from structural dilemmas that cannot be overcome simply by institutional fixes. For example, much of the transatlantic divergence on Iraq stemmed from the simple but powerful fact that since 9/11 the United States has been psychologically at war, whereas Europe has not. Thus, Americans and Europeans will almost certainly continue to argue over the origins of, and the response to, terrorism. Nor will there be complete convergence in threat perceptions regarding weapons of mass destruction. The Europeans share neither the US urgency to act against "axis of evil" proliferants, nor do they share the American proclivity to write off deterrence as unworkable. And asymmetries in military capabilities will remain, even if the Europeans fulfill their Prague Capabilities Commitment pledges to the letter.

The Prague Summit was nonetheless highly significant. It sent a clear signal that irrespective of disagreements on individual issues, working together remains the preferred option for both sides of the Atlantic. As the transatlantic relationship enters another period of fundamental transition, NATO's Prague Summit demonstrated that the institutional underpinnings of this relationship are still solid.

Part IV
Background Information on the WTO

The Mark Amstutz 's article is supplemental information for Hegemonic Stability Theory and the WTO debate. It describes the history and provides background information to the Breton Woods Agreements—creating the GATT, IMF and World Bank.

The Bretton Woods System:
The System of International Trade

By Mark Amstutz

In the aftermath of World War II, the major democratic powers, led by the United States, established an international economic order designed to facilitate international trade and promote efficient monetary transactions. This economic order—known as the Bretton Woods system[1]—involved three major institutions:

1. The General Agreement on Tariffs and Trade (GATT)[2]
2. The International Monetary Fund (IMF)
3. The International Bank for Reconstruction and Development (IBRD), or World Bank

The purpose of GATT was to foster freer international commerce by reducing trade barriers. The aim of the IMF was to facilitate international economic transactions by assuring an adequate source of international reserves and by regulating the interrelationship of foreign currencies. Finally, the IBRD was created to provide capital for the reconstruction of Europe and to foster the economic growth of other nations. Although the international economic order has of course undergone a number of significant modifications since it was established nearly fifty years ago, the institutions and liberal procedures created in the late 1940s continue to function largely as they were designed. In the following sections we examine the nature and evolution of GATT, and the role of the IMF in facilitating international financial transactions. . . [and] the role of the World Bank in facilitating Third World development.

GATT AND TRADE LIBERALIZATION

The most important rules governing international trade in the postwar decades have been established by the *General Agreement on Tariffs and Trade* (**GATT**). Since its creation in 1947, this Geneva-based multilateral institution, which has grown from 19 members to 123 in 1996,[3] has contributed significantly to the reduction of tariff and nontariff barriers to trade. GATT's most basic working norm—the "most-favored-nation" **(MFN) principle**—calls on states to carry out trade policies on a reciprocal and nondiscriminatory basis. This means that when a GATT member-state accords a trade preference, it is obligated to give that same preference to all member-states.

MARK AMSTUTZ is a professor of political science at Wheaton College.

Mark R. Amstutz *International Conflict and Cooperation* New York: McGraw-Hill/Dushkin, 2000, pp. 399-404, 408-410, 431.
Copyright by McGraw-Hill. Reprinted with Permission.

GATT has been successful in bringing about major reductions in tariff and nontariff trade barriers. The liberalization of international trade has been undertaken through a number of negotiations, known as *"rounds"*. The two most successful of these have been the Kennedy and Uruguay Rounds, which resulted in tariff reductions on most exports of 35 to 40 percent each. As a result of the GATT's significant reductions in trade barriers, international trade has increased greatly in the last half of this century, rising from $94 billion in 1955 to more than $4 trillion in 1994. Indeed, since the 1980s, the growth rate of global trade has been much greater than the growth rate of the world's total economic output.

Despite the considerable success of GATT during the early postwar period, protectionism began to reemerge in the early 1980s, thereby threatening continued trade liberalization. Four developments contributed to the reemergence of protectionist pressures: first, the extraordinary increases in petroleum prices; second, the increasing instability of the international monetary system (caused in part by the shift from fixed to flexible exchange rates); third, the extraordinary growth in exports of industrial commodities from Japan and the newly industrializing countries (NICs); and fourth, the continuation of preferential trade policies by the European Economic Community. Moreover, the global economic slow-down in the early 1980s further threatened trade liberalization. As governments adjusted to increasing international competition and slower growth rates, governments had to face growing domestic protectionist pressures from constituencies threatened by job displacement and unemployment.

This growing protectionism was evident in the United States in the late 1980s and early 1990s as the government sought to respond to large and persistent trade deficits. Beginning in 1980 with a trade deficit of more than $25 billion, the U.S. trade imbalance increased to $160 billion in 1987. The trade deficit then declined to $74 billion in 1991 before rising again to a record $183 billion in 1995. A principal reason for this large trade imbalance has been the major deficits with Japan, accounting for 30 to 50 percent of the total.

Notwithstanding growing international commercial tensions, the major powers persisted in further reducing trade barriers. During the Uruguay Round (1986-1993) the hundred participating states sought to extend trade liberalization to agriculture, services, and intellectual property (patents, copyrights, trademarks). Because these areas were complex and politically sensitive, the negotiations were intense and protracted. In 1992 trade conflict came to a head over agriculture, precipitating an intense dispute between the European Community and the United States that threatened not only the trade talks but also the collapse of GATT itself. Fortunately the so-called "chablis war" was averted, and consensus between the major industrial economies was achieved on agricultural trade liberalization, thereby paving the way for the Uruguay Accord.

The Uruguay Round was especially significant for two reasons. First, it extended GATT rules to intellectual property (e.g., patents, copyrights, and trademarks) and to agricultural products. Until July 1, 1995, when the Uruguay Agreement went into effect, GATT norms had applied only to industrial goods. Because of the new trade accord, about one-fourth of the world's total annual trade (more than $1 trillion) that was formerly excluded from GATT coverage is now governed by GATT rules. As a result of the further reduction in trade barriers, it has been estimated that the Uruguay trade liberalization will increase global income by $235 billion.[4] Second, the Uruguay Agreement is important because it created a more powerful trade-enforcement institution, the **World Trade Organization (WTO)**. The WTO, an umbrella organization that now oversees GATT and two new sister institutions covering services and intellectual property, is responsible for monitoring implementation of the Uruguay Accord and for settling trade disputes among member-states. Although it is still too soon to know how effective the new organization will be in policing the international trading system, WTO rules give the new organization far more authority in settling trade disputes than the less formal GATT structure.[5] As of July 1996, fifty-four trade disputes had been brought to the WTO for arbitration. Of these, thirty-three were launched by the developed states, with the United States initiating the largest (eighteen) number of complaints. The developing nations were responsible for initiating twenty-one trade complaints. As of 1997, the WTO had 132 members, with another 29 states, including China and Russia, having observer status.

One of the most effective approaches to trade liberalization has been at the regional level. Neighboring states in Africa, Asia, Europe, North and South America, and the Pacific Basin have established a variety of regional organizations, including common markets and free trade associations, aimed at fostering economic expansion through trade liberalization. To date, the most successful of these experiments has been the European Union (EU) . . . after creating a common market among its members, the EU has moved toward the establishment of full economic union among its fifteen member-states by seeking to create a single European currency, as well as common defense policies and foreign policies.

Another important regional economic development has been the establishment of the North American Free Trade Agreement (NAFTA). Created in 1994, **NAFTA** is a trade accord among Canada, Mexico, and the United States that seeks to increase regional economic output through trade liberalization. The accord calls for the removal over ten years of all restrictions on manufacturing trade and most cross-border investment barriers. In addition, tariffs and quotas on agricultural goods are to be eliminated within fifteen years. Because some American political leaders claimed that NAFTA would lead to job losses in the United States, the adoption of NAFTA by the U.S. government was a highly contentious political issue. NAFTA critics, led by business leaders and 1992 and 1996 U.S. presidential candidate Ross Perot, argued that the accord would lead to massive job migration to Mexico and harmful environmental consequences. By contrast, NAFTA advocates argued that greater trade with Canada and Mexico would increase American economic efficiency, foster domestic economic expansion, and improve living standards in all three countries, especially in Mexico. As of 1997, the effects of NAFTA in the United States have been hardly perceptible, calling into question the predictions of both its critics and supporters. At the same time, some studies suggest that the preferential treatment now being given Mexican exports has been harmful to developing economies in the region, especially Caribbean countries. A study by the World Bank, for example, has estimated that Caribbean nations lost 123,000 jobs to Mexico during the first two years of NAFTA because of diversion of foreign investment and trade. According to this study, the Caribbean apparel industry has been especially damaged, with the forced closure of some 150 clothing manufacturing plants in 1995 and 1996 alone.[6]

THE GLOBAL MONETARY SYSTEM

One requirement for efficient trade among states is a flexible and stable international monetary system. Just as money is the major means of domestic exchange, so money is the major instrument of international trade. But even though each country has a government-regulated currency, the world economy has neither a common currency nor a governmental institution with the authority to regulate international monetary affairs.

THE NATURE AND ROLE OF FOREIGN EXCHANGE

If a state is to effectively meet its foreign financial obligations, it will have to acquire foreign exchange—that is, foreign currencies with which to pay for imports and cover other financial obligations. The principal means by which states generate foreign exchange is by accumulating financial reserves through trade. These surplus funds can therefore be exchanged for foreign currencies to buy foreign goods and services. The aim of an effective international monetary system is to facilitate efficient currency convertibility.

Because each country has its own money, states acquire needed foreign currencies by trading currencies in foreign exchange markets. Because the U.S. economy is the largest, the U.S. dollar is the major international currency, accounting for more than 60 percent of world currency reserves. It has been estimated that 80 percent of all trading in foreign exchange markets involves four currencies: the U.S. dollar (41%), the German mark (20%), the Japanese yen (12%), and the British pound (7%).[7] Most foreign exchange trading is carried out in the world's principal financial centers—namely, London, New York, Tokyo, Zurich, Frankfurt, Paris, Hong Kong, with London accounting for nearly a third of all currency exchange.

THE BRETTON WOODS MONETARY SYSTEM

If international trade is to be carried out efficiently, there needs to be widely accepted rules governing international financial transactions. Benjamin Cohen, a leading political economist, argues that an efficient and stable international monetary system must provide three elements: *liquidity, adjustment*, and *confidence*.[8] To assure liquidity, a system must provide an adequate supply of international money (reserves) to finance trade and facilitate balance of payments adjustments among states. To assist adjustment, the system must provide an accepted means to resolve temporary national payments imbalances. And finally, the system along with the international reserve currency must enjoy the confidence of other states.

Given the absence of world government, the creation and maintenance of an international monetary system has depended on the voluntary cooperation of major powers. During the late nineteenth and early twentieth centuries, for example, the international monetary system was based on gold. Under the so-called *gold standard*, states pegged their currencies to gold, promising to redeem their currency for a particular quantity of gold. The system collapsed with the outbreak of World War I, when European powers moved to protect their gold stockpiles and ceased to back up their currencies with it. After a period of significant international monetary confusion, a new international monetary system was created toward the end of World War II. This arrangement, known as the **Bretton Woods monetary system**, was established by the Allied powers to facilitate international financial transactions, to foster global monetary stability, and to inhibit harmful, competitive monetary policies, such as those prevalent during the interwar period. The system operated in accordance with four rules:

1. Exchange rates were to be fixed, allowing only for small shifts.
2. States could alter their exchange rate when fundamental balance of payments disequilibria developed, provided international consent was given beforehand.
3. A pool of international reserves would be created to assist states during periods of temporary balance of payments disequilibria.
4. The U.S. dollar would serve as the major currency of international exchange, with confidence in this currency assured by the United States' guarantee of convertibility of dollars into gold at $35.00 an ounce.

To implement these rules, the major powers established an international financial institution, the International Monetary Fund (**IMF**), to foster international financial coordination. In particular, the IMF was to monitor and coordinate exchange rates and ensure international liquidity for carrying out transnational economic transactions. To assure an adequate pool of international reserves, an IMF reserve fund was created from member-states' contributions, which were to be assigned on the basis of countries' relative economic capabilities. The major powers' quotas, which determine their voting power in IMF decision making, were as follows in 1995: United States—17 percent, Japan—7 percent, United Kingdom—5 percent, Germany—5 percent, France—5 percent, and Canada—3 percent.[9] Three-fourths of each state's quota contributions are paid in the member-state's own currency and one-fourth in gold. In 1993, the IMF pool of international reserves was estimated at nearly $187 billion.

States are allowed to borrow from the IMF in order to settle international debts, up to 125 percent of their quota. As a precondition for loans, the IMF ordinarily insists on domestic austerity measures that will help correct the balance of payments disequilibria. Because IMF loans are normally associated with stringent financial requirements, developing nations often resent the economic demands of the IMF, especially when reduction in public expenditures leads to domestic strife, as was the case in Caracas, Venezuela, in March 1989 following the government's imposition of austerity measures.

Because the dollar was the key reserve currency under the Bretton Woods system, the increasing need for international reserves could only be satisfied through continued U.S. balance of payments deficits. In 1960 economist Robert Triffin pointed out that the dollar-exchange standard was fundamentally flawed because the availability of dollars could only be achieved through increasing U.S. indebtedness, a condition that would ultimately undermine confidence in the dollar.[10] By the late 1960s this is exactly what happened. As Western European economies gained strength relative to the U.S. economy, their currencies became undervalued relative to the dollar, thereby further exacerbating the U.S. balance of payments disequilibria. As a result of declining confidence in the dollar, foreigners converted their dollar holdings into gold.

In 1971 the U.S. balance of payments deficit soared to more than $10 billion, more than doubling what it had been at any time in the previous five years. To rectify this imbalance between the U.S. economy and that of other industrial states, President Richard Nixon imposed a number of radical economic changes on August 15, 1971. Specifically, Nixon stopped the convertibility of the dollar into gold and imposed a surcharge on U.S. imports from Europe and Japan until the dollar was devalued (decreased in value in relation to other currencies). Although Nixon's actions strengthened the American economy, ending the dollar's convertibility destroyed a key pillar of the Bretton Woods system. And when the IMF adopted a more flexible system of exchange rates in March 1973, it in effect brought the Bretton Woods system to an end.

THE POST BRETTON WOODS MONETARY SYSTEM

Since the demise of the Bretton Woods system, no orderly monetary system has replaced it. The post-Bretton Woods regime is essentially a "nonsystem" based on a mixture of exchange rates. The basis for this regime was laid at the IMF meeting in Kingston, Jamaica, in 1976. At the Jamaica conference, IMF member-states made the following decisions:

1. Floating exchange rates were legalized.
2. The role of gold in international reserves was reduced.
3. IMF quotas—that amount of money members contribute to the IMF—were increased, especially for OPEC members.
4. Economic aid to the Third World was increased.
5. The establishment of a currency's international value became the sole responsibility of each state.

According to one leading scholar, the actions taken at the Jamaica meeting represented the triumph of domestic autonomy over international rules.[11]

Although the post-Bretton Woods system does not provide the financial stability of the former dollar-gold system, the current norms have the advantage of greater flexibility in responding to the balance of payments disequilibria. Theoretically, under the new regime, a significant balance of payments deficit should result in less confidence in a state's national currency, and this should, in turn, lead to a currency's loss of value—either through the behavior of foreign exchange markets or through deliberate governmental action in lowering the value of a currency through *devaluation*. The decline in the currency's relative value should make exports more competitive, thereby contributing to the reestablishment of a balanced foreign trade account.

But the system has not worked this way, at least for the United States. The U.S. trade position shifted dramatically during the 1980s, moving from a modest surplus in the late 1970s; to a soaring deficit of close to $160 billion in 1987, and to more than $180 billion in 1995. As noted before, the perpetuation of a trade deficit normally leads to the weakening of a state's currency, but this has not happened to the dollar, in part because of heavy foreign (especially Japanese) investment in U.S. securities, and also because of the continuing confidence in the long-term prosperity and stability of the U.S. economy. As a result, foreign governments along with foreign exchange traders have maintained a high demand for dollars.

In order to cope with the expanding global trade, international reserves have increased greatly, rising from an estimated $129 billion in 1971 to more than $1.1 trillion in 1993. Most of these reserves are in the form of foreign currencies, with gold providing nearly one-third of the total. To meet the growing demand for international liquidity, the IMF established in 1969 a new reserve asset known as Special Drawing Rights (**SDRs**). The SDRs are a form of international "paper gold" assigned to IMF members in proportion to their institutional quotas in order to meet "paper" obligations among central banks of IMF member-states. Unlike gold, dollars, and other international currencies, SDRs are not used for meeting commercial and other financial obligations but only for settling accounts among central banks. As of 1993, total SDRs were valued at about $21.4 billion, or roughly 2 percent of the world's total international reserves.

Despite international pressures on the U.S. economy, the dollar remains the major international currency, accounting for more than 60 percent of total foreign exchange reserves. The German mark and the Japanese yen, by contrast, accounts for only 16 and 7 percent of the world's foreign exchange reserves, respectively.[12] The major reason for the dollar's preeminence is that the U.S. economy is still the strongest in the world. Two economists have written that the United States "remain in a class by itself in terms of international monetary relations by virtue of its immense economic size."[13]

. . . The International Bank for Reconstruction and Development (IBRD), or **World Bank**, was established in the aftermath of World War II as part of the original Bretton Woods system. The IBRD is owned by the more than 150 states that have contributed to its capital stock, which in 1993 totaled $166 billion. To finance its loans, the World Bank borrows money from the international capital markets, using its existing capital to provide concessionary lending to poor countries. In its early years, the IBRD provided loans for the rebuilding of European economies. Once this was accomplished, the World Bank turned its attention to the development of the Third World.

The World Bank makes loans to governments only, and its charter requires that all loans must be for "productive purposes" that are likely to foster economic expansion. As a result, IBRD makes loans for particular projects, such as infrastructure development, but it does not provide financial help to alleviate a trade deficit or a balance of payments problem. During the 1990-1994 period, new World Bank lending averaged $15.8 billion per year.[14] Although lending by the World Bank and other international financial institutions remains essential to many poor developing nations, the relative significance of public international financial transfers has decreased since the 1980s. In 1993, for example, net private capital flows (e.g., FDI, indirect or portfolio investment, commercial loans) were many times larger than public capital flows to the developing nations.[15]

To more effectively meet the financial needs of developing nations, the World Bank established three subsidiary institutions. The first, the *International Development Association (IDA)*, provides concessionary loans to the poorest developing nations. Borrowers typically have fifty years to repay the loan, and the interest rate is generally less than 1 percent a year. About 40 percent of all World Bank lending is channeled through the IDA. The second institution, the *International Finance Corporation (IFC)*, fosters private sector development in Third World nations. The IFC functions much like an investment bank, facilitating and supplementing equity loans for commercial developments. The third World Bank affiliate is the *Multilateral Investment Guarantee Agency (MIGA)*, established in 1988 to encourage FDI in low-income countries by providing insurance against noncommercial risks. The aim of MIGA is to provide protection against political risks in developing nations.

Notes

1. The name "Bretton Woods system" comes from an international planning conference, attended by delegates from forty-four countries, held in Bretton Woods, New Hampshire, in 1944. At the meeting the fundamental elements of the postwar liberal international economic order were worked out.

2. Originally, the Bretton Woods plan called for the establishment of the International Trade Organization (ITO), with GATT functioning within the structure of that organization. Because the ITO treaty was never ratified, GATT functioned as the principal trade institution in the global economy.

3. *The Economist* (August 3, 1996), pp. 17-18.

4. *New York Times* (April 16, 1994), pp. 1 and 25.

5. Under GATT, a member could veto the verdict of a panel set up to rule on a quarrel, even if it was a party to the dispute. But under the WTO, panel decisions can be overturned only by consensus.

6. *New York Times* (January 30, 1997), p. 1.

7. *Washington Post National Weekly* (June 19-25, 1995), p. 20.

8. Benjamin J. Cohen, *Organizing the World's Money, The Political Economy of International Monetary Relations* (New York: Basic Books, 1977), p. 28.

9. Ricky W. Griffin and Michael W. Pustay, *International Business: A Managerial Perspective* (New York: Addison-Wesley, 1996), p. 123.

10. Robert Triffin, *Gold and the Dollar Crisis: The Future of Convertibility* (New Haven: Yale University Press, 1960).

11. Gilpin, *The Political Economy*, p.141.

12. Ibid., p, 85.

13. Ibid.

14. United Nations, *World Economic and Social Survey, 1995* (New York: United Nations, 1995), p. 334.

15. *The Economist* (July 23, 1944), p. 73.

Part V

How Governments Make Decisions and Foreign Policy

By readings these two articles, you will clearly see that governmental policy is Not decided by a "unitary" actor that possess all of the information and acts on that information using value-free cost-benefit analysis. These readings supplement Graham Allison's reading in the UIR on Organizational Processes and Bureaucratic Politics.

Bob Woodward and Dan Balz's *10 Days in September: Inside the War Cabinet at Camp David, Advise and Dissent* shows that the personalities & interests of key leaders in government matter DO affect our country's foreign policy.

Richard Shultz's article argues that the United States did not use its highly-trained and efficient Special Operations Forces—such as the Army's "Delta Force" and Seal Team 6—before 9/11 because of organizational culture and preferences within the Department of Defense.

10 Days In September: Inside The War Cabinet at Camp David, Advise And Dissent

Bush, Aides Grapple With War Plan

Bob Woodward and Dan Balz

FIFTH IN A SERIES

Saturday, September 15

CIA Director George J. Tenet arrived at Camp David with a briefcase stuffed with top-secret documents and plans, in many respects the culmination of more than four years of work on Osama bin Laden, the al Qaeda network and worldwide terrorism.

The briefing packet he handed to President Bush and other members of the war cabinet carried a cover sheet entitled "Going to War." In the upper left corner was a picture of bin Laden inside a red circle. A red slash was superimposed over his face in the CIA's adaptation of the universal symbol of warning and prohibition.

Bush had assembled his advisers in Laurel Lodge at the 125-acre presidential retreat in the Catoctin Mountains of Maryland for a day of intensive discussions about how to respond to the attacks of Sept. 11. They had been conferring regularly but mostly in short meetings. This session would give them a chance to talk at length without interruption and to revisit some of the questions they had been wrestling with the past four days.

Tenet was just one of several advisers called on to offer ideas and options on a day designed more for deliberation and recommendations than presidential decision. But Tenet's 30-minute presentation, an expanded version of what he had told Bush and the war cabinet on Sept. 13, sketched the architecture of what the president was looking for: a worldwide campaign on terrorism with an opening phase focused on bin Laden, al Qaeda and the Taliban regime in Afghanistan.

Tenet brought with him a detailed master plan for covert war in Afghanistan and a top-secret "Worldwide Attack Matrix" outlining a clandestine anti-terror campaign in 80 countries around the world. What he was ready to propose represented a striking and risky departure for U.S. policy and would give the CIA the broadest and most lethal authority in its history.

BOB WOODWARD and DAN BALZ are staff writers for the Washington Post.

© 2002, *The Washington Post*. Reprinted with permission. Washington Post, January 31, 2002. *Staff researcher Jeff Himmelman contributed to this report.*

Another option discussed by Bush's advisers during the week—a military campaign against Iraq—also would be considered at Camp David. But at a key moment, when asked by Bush, four of his five top advisers would recommend that Iraq not be included in an initial round of military strikes.

Seated around a large table in the wood-paneled conference room, Bush and his advisers were informally dressed, many wearing jackets because of the chilly temperatures that morning. Bush was flanked on his right by Vice President Cheney and his left by Secretary of State Colin L. Powell, with Secretary of Defense Donald H. Rumsfeld next to Powell.

Bush had recorded his weekly radio address from the same cabin earlier in the day, and conferred with Chief of Staff Andrew H. Card Jr. and national security adviser Condoleezza Rice. At 9:19 a.m. he invited reporters into the conference room for a few questions. He was pointing toward war but deliberately circumspect about what he intended to do—and when.

"This is an administration that will not talk about how we gather intelligence, how we know what we're going to do, nor what our plans are," he said. "When we move, we will communicate with you in an appropriate manner. We're at war."

The morning agenda called for a series of presentations, with each followed by a period of free-wheeling discussion—sometimes brief, sometimes lengthy, other times focused, in many cases quite unfocused. By the end of the morning, the unstructured format sometimes seemed to leave the president's team even farther from consensus.

9:30 a.m.—Tenet Makes the Case for Wider CIA Role

The session began with a prayer, followed by the first presentations—from Powell and Treasury Secretary Paul H. O'Neill. Powell talked about the international coalition, with special emphasis on Pakistan. O'Neill reviewed Treasury's efforts to develop a plan to attack al Qaeda's financial assets.

Then came Tenet with his professionally packaged briefing papers. He flipped past the cover to the first page, which read, "Initial Hook: Destroying al Qaeda, Closing the safe haven." The haven was Afghanistan. Then he went methodically, page by page, through the briefing material, providing for the president and the others the basic covert-action foundation for an unconventional war on terrorism.

It would start with a half-dozen small CIA paramilitary teams on the ground in Afghanistan. They could eventually link up with military Special Forces units, who would bring firepower and technology to aid the opposition fighters in Afghanistan. The plan called for intelligence-sharing with other nations and a full-scale attack on the financial underpinnings of the terrorist network, plus covert operations across the globe.

At the heart of the proposal was a recommendation that the president give the CIA what Tenet labeled "exceptional authorities" to attack and destroy al Qaeda in Afghanistan and the rest of the world. Tenet wanted a broad, general intelligence order that would allow the CIA to conduct the necessary covert operations without having to come back for formal approval for each specific operation. Tenet said he needed the new authority to allow the agency to operate without restraint—and he wanted encouragement from the president to take risks.

Tenet had with him a draft of a presidential intelligence order that would give the CIA power to use the full range of covert instruments, including deadly force.

For more than two decades, the CIA had simply modified previous presidential findings to obtain formally its authority for counterterrorism. Tenet's new proposal, technically called a Memorandum of Notification, was presented as a modification to the worldwide counterterrorism intelligence finding signed on May 12, 1986, by President Ronald Reagan. As if symbolically erasing the more recent past, it superseded five such memoranda signed by President Bill Clinton.

Another proposal was that the CIA increase liaison work with key foreign intelligence services. Tenet hoped to obtain the assistance of these agencies with some of the hundreds of millions of dollars in new funding he was seeking. Using such intelligence services as surrogates could triple or quadruple the CIA's effectiveness.

Like much of the world of covert activity, these kinds of arrangements carried risks: It would put the United States in league with questionable agencies, some with dreadful human rights records. Some of these intelligence services had a reputation for ruthlessness and they used torture to obtain confessions. Tenet acknowledged that these were not people you were likely to be sitting next to in church on Sunday.

Tenet also said the United States already had a "large asset base," given the work the CIA had been doing in countries near Afghanistan.

The unmanned Predator surveillance aircraft that was now armed with Hellfire missiles had been operating for more than a year out of Uzbekistan to provide real-time video of Afghanistan. It could be used to kill bin Laden and his key lieutenants from the air—a major focus of what Tenet now proposed.

In addition, he said, the United States should seek to work closely with Tajikistan, Turkmenistan and Pakistan to stop the travel of al Qaeda leaders and "close all border crossings" to them. Tenet called for initiating intelligence contact with some rogue states that he said might be helpful in trying to destroy al Qaeda.

A key portion of Tenet's briefing covered operations inside Afghanistan, and here he presented in more detail how the Northern Alliance, the loose amalgam of forces that had been fighting the Taliban for years, could be used. The CIA believed the alliance was potentially a powerful force but was desperate for money, weapons and intelligence. Tenet advocated substantially stepping up "direct support of the Northern Alliance," a proposal the president had said he would approve. U.S. ground forces could then link up with the Northern Alliance fighters.

Operationally, Tenet envisioned a strategy to create "a northern front, closing the safe haven." His idea was that Afghan opposition forces, aided by the United States, would move first against the northern city of Mazar-e Sharif, try to break the Taliban's grip on that city and open up the border with Uzbekistan. From there the campaign could move to other cities in the north, he said.

The CIA director also described a role for the opposition tribes in the southern part of Afghanistan, groups hostile to the northern opposition forces but crucial to a campaign against al Qaeda and the Taliban. Tenet said the CIA had begun working with a number of tribal leaders in the south the previous year. Some would try to play on both sides, he said, but once the war began, they could be enticed by money, food, ammunition and supplies to join the U.S.-led campaign.

On the financial front, Tenet called for clandestine computer surveillance and electronic eavesdropping to locate the assets of al Qaeda and other terrorist groups, with a particular focus on the charitable groups that were a critical element in bin Laden's funding.

Tenet then turned to another top secret document, called the "Worldwide Attack Matrix," which described covert operations in 80 countries that were either underway or that he was now recommending. The actions ranged from routine propaganda to lethal covert action in preparation for military attacks. Included were efforts to disrupt terrorist plots or attacks in countries in Asia, the Middle East and Africa. In some countries, CIA teams would break into facilities to obtain information.

Because the CIA had been working aggressively against terrorism for years, Tenet said, the agency had done extensive target development and network analysis. What it needed was money and flexibility—so the CIA could move quickly, even instantly, if it discovered terrorist targets—and broad authority.

Rumsfeld was enthusiastic about what Tenet laid out that morning, despite potential friction between the CIA and the Pentagon over roles and responsibilities in any military campaign. "I was convinced we had to get people on the ground," Rumsfeld said in an interview. "And to the extent the CIA had relationships or could develop relationships that would facilitate that, [then] that would be critically important."

"Rumsfeld understood the utility of having the CIA involved," the president said in an interview last month. "I think he quickly grasped what I grasped. . . . It was near unanimity on the immediate plan for Afghanistan, which was to mate up our assets with the Northern Alliance troops."

When the CIA director finished his presentation, Bush left no doubt what he thought of it, virtually shouting with enthusiasm: "Great job."

After a break, Bush turned to Robert S. Mueller III, who had taken over as FBI director the week before the attacks.

Mueller, a former federal prosecutor, had spent years working on the 1988 terrorist bombing of Pan Am Flight 103. He knew that the worst thing that could happen to an FBI director was to have a major domestic terrorist incident on his watch. The second thing he knew was that he had not prepared a presentation. He had been shocked that he had been invited to the Camp David war-planning session and expected to be called on somewhat later, if at all.

Not used to the company and slightly intimidated by the presence of the nation's top leadership, Mueller soon found himself giving a routine summary of the investigation into the four Sept. 11 hijackings. He told other FBI officials afterward that he was so unhappy with his own performance that he brought his remarks to an early close. At least one of the president's advisers concluded that the FBI was still too focused on prosecuting terrorists and not on preventing them from acting.

Attorney General John D. Ashcroft provided an update to the group on his efforts to develop a legislative package to expand the powers of law enforcement to fight terrorism. He outlined a two-phase strategy, aimed first at "immediate disruption and prevention of terrorism" and followed by longer-term efforts to put terrorists "off keel." Ashcroft warned that it was "important to disrupt" the terrorists now, but added, "We need to remember these are patient people," noting that eight years passed between the two attacks on the World Trade Center. The administration needed a new long-term strategy, he said, "because that's the kind of strategy they have in place."

The final presentation of the morning came from Gen. Henry H. Shelton, chairman of the Joint Chiefs of Staff, who had also brought a big briefcase to Camp David. Bush had ordered the Pentagon to come to the meeting with plenty of options, and Shelton was prepared to talk about military action against both Afghanistan and, if pressed, Iraq, although he opposed that step then. But as the day developed, he discussed only three options, all aimed at Afghanistan.

The first called for a strike with cruise missiles, a plan the military could execute quickly if speed was the president's overriding priority. The missiles could be launched by Navy ships or Air Force planes from hundreds of miles away. The targets included al Qaeda's training camps.

The problem, Shelton said, was that the camps were virtually empty and therefore the missile attacks would not be that effective. Clearly, Shelton was not enamored of this idea, nor were the others. Bush had brushed off the possibility from Day One that his response would be an antiseptic "pin-prick" attack.

Option Two combined cruise missiles with manned bomber attacks. Shelton said Bush could initially choose a strike lasting three or four days or something longer, maybe up to 10 days. The targets included al Qaeda training camps and some Taliban targets, depending on whether the president wanted to go after the Taliban militarily at the start. But this too had limits. As Cheney had said the first night of the crisis, there were few high-value targets in Afghanistan, a country devastated by two decades of war. Another disadvantage was that it could reinforce perceptions that the United States wanted a largely risk-free war on terrorism.

Shelton described the third and most robust option as cruise missiles, bombers and what the planners like to call "boots on the ground." This option included all the elements of the second option along with U.S. Special Forces, the elite commandos, and possibly the Army and Marines being deployed inside Afghanistan. But he said it would take a minimum of 10 to 12 days just to get initial forces on the ground—in reality it took far longer—because bases and overflight rights would be needed for search-and-rescue teams to bring out any downed pilots.

If there was already a consensus to go to war, the discussions that followed many of the morning's presentations underscored to the participants the complexity and uncertainty of their undertaking.

Bush and his team faced a far different situation than Bush's father, George H.W. Bush, had 11 years earlier, after Iraq had invaded Kuwait in 1990. On Saturday, Aug. 4, 1990, again at Camp David and in the same lodge, Gen. Norman Schwarzkopf, then commander of the Central Command, had presented a detailed, off-the-shelf proposal for military action. It was called Operations Plan 90-1002, and it was the basic military plan that had been executed over the next seven months to oust Iraq from Kuwait.

In the case of Afghanistan, a military plan would have to be devised quickly, once the president made decisions about the shape of the war, the initial focus of the campaign and the relationship between the CIA and the Pentagon.

Based on the recollections of many of the participants and some notes taken at the meeting, the topics that morning included the politics of the region—Afghanistan and the surrounding countries; the shaping of a coalition; the need to think unconventionally about fighting the war; and whether Iraq should be included in the war's first phase.

At one point, as they discussed the inherent risks of any operation in Afghanistan, someone said this was not likely to be like the Balkans, where ethnic hatreds had occupied the Clinton administration for most of its tenure. Rice said the problems of Afghanistan and the surrounding region were so complicated, "We're going to wish this was the Balkans."

The ideal result from this campaign, the president said, would be to kick terrorists out of some places like Afghanistan and through that action persuade other countries that had supported terrorism in the past, such as Iran, to change their behavior.

Powell noted that everyone in the international coalition was ready to go after al Qaeda, but that extending the war to other terrorist groups or countries could cause some of them to drop out.

The president said he didn't want other countries dictating terms or conditions for the war on terrorism. "At some point," the president said, "we may be the only ones left. That's okay with me. We are America."

Powell didn't reply, but going it alone was precisely what he wanted to avoid if possible. In Powell's view, the president's formulation was not realistic. The United States could not launch an effective war in Afghanistan or worldwide without a coalition. He believed the president made such statements knowing they might not withstand a second analysis. The tough talk might be necessary but it was not policy.

In contrast, Cheney took the president at his word, and was convinced the president was absolutely serious when he said they would go it alone if necessary.

Rumsfeld raised another problem. Although everyone agreed that destroying al Qaeda was the first priority, singling out bin Laden, particularly by the president, would elevate bin Laden the way Iraqi President Saddam Hussein had been elevated during the Gulf War.

Rumsfeld told the others the worst thing they could do in such a situation was to misstate their objective. It would not be effective to succeed in your objective of removing or killing bin Laden or Taliban leader Mohammad Omar without solving the basic problem of terrorism. Vilification of bin Laden could rob the United States of its ability to frame this as a larger war.

Another puzzle to the group was the Taliban itself. The Taliban clearly would be pressured in hopes that it would break with al Qaeda and perhaps give up bin Laden. Few thought this was likely, but they agreed they had to make the effort. Some of Bush's advisers believed the Taliban might fracture, that some faction might break off and help in rounding up bin Laden, but there was no reliable evidence or intelligence to support this notion.

Bush noted that British Prime Minister Tony Blair had suggested giving the Taliban not just an ultimatum but also a deadline.

Several others argued against a deadline; they did not want a deadline to dictate the timing of when to start military action. As Bush had said the previous day at Washington National Cathedral, the military campaign would begin at "an hour of our choosing." During this part of the discussion,

Bush said, according to notes of one participant, "I want to give the Taliban a right to turn over al Qaeda; if they don't, there have to be consequences that show the United States is serious."

Afghanistan's history nagged at the president's advisers. Its geography was forbidding and its record of rebuffing outside forces was real. Despite attractive options presented earlier in the morning, several advisers seemed worried. Bush asked his advisers: What are the worst cases out there? What are the real downside risks?

One was triggering chaos in Afghanistan that would spill over into Pakistan. This was seen as a great danger by many, particularly Rice and Cheney. Afghanistan was already a mess, Cheney noted. If Pakistan went, then you have unleashed a whole other set of demons. He was worried that Pakistan's choice to support the United States could lead to internal unrest that might bring down the government—and give Islamic fundamentalists access to Pakistan's nuclear weapons.

The discussion highlighted the critical importance of Pakistan's president, Gen. Pervez Musharraf, who, everyone now understood, was the most important barrier between stability and a worst-case scenario. Have the Pakistanis fully thought through the risks of supporting the United States, Bush asked.

Powell said he believed they had. First, Musharraf had seen how serious the administration was about terrorism. Second, he said, the general realizes he has gradually been losing control of his country, and he may see this as an opportunity to stop the slide into extremism. Musharraf did not want Pakistan to turn into a rogue state, Powell believed. He wanted a more secular, westernized country.

President Musharraf is taking a tremendous risk, the president said. We need to make it worth his while. We should help him with a number of things, including nuclear security. Put together a package of support for Pakistan, he directed.

Another risk they faced was getting bogged down in Afghanistan. Rice knew it had been the nemesis of the British in the 19th century and the Soviets in the 20th. She wondered whether it might be the same for the United States in the 21st.

These fears were shared by others, which led to a different discussion: Should they think about launching military action elsewhere as an insurance policy in case things in Afghanistan went bad? They would need successes early in any war to maintain domestic and international support. Rice asked whether they could envision a successful military campaign beyond Afghanistan.

In this context, the issue of Iraq once again was on the table. The full sequence is not clear from the recollections and notes of several key participants. But all agree that the Iraq strategy's principal advocate in the group was Deputy Defense Secretary Paul Wolfowitz. He had been the department's third-ranking official under Cheney during the Gulf War and believed that the abrupt and incomplete end to the ground campaign, with Hussein still in power, had been a mistake.

The Bush administration had been seeking to undermine Hussein from the start, with Wolfowitz pushing efforts to aid opposition groups and Powell seeking support for a new set of sanctions. Rumsfeld and Wolfowitz had been examining military options in Iraq for months but nothing had emerged. The fear was that Hussein was still attempting to develop weapons of mass destruction, and without United Nations inspectors in the country, there was no way to know the exact nature of the threat they faced.

Wolfowitz argued that the real source of all the trouble and terrorism was probably Hussein. The terrorist attacks of Sept. 11 created an opportunity to strike. Hussein was a bad guy, a dangerous leader bent on obtaining and probably using weapons of mass destruction. He also likely was culpable in the attacks of the previous Tuesday, at least indirectly, and all of them ought to acknowledge it.

Rumsfeld had helped raise the Iraq issue in previous meetings, but not as vehemently as his deputy. Now, Rumsfeld asked again: Is this the time to attack Iraq? He noted that there would be a big buildup of forces, with not that many good targets in Afghanistan. At some point, if the United States was serious about terrorism, it would have to deal with Iraq. Is this the opportunity?

Powell objected. You're going to hear from your coalition partners, he told the president. They're all with you, every one, but they will go away if you hit Iraq. If you get something pinning Sept. 11

on Iraq, great—let's put it out and kick them at the right time. But let's get Afghanistan now. If we do that, we will have increased our ability to go after Iraq—if we can prove Iraq had a role.

Bush let the discussion continue but he had strong reservations about Iraq. He was concerned about two things, which he described in an interview last month. "My theory is you've got to do something and do it well and that . . . if we could prove that we could be successful in this theater, then the rest of the task would be easier," he said. "If we tried to do too many things—two things, for example, or three things—militarily, then . . . the lack of focus would have been a huge risk."

His other concern was one that he did not express to his war cabinet but that he said later was part of his own thinking. He knew that around the table were a number of advisers—Powell, Cheney and Wolfowitz—who had been with his father during the Gulf War deliberations. "And one of the things I wasn't going to allow to happen is, that we weren't going to let their previous experience in this theater dictate a rational course for the new war," the president said.

Bush also noted that, whatever his comments were about Iraq that morning, they seemed to bring the debate to a close. "There wasn't a lot of talk about Iraq in the second [afternoon] round," he said. "The second round of discussion was focused only on Afghanistan, let me put it to you that way."

Wolfowitz had persisted in making his arguments about Iraq and other issues, and had annoyed some of his colleagues by showing up at meetings that were called for principals only—not for deputies. To Card, the president's chief of staff, it seemed as if Wolfowitz was just banging a drum, not providing additional information or new arguments.

At one point during the morning, Wolfowitz interrupted his boss, Rumsfeld, and repeated a point he had made earlier in the discussion. There was an awkward silence around the table. Rumsfeld seemed to ignore the interruption but his eyes narrowed. Some thought he might be annoyed; others thought he was just listening carefully.

Bush flashed a pointed look in Card's direction. During a break in the meeting, the chief of staff took Rumsfeld and Wolfowitz aside.

"The president will expect one person to speak for the Department of Defense," Card said.

12:45 p.m.'—After Today, We'll Have a Plan for Action'

Lunch was finally served, and Bush told his advisers that they should take some time to exercise or rest. He said: Then I want everybody back here at 4 o'clock, and I want to hear what you think we ought to do.

Rice was concerned about the apparent lack of focus during the last part of the morning. The National Security Council meetings usually were more structured, with the principals reporting on their departments or agencies, and then together they would work through the problem and come up with options. The morning meeting had started well, but then had become repetitive, unusually free-wheeling. She didn't know where the morning discussion had left them.

How are we going to get a plan out of this? she wondered. Have we got anything here?

She had listened carefully to the president that morning and she could tell he was heading toward action. He had remarked, "After today, we'll have a plan of action now," and referred to the session as "an action meeting."

Rice convened the principals—Powell, Rumsfeld, Tenet, Card—without the president. She expressed her concerns to the others. We need to bring more discipline to the discussion in the afternoon, she said.

Powell went back to his cabin, where Alma, his wife, was reading a book. As he saw it, the big questions were still on the table: what to do, when to do it, and do you go after this one thing—al Qaeda and Afghanistan—that they knew was out there, or do you expand the war at this time? Back in the cabin, he sat down in a chair and closed his eyes for half an hour.

Rice went back to her cabin, returned some phone calls and went off to exercise. About 3:45 p.m., she ran into the president outside his cabin. He had worked out on the elliptical machine and lifted weights. Now he told his national security adviser he had a plan for the afternoon. "I'm going to go around the table and I'm going to ask people what they think," the president said. "What do you think about that?"

"That's fine," she replied. "Do you want me just to listen?"

"I want you to listen," Bush said.

That was consistent with their usual working arrangement. Rice would listen for him and then offer assessments in private. Her principal role was to help make the decision-making process orderly, to ensure that Bush had received all the information he needed. Every morning about 7:15, she, Powell and Rumsfeld were on the phone together to share information and ideas.

4 P.M.—Back in Laurel Lodge, the Advisers Have Their Say

The entire team reconvened in Laurel Lodge. The president said he wanted to hear recommendations from the principals—Powell, Rumsfeld, Tenet, Card and the vice president. Okay, who will start? He looked at Powell.

Powell expected more general discussion but plunged ahead. The focus ought to be on bin Laden and al Qaeda, he said, their camps and their infrastructure. Make them the target. All the states that supported terror, you can do at a time of your choosing. They are not going anywhere. The coalition and the energy that had been created were directed against Sept. 11.

It looked as if 6,000 people were dead from the World Trade Center and Pentagon attacks (by January, the estimate was down to 3,100). To do anything that did not focus on al Qaeda would not be understood, either by the American people, the coalition or, he argued, international opinion.

If we weren't going after Iraq prior to Sept. 11, why would we be going after them now when the current outrage is not directed at Iraq, Powell asked. Nobody could look at Iraq and say it was responsible for Sept. 11. It was important not to lose focus.

Powell also felt that the Defense Department was overestimating its ability to do two things at the same time from the same command, with the same commander and staff. Military attacks on both Afghanistan and Iraq would be under the jurisdiction of the Central Command, which is responsible for the region that included the Middle East and South Asia.

He didn't make that point, but figured it was his ace in the hole. Powell also noticed that no military plan had been presented for Iraq. No one, neither Rumsfeld nor Wolfowitz, had told the president precisely what should be done in Iraq and how it might be done. Nobody had taken it to the next step and said, This is what we're talking about. The absence of a plan was a gaping hole.

Continuing, Powell said, tell the Taliban, "You're responsible." Be firm with the Taliban's leaders. If they don't act and throw bin Laden and his terrorists out of Afghanistan, then we tell them, "We're going to hold you accountable." The focus should be on military targets. Also, a public case should be made that bin Laden was the guilty one. That was important. Evidence mattered.

Rumsfeld was next. We must not undercut our ability to act over the long term, he said, which meant they should keep thinking about what to do about terrorism in general. Patience was important. Rooting out bin Laden would take very different intelligence than they had. The doctrine of "hit, talk, hit," in which the United States would strike, pause to see the reaction, and then hit again, sounded too much like Vietnam. Rumsfeld said there was a need for unconventional approaches, especially the Special Forces information operations, in gathering intelligence on the ground.

But Rumsfeld, significantly, did not make a recommendation on Iraq.

Tenet attempted to summarize. The plan, he said, should include the elements of strike, strangle, surround and sustain. He mentioned his own plan for a global approach but basically supported the position that the initial military focus should be on Afghanistan.

Card was next. He did not have much foreign policy experience, so he began by speaking generally. "What is the definition of success?" he asked. He said it would first be proving that this was not just an effort to pound sand—as the president had repeatedly made clear. They should demonstrate to the world that the effort was directed at terrorists beyond Afghanistan.

Consideration should be given to contemporaneous actions in other parts of the world—that could be in Indonesia, the Philippines, Malaysia, Yemen or Somalia, he said. This could be covert, not overt military action, though it was important to consider a plan that would demonstrate to the world relatively quickly the worldwide nature of the problem.

Card also said he didn't think the case had been made for Iraq to be a principal target.

Cheney was last and, according to notes from that day, talked the longest and most comprehensively. We need to do everything we can to stop the next attack, he said. Are we being aggressive enough? We need a group now that's going to look at lessons learned from where we've been. And in going after bin Laden we need to consider the broader context. A week ago, before Sept. 11, we were worried about the strength of our whole position in the Middle East—where we stood with the Saudis, the Turks and others in the region. Now they all want to be part of our efforts, and that's an opportunity. We need to reach out for that opportunity.

Building a coalition to take advantage of the opportunities, he said, suggests that this may be a bad time to take on Saddam Hussein in Iraq. We would lose momentum.

Cheney thus joined Powell, Tenet and Card in opposing action on Iraq. Rumsfeld had not committed one way or the other. To anyone keeping a tally it was 4 to 0 with Rumsfeld abstaining—a heavy body of advice against Iraq.

Still, the vice president expressed deep concern about Hussein and said he was not going to rule out going after Iraq at some point—just not now.

Earlier in the day he had told the group, "We've indicted bin Laden, but now we must wage war against him." He said the CIA must push every button it could and said it was also crucial to deal with the charitable organizations that helped finance bin Laden. He recommended strengthening the Northern Alliance in Afghanistan and hitting the Taliban—but not necessarily in a massive way at first. We need to knock out their air defenses and their air power at the start, he said. We need to be ready to put boots on the ground. There are some places only special operations forces will get them, he added. And we need to ask: Do we have the right mix of forces?

Finally, he returned to the question of homeland defense. They must do everything possible to defend, prevent or disrupt the next attack on America, he said. The issue was very worrisome. He had reviewed the work of five government commissions that had recently studied terrorism. The president had assigned him the task of coming up with a homeland security plan back in May. It's not just borders and airline security, but biological and other threats that they had to think about, he said.

Cheney was the last to make any recommendations. There was some additional discussion, including the themes to strike on the Sunday morning talk shows where Cheney, Powell, Rumsfeld and Ashcroft would be appearing. At the end of the meeting, Bush went around the table and thanked everyone. No one was quite certain where things stood.

"I'm going to go think about it and I'll let you know what I've decided," Bush said.

Powell and Rumsfeld left Camp David, but most of the others stayed over for dinner and the night. Bush had invited his advisers to bring their spouses, and after dinner that evening someone suggested to Ashcroft, who in the Senate had been a member of a group called the Singing Senators, that he sing some songs.

"I don't want to sing," he said, "but if you'll sing, I'll play."

He sat down at the piano and began playing a number of traditional American melodies, from "Old Man River" and "Nobody Knows the Trouble I've Seen" to "America the Beautiful" and "God Bless America." Rice, herself an accomplished pianist, was the principal vocalist. Bush was at a table nearby, joining in trying to assemble an elaborate wooden jigsaw puzzle.

Showstoppers:
Nine reasons why we never sent our Special Operations Forces after al Qaeda before 9/11

Richard H. Shultz Jr.

Since 9/11, Secretary of Defense Donald Rumsfeld has repeatedly declared that the United States is in a new kind of war, one requiring new military forces to hunt down and capture or kill terrorists. In fact, for some years, the Department of Defense has gone to the trouble of selecting and training an array of Special Operations Forces, whose forte is precisely this. One president after another has invested resources to hone lethal "special mission units" for offensive—that is, preemptive—counterterrorism strikes, with the result that these units are the best of their kind in the world. While their activities are highly classified, two of them—the Army's Delta Force and the Navy's SEAL Team 6—have become the stuff of novels and movies.

Prior to 9/11, these units *were never used even once* to hunt down terrorists who had taken American lives. Putting the units to their intended use proved impossible —even after al Qaeda bombed the World Trade Center in 1993, bombed two American embassies in East Africa in 1998, and nearly sank the USS *Cole* in Yemen in 2000. As a result of these and other attacks, operations were planned to capture or kill the ultimate perpetrators, Osama bin Laden and his top lieutenants, but each time the missions were blocked. A plethora of self-imposed constraints—I call them showstoppers—kept the counterterrorism units on the shelf.

I first began to learn of this in the summer of 2001, after George W. Bush's election brought a changing of the guard to the Department of Defense. Joining the new team as principal deputy assistant secretary of defense for special operations and low-intensity conflict was Bob Andrews, an old hand at the black arts of unconventional warfare. During Vietnam, Andrews had served in a top secret Special Forces outfit codenamed the Studies and Observations Group that had carried out America's largest and most complex covert paramilitary operation in the Cold War. Afterwards, Andrews had joined the CIA, then moved to Congress as a staffer, then to the defense industry.

I'd first met him while I was writing a book about the secret war against Hanoi, and we hit it off. He returned to the Pentagon with the new administration, and in June 2001 he called and asked me to be his consultant. I agreed, and subsequently proposed looking into counterterrorism policy. Specifically, I wondered why had we created these superbly trained Special Operations Forces to fight terrorists, but had never used them for their primary mission. What had kept them out of action?

Richard H. Shultz Jr. is director of international security studies at the Fletcher School, Tufts University, and director of research at the Consortium for the Study of Intelligence in Washington, D.C.

Andrews was intrigued and asked me to prepare a proposal. I was putting the finishing touches on it on the morning of September 11, when al Qaeda struck. With that blow, the issue of America's offensive counterterrorist capabilities was thrust to center stage.

By early November, I had the go-ahead for the study. Our question had acquired urgency: Why, even as al Qaeda attacked and killed Americans at home and abroad, were our elite counterterrorism units not used to hit back and prevent further attacks? That was, after all, their very purpose, laid out in the official document *Special Operations in Peace and War* (1996). To find the answer, I interviewed civilian and military officials, serving and retired, at the center of U.S. counterterrorism policy and operational planning in the late 1980s and 1990s.

They included senior members of the National Security Council's Counterterrorism and Security Group, the interagency focal point for counterterrorism policy. In the Pentagon, I interviewed the top leaders of the offices with counterterrorism responsibility, as well as second-tier professionals, and their military counterparts in the Joint Staff. Finally, the U.S. Special Operations Command, head-quartered in Tampa, Florida, is responsible for planning and carrying out counterterrorism strikes, and I interviewed senior commanders who served there during the 1990s.

Some were willing to speak on the record. Others requested anonymity, which I honored, in order to put before the top leadership of the Pentagon the detailed report from which this article is drawn. My findings were conveyed to the highest levels of the Department of Defense in January 2003.

Among those interviewed, few were in a better position to illuminate the conundrum than General Pete Schoomaker. An original member of the Delta Force, he had commanded the Delta Force in 1991-92, then led the Special Operations Command in the late 1990s. "Counterterrorism, by Defense Department definition, is offensive," Schoomaker told me during a discussion we had over two days in the summer of 2002. "But Special Operations was never given the mission. It was very, very frustrating. It was like having a brand-new Ferrari in the garage, and nobody wants to race it because you might dent the fender."

*   *   *

As terrorist attacks escalated in the 1990s, White House rhetoric intensified. President Clinton met each successive outrage with a vow to punish the perpetrators. After the *Cole* bombing in 2000, for example, he pledged to "find out who is responsible and hold them accountable." And to prove he was serious, he issued an increasingly tough series of Presidential Decision Directives. The United States would "deter and preempt . . . individuals who perpetrate or plan to perpetrate such acts," said Directive 39, in June 1995. Offensive measures would be used against foreign terrorists posing a threat to America, said Directive 62, in May 1998. Joint Staff contingency plans were revised to provide for offensive and preemptive options. And after al Qaeda's bombings of the U.S. embassies in Kenya and Tanzania, President Clinton signed a secret "finding" authorizing lethal covert operations against bin Laden.

These initiatives led to the planning of several operations. Their details rest in the classified records of the National Security Council's Counterterrorism and Security Group. Its former coordinator, Dick Clarke, described them as providing the White House with "more aggressive options," to be carried out by Special Operations Forces (or SOF, a category that includes the Green Berets, the Rangers, psychological operations, civilian affairs, the SEALS, special helicopter units, and special mission units like the Delta Force and SEAL Team 6).

Several plans have been identified in newspaper accounts since 9/11. For example, "snatch operations" in Afghanistan were planned to seize bin Laden and his senior lieutenants. After the 1998 embassy bombings, options for killing bin Laden were entertained, including a gunship assault on his compound in Afghanistan.

SOF assaults on al Qaeda's Afghan training camps were also planned. An official very close to Clinton said that the president believed the image of American commandos jumping out of helicopters and killing terrorists would send a strong message. He "saw these camps as conveyor belts pushing radical Islamists through," the official said, "that either went into the war against the Northern Alliance [an Afghan force fighting the Taliban in northern Afghanistan] or became sleeper cells in Germany, Spain, Britain, Italy, and here. We wanted to close these camps down. We had to make it unattractive to go to these camps. And blowing them up, by God, would make them unattractive."

And preemptive strikes against al Qaeda cells outside Afghanistan were planned, in North Africa and the Arabian Gulf. Then in May 1999, the White House decided to press the Taliban to end its support of bin Laden. The Counterterrorism and Security Group recommended supporting the Northern Alliance.

These examples, among others, depict an increasingly aggressive, lethal, and preemptive counterterrorist policy. But *not one* of these operations—all authorized by President Clinton—was ever executed. General Schoomaker's explanation is devastating. "The presidential directives that were issued," he said, "and the subsequent findings and authorities, in my view, were done to check off boxes. The president signed things that everybody involved knew full well were never going to happen. You're checking off boxes, and have all this activity going on, but the fact is that there's very low probability of it ever coming to fruition. . . ." And he added: "The military, by the way, didn't want to touch it. There was great reluctance in the Pentagon."

* * *

From my interviews, I distilled nine mutually reinforcing, self-imposed constraints that kept the special mission units sidelined, even as al Qaeda struck at American targets around the globe and trumpeted its intention to do more of the same. These showstoppers formed an impenetrable phalanx ensuring that all high-level policy discussions, tough new presidential directives, revised contingency plans, and actual dress rehearsals for missions would come to nothing.

1. Terrorism as Crime

During the second half of the 1980s, terrorism came to be defined by the U.S. government as a crime, and terrorists as criminals to be prosecuted. The Reagan administration, which in its first term said that it would meet terrorism with "swift and effective retribution," ended its second term, in the political and legal aftermath of Iran-contra, by adopting a counterterrorism policy that was the antithesis of that.

Patterns of Global Terrorism, a report issued by the State Department every year since 1989, sets forth guidance about responding to terrorism. Year after year prior to 9/11, a key passage said it was U.S. policy to "treat terrorists as criminals, pursue them aggressively, and apply the rule of law." Even now, when President Bush has defined the situation as a war on terrorism, *Patterns of Global Terrorism* says U.S. policy is to "bring terrorists to justice for their crimes."

Criminalization had a profound impact on the Pentagon, said General Schoomaker. It came to see terrorism as "not up to the standard of our definition of war, and therefore not worthy of our attention." In other words, militaries fight other militaries. "And because it's not war," he added, "and we don't act like we're at war, many of the Defense Department's tools are off the table." The Pentagon's senior leadership made little if any effort to argue against designating terrorism as a crime, Schoomaker added derisively.

"If you declare terrorism a criminal activity, you take from Defense any statutory authority to be the leader in responding," a long-serving department official agreed. Whenever the White House proposed using SOF against terrorists, it found itself facing "a band of lawyers at Justice defending their

Special Operations soldiers crossing into Afghanistan from Tajikistan, November 15, 2001

turf." They would assert, said this old hand at special operations, that the Pentagon lacked authority to use force—and "lawyers in the Defense Department would concur. They argued that we have no statutory authority because this is essentially a criminal matter."

In effect, the central tool for combating terrorism would not be military force. Extradition was the instrument of choice. This reduced the Pentagon's role to providing transportation for the Justice Department.

To be sure, Justice had its successes. With the help of the Pakistani government, it brought back Mir Amal Kansi, the gunman who opened fire outside CIA headquarters in 1993; with the help of the governments of the Philippines and Kenya, it brought several of the terrorists responsible for the first World Trade Center bombing and the attacks on the U.S. embassies in East Africa back to stand trial. But those were lesser al Qaeda operatives. Against the group's organizational infrastructure and leadership, there were no such successes. Law enforcement had neither the access nor the capability to go after those targets.

2. Not a Clear and Present Danger or War

Since terrorism had been classified as crime, few Pentagon officials were willing to call it a clear and present danger to the United States—much less grounds for war. Any attempt to describe terrorism in those terms ran into a stone wall.

For instance, on June 25, 1996, a truck bomb killed 19 Americans and wounded another 250 at the U.S. military's Khobar Towers housing facility near Dhahran, Saudi Arabia. In the aftermath, a tough-minded subordinate of Allen Holmes, then the assistant secretary of defense for special operations and low-intensity conflict, asserted that the Defense Department needed a more aggressive counterterrorism policy to attack those responsible for these increasingly lethal terrorist attacks. Holmes told him, "Write it down, and we'll push it."

The aide laid out a strategy that pulled no punches. Khobar Towers, the World Trade Center bombing, and other attacks were acts of war, he wrote, and should be treated as such. He called for "retaliatory and preemptive military strikes against the terrorist leadership and infrastructure responsible, and even against states assisting them." In his strategy, he assigned a central role for this to SOF.

Holmes ran the proposal up the flagpole. A meeting to review it was held in the office of the undersecretary of defense for policy. As the hard-charging aide explained his recommendations, a senior policy official blurted out: "Are you out of your mind? You're telling me that our Middle East policy is not important and that it's more important to go clean out terrorists? Don't you understand what's going on in terms of our Middle East policy? You're talking about going after terrorists backed by Iran? You just don't understand." And that was that.

In the wake of Khobar Towers, Secretary of Defense William Perry asked retired General Wayne Downing to head a task force to assess what had happened. Formerly the head of the U.S. Special Operations Command, Downing had been in counterterrorism a long time. He was more than willing to pull the trigger and cajole policymakers into giving him the authority to do so. Interviewed in 2002 during a year-long stint as President Bush's deputy national security adviser for combating terrorism, he reflected on his report: "I emphasized that people are at war with us, and using terrorism as an asymmetrical weapon with which to attack us because they can't in a direct or conventional manner." It *was* war, he told the department's senior leadership; they needed to wake up to that fact. But his plea fell on deaf ears. He lamented, "No one wanted to address terrorism as war."

Even after bin Laden declared war on America in a 1998 *fatwa*, and bombed U.S. embassies to show his followers that he meant business in exhorting them to "abide by Allah's order by killing Americans . . . anywhere, anytime, and wherever possible," the Pentagon still resisted calling terrorism war. It wasn't alone. A CIA assessment of the *fatwa* acknowledged that if a *government* had issued such a decree, one would have had to consider it a declaration of war, but in al Qaeda's case it was only propaganda.

During the late 1990s, the State Department coordinator for counterterrorism was Mike Sheehan. A retired Special Forces officer who had learned unconventional warfare in El Salvador in the late 1980s, he was considered one of the most hawkish Clinton officials, pushing for the use of force against the Taliban and al Qaeda. His mantra was "drain the Afghan swamp of terrorists."

I visited Sheehan at his office at the U.N. building in New York, where he had become assistant secretary-general for peacekeeping. He recounted how aggressive counterterrorism proposals were received in the Defense Department: "The Pentagon wanted to fight and win the nation's wars, as Colin Powell used to say. But those were wars against the armies of other nations—not against diffuse transnational terrorist threats. So terrorism was seen as a distraction that was the CIA's job, even though DOD personnel were being hit by terrorists. The Pentagon way to treat terrorism against Pentagon assets abroad was to cast it as a force protection issue."

"Force protection" is Pentagon lingo for stronger barriers to shield troops from Khobar Towers-type attacks. Even the attack on the USS *Cole* did not change that outlook. As far as causing anyone to consider offensive measures against those responsible, "the *Cole* lasted only for a week, two weeks," Sheehan lamented. "It took a 757 crashing into the Pentagon for them to get it." Shaking his head, he added: "The near sinking of a billion-dollar warship was not enough. Folding up a barracks full of their troops in Saudi Arabia was not enough. Folding up two American embassies was not enough."

Of course, Washington continued to try to arrest those who had carried out these acts. But the places where terrorists trained and planned—Afghanistan, Lebanon, Sudan, Yemen—remained off-limits. Those were not areas where the Defense Department intended to fight. A very senior SOF officer who had served on the Joint Staff in the 1990s told me that more than once he heard terrorist strikes characterized as "a small price to pay for being a superpower."

3. The Somalia Syndrome

In the first year of his presidency, Bill Clinton suffered a foreign policy debacle. The "Fire Fight from Hell," *Newsweek* called it. The *Los Angeles Times* described it as culminating in "dozens of cheering, dancing Somalis dragging the body of a U.S. soldier through the city's streets." Those reports followed the 16-hour shootout portrayed in the movie *Black Hawk Down*, pitting SOF units against Somali warriors in the urban jungle of Mogadishu on October 3-4, 1993. The American objective had been capturing Mohammed Aidid, a warlord who was interfering with the U.N.'s humanitarian mission. The new administration had expected a quick surgical operation.

The failure caused disquieting questions and bad memories. How could this happen? What had gone wrong? Some Clinton officials recalled that the last time the Democrats had held the White House, similar forces had failed in their attempt to rescue American hostages in Tehran ("Desert One"), a catastrophe instrumental in President Carter's 1980 reelection defeat.

Some senior generals had expressed doubts about the Mogadishu operation, yet as it had morphed from a peacekeeping mission into a manhunt for Aidid, the new national security team had failed to grasp the implications. The Mogadishu disaster spooked the Clinton administration as well as the brass, and confirmed the Joint Chiefs in the view that SOF should never be entrusted with independent operations.

After Mogadishu, one Pentagon officer explained, there was "reluctance to even discuss proactive measures associated with countering the terrorist threat through SOF operations. The Joint Staff was very happy for the administration to take a law enforcement view. They didn't want to put special ops troops on the ground. They hadn't wanted to go into Somalia to begin with. The Joint Staff was the biggest foot-dragger on all of this counterterrorism business."

Another officer added that Somalia heightened a wariness, in some cases outright disdain, for SOF in the senior ranks. On the Joint Staff, the generals ranged from those who "did not have a great deal of respect" for SOF, to those who actually "hated what it represented, . . . hated the independent thought process, . . . hated the fact that the SOF guys on the Joint Staff would challenge things, would question things."

During Desert Storm, for example, General Norman Schwarzkopf was reluctant to include SOF in his war plan. He did so only grudgingly, and kept SOF on a short leash, wrote the commander of all Special Operations Forces at the time, General Carl Stiner, in his book *Shadow Warriors*. But SOF performed well in Desert Storm, and afterwards Schwarzkopf acknowledged their accomplishments. In 1993, Mogadishu turned back the clock.

4. No Legal Authority

August 1998 was a watershed for the White House. The embassy bombings led to the reexamination of preemptive military options. President Clinton proposed using elite SOF counterterrorism units to attack bin Laden, his lieutenants, and al Qaeda's infrastructure.

Also considered was unconventional warfare, a core SOF mission very different from counterterrorism. The Special Operations Command's *Special Operations in Peace and War* defines unconventional warfare as "military and paramilitary operations conducted by indigenous or surrogate forces who are organized, trained, equipped, and directed by an external source." For the White House, this meant assisting movements like the Northern Alliance in Afghanistan.

Both the Special Operations Command's counterterrorism units and Special Forces training for and executing unconventional warfare operate clandestinely. That is what their doctrine specifies. But because such operations are secret, the question arose in the 1990s whether the department had the legal authority to execute them.

This may seem baffling. If these missions are specified in the military doctrine of the Special Operations Command, and actual units train for them, isn't it obvious that the Department of Defense must have the authority to execute them? Perhaps, yet many in government emphatically deny it.

A gap exists, they believe, between DOD's *capability* for clandestine operations and its *authority* under the United States Code. In the 1990s, some Pentagon lawyers and some in the intelligence community argued that Title 10 of the U.S. Code, which covers the armed forces, did not give Defense the legal authority for such missions, while Title 50, which spells out the legal strictures for covert operations, gave this power exclusively to the CIA.

Title 50 defines covert action as "an activity of the United States Government to influence political, economic, or military conditions abroad, where it is intended that the role of the United States Government will not be apparent or acknowledged publicly." Covert action and deniability go hand in hand. If a story about a covert action hits the newspapers, the president must be able to avow that the United States is not mixed up in it.

But is it the case that *only* the CIA has this authority? Title 50, Chapter 15, Section 413b of the U.S. Code stipulates: "The President may not authorize the conduct of a covert action by departments, agencies, or entities of the United States Government unless the President determines such an action is necessary to support identifiable foreign policy objectives of the United States and is important to the national security of the United States, which determination shall be set forth in a finding that shall meet each of the following conditions." The key condition is: "Each finding shall specify each department, agency, or entity of the United States Government authorized to fund or otherwise participate in any significant way in such action." Title 50 leaves the choice of agency to the president and does not exclude the Pentagon.

At the heart of this debate, said a former senior Defense official, was "institutional culture and affiliation." The department took the position that it lacked the authority because it did not *want* the authority—or the mission. He told me, "All of its instincts push it in that direction."

One senior member of the National Security Council's counterterrorism group recalled encountering this attitude during deliberations over counterterrorism operations and clandestine support for the Northern Alliance. To the Joint Staff, neither was "in their minds a military mission. It was a covert action. The uniformed military was adamant that they would not do covert action." And, he added, if you presented them with "a legal opinion that says 'You're wrong,'" then they would say, "Well, we're not going to do it anyway. It's a matter of policy that we don't.'"

The authority argument was a "cop-out," said a retired officer who served in the Pentagon from 1994 to 2000. Sure enough, the Defense Department could have bypassed Title 50 by employing SOF on a *clandestine* basis. While both clandestine and covert missions are secret, only the latter require that the U.S. role not be "acknowledged publicly," which is Title 50's key requirement. Using SOF to preempt terrorists or support resistance movements clandestinely in peacetime is within the scope of Title 10, as long as the U.S. government does not deny involvement when the mission is over.

But this interpretation of Title 10 was considered beyond the pale in the 1990s. The Pentagon did not want the authority to strike terrorists secretly or to employ Special Forces against states that aided and sheltered them.

5. Risk Aversion
The mainstream military often dismisses special operations as too risky. To employ SOF requires open-minded political and military leadership willing to balance risks against potential gains. Supple judgment was in short supply in the Pentagon in the 1990s.

Walter Slocombe served as Clinton's undersecretary of defense for policy, and took part in all coun-terterrorism policy discussions in the Department of Defense. "We certainly looked at lots of options which involved the possible use of SOF," he stressed. But in the end they were never selected because they seemed too hard to pull off, he acknowledged. Options that put people on the ground to go after bin Laden were "much too hard." It was much easier and much less risky to fire off cruise missiles.

During Clinton's first term, someone would always find something wrong with a proposed oper-ation, lamented General Downing. The attitude was: "Don't let these SOF guys go through the door because they're dangerous. . . . They are going to do something to embarrass the country." Downing recalls that during his years in command, he "sat through the preparation of maybe 20 operations where we had targeted people who had killed Americans. Terrorists who had done bad things to this country, and needed either to be killed or apprehended and brought back here, and we couldn't pull the trigger." It was too risky for the Pentagon's taste.

The other side of the risk-aversion coin is policymakers' demand for fail-safe options. A general who served in the Special Operations Command in the 1990s encountered "tremendous pressure to do something," he said, but at the same time, the requirement was for "perfect operations, no casu-alties, no failure." There were some "great opportunities" to strike at al Qaeda, "but you couldn't take any risk in doing so. You couldn't have a POW, you couldn't lose a man. You couldn't have anybody hurt." It was Catch-22. There were frequent "spin-ups" for SOF missions, but "in the end, the senior political and military leadership wouldn't let you go do it."

In the mid-1990s, and again at the end of the decade, the Clinton administration flirted with supporting the Iraqi resistance and then the Northern Alliance. An officer who served on the Joint Staff recounted how the senior military leadership put the kibosh on these potentially bold moves.

The CIA ran the Iraqi operation. But its unconventional warfare capabilities were paltry, and it turned to the military for help, requesting that SOF personnel be seconded to bolster the effort. The Joint Staff and its chairman wanted nothing to do with it, he said. "The guidance I got from the chair-man's director of operations was that we weren't going to support this, and do everything you can to stall or keep it in the planning mode, don't let it get to the point where we're briefing this at the National Security Council or on the Hill."

Later, the National Security Council's counterterrorism group proposed supporting the Northern Alliance. They pushed the proposal up to the "principals" level. But attached to it was a "non-con-currence" by the Joint Staff, opposing it as too complex and risky. That was the kiss of death.

None of this was new to the Joint Staff officer, who had been in special operations for a long time. "Risk aversion emerges as senior officers move into higher positions," he explained. "It's a very common thing for these guys to become non-risk takers. They get caught up in interagency politics and the bureaucratic process, and get risk averse."

A member of the counterterrorism group in the late 1990s noted that General Hugh Shelton, a former commander of the Special Operations Command, considered the use of SOF for counterter-rorism less than anyone when he was chairman of the Joint Chiefs. The official said Shelton directed the Joint Staff "not to plan certain operations, I'm sure you've heard this from others." In fact, I had. "It got to the point," he said, where "the uniforms had become the suits, they were more the bureau-crats than the civilians."

6. Pariah Cowboys

When events finally impelled the Clinton administration to take a hard look at offensive operations, the push to pursue them came from the civilians of the National Security Council's Counterterrorism and Security Group.

One of the hardest of the hard-liners was the group's chief, Dick Clarke. For nearly a decade, this career civil servant began and ended his work day with the burgeoning terrorist threat to America. He knew in detail the danger the bin Ladens of the world posed, and it worried him greatly. Defensive measures were just not enough. "Clarke's philosophy was to go get the terrorists," one former senior Pentagon special operations official told me, "Go get them anywhere you can."

Asked if that meant using SOF, he replied: "Oh yeah. In fact, many of the options were with special mission units." But "Dick Clarke was attempting to take on a Pentagon hierarchy that wasn't of the same philosophical mindset."

Clarke was not alone. Mike Sheehan also pushed for assisting the Northern Alliance and striking al Qaeda with SOF. Such measures worried the senior brass, who proceeded to weaken those officials by treating them as pariahs. That meant portraying them as cowboys, who proposed reckless military operations that would get American soldiers killed.

Sheehan explained: Suppose one civilian starts beating the drum for special operations. The establishment "systematically starts to undermine you. They would say, 'He's a rogue, he's uncooperative, he's out of control, he's stupid, he makes bad choices.' It's very damaging. . . . You get to the point where you don't even raise issues like that. If someone did, like me or Clarke, we were labeled cowboys, way outside our area of competence."

Several officials who served on the Joint Staff and in the Pentagon's special operations office remembered the senior brass characterizing Clarke in such terms. "Anything Dick Clarke suggested, the Joint Staff was going to be negative about," said one. Some generals had been vitriolic, calling Clarke "a madman, out of control, power hungry, wanted to be a hero, all that kind of stuff." In fact, one of these former officials emphasized, "when we would carry back from the counterterrorism group one of those SOF counterterrorism proposals, our job was to figure out not how to execute it, but how we were going to say no."

By turning Clarke into a pariah, the Pentagon brass discredited precisely the options that might have spared us the tragedy of September 11, 2001. And when Clarke fought back at being branded "wild" and "irresponsible," they added "abrasive" and "intolerant" to the counts against him.

7. Intimidation of Civilians

Another way the brass stymied hard-line proposals from civilian policymakers was by highlighting their own military credentials and others' lack of them. One former defense official recounted a briefing on counterterrorism options given the secretary of defense by senior civilians and military officers. "The civilian, a political appointee with no military experience, says, 'As your policy adviser, let me tell you what you need to do militarily in this situation.' The chairman sits there, calmly listening. Then it's his turn. He begins by framing his sophisticated Power- Point briefing in terms of the 'experience factor,' his own judgment, and those of four-star associates. The 'experience factor' infuses the presentation. Implicitly, it raises a question intended to discredit the civilian: 'What makes you qualified? What makes you think that your opinion is more important than mine when you don't have the experience I have?' 'Mr. Secretary,' concludes the chairman, 'this is my best military advice.'" In such situations, the official said, civilians were often dissuaded from taking on the generals.

Wayne Downing, the former special operations commander, had plenty of experience providing such briefings. "Occasionally you would get a civilian champion," he said, who would speak up enthusiastically in favor of the mission being presented. "And then the chairman or the vice chairman would say, 'I don't think this is a good idea. Our best military judgment is that you not do this.' That champion is not going any further."

During the 1990s, the "best military advice," when it came to counterterrorism, was always wary of the use of force. Both risk-aversion and a deep-seated distrust of SOF traceable all the way back to World War II informed the military counsel offered to top decision makers. Almost all those I consulted confirmed this, and many, including General Stiner, have described it in print.

When President Clinton began asking about special operations, one former senior official recounted, "those options were discussed, but never got anywhere. The Joint Staff would say, 'That's cowboy Hollywood stuff.' The president was intimidated because these guys come in with all those medals, [and] the White House took the 'stay away from SOF options' advice of the generals."

Another former official during both Clinton terms described several instances where "best military advice" blocked SOF options under White House review. "The Pentagon resisted using Special Forces. Clinton raised it several times with [Joint Chiefs chairmen] Shalikashvili and Shelton. They recommended against it, and never really came up with a do-able plan."

Occasionally, policymakers kept pushing. When support for the Northern Alliance was on the table after the embassy bombings in Africa, the senior military leadership "refused to consider it," a former counterterrorism group member told me. "They said it was an intelligence operation, not a military mission."

The counterterrorism group at the National Security Council pushed the proposal anyway, but the Joint Staff strongly demurred and would not support it. They argued that supporting the Northern Alliance would entangle the United States in a quagmire. That was the end of the line. Let's suppose, said the former counterterrorism group member, that the president had ordered a covert strike "despite the chairman going on record as opposing it. Now, if the president orders such an operation against the best military advice of his chief military adviser, and it gets screwed up, they will blame the president who has no military experience, who was allegedly a draft dodger." The Northern Alliance was left to wither on the vine.

8. Big Footprints

The original concept for SOF counterterrorism units was that they would be unconventional, small, flexible, adaptive, and stealthy, suited to discreet and discriminate use, say those "present at the creation" following the Desert One disaster. Force packages were to be streamlined for surgical operations. The "footprint" of any operation was to be small, even invisible.

By the 1990s, this had dropped by the wayside. One former official recalled that when strikes against al Qaeda cells were proposed, "the Joint Staff and the chairman would come back and say, 'We highly recommend against doing it. But if ordered to do it, this is how we would do it.' And usually it involved the 82nd and 101st Airborne Divisions. The footprint was ridiculous." In each instance the civilian policymakers backed off.

To some extent, SOF planners themselves have been guilty of this. "Mission-creep," one official called it. Since you can't "totally suppress an environment with 15 guys and three helicopters," force packages became "five or six hundred guys, AC-130 gunships, a 900-man quick-reaction force ready to assist if you get in trouble, and F-14s circling over the Persian Gulf." The policymakers were thinking small, surgical, and stealthy, so they'd take one "look at it and say that's too big."

One original Delta Force member traced this problem back to Desert One. "We took some bad lessons from that," he said. ". . . One was that we needed more. That maybe it would have been successful if we'd had more helicopters. That more is better. And now we add too many bells and whistles. We make our footprint too large. We price ourselves out of the market."

It's a way of dealing with the military's aversion to risk. "One way we tend to think we mitigate risk," he said, "is by adding more capabilities for this contingency and that contingency." Asked if this thinking had found its way into the Special Operations Command, he replied, "Yes. Absolutely."

9. No Actionable Intelligence

A top official in the Office of the Under Secretary of Defense for Policy in the 1990s described the intelligence deficit with respect to targeting Osama bin Laden: "If you get intelligence, it's by definition very perishable. He moves all the time and he undoubtedly puts out false stories about where he's moving," making it extremely difficult "to get somebody from anyplace outside of Afghanistan into Afghanistan in time. The biggest problem was always intelligence."

But if the target had been broadened to al Qaeda's infrastructure, the intelligence requirements would have been less demanding, noted Dick Clarke. "There was plenty of intelligence. We had incredibly good intelligence about where bin Laden's facilities were. While we might never have been able to say at any given moment where he was, we knew half a dozen places that he moved among. So there was ample opportunity to use Special Forces."

In effect, to turn the need for "actionable intelligence" into a showstopper, all you have to do is define the target narrowly. That makes the intelligence requirements nearly impossible to satisfy. Broaden the picture, and the challenge of actionable intelligence became more manageable.

Special Operators are actually the first to seek good intelligence. But according to an officer on the Joint Staff at the time, "no actions [were] taken to pre-position or deploy the kinds of people that could have addressed those intelligence shortfalls"—people who could have provided the operational-level intelligence needed for SOF to deploy rapidly against fleeting targets in the safe havens where terrorists nest.

What was essential for counterterrorism operations was to establish intelligence networks in places harboring targets. This "operational preparation of the battlespace" is accomplished by infiltrating special operators who pass for locals. Their job includes recruiting indigenous elements who can help SOF units enter an area of interest, and organize, train, and equip local resistance and surrogate forces to assist them.

But no such preparation took place in the 1990s in terrorist havens like Afghanistan, Yemen, Lebanon, and Sudan. Operating in those lands "would have taken official approval that prior to 9/11 would have never been given to us," one knowledgeable individual explained. "Prior to 9/11 there was no willingness to put Department of Defense personnel in such places. No such request would have been authorized."

Why? Because it's dicey, was the bottom line for a former senior Clinton appointee at the Pentagon. Asked if there were proposals at his level for it, he said: "Not that I remember," adding, "I can understand why. It raises a lot of questions. Without saying you shouldn't do it, it is one of those things that is going to cause concern. . . . You're talking not just about recruiting individuals to be sent, but recruiting whole organizations, and you think about it in the context of Somalia. I'm sure that would have raised a lot of questions. I can see why people would have been reluctant."

*　*　*

During Clinton's second term, then, the possibility of hunting down the terrorists did receive ample attention at the top echelons of government. But somewhere between inception and execution, the SOF options were always scuttled as too problematic.

War and tragedy have a way of breaking old attitudes. September 11, 2001, should have caused a sea change in SOF's role in fighting terrorism. To some extent, it has. Consider the stellar contribution of Special Operations Forces to the campaign in Afghanistan in 2001-02. In the early planning stages, SOF were only ancillary to the war plan; but by the end of October 2001, they had moved to center stage. They played a decisive role in toppling the Taliban and routing al Qaeda.

Since then, SOF have deployed to places like Yemen and the Philippines to train local militaries to fight al Qaeda and its affiliates. And last year, Secretary Rumsfeld ordered the Special Operations Command to track down and destroy al Qaeda around the globe. In effect, he ordered a global manhunt to prevent future 9/11s, including attacks with weapons of mass destruction.

In the war against terrorism, a global SOF campaign against al Qaeda is indispensable. Happily, our special counterterrorism units are tailor-made for this. And now that the United States is at war, it should be possible to overcome the showstoppers that blocked the "peacetime" use of those forces through the 1990s.

It should be—but will it? The answer is mixed. Some showstoppers have been neutralized. While law enforcement still has a role to play, we are clearly fighting a war, in which the Department of Defense and the armed forces take the lead. Thus, there should be far less latitude for turning advocates of tough counterterrorism missions into pariahs. September 11 and the president's response to it changed the terms of the policy discussion.

Yet the other showstoppers have not ceased to matter. Competing power centers continue to jockey for influence over counterterrorism policy. In a war in which the CIA may feel it has both a role to play and lost ground to regain, the Title 10/Title 50 debate and arguments over actionable intelligence are likely to persist. In our democratic society, fear of another Somalia remains. And the conventional military's mistrust of SOF has not evaporated.

Once again, a civilian is pushing for greater use of Special Operations Forces. Secretary of Defense Rumsfeld wants the Special Operations Command, for the first time in its history, to play the role of a "supported command," instead of supporting the geographic commands, as it has in the past. Neither those commands nor their friends on the Joint Staff are likely to welcome a reversal of the relationship in order to facilitate SOF missions. "Who's in command here?" could become a new wartime showstopper. Some in SOF believe it already has.

Once again, the problem involves institutions, organizational cultures, and entrenched ways of thinking. "Rumsfeld might think we're at war with terrorism," observed one former general, "but I'll bet he also thinks he is at war within the Pentagon. . . . The real war's happening right there in his building. It's a war of the culture. He can't go to war because he can't get his organization up for it."

Donald Rumsfeld may believe that Special Operations Forces should be in the forefront of the global war on terrorism. But for that to happen, he will have to breach what remains of the phalanx of resistance that blocked the offensive use of special mission units for over a decade— and he'll have to overcome the new showstoppers as well.

For now, it appears that the most powerful defense secretary ever has failed in his attempt to do this. In a disquieting October 16, 2003, memo to the Pentagon elite in the war on terror—General Dick Meyers, Joint Chiefs chairman; Deputy Defense Secretary Paul Wolfowitz; General Pete Pace, vice chairman of the Joint Chiefs; and Doug Feith, undersecretary of defense for policy—Rumsfeld laments that progress has been slow and the Defense Department has not "yet made truly bold moves" in fighting al Qaeda. And he wonders whether his department "is changing fast enough to deal with the new 21st century security environment."

It's a good question. As al Qaeda regroups and deploys to new battlefields in Iraq and elsewhere, our special mission units—the Delta boys, the SEALs, and the rest— remain on the shelf. It's time to take them off.

Part VI
Globalization and its Effects

Benjamin Barber's *Jihad vs. McWorld* continue the predictions of Samuel Huntington's *Clash of Civilizations* on what will cause conflict and cooperation among states in the new, post-Cold War world.

Barber's *globalization* and *tribalization* dovetail nicely into Huntington's third and fourth causal factors explaining why different civilizations are doomed to conflict—that tribalization is a back-lash against globalization.

Jihad vs. McWorld

Benjamin R. Barber

The two axial principles of our age—tribalism and globalism—clash at every point except one: they may both be threatening to democracy

Just beyond the horizon of current events lie two possible political futures—both bleak, neither democratic. The first is a retribalization of large swaths of humankind by war and bloodshed: a threatened Lebanonization of national states in which culture is pitted against culture, people against people, tribe against tribe—a Jihad in the name of a hundred narrowly conceived faiths against every kind of interdependence, every kind of artificial social cooperation and civic mutuality. The second is being borne in on us by the onrush of economic and ecological forces that demand integration and uniformity and that mesmerize the world with fast music, fast computers, and fast food—with MTV, Macintosh, and McDonald's, pressing nations into one commercially homogenous global network: one McWorld tied together by technology, ecology, communications, and commerce. The planet is falling precipitantly apart *AND* coming reluctantly together at the very same moment.

. . . The old interwar national state based on territory and political sovereignty looks to be a mere transitional development.

The tendencies of what I am here calling the forces of Jihad and the forces of McWorld operate with equal strength in opposite directions, the one driven by parochial hatreds, the other by universalizing markets, the one re-creating ancient subnational and ethnic borders from within, the other making national borders porous from without. They have one thing in common: neither offers much hope to citizens looking for practical ways to govern themselves democratically. . . .

MCWORLD, OR THE GLOBALIZATION OF POLITICS

Four imperatives make up the dynamic of McWorld: a market imperative, a resource imperative, an information-technology imperative, and an ecological imperative. By shrinking the world and diminishing the salience of national borders, these imperatives have in combination achieved a considerable victory over factiousness and particularism, and not least of all over their most virulent traditional form—nationalism. . . .

BENJAMIN R. BARBER is the Professor of Civil Society at the Maryland School of Public Affairs and the College of Behavioral and Social Sciences, University of Maryland. When this article was written, he was the Whitman Professor of Political Science and director of the Whitman Center for the Culture and Politics of Democracy at Rutgers University.

The Atlantic Monthly Volume 269, Number 3 (March 1992), pp 53-65. Copyright 1992 by The Atlantic Monthly. Reprinted with Permission.

The Market Imperative

Marxist and Leninist theories of imperialism assumed that the quest for ever-expanding markets would in time compel nation-based capitalist economies to push against national boundaries in search of an international economic imperium. Whatever else has happened to the scientistic predictions of Marxism, in this domain they have proved farsighted. All national economies are now vulnerable to the inroads of larger, transnational markets within which trade is free, currencies are convertible, access to banking is open, and contracts are enforceable under law. In Europe, Asia, Africa, the South Pacific, and the Americas such markets are eroding national sovereignty and giving rise to entities—international banks, trade associations, transnational lobbies like OPEC and Greenpeace, world news services like CNN and the BBC, and multinational corporations that increasingly lack a meaningful national identity—that neither reflect nor respect nationhood as an organizing or regulative principle.

The market imperative has also reinforced the quest for international peace and stability, requisites of an efficient international economy. Markets are enemies of parochialism, isolation, fractiousness, war. Market psychology attenuates the psychology of ideological and religious cleavages and assumes a concord among producers and consumers—categories that ill fit narrowly conceived national or religious cultures. . . .

Common markets demand a common language, as well as a common currency, and they produce common behaviors of the kind bred by cosmopolitan city life everywhere. Commercial pilots, computer programmers, international bankers, media specialists, oil riggers, entertainment celebrities, ecology experts, demographers, accountants, professors, athletes—these compose a new breed of men and women for whom religion, culture, and nationality can seem only marginal elements in a working identity. Although sociologists of everyday life will no doubt continue to distinguish a Japanese from an American mode, shopping has a common signature throughout the world. Cynics might even say that some of the recent revolutions in Eastern Europe have had as their true goal not liberty and the right to vote but well-paying jobs and the right to shop (although the vote is proving easier to acquire than consumer goods). The market imperative is, then, plenty powerful; but, notwithstanding some of the claims made for "democratic capitalism," it is not identical with the democratic imperative.

The Resource Imperative

Democrats once dreamed of societies whose political autonomy rested firmly on economic independence. The Athenians idealized what they called autarky, and tried for a while to create a way of life simple and austere enough to make the polis genuinely self-sufficient. To be free meant to be independent of any other community or polis. Not even the Athenians were able to achieve autarky, however: human nature, it turns out, is dependency. Master and slave, it turned out, were bound together by mutual insufficiency.

The dream of autarky briefly engrossed nineteenth-century America as well, for the underpopulated, endlessly bountiful land, the cornucopia of natural resources, and the natural barriers of a continent walled in by two great seas led many to believe that America could be a world unto itself. Given this past, it has been harder for Americans than for most to accept the inevitability of interdependence. But the rapid depletion of resources even in a country like ours, where they once seemed inexhaustible, and the maldistribution of arable soil and mineral resources on the planet, leave even the wealthiest societies ever more resource-dependent and many other nations in permanently desperate straits.

Every nation, it turns out, needs something another nation has; some nations have almost nothing they need.

The Information-Technology Imperative

. . . Scientific progress embodies and depends on open communication, a common discourse rooted in rationality, collaboration, and an easy and regular flow and exchange of information. . . .

Business, banking, and commerce all depend on information flow and are facilitated by new communication technologies. The hardware of these technologies tends to be systemic and integrated—computer, television, cable, satellite, laser, fiber-optic, and microchip technologies combining to create a vast interactive communications and information network that can potentially give every person on earth access to every other person, and make every datum, every byte, available to every set of eyes. If the automobile was, as George Ball once said (when he gave his blessing to a Fiat factory in the Soviet Union during the Cold War), "an ideology on four wheels," then electronic telecommunication and information systems are an ideology at 186,000 miles per second—which makes for a very small planet in a very big hurry. Individual cultures speak particular languages; commerce and science increasingly speak English; the whole world speaks logarithms and binary mathematics.

Moreover, the pursuit of science and technology asks for, even compels, open societies. Satellite footprints do not respect national borders; telephone wires penetrate the most closed societies. With photocopying and then fax machines having infiltrated Soviet universities and *samizdat* literary circles in the eighties, and computer modems having multiplied like rabbits in communism's bureaucratic warrens thereafter, *glasnost* could not be far behind. In their social requisites, secrecy and science are enemies.

The new technology's software is perhaps even more globalizing than its hardware. The information arm of international commerce's sprawling body reaches out and touches distinct nations and parochial cultures, and gives them a common face chiseled in Hollywood, on Madison Avenue, and in Silicon Valley. Throughout the 1980s one of the most-watched television programs in South Africa was *The Cosby Show*. The demise of apartheid was already in production. Exhibitors at the 1991 Cannes film festival expressed growing anxiety over the "homogenization" and "Americanization" of the global film industry when, for the third year running, American films dominated the awards ceremonies. America has dominated the world's popular culture for much longer, and much more decisively. In November of 1991 Switzerland's once insular culture boasted best-seller lists featuring *Terminator 2* as the No. 1 movie, *Scarlett* as the No. 1 book, and Prince's *Diamonds and Pearls* as the No. 1 record album. No wonder the Japanese are buying Hollywood film studios even faster than Americans are buying Japanese television sets. This kind of software supremacy may in the long term be far more important than hardware superiority, because culture has become more potent than armaments. What is the power of the Pentagon compared with Disneyland? Can the Sixth Fleet keep up with CNN? McDonald's in Moscow and Coke in China will do more to create a global culture than military colonization ever could. It is less the goods than the brand names that do the work, for they convey life-style images that alter perception and challenge behavior. They make up the seductive software of McWorld's common (at times much too common) soul. . . .

The Ecological Imperative

The impact of globalization on ecology is a cliche even to world leaders who ignore it. We know well enough that the German forests can be destroyed by Swiss and Italians driving gas-guzzlers fueled by leaded gas. We also know that the planet can be asphyxiated by greenhouse gases because Brazilian farmers want to be part of the twentieth century and are burning down tropical rain forests to clear a little land to plough, and because Indonesians make a living out of converting their lush jungle into toothpicks for fastidious Japanese diners, upsetting the delicate oxygen balance and in effect puncturing our global lungs. Yet this ecological consciousness has meant not only greater awareness but also greater inequality, as modernized nations try to slam the door behind them, saying to developing nations, "The world cannot afford your modernization; ours has wrung it dry!"

Each of the four imperatives just cited is transnational, transideological, and transcultural. Each applies impartially to Catholics, Jews, Muslims, Hindus, and Buddhists; to democrats and totalitarians; to capitalists and socialists. The Enlightenment dream of a universal rational society has to a remarkable degree been realized—but in a form that is commercialized, homogenized, depoliticized, bureaucratized, and, of course, radically incomplete, for the movement toward McWorld is in competition with forces of global breakdown, national dissolution, and centrifugal corruption. These forces, working in the opposite direction, are the essence of what I call Jihad.

JIHAD, OR THE LEBANONIZATION OF THE WORLD

OPEC, the World Bank, the United Nations, the International Red Cross, the multinational corporation . . . there are scores of institutions that reflect globalization. But they often appear as ineffective reactors to the world's real actors: national states and, to an ever greater degree, subnational factions in permanent rebellion against uniformity and integration—even the kind represented by universal law and justice. The headlines feature these players regularly: they are cultures, not countries; parts, not wholes; sects, not religions; rebellious factions and dissenting minorities at war not just with globalism but with the traditional nation-state. Kurds, Basques, Puerto Ricans, Ossetians, East Timoreans, Quebecois, the Catholics of Northern Ireland, Abkhasians, Kurile Islander Japanese, the Zulus of Inkatha, Catalonians, Tamils, and, of course, Palestinians—people without countries, inhabiting nations not their own, seeking smaller worlds within borders that will seal them off from modernity.

A powerful irony is at work here. Nationalism was once a force of integration and unification, a movement aimed at bringing together disparate clans, tribes, and cultural fragments under new, assimilationist flags. But as Ortega y Gasset noted more than sixty years ago, having won its victories, nationalism changed its strategy. In the 1920s, and again today, it is more often a reactionary and divisive force, pulverizing the very nations it once helped cement together. . . .

. . . The international scene is little more unified than it was at the end of the Great War, in Ortega's own time. There were more than thirty wars in progress last year, most of them ethnic, racial, tribal, or religious in character, and the list of unsafe regions doesn't seem to be getting any shorter. Some new world order!

The aim of many of these small-scale wars is to redraw boundaries, to implode states and resecure parochial identities: to escape McWorld's dully insistent imperatives. The mood is that of Jihad: war not as an instrument of policy but as an emblem of identity, an expression of community, an end in itself. Even where there is no shooting war, there is fractiousness, secession, and the quest for ever smaller communities. Add to the list of dangerous countries those at risk: In Switzerland and Spain, Jurassian and Basque separatists still argue the virtues of ancient identities, sometimes in the language of bombs. . . . Kurdish independence would threaten the territorial integrity of four Middle Eastern nations. . . . Even the good will established by Canada's once promising Meech Lake protocols is in danger, with Francophone Quebec again threatening the dissolution of the federation. In South Africa the emergence from apartheid was hardly achieved when friction between Inkatha's Zulus and the African National Congress's tribally identified members threatened to replace Europeans' racism with an indigenous tribal war. After thirty years of attempted integration using the colonial language (English) as a unifier, Nigeria is now playing with the idea of linguistic multiculturalism—which could mean the cultural breakup of the nation into hundreds of tribal fragments. . . .

The passing of communism has torn away the thin veneer of internationalism (workers of the world unite!) to reveal ethnic prejudices that are not only ugly and deep-seated but increasingly murderous. Europe's old scourge, anti-Semitism, is back with a vengeance, but it is only one of many antagonisms. It appears all too easy to throw the historical gears into reverse and pass from a Communist dictatorship back into a tribal state.

Among the tribes, religion is also a battlefield. ("Jihad" is a rich word whose generic meaning is "struggle"—usually the struggle of the soul to avert evil. Strictly applied to religious war, it is used only in reference to battles where the faith is under assault, or battles against a government that denies the practice of Islam. My use here is rhetorical, but does follow both journalistic practice and history.) Remember the Thirty Years War? Whatever forms of Enlightenment universalism might once have come to grace such historically related forms of monotheism as Judaism, Christianity, and Islam, in many of their modern incarnations they are parochial rather than cosmopolitan, angry rather than loving, proselytizing rather than ecumenical, zealous rather than rationalist, sectarian rather than deistic, ethnocentric rather than universalizing. As a result, like the new forms of hypernationalism, the new expressions of religious fundamentalism are fractious and pulverizing, never integrating. This is religion as the Crusaders knew it: a battle to the death for souls that if not saved will be forever lost.

The atmospherics of Jihad have resulted in a breakdown of civility in the name of identity, of comity in the name of community. International relations have sometimes taken on the aspect of gang war—cultural turf battles featuring tribal factions that were supposed to be sublimated as integral parts of large national, economic, postcolonial, and constitutional entities.

THE DARKENING FUTURE OF DEMOCRACY

These rather melodramatic tableaux vivants do not tell the whole story, however. For all their defects, Jihad and McWorld have their attractions. Yet, to repeat and insist, the attractions are unrelated to democracy. Neither McWorld nor Jihad is remotely democratic in impulse. Neither needs democracy; neither promotes democracy.

McWorld does manage to look pretty seductive in a world obsessed with Jihad. It delivers peace, prosperity, and relative unity—if at the cost of independence, community, and identity (which is generally based on difference). The primary political values required by the global market are order and tranquillity, and freedom—as in the phrases "free trade," "free press," and "free love." Human rights are needed to a degree, but not citizenship or participation—and no more social justice and equality than are necessary to promote efficient economic production and consumption. Multinational corporations sometimes seem to prefer doing business with local oligarchs, inasmuch as they can take confidence from dealing with the boss on all crucial matters. Despots who slaughter their own populations are no problem, so long as they leave markets in place and refrain from making war on their neighbors (Saddam Hussein's fatal mistake). In trading partners, predictability is of more value than justice.

. . . Jihad delivers a different set of virtues: a vibrant local identity, a sense of community, solidarity among kinsmen, neighbors, and countrymen, narrowly conceived. But it also guarantees parochialism and is grounded in exclusion. Solidarity is secured through war against outsiders. And solidarity often means obedience to a hierarchy in governance, fanaticism in beliefs, and the obliteration of individual selves in the name of the group. Deference to leaders and intolerance toward outsiders (and toward "enemies within") are hallmarks of tribalism—hardly the attitudes required for the cultivation of new democratic women and men capable of governing themselves. Where new democratic experiments have been conducted in retribalizing societies, in both Europe and the Third

World, the result has often been anarchy, repression, persecution, and the coming of new, noncommunist forms of very old kinds of despotism. . . .

THE CONFEDERAL OPTION

How can democracy be secured and spread in a world whose primary tendencies are at best indifferent to it (McWorld) and at worst deeply antithetical to it (Jihad)? My guess is that globalization will eventually vanquish retribalization. The ethos of material "civilization" has not yet encountered an obstacle it has been unable to thrust aside. Ortega may have grasped in the 1920s a clue to our own future in the coming millennium.

"Everyone sees the need of a new principle of life. But as always happens in similar crises—some people attempt to save the situation by an artificial intensification of the very principle which has led to decay. This is the meaning of the 'nationalist' outburst of recent years. . . . things have always gone that way. The last flare, the longest; the last sigh, the deepest. On the very eve of their disappearance there is an intensification of frontiers—military and economic."

Jihad may be a last deep sigh before the eternal yawn of McWorld. On the other hand, Ortega was not exactly prescient; his prophecy of peace and internationalism came just before blitzkrieg, world war, and the Holocaust tore the old order to bits. Yet democracy is how we remonstrate with reality, the rebuke our aspirations offer to history. . . .

By the same token, the participatory and direct form of democracy that engages citizens in civic activity and civic judgment and goes well beyond just voting and accountability—the system I have called "strong democracy"—suits the political needs of decentralized communities as well as theocratic and nationalist party dictatorships have done. Local neighborhoods need not be democratic, but they can be. Real democracy has flourished in diminutive settings: the spirit of liberty, Tocqueville said, is local. Participatory democracy, if not naturally apposite to tribalism, has an undeniable attractiveness under conditions of parochialism.

Democracy in any of these variations will, however, continue to be obstructed by the undemocratic and antidemocratic trends toward uniformitarian globalism and intolerant retribalization which I have portrayed here. For democracy to persist in our brave new McWorld, we will have to commit acts of conscious political will—a possibility, but hardly a probability, under these conditions. Political will requires much more than the quick fix of the transfer of institutions. Like technology transfer, institution transfer rests on foolish assumptions about a uniform world of the kind that once fired the imagination of colonial administrators. Spread English justice to the colonies by exporting wigs. Let an East Indian trading company act as the vanguard to Britain's free parliamentary institutions. Today's well-intentioned quick-fixers in the National Endowment for Democracy and the Kennedy School of Government, in the unions and foundations and universities zealously nurturing contacts in Eastern Europe and the Third World, are hoping to democratize by long distance. Post Bulgaria a parliament by first-class mail. Fed Ex the Bill of Rights to Sri Lanka. Cable Cambodia some common law.

Yet Eastern Europe has already demonstrated that importing free political parties, parliaments, and presses cannot establish a democratic civil society; imposing a free market may even have the opposite effect. Democracy grows from the bottom up and cannot be imposed from the top down. Civil society has to be built from the inside out. The institutional superstructure comes last. Poland may become democratic, but then again it may heed the Pope, and prefer to found its politics on its Catholicism, with uncertain consequences for democracy. Bulgaria may become democratic, but it may prefer tribal war. . . .

It certainly seems possible that the most attractive democratic ideal in the face of the brutal realities of Jihad and the dull realities of McWorld will be a confederal union of semi-autonomous communities smaller than nation-states, tied together into regional economic associations and markets larger than nation-states—participatory and self-determining in local matters at the bottom, representative and accountable at the top. The nation-state would play a diminished role, and sovereignty would lose some of its political potency. The Green movement adage "Think globally, act locally" would actually come to describe the conduct of politics.

This vision reflects only an ideal, however—one that is not terribly likely to be realized. Freedom, Jean-Jacques Rousseau once wrote, is a food easy to eat but hard to digest. Still, democracy has always played itself out against the odds. And democracy remains both a form of coherence as binding as McWorld and a secular faith potentially as inspiriting as Jihad.

Part VII
Future American Foreign Policy Debate

As the course enters the last block, we will transition from studying theories to applying those theories to come up with prescriptions to develop a foreign policy for the United States.

Juan Alsace debates the old concept of isolationism in *In Search of Monsters to Destroy.* He bases his conclusion of supporting or not supporting a return to American isolationism on the Realist premise of national security and survival. But he also asses the United States' power in Liberal-ish non-military terms.

In *Democratic Realism,* Charles Krauthammer offers up four possible foreign policy constructs for this new unipolar world—all based on different conceptual visualizations of the world: isolationism, liberal internationalism, realism, and democratic globalism/realism. Each of these positions is based on Liberalism, Realism . . . or both.

In *The Atlantic Century,* Ralph Peters argues that while the US will continue to have interests to the East & West—towards Europe and Asia—the focus of its foreign policy should be towards Latin America and Africa. See how he uses arguments from both Realism and Liberalism to support to foreign policy prescription.

In Search of Monsters to Destroy:
American Empire in the New Millennium

Juan A. Alsace

"We have had an Imperial lesson; it may make us an Empire yet!"

— *Rudyard Kipling[1]*

With the coldly calculated use of terror, the perpetrators of 11 September 2001 served abrupt notice of challenge to US global dominance. The seemingly easy path before Americans that had appeared to stretch out well into the 21st century—promising boundless economic growth, a worldwide embrace of US values, an absence of rivals—stood blocked by the rubble in New York and Washington. In tallying the costs buried within the debris of 9/11, Americans need to look beyond the lost lives and shattered dreams and recognize that defense of the empire they possess will not come cheaply. But first they must accept the fact of empire. Those who argue the United States has no empire to uphold whistle past the graveyard, ignoring the historically unparalleled confluence of political, economic, military, and information power that have come together in the American imperial construct. To a great extent, the United States holds sway over the world—or at least influence over much of it—an empire inviting admiration, envy, and, as with all empires before it, challenge.

John Quincy Adams warned in 1821 that Americans should resist the temptation of going abroad "in search of monsters to destroy."[2] But in September 2001, monsters literally came to the United States, threatening political instability, economic malaise, and chaos. Even with al Qaeda on the run and Baghdad now fallen, the world remains dangerous and unstable, with vital US interests challenged by committed actors and unrelenting forces. North Korea pursues its nuclear ambition; Israelis and Palestinians remain locked in a death embrace; Islamic fundamentalists scheme to force the world back to the seventh century; Colombia teeters at the edge of failure; and the whole of the African continent stares at virtual extinction occasioned by a plague of Biblical proportion. Only the United States has the capability to restore order, imposing its will when and where necessary. This imperial path holds danger and difficulty, but it is a choice the nation must embrace, even if reluctantly and at certain cost.

Juan Alsace is the US Consul General in Barcelona. A career diplomat, he has previously served overseas as the Deputy Principal Officer in Istanbul, as well as political officer tours in Karachi, Santo Domingo, and Quito. Mr. Alsace's Washington assignments include a Pearson Fellowship in the office of Senator Russell Feingold. Mr. Alsace is a Distinguished Graduate of the National War College (2003). As with all *Parameters* articles, the views expressed are the author's own, and do not necessarily reflect the position of any agency of the US government.

TAKING UP THE GAUNTLET

In September 2002, the Bush Administration released its carefully crafted National Security Strategy (NSS), affirmatively answering the question of whether the United States would meet the challenges posed by a disordered world, seemingly accepting the mantle and responsibility of empire. The Administration determined, not unreasonably, that the doctrines of containment and deterrence that had served the nation throughout the Cold War would not be effective in protecting Americans against asymmetric threats posed by irrational or ideologically motivated non-state actors or rogue states, foes who would be neither contained nor deterred.[3] The new "Bush Doctrine" of preemption, as enunciated in the NSS, drew attention (and criticism) as proof that the United States would act unilaterally —indeed, with imperial "arrogance"—in defense of its interests.

If truth be told, preemption is not so radical a concept; at heart it is simply self-defense. Controversy lies, however, in the robust version of self-defense espoused in the NSS. Therein preemption has moved from the classic, internationally recognized "anticipatory self-defense" in the face of imminent danger to a flat assertion that the United States can even change regimes in order to obviate dangers not yet operational, as exemplified by the war against Iraq.[4]

But even "more ambitious than preemption is the sometimes overlooked assertion that the United States will remain powerful enough to keep potential adversaries from a military buildup that would surpass or equal the power of the United States."[5] Herein truly lies assertion of imperial prerogative: the United States will "have all the power and no one else shall have the capacity to provide a balance. . . . [It is a] declaration of absolute military supremacy throughout the globe."[6] Max Boot, senior fellow at the Council on Foreign Relations, observes that this "predominance doctrine" reflects the American preference to go it alone, unconstrained by allies.[7] Many in the world—the French come to mind—view the combination of preemption and predominance as insidious, an imperial overreach that goes beyond a war on terror to establish the United States not only as the world's constable but as its final arbiter of state legitimacy.[8]

The National Security Strategy seeks to soften such opposition with repeated assertions that the United States acts only with the most benevolent of motives: to "create a balance of power that favors human freedom: conditions in which all nations and societies can choose for themselves the rewards and challenges of political and economic freedom."[9] Such pieties are very likely neither convincing nor comforting to European or Chinese practitioners of realpolitik (nor to al Qaeda, for that matter), given the insistence in the NSS that the American vision of democratic governance and economic policy is the "single sustainable model for national success."[10] But they do serve to make empire palatable to a US populace that has "tended to reject the idea that our own high-minded republic might be imperial (much less imperialist) . . . [certain that Washington] did not seek to conquer territory nor, supposedly, to dominate other societies."[11]

It may be true that American dominion lacks many of the indicia of classic empire—the United States does not, for example, forcibly extract resources from colonies, impose its political values and institutions by force, or direct the foreign policies of client states.[12] While the operation in Iraq lends pause to the claim that the United States will not impose its values, as a general proposition America exercises its authority indirectly, preferring "seduction to coercion" (albeit perfectly prepared to use force as necessary), always with the goal of maintaining supremacy. As Andrew Bacevich notes, this preference "befits a nation founded on the conviction of its own uniqueness, [an] empire . . . like no other in history."[13] In sum, rigid academic classification should not deter "Americans [from] admitting the truth and facing up to their responsibilities as the undisputed masters of the world."[14]

This American mastery comes in several forms. US economic might drives the world's trade and markets and American political power can often shape the decisions of international bodies. In the

21st century, American "soft power" surely influences the course of human events, creating an enticing culture driven by US command of the information network. But that attractive velvet glove hides a mailed fist, the nexus of American power. The United States "has overwhelming superiority in military power, and uses that power to influence the internal behavior of other states, [acting as] an empire."[15] Televised images of American tanks rolling through the streets of Baghdad evinced the "centrality of military power to present-day American policy . . . to convey disapproval, change attitudes, and dictate behavior."[16] As one reviews current American military strategy and planning for the future, defense of empire, if not its expansion, seems a clear if unspoken objective.

A RULING CAPABILITY

In the Cold War years, US military planning was "threat-based," focused mainly on the specter of Soviet-bloc tanks racing through the Fulda Gap. With the collapse of the Soviet threat—and the subsequent seeming absence of any real threat at all—the military moved toward a "capabilities-based" posture, a shift in focus consistent with the 2002 National Security Strategy.[17] A "threat-based" force was reactive and defensive in nature: the United States awaited the thrust. In contrast, a "capabilities-based" force carries with it an implication of offensive capability if not intent: the US focus is not on any particular threat as it prepares for any and all contingencies by adopting an aggressive, forward-leaning posture.

In *Joint Vision 2020*, the US military posits "Full Spectrum Dominance," a doctrine that moves beyond fighting and winning conventional wars, past confronting weapons of mass destruction, to a particular attention to the "asymmetric threats—terrorists, criminals, religious crazies, two-bit strongmen with big ambitions, anarchy-minded hackers, and unscrupulous scientists peddling weapons secrets to make a buck."[18] This "capabilities-based" force provides policymakers with a suite of options to fight what Boot calls "the savage wars of peace . . . necessary to enlarge the 'empire of liberty.'"[19]

The US ability to bend wills derives from several key elements, but perhaps the most important is the ubiquity of its presence worldwide, with "military bases, or base rights, in some 40 countries—giving it the same global muscle it would enjoy if it ruled those countries directly."[20] The US footprint is innocuous in most cases (often treaty rights without a physical presence, except as needed), allowing for a light touch that minimizes local resentments. Next, the United States projects power and imperial influence through its Special Forces and intelligence capabilities. Since 9/11, the United States has quietly dispersed such forces worldwide, moving "deeply into the governments, intelligence agencies, and security apparatus of many countries . . . [with] small numbers of US forces 'advising'(i.e., commanding) native forces, . . . in effect usurping sovereignty."[21]

The use of proxies is a time-honored tradition of empire: Bacevich devotes an entire chapter of his book *American Empire* to comparing US proxies fighting, inter alia, in Afghanistan, to the British employing Gurkhas during the time of the Raj. When Australian Prime Minister John Howard asserted his own nation's right to strike preemptively (following the 12 October 2002 terror attacks in Bali), his alarmed Asian neighbors accused him of playing America's "deputy sheriff" in Southeast Asia.[22]

A rapid response capability, intelligence/information dominance, proxies, and air and naval power are all evolving components of American imperial power projection. That said, "lesson one in the Roman handbook for imperial success would be a realization that it is not enough to have great military strength; the rest of the world must know that strength—and fear it."[23] The war on terror, as the Administration has oft-noted, is being fought in the shadows, as it should be. But the war against Iraq has been front-page news for nearly all of 2003, dominating the world's consciousness, underscoring the reality of American suzerainty. The willingness on the part of the United States to use credible and massive force against Saddam Hussein, as *The Washington Post* speculated on 13 April 2003, did more than topple a dictator: it served notice in Pyongyang, Tehran, and Damascus that Washington will remove those who threaten US interests. 24 That action is truly an exercise of imperial power, a "demonstration that the empire cannot be challenged with impunity."[25]

SHOCKED AND AWED . . . BY THE CHECK

The image of Saddam's statue tumbling from its pedestal brings with it a visceral satisfaction; the American psyche, scarred by 9/11, anthrax attacks, color-coded security alerts, economic woes, and a general sense of unease, restored to a confident, imperial swagger. Watch out, world! But the victory comes at a cost, and the bill has yet to be paid. As Boot noted in October 2002:

> [As] impressive as the American military dominance of the past decade has been, it was acquired, relatively speaking, on the cheap. America spends only about 3.5 percent of its GDP on defense, down from 4.4 percent as recently as 1993 . . . but [now] there aren't enough troops to carry out all our commitments, and the equipment they use is aging fast. . . . [N]ext year's [2003] defense budget increase won't begin to cover this shortfall. . . . If America is serious about remaining the Big Enchilada, it will have to spend more on defense."[26]

The expense of bases abroad, of massive deployments, of "full spectrum dominance," is going to fall on the American taxpayer, with an economy still in the doldrums. In spending for imperial defense, the United States may shortchange domestic priorities for, as Michael Ignatieff observes, "What empires lavish abroad, they cannot spend on good republican government at home: on hospitals or roads or schools."[27] To the defense bill, add also the cost of homeland security and, of course, the as-yet-uncalculated costs of Iraqi reconstruction.

The Romans, Ottomans, and British resolved this issue easily and brutally, through the imposition of imperial levies. The US approach, bowing to both domestic and international sensibilities, is of necessity subtler, based on the principle of what Norwegian historian Geir Lundestad has characterized as "empire by invitation."[28] A good example is the arrangement that the United States has with Singapore, which agreed to pay for the construction of a naval facility that could accommodate American carriers. Singaporeans have now both an economic and security stake in the empire (not to mention plausible deniability, as they can claim that the facilities are open to any nation, even if the United States is the only likely occupant). While such direct subsidies are welcome, the costs of the imperial construct are in the last analysis defrayed on a grander scale, through globalization and a stable, open economic order that furthers, first and foremost, American prosperity. This is the aim US power ultimately means to impose and protect.

NON, NYET, NEIN

In addition to the economic accounting, there is also an intangible levy, best summed up by President Bush's question in the aftermath of 9/11: "Why do they hate us so?" He answered the question in a typically American manner that underscores the sense of exceptionalism that informs US policy: "They hate our freedoms." Perhaps. But a more honest answer might be that "they" hate US power and a system that "no matter how benevolent the intentions . . . will generate some violence . . . [by] those left outside the expanding walls [of empire]."[29] More to the point, the weak have always envied the strong; it is a natural human reaction.

If foreign envy were the only concern of US policymakers, the wailings of the French, Russians, or Germans would be as ephemeral whispers lost in the rising American chorus. But these allied fulminations represent only the least threatening manifestation of challenge to the American empire. There are potential great-power rivals. China is most often cited as the likeliest candidate. Several respected US research institutions have concluded, however, that, "China [remains far] from the threshold of global military power . . . [and that] the formidable US lead over China in military technology may well expand in the 21st century."[30] Hobbled by a shrinking population and a bankrupt social infrastructure, Russia's bleak demographics leave it weak into the foreseeable future. The European Union, wired into the information age and potentially militarily capable, could emerge as a peer competitor, assuming it achieves actual political integration. But EU nations share US democratic values and a commitment to open trade and market systems. They grumble at US dominance, but they are unlikely to truly undermine an order that has brought them prosperity as well.

The absence of great power rivals provides little comfort, however. In their place, "a viper's nest of perils . . . that run the gamut from terror and international organized crime to rogue states and genocidal violence fueled by ethnic hatred" challenges the established order.[31] Professor John Keegan recommends that, in response, "the great work of disarming tribes, sects, warlords, and criminals —a principal achievement of monarchs in the 17th century and empires in the 19th" be revived today.[32] Combating forces that have typically nibbled at the edges of empire has heretofore "been trivialized as hovering somehow beneath the dignity of serious strategists and military planners."[33] The physical scars of 9/11—as well as its lingering economic aftershocks—make clear that the United States can no longer afford the luxury of that conceit.

Still and all, militarily engaging the Lilliputians might be the easiest element of a complex problem. Even in their most terrible forms, transnational terrorism, rogue states, and international crime are dwarfed by American power. The counterstrikes the United States can expect from al Qaeda, the narco-traffickers, and the disaffected will be as pinpricks in the flanks of empire. It is crucial that US responses, while firm, be measured against other interests. The danger ultimately lies not so much in what others do, but in what the United States does or does not.

OF THIS WORLD AND IN IT

Ironically, the United States, the nation of immigrants, "remains a profoundly provincial, monolingual nation . . . not [much] interested in the rest of the world and certainly [not knowing] much about it."[34] Yet, as Bacevich argues, "America's purpose is the creation of an open and integrated international order based on the principles of democratic capitalism, with the United States as the ultimate guarantor of order and enforcer of norms."[35] Can the United States restore order and lead a world in which it has little interest and knowledge?

It is a critical question because the nature and ultimate success or failure of the American empire depends on its answer. If Americans become a truly insular people, suspicious of the world and of its motives, the nation is likely to head down unsavory paths, to an empire bereft of the values that give the United States a legitimate claim to leadership. In the end, in that event, it will become an empire that will have drifted from its bedrock moorings and it will fail. The better road would have Americans undertake their responsibility to genuinely engage the world they purport to lead, building relationships that will both facilitate the restoration of imperial order and soften the resentments that breed chaos. There is no guarantee that such an empire will succeed—history has no precedent—but in the effort Americans will have put behind them the rubble of 9/11, returning to the path upon which they were embarked, while remaining true to themselves.

NOTES

1. Rudyard Kipling, "The Lesson," accessible at http://whitewolf.newcastle.edu.au/words/authors/K/KiplingRudyard/verse/p1/lesson.html.

2. John Quincy Adams, 1821, while Secretary of State under President James Monroe, in a speech at the US House of Representatives in honor of Independence Day. Excerpt at http://www.uiowa.edu/~c030162/Common/Handouts/Other/JQ-ADAMS.html.

3. Michael Ignatieff, "The American Empire: The Burden," *The New York Times Magazine*, 5 January 2003, p. 4, http://www.ksg.harvard.edu/news/opeds/america_burden_ignatieff_nyt_010503.htm.

4. W. Michael Reisman, "Pre-emptive Force: When Can It Be Used?" Foreign Policy Association, 13 January 2003, transcript of panel discussion, p. 4.

5. Jay Tolson, "The New American Empire? Americans Have an Enduring Aversion to Planting the Flag on Foreign Soil: Is that Attitude Changing?" *U.S. News and World Report*, 13 January 2003, p. 37.

6. Robert N. Bellah, "The New American Empire," *Commonweal*, 25 October 2002, p. 12.

7. Max Boot, "Doctrine of the 'Big Enchilada,'" *the Washington Post*, 14 October 2002, sec. A, p. 29.

8. Discussions between the author and several French colonels, 7-10 April 2003, in Paris, as part of annual exchange between students of the National War College and students of the Centre des Hautes Etudes Militaires (CHEM). The French counterparts carefully adhered to national policy as set forth by French civilian authorities. Even given the expected fidelity to policy, however, the author was struck by the clear discomfort of the French military vis-à-vis the "unilateral" nature of the US action in Iraq. While sympathetic to the specific goal of removing Saddam Hussein and acknowledging that US values were consonant with those of the French, the notion that US goals and values could be imposed was perceived as, in the last analysis, dangerous.

9. George W. Bush, *The National Security Strategy of the United States of America*, President Bush's transmittal letter to the US Congress, 17 September 2002, p. 1.

10. Ibid.

11. Charles S. Maier, "An American Empire? The Problems of Frontiers and Peace in 21st Century World Politics," *Harvard Magazine*, November-December 2002, p. 28.

12. Discussions between the author and Colonel Richard Hooker (USA), 7-10 April 2003, in Paris. Colonel Hooker, a fellow National War College student, firmly adheres to the view that "the word 'empire' has a defined meaning" and that it is intellectual sleight-of-hand to shoehorn US actions into that definition. His view reflects that of many Americans. The point is clear, however, that whatever the name, the US government must deal with the view abroad—and the actions that spring from those perceptions—that America is an empire, and has to act accordingly if it is going to protect its vital interests.

13. Andrew S. Bacevich, "New Rome, New Jerusalem," *The Wilson Quarterly*, 26 (Summer 2002), 50.

14. Jonathan Freedland, "Hail Bush: A New Roman Empire," *The Guardian*, 22 September 2002, p. 1, http://www.smh.com.au/articles/2002/09/19/1032054915705.html.

15. Stephen Peter Rosen, "The Future of War and the American Military: Demography, Technology and the Politics of Modern Empire," *Harvard Magazine*, May-June 2002, p. 31, http://www.harvard-magazine.com/on-line/050218.html.

16. Andrews S. Bacevich, "Policing Utopia: The Military Imperatives of Globalization," *The National Interest*, No. 56 (Summer 1999), p. 1, http://www.ciaonet.org/olj/ni/ni_99baa01.html.

17. US Department of Defense, *Quadrennial Defense Review Report*, 30 September 2001, p. IV, http://www.defenselink.mil/pubs/qdr2001.pdf.

18. Bacevich, "Policing Utopia," p. 6.

19. Thomas Donnelly, "The Past as Prologue: An Imperial Manual," *Foreign Affairs*, 81 (July/August 2002), 2, http://www.foreignaffairs.org/20027701fareviewessay8529/thomas-donnelly/the-past-as-prologue.html.

20. Freedland, p. 2. Certainly the presence of US military bases is not always a guarantee of acquiescence; consider the difficulties the United States encountered with Turkey and Saudi Arabia in the war against Iraq.

21. "The American Empire," STRATFOR, 2 April 2003, p. 4, http://www.stratfor.biz/1Story.neo.

22. "Howard Defends Terror Stance," Reuters, 12 December 2002, http://onenews.nzoom.com/onenews_detail/0,1227,152638-1-9,00.html. The "deputy sheriff" phrase was used previously, in 1999, when an Australian media report suggested he would serve in that role in the region in support of the US alliance. See "Howard Dubbed 'Deputy Sheriff,'" http://www.smh.com.au/articles/2002/12/02/1038712881405.html.

23. Freedland, p. 2.

24. Glenn Kessler and Karen DeYoung, "Foreign Policy: After Iraq, U.S. Debates Next Steps," *the Washington Post*, 13 April 2003, sec A.

25. Rosen, p. 4.

26. Boot, p. 3.

27. Ignatieff, p. 3.

28. Robert S. Litwak, "The Imperial Republic After 9/11," *The Wilson Quarterly*, 26 (Summer 2002), 78.

29. Maier, p. 31.

30. Paul Mann, "U.S. Military Technology Forecast to Outpace China's for Decades," *Aviation Week & Space Technology*, 17 January 2000, p. 432.

31. Bacevich, "Policing Utopia," p. 5.

32. William Anthony Hay, "Challenges of Empire," *Foreign Policy Research Institute:Watch on the West, A Newsletter of FPRI's Center for the Study of America and the West*, 3 (May 2002), 1, http://www.fpri.org/ww/0305.200205.hay.challengesofempire.html.

33. Donnelly, p. 2.

34. Bellah, pp. 3-4.

35. Andrew S. Bacevich, *American Empire: The Realities and Consequences of U.S. Diplomacy* (Cambridge, Mass.: Harvard Univ. Press, 2002), p. 3.

Democratic Realism: An American Foreign Policy for a Unipolar World

Charles Krauthammer

A UNIPOLAR WORLD

Americans have a healthy aversion to foreign policy. It stems from a sense of thrift: Who needs it? We're protected by two great oceans. We have this continent practically to ourselves. And we share it with just two neighbors, both friendly, one so friendly that its people seem intent upon moving in with us.

It took three giants of the twentieth century to drag us into its great battles: Wilson into World War I, Roosevelt into World War II, Truman into the Cold War. And then it ended with one of the great anticlimaxes in history. Without a shot fired, without a revolution, without so much as a press release, the Soviet Union simply gave up and disappeared.

It was the end of everything—the end of communism, of socialism, of the Cold War, of the European wars. But the end of everything was also a beginning. On December 26, 1991, the Soviet Union died and something new was born, something utterly new—a unipolar world dominated by a single superpower unchecked by any rival and with decisive reach in every corner of the globe.

This is a staggering new development in history, not seen since the fall of Rome. It is so new, so strange, that we have no idea how to deal with it. Our first reaction—the 1990s—was utter confusion. The next reaction was awe. When Paul Kennedy, who had once popularized the idea of American decline, saw what America did in the Afghan war—a display of fully mobilized, furiously concentrated unipolar power at a distance of 8,000 miles—he not only recanted, he stood in wonder: "Nothing has ever existed like this disparity of power;" he wrote, "nothing. . . . No other nation comes close. . . . Charlemagne's empire was merely western European in its reach. The Roman empire stretched farther afield, but there was another great empire in Persia, and a larger one in China. There is, therefore, no comparison."

Even Rome is no model for what America is today. First, because we do not have the imperial culture of Rome. We are an Athenian republic, even more republican and infinitely more democratic than Athens. And this American Republic has acquired the largest seeming empire in the history of

Charles Krauthammer is an essayist and syndicated columnist. His *Washington Post* column appears in more than 130 newspapers worldwide. He writes a monthly essay for *Time* magazine and contributes frequently to *The Weekly Standard, The New Republic, The National Interest* and other journals. His columns have been awarded the Pulitzer Prize for distinguished commentary; his essays, the National Magazine Award for essays and criticism. He is the recipient of the Bradley Prize for promotion of liberal democracy and American institutions, and, on the occasion of the presentation of this essay, the American Enterprise Institute's highest honor, the Irving Kristol Award.

the world—acquired it in a fit of absent-mindedness greater even than Britain's. And it was not just absent-mindedness; it was sheer inadvertence. We got here because of Europe's suicide in the world wars of the twentieth century, and then the death of its Eurasian successor, Soviet Russia, for having adopted a political and economic system so inhuman that, like a genetically defective organism, it simply expired in its sleep. Leaving us with global dominion.

Second, we are unlike Rome, unlike Britain and France and Spain and the other classical empires of modern times, in that *we do not hunger for territory.* The use of the word "empire" in the American context is ridiculous. It is absurd to apply the word to a people whose first instinct upon arriving on anyone's soil is to demand an exit strategy. I can assure you that when the Romans went into Gaul and the British into India, they were not looking for exit strategies. They were looking for entry strategies.

In David Lean's *Lawrence of Arabia,* King Faisal says to Lawrence: "I think you are another of these desert-loving English. . . . The English have a great hunger for desolate places." Indeed, for five centuries, the Europeans did hunger for deserts and jungles and oceans and new continents. Americans do not. We like it here. We like our McDonald's. We like our football. We like our rock-and-roll. We've got the Grand Canyon and Graceland. We've got Silicon Valley and South Beach. We've got everything. And if that's not enough, we've got Vegas—which is a facsimile of everything. What could we possibly need anywhere else? We don't like exotic climates. We don't like exotic languages—lots of declensions and moods. We don't even know what a mood is. We like Iowa corn and New York hot dogs, and if we want Chinese or Indian or Italian, we go to the food court. We don't send the Marines for takeout.

That's because we are not an imperial power. We are a commercial republic. We don't take food; we trade for it. Which makes us something unique in history, an anomaly, a hybrid: a commercial republic with overwhelming global power. A commercial republic that, by pure accident of history, has been designated custodian of the international system. The eyes of every supplicant from East Timor to Afghanistan, from Iraq to Liberia; Arab and Israeli, Irish and British, North and South Korean are upon us.

That is who we are. That is where we are.

Now the question is: What do we do? What is a unipolar power to do?

ISOLATIONISM

The oldest and most venerable answer is to hoard that power and retreat. This is known as isolationism. Of all the foreign policy schools in America, it has the oldest pedigree, not surprising in the only great power in history to be isolated by two vast oceans.

Isolationism originally sprang from a view of America as spiritually superior to the Old World. We were too good to be corrupted by its low intrigues, entangled by its cynical alliances.

Today, however, isolationism is an ideology of fear. Fear of trade. Fear of immigrants. Fear of the Other. Isolationists want to cut off trade and immigration, and withdraw from our military and strategic commitments around the world. Even isolationists, of course, did not oppose the war in Afghanistan, because it was so obviously an act of self-defense—only a fool or a knave or a Susan Sontag could oppose that. But anything beyond that, isolationists oppose.

They are for a radical retrenchment of American power—for pulling up the drawbridge to Fortress America.

Isolationism is an important school of thought historically, but not today. Not just because of its brutal intellectual reductionism, but because it is so obviously inappropriate to the world of today—a world of export-driven economies, of massive population flows, and of 9/11, the definitive demonstration that the combination of modern technology and transnational primitivism has erased the barrier between "over there" and over here.

Classical isolationism is not just intellectually obsolete; it is politically bankrupt as well. Four years ago, its most public advocate, Pat Buchanan, ran for president of the United States, and carried Palm Beach. By accident.

Classic isolationism is moribund and marginalized. Who then rules America?

LIBERAL INTERNATIONALISM

In the 1990s, it was liberal internationalism. Liberal internationalism is the foreign policy of the Democratic Party and the religion of the foreign policy elite. It has a peculiar history. It traces its pedigree to Woodrow Wilson's utopianism, Harry Truman's anticommunism, and John Kennedy's militant universalism. But after the Vietnam War, it was transmuted into an ideology of passivity, acquiescence and almost reflexive anti-interventionism.

Liberals today proudly take credit for Truman's and Kennedy's roles in containing communism, but they prefer to forget that, for the last half of the Cold War, liberals used "cold warrior" as an epithet. In the early 1980s, they gave us the nuclear freeze movement, a form of unilateral disarmament in the face of Soviet nuclear advances. Today, John Kerry boasts of opposing, during the 1980s, what he calls Ronald Reagan's "illegal war in Central America"—and oppose he did what was, in fact, an indigenous anticommunist rebellion that ultimately succeeded in bringing down Sandinista rule and ushering in democracy in all of Central America.

That boast reminds us how militant was liberal passivity in the last half of the Cold War. But that passivity outlived the Cold War. When Kuwait was invaded, the question was: Should the United States go to war to prevent the Persian Gulf from falling into hostile hands? The Democratic Party joined the Buchananite isolationists in saying No. The Democrats voted No overwhelmingly—two to one in the House, more than four to one in the Senate.

And yet, quite astonishingly, when liberal internationalism came to power just two years later in the form of the Clinton administration, it turned almost hyperinterventionist. It involved us four times in military action: deepening intervention in Somalia, invading Haiti, bombing Bosnia, and finally going to war over Kosovo.

How to explain the amazing transmutation of Cold War and Gulf War doves into Haiti and Balkan hawks? The crucial and obvious difference is this: Haiti, Bosnia and Kosovo were humanitarian ventures—fights for right and good, *devoid of raw national interest*. And only humanitarian interventionism—disinterested interventionism devoid of national interest—is morally pristine enough to justify the use of force. The history of the 1990s refutes the lazy notion that liberals have an aversion to the use of force. They do not. They have an aversion to using force for reasons of pure national interest.

And by national interest I do not mean simple self-defense. Everyone believes in self-defense, as in Afghanistan. I am talking about national interest as defined by a Great Power: shaping the international environment by projecting power abroad to secure economic, political, and strategic goods. Intervening militarily for *that* kind of national interest, liberal internationalism finds unholy and unsupportable. It sees that kind of national interest as merely self-interest writ large, in effect, a form of grand national selfishness. Hence Kuwait, no; Kosovo, yes.

The other defining feature of the Clinton foreign policy was multilateralism, which expressed itself in a mania for treaties. The Clinton administration negotiated a dizzying succession of parchment promises on bioweapons, chemical weapons, nuclear testing, carbon emissions, antiballistic missiles, etc.

Why? No sentient being could believe that, say, the chemical or biological weapons treaties were anything more than transparently useless. Senator Joseph Biden once defended the Chemical Weapons

Convention, which even its proponents admitted was unenforceable, on the grounds that it would "provide us with a valuable tool"—the "moral suasion of the entire international community."

Moral suasion? Was it moral suasion that made Qaddafi see the wisdom of giving up his weapons of mass destruction? Or Iran agree for the first time to spot nuclear inspections? It was the suasion of the bayonet. It was the ignominious fall of Saddam—and the desire of interested spectators not to be next on the list. The whole point of this treaty was to keep *rogue states* from developing chemical weapons. Rogue states are, by definition, impervious to moral suasion.

Moral suasion is a farce. Why then this obsession with conventions, protocols, legalisms? Their obvious net effect is to temper American power. Who, after all, was really going to be most constrained by these treaties? The ABM amendments were aimed squarely at American advances and strategic defenses, not at Russia, which lags hopelessly behind. The Kyoto Protocol exempted India and China. The nuclear test ban would have seriously degraded the American nuclear arsenal. And the land mine treaty (which the Clinton administration spent months negotiating but, in the end, met so much Pentagon resistance that even Clinton could not initial it) would have had a devastating impact on U.S. conventional forces, particularly at the DMZ in Korea.

But that, you see, is the whole point of the multilateral enterprise: To reduce American freedom of action by making it subservient to, dependent on, constricted by the will—and interests—of other nations. To tie down Gulliver with a thousand strings. To domesticate the most undomesticated, most outsized, national interest on the planet—ours.

Today, multilateralism remains the overriding theme of liberal internationalism. When in power in the 1990s, multilateralism expressed itself as a mania for treaties. When out of power in this decade, multilateralism manifests itself in the slavish pursuit of "international legitimacy"—and opposition to any American action undertaken without universal foreign blessing.

Which is why the Democratic critique of the war in Iraq is so peculiarly one of process and not of policy. The problem was that we did not have the permission of the UN; we did not have a large enough coalition; we did not have a second Security Council resolution. Kofi Annan was unhappy and the French were cross.

The Democratic presidential candidates all say that we should have internationalized the conflict, brought in the UN, enlisted the allies. Why? Two reasons: assistance and legitimacy. First, they say, we could have used these other countries to help us in the reconstruction.

This is rich. Everyone would like to have more help in reconstruction. It would be lovely to have the Germans and the French helping reconstruct Baghdad. But the question is moot, and the argument is cynical: France and Germany made absolutely clear that they would never support the overthrow of Saddam. So, accommodating them was not a way to get them into the reconstruction, it was a way to ensure that there would never be any reconstruction, because Saddam would still be in power.

Of course it would be nice if we had more allies rather than fewer. It would also be nice to be able to fly. But when some nations are not with you on your enterprise, including them in your coalition is not a way to broaden it; it's a way to abolish it.

At which point, liberal internationalists switch gears and appeal to legitimacy—on the grounds that multilateral action has a higher moral standing. I have always found this line of argument incomprehensible. By what possible moral calculus does an American intervention to liberate 25 million people forfeit moral legitimacy because it lacks the blessing of the butchers of Tiananmen Square or the cynics of the Quai d'Orsay?

Which is why it is hard to take these arguments at face value. Look: We know why liberal internationalists demanded UN sanction for the war in Iraq. It was a way to stop the war. It was the Gulliver effect. Call a committee meeting of countries with hostile or contrary interests—i.e., the Security Council—and you have guaranteed yourself another twelve years of inaction.

Historically, multilateralism is a way for weak countries to multiply their power by attaching themselves to stronger ones. But multilateralism imposed on Great Powers, and particularly on a unipolar power, is intended to *restrain* that power. Which is precisely why France is an ardent multi-lateralist. But why should America be?

Why, in the end, *does* liberal internationalism want to tie down Gulliver, to blunt the pursuit of American national interests by making them subordinate to a myriad of other interests?

In the immediate post-Vietnam era, this aversion to national interest might have been attributed to self-doubt and self-loathing. I don't know. What I do know is that today it is a mistake to see liberal foreign policy as deriving from anti- Americanism or lack of patriotism or a late efflorescence of 1960s radicalism.

On the contrary. The liberal aversion to national interest stems from an idealism, a larger vision of country, a vision of some ambition and nobility—the ideal of a true international community. And that is: To transform the international system from the Hobbesian universe into a Lockean universe. To turn the state of nature into a norm-driven community. To turn the law of the jungle into the rule of law—of treaties and contracts and UN resolutions. In short, to remake the international system in the image of domestic civil society.

They dream of a new world, a world described in 1943 by Cordell Hull, FDR's secretary of state—a world in which "there will no longer be need for spheres of influence, for alliances, for balance of power, or any other of the special arrangements by which, in the unhappy past, the nations strove to safeguard their security or promote their interests."

And to create such a true international community, you have to temper, transcend, and, in the end, abolish the very idea of state power and national interest. Hence the antipathy to American hegemony and American power. If you are going to break the international arena to the mold of domestic society, you have to domesticate its single most powerful actor. You have to abolish American dominance, not only as an affront to fairness, but also as the greatest obstacle on the whole planet to a democratized international system where all live under self-governing international institutions and self-enforcing international norms.

REALISM

This vision is all very nice. All very noble. And all very crazy. Which brings us to the third great foreign policy school: realism.

The realist looks at this great liberal project and sees a hopeless illusion. Because turning the Hobbesian world that has existed since long before the Peloponnesian Wars into a Lockean world, turning a jungle into a suburban subdivision, requires a revolution in human nature. Not just an erector set of new institutions, but a revolution in human nature. And realists do not believe in revolutions in human nature, much less stake their future, and the future of their nation, on them.

Realism recognizes the fundamental fallacy in the whole idea of the international system being modeled on domestic society.

First, what holds domestic society together is a supreme central authority wielding a monopoly of power and enforcing norms. In the international arena there is no such thing. Domestic society may look like a place of self-regulating norms, but if somebody breaks into your house, you call 911, and the police arrive with guns drawn. That's not exactly self-enforcement. That's law enforcement.

Second, domestic society rests on the shared goodwill, civility and common values of its individual members. What values are shared by, say, Britain, Cuba, Yemen and Zimbabwe—all nominal members of this fiction we call the "international community"?

Of course, you can have smaller communities of shared interests—NAFTA, ANZUS, or the European Union. But the European conceit that relations with all nations—regardless of ideology, regardless of culture, regardless even of open hostility—should be transacted on the EU model of suasion and norms and negotiations and solemn contractual agreements is an illusion. A fisheries treaty with Canada is something real. An Agreed Framework on plutonium processing with the likes of North Korea is not worth the paper it is written on.

The realist believes the definition of peace Ambrose Bierce offered in *The Devil's Dictionary:* "Peace: *noun,* in international affairs, a period of cheating between two periods of fighting."

Hence the realist axiom: The "international community" is a fiction. It is not a community, it is a cacophony—of straining ambitions, disparate values and contending power.

What does hold the international system together? What keeps it from degenerating into total anarchy? Not the phony security of treaties, not the best of goodwill among the nicer nations. In the unipolar world we inhabit, what stability we do enjoy today is owed to the overwhelming power and deterrent threat of the United States.

If someone invades your house, you call the cops. Who do you call if someone invades your country? You dial Washington. In the unipolar world, the closest thing to a centralized authority, to an enforcer of norms, is America—American power. And ironically, American power is precisely what liberal internationalism wants to constrain and tie down and subsume in pursuit of some brave new Lockean world.

Realists do not live just in America. I found one in Finland. During the 1997 negotiations in Oslo over the land mine treaty, one of the rare hold-outs, interestingly enough, was *Finland*. The Finnish prime minister stoutly opposed the land mine ban. And for that he was scolded by his Scandinavian neighbors. To which he responded tartly that this was a "very convenient" pose for the "other Nordic countries"—after all, Finland is their land mine.

Finland is the land mine between Russia and Scandinavia. America is the land mine between barbarism and civilization.

Where would South Korea be without America and its land mines along the DMZ? Where would Europe—with its cozy arrogant community—be had America not saved it from the Soviet colossus? Where would the Middle East be had American power not stopped Saddam in 1991?

The land mine that protects civilization from barbarism is not parchment but power, and in a unipolar world, American power—wielded, if necessary, unilaterally. If necessary, preemptively,

Now, those uneasy with American power have made these two means of wielding it—preemption and unilateralism—the focus of unrelenting criticism. The doctrine of preemption, in particular, has been widely attacked for violating international norms.

What international norm? The one under which Israel was universally condemned—even the Reagan administration joined the condemnation at the Security Council—for preemptively destroying Iraq's Osirak nuclear reactor in 1981? Does anyone today doubt that it was the right thing to do, both strategically and morally?

In a world of terrorists, terrorist states and weapons of mass destruction, the option of preemption is especially necessary. In the bipolar world of the Cold War, with a stable nonsuicidal adversary, deterrence could work. Deterrence does not work against people who ache for heaven. It does not work against *undeterrables*. And it does not work against undetectables: nonsuicidal enemy regimes that might attack through clandestine means—a suitcase nuke or anonymously delivered anthrax. Against both undeterrables and undetectables, preemption is the only possible strategy.

Moreover, the doctrine of preemption against openly hostile states pursuing weapons of mass destruction is an improvement on classical deterrence. Traditionally, we deterred the use of WMDs by the threat of retaliation after we'd been attacked—and that's too late; the point of preemption is to deter the very acquisition of WMDs in the first place.

Whether or not Iraq had large stockpiles of WMDs, the very fact that the United States overthrew a hostile regime that repeatedly refused to come clean on its weapons has had precisely this deterrent effect. We are safer today not just because Saddam is gone, but because Libya and any others contemplating trafficking with WMDs, have—for the first time—seen that it carries a cost, a very high cost.

Yes, of course, imperfect intelligence makes preemption problematic. But that is not an objection on principle, it is an objection in practice. Indeed, the objection concedes the principle. We need good intelligence. But we remain defenseless if we abjure the option of preemption.

The other great objection to the way American unipolar power has been wielded is its unilateralism. I would dispute how unilateralist we have in fact been. Constructing ad hoc "coalitions of the willing" hardly qualifies as unilateralism just because they do not have a secretariat in Brussels or on the East River.

Moreover, unilateralism is often the very road to multilateralism. As we learned from the Gulf War, it is the leadership of the United States—indeed, its willingness to act unilaterally if necessary—that galvanized the Gulf War coalition into existence. Without the president of the United States declaring "This will not stand" about the invasion of Kuwait—and making it clear that America would go it alone if it had to—there never would have been the great wall-to-wall coalition that is now so retroactively applauded and held up as a model of multilateralism.

Of course one acts in concert with others if possible. It is nice when others join us in the breach. No one seeks to be unilateral. Unilateralism simply means that one does not allow oneself to be held hostage to the will of others.

Of course you build coalitions when possible. In 2003, we garnered a coalition of the willing for Iraq that included substantial allies like Britain, Australia, Spain, Italy and much of Eastern Europe. France and Germany made clear from the beginning that they would never join in the overthrow of Saddam. Therefore the choice was not a wide coalition versus a narrow one, but a narrow coalition versus none. There were serious arguments against war in Iraq—but the fact France did not approve was not one of them.

Irving Kristol once explained that he preferred the Organization of American States to the United Nations because in the OAS we can be voted down in only three languages, thereby saving translators' fees. Realists choose not to be Gulliver. In an international system with no sovereign, no police, no protection—where power is the ultimate arbiter and history has bequeathed us unprecedented power—we should be vigilant in preserving that power. And our freedom of action to use it.

But here we come up against the limits of realism: You cannot live by power alone. Realism is a valuable antidote to the woolly internationalism of the 1990s. But realism can only take you so far.

Its basic problem lies in its definition of national interest as classically offered by its great theorist, Hans Morgenthau: interest defined as power. Morgenthau postulated that what drives nations, what motivates their foreign policy, is the will to power—to keep it and expand it.

For most Americans, will to power might be a correct description of the world—of what motivates other countries—but it cannot be a prescription for America. It cannot be our purpose. America cannot and will not live by realpolitik alone. Our foreign policy must be driven by something beyond power. Unless conservatives present ideals to challenge the liberal ideal of a domesticated international community, they will lose the debate.

Which is why among American conservatives, another, more idealistic, school has arisen that sees America's national interest as an expression of values.

DEMOCRATIC GLOBALISM

It is this fourth school that has guided U.S. foreign policy in this decade. This conservative alternative to realism is often lazily and invidiously called neoconservatism, but that is a very odd name for a school whose major proponents in the world today are George W. Bush and Tony Blair—if they are neoconservatives, then Margaret Thatcher was a liberal. There's nothing neo about Bush, and there's nothing con about Blair.

Yet they are the principal proponents today of what might be called democratic globalism, a foreign policy that defines the national interest not as power but as values, and that identifies one supreme value, what John Kennedy called "the success of liberty." As President Bush put it in his speech at Whitehall last November: "The United States and Great Britain share a mission in the world beyond the balance of power or the simple pursuit of interest. We seek the advance of freedom and the peace that freedom brings."

Beyond power. Beyond interest. Beyond interest defined as power. That is the credo of democratic globalism. Which explains its political appeal: America is a nation uniquely built not on blood, race or consanguinity, but on a proposition—to which its sacred honor has been pledged for two centuries. This American exceptionalism explains why non-Americans find this foreign policy so difficult to credit; why Blair has had more difficulty garnering support for it in his country; and why Europe, in particular, finds this kind of value-driven foreign policy hopelessly and irritatingly moralistic.

Democratic globalism sees as the engine of history not the will to power but the will to freedom. And while it has been attacked as a dreamy, idealistic innovation, its inspiration comes from the Truman Doctrine of 1947, the Kennedy inaugural of 1961, and Reagan's "evil empire" speech of 1983. They all sought to recast a struggle for power between two geopolitical titans into a struggle between freedom and unfreedom, and yes, good and evil.

Which is why the Truman Doctrine was heavily criticized by realists like Hans Morgenthau and George Kennan—and Reagan was vilified by the entire foreign policy establishment: for the sin of ideologizing the Cold War by injecting a moral overlay.

That was then. Today, post-9/11, we find ourselves in a similar existential struggle but with a different enemy: not Soviet communism, but Arab-Islamic totalitarianism, both secular and religious. Bush and Blair are similarly attacked for naively and crudely casting this struggle as one of freedom versus unfreedom, good versus evil.

Now, given the way not just freedom but human decency were suppressed in both Afghanistan and Iraq, the two major battles of this new war, you would have to give Bush and Blair's moral claims the decided advantage of being obviously true.

Nonetheless, something can be true and still be dangerous. Many people are deeply uneasy with the Bush-Blair doctrine—many conservatives in particular. When Blair declares in his address to Congress: "The spread of freedom is . . . our last line of defense and our first line of attack," they see a dangerously expansive, aggressively utopian foreign policy. In short, they see Woodrow Wilson.

Now, to a conservative, Woodrow Wilson is fightin' words. Yes, this vision is expansive and perhaps utopian. But it ain't Wilsonian. Wilson envisioned the spread of democratic values through as-yet-to-be invented international institutions. He could be forgiven for that. In 1918, there was no way to know how utterly corrupt and useless those international institutions would turn out to be. Eight decades of bitter experience later—with Libya chairing the UN Commission on Human Rights—there is no way *not* to know.

Democratic globalism is not Wilsonian. Its attractiveness is precisely that it shares realism's insights about the centrality of power. Its attractiveness is precisely that it has appropriate contempt for the fictional legalisms of liberal internationalism.

Moreover, democratic globalism is an improvement over realism. What it can teach realism is that the spread of democracy is not just an end but a means, an indispensable means for securing American interests. The reason is simple. Democracies are inherently more friendly to the United States, less belligerent to their neighbors, and generally more inclined to peace. Realists are right that to protect your interests you often have to go around the world bashing bad guys over the head. But that technique, no matter how satisfying, has its limits. At some point, you have to implant something, something organic and self-developing. And that something is democracy.

But where? The danger of democratic globalism is its universalism, its open-ended commitment to human freedom, its temptation to plant the flag of democracy everywhere. It must learn to say no.

And indeed, it does say no. But when it says no to Liberia, or Congo, or Burma, or countenances alliances with authoritarian rulers in places like Pakistan or, for that matter, Russia, it stands accused of hypocrisy. Which is why we must articulate criteria for saying yes.

Where to intervene? Where to bring democracy? Where to nation-build? I propose a single criterion: where it counts.

Call it democratic *realism*. And this is its axiom: *We will support democracy everywhere, but we will commit blood and treasure only in places where there is a strategic necessity—meaning, places central to the larger war against the existential enemy, the enemy that poses a global mortal threat to freedom.*

Where does it count? Fifty years ago, Germany and Japan counted. Why? Because they were the seeds of the greatest global threat to freedom in midcentury—fascism—and then were turned, by nation building, into bulwarks against the next great threat to freedom, Soviet communism.

Where does it count today? Where the overthrow of radicalism and the beginnings of democracy can have a decisive effect in the war against the new global threat to freedom, the new existential enemy, the Arab-Islamic totalitarianism that has threatened us in both its secular and religious forms for the quarter-century since the Khomeini revolution of 1979.

Establishing civilized, decent, nonbelligerent, pro-Western polities in Afghanistan and Iraq and ultimately their key neighbors would, like the flipping of Germany and Japan in the 1940s, change the strategic balance in the fight against Arab-Islamic radicalism.

Yes, it may be a bridge too far. Realists have been warning against the hubris of thinking we can transform an alien culture because of some postulated natural and universal human will to freedom. And they may yet be right. But how do they know in advance? Half a century ago, we heard the same confident warnings about the imperviousness to democracy of Confucian culture. That proved stunningly wrong. Where is it written that Arabs are incapable of democracy?

Yes, as in Germany and Japan, the undertaking is enormous, ambitious and arrogant. It may yet fail. But we cannot afford not to try. There is not a single, remotely plausible, alternative strategy for attacking the monster behind 9/11. It's not Osama bin Laden; it is the cauldron of political oppression, religious intolerance, and social ruin in the Arab-Islamic world—oppression transmuted and deflected by regimes with no legitimacy into virulent, murderous anti-Americanism. It's not one man; it is a condition. It will be nice to find that man and hang him, but that's the cops-and-robbers law-enforcement model of fighting terrorism that we tried for twenty years and that gave us 9/11. This is war, and in war arresting murderers is nice. But you win by taking territory—and leaving something behind.

SEPTEMBER 11

We are the unipolar power and what do we do?

In August 1900, David Hilbert gave a speech to the International Congress of Mathematicians naming twenty-three still unsolved mathematical problems bequeathed by the nineteenth century to the twentieth. Had he presented the great unsolved geopolitical problems bequeathed to the twentieth century, one would have stood out above all—the rise of Germany and its accommodation within the European state system.

Similarly today, at the dawn of the twenty-first century, we can see clearly the two great geopolitical challenges on the horizon: the inexorable rise of China and the coming demographic collapse of Europe, both of which will irrevocably disequilibrate the international system.

But those problems come later. They are for midcentury. They are for the next generation. And that generation will not even get to these problems unless we first deal with our problem.

And our problem is 9/11 and the roots of Arab-Islamic nihilism. September 11 felt like a new problem, but for all its shock and surprise, it is an old problem with a new face. September 11 felt like the initiation of a new history, but it was a return to history, the twentieth-century history of radical ideologies and existential enemies.

The anomaly is not the world of today. The anomaly was the 1990s, our holiday from history. It felt like peace, but it was an interval of dreaming between two periods of reality.

From which 9/11 awoke us. It startled us into thinking everything was new. It's not. What is new is what happened not on 9/11 but ten years earlier on December 26, 1991: the emergence of the United States as the world's unipolar power. What is unique is our advantage in this struggle, an advantage we did not have during the struggles of the twentieth century. The question for our time is how to press this advantage, how to exploit our unipolar power, how to deploy it to win the old/new war that exploded upon us on 9/11.

What is the unipolar power to do?

Four schools, four answers.

The isolationists want simply to ignore unipolarity, pull up the drawbridge, and defend Fortress America. Alas, the Fortress has no moat—not after the airplane, the submarine, the ballistic missile—and as for the drawbridge, it was blown up on 9/11.

Then there are the liberal internationalists. They like to dream, and to the extent they are aware of our unipolar power, they don't like it. They see its use for anything other than humanitarianism or reflexive self-defense as an expression of national selfishness. And they don't just want us to ignore our unique power, they want us to yield it piece by piece, by subsuming ourselves in a new global architecture in which America becomes not the arbiter of international events, but a good and tame international citizen.

Then there is realism, which has the clearest understanding of the new unipolarity and its uses— unilateral and preemptive if necessary. But in the end, it fails because it offers no vision. It is all means and no ends. It cannot adequately define our mission. Hence, the fourth school: democratic globalism. It has, in this decade, rallied the American people to a struggle over values. It seeks to vindicate the American idea by making the spread of democracy, the success of liberty, the ends and means of American foreign policy.

I support that. I applaud that. But I believe it must be tempered in its universalistic aspirations and rhetoric from a democratic globalism to a democratic realism. It must be targeted, focused and limited. We are friends to all, but we come ashore only where it really counts. And where it counts today is that Islamic crescent stretching from North Africa to Afghanistan.

In October 1962, during the Cuban Missile Crisis, we came to the edge of the abyss. Then, accompanied by our equally shaken adversary, we both deliberately drew back. On September 11, 2001, we saw the face of Armageddon again, but this time with an enemy that does not draw back. This time the enemy knows no reason.

Were that the only difference between now and then, our situation would be hopeless. But there is a second difference between now and then: the uniqueness of our power, unrivaled, not just today but ever. That evens the odds. The rationality of the enemy is something beyond our control. But the use of our power is within our control. And if that power is used wisely, constrained not by illusions and fictions but only by the limits of our mission—which is to bring a modicum of freedom as an antidote to nihilism—we can prevail.

The Atlantic Century

Ralph Peters

Throughout the previous decade, strategists and statesmen asserted that we were about to enter the "Pacific Century." Global power and wealth would shift to East Asia. American interests, power, and investments would follow. The Atlantic would become a dead sea strategically, its littoral states and their continents declining to marginal status. Economic opportunities, crucial alliances, and the gravest threats would rise in the east, as surely as the morning sun.

An alternative view of the evidence suggests that the experts were wrong. Although the United States will remain engaged in the Far East—as well as in the Middle East, Europe, and nearly everywhere else—the great unexplored opportunities for human advancement, fruitful alliances, strategic cooperation, and creating an innovative, just, and mutually beneficial international order still lie on the shores of the Atlantic. The difference is that the potential for future development lies not across the North Atlantic in "Old Europe," but on both sides of the South Atlantic, in Africa and Latin America.

Especially since 9/11, the deteriorating civilization of the Middle East has demanded our attention. But we must avoid a self-defeating strategic fixation on the Arab Muslim world and self-destructive states nearby. Any signs of progress in the Middle East will be welcome, but the region overall is fated to remain an inexhaustible source of disappointments. While Africa suffers from an undeserved reputation for hopelessness (often a matter of racism couched in diplomatic language) and Latin America is dismissed as a backwater, the aggressive realms of failure in the Middle East always get the benefit of the doubt. When the United States places a higher priority on relations with Egypt than on those with Mexico or Brazil, and when Jordan attracts more of our attention than does South Africa, our foreign policy lacks common sense as much as it does foresight.

Our obsession with the Middle East is not just about oil. It's about intellectual habit. We assign unparalleled strategic importance to the survival of the repugnant Saudi regime because that's the way we've been doing things for half a century, despite the complete absence of political, cultural, or elementary human progress on the Arabian Peninsula.

Certainly, the United States has genuine strategic interests between the Nile and the Indus, and the threats from the region's apocalyptic terrorists and rogue regimes are as deadly as they are likely to be enduring. But we must stop pretending there is a bright, magical solution for the darkest region on earth, if only we Americans could discover the formula. The Middle East will remain a strategic basket case beyond our lifetimes.We will need to remain engaged, but we must be careful not to be consumed. If you are looking for hope, look elsewhere.

Ralph Peters retired from the US Army shortly after his promotion to lieutenant colonel. A contributor to *Parameters* for 15 years, he is the author of 17 books, written under his own name or under the pen-name "Owen Parry," as well as hundreds of essays, articles, and commentaries. Last winter, he visited South Africa and Zimbabwe. Previous journeys have taken him to every continent except Antarctica. His next book, *Beyond Baghdad: Postmodern War and Peace*, will be published in October.

Apart from crisis intervention and measured support for any promising regimes that may emerge in the region (such as, perhaps, an independent, democratic Kurdistan), we need to begin shifting our practical as well as our emotional commitments away from the Middle East—and even away from Europe and northeast Asia—in order to help Africa and Latin America begin to realize their enormous strategic potential. Our past lies to the east and west, but our future lies to the south.

This is not a utopian vision. On the contrary, the returns of such a shift in our commitments would be practical and tangible. Turning our focus to Africa and Latin America would be the strategic equivalent of a "dogs of the Dow" approach, investing in "stocks" that are out of favor and unwanted, and placing our resources where the potential returns are highest, instead of continuing to throw them at strategic investments with, at best, marginal rates of return.

Nor is this about forging a neo-classical American empire. Rather, it's about creating strategic partnerships to supercede our waning relations with continental Europe and about structuring alternatives to an overreliance on the states, populations, and markets of East Asia. Although the United States, where all the relevant cultures converge, would be the most powerful member of an Afro-Latin-Anglo-American web of alliances, this would be a new kind of informal, democratic network, based on shared interests, aligning values, cultural fusion, and mutual advantage.

Turning our attention to Africa and Latin America is also the right thing to do, although that will not impress the advocates of Realpolitik. For them, the argument would lie in the security advantages, the profit potential in developing human capital, the expanded markets, and the enhancement of American influence even beyond our current "hyper-power" status.

Old Asia and Old Europe have devoured American lives and consumed our wealth. The regressive societies of the Middle East are sick—and contagious— with hatred, jealousy, and congenital disrepair. Whenever the United States is forced to engage cultures whose glory days are behind them, we win, but we often pay a bitter price.

America always has done best on frontiers, from our own West through technological frontiers to our pioneering of the society of the future, in which gender, racial, and religious equality increasingly prevail (to the horror of our enemies, foreign and domestic). And the great human frontiers of the 21st century lie to our south.

*   *   *

As this essay is written, President Bush visits Africa, having asked Congress to increase our funding for counter-AIDS initiatives in Africa and the Caribbean to $15 billion. The Administration is contemplating the dispatch of Marines to Liberia, and the people of that long-abandoned country are begging for the Yankees to come and stay. During a visit to Zimbabwe last winter, the commonest question asked of me was, "Why, please, does the American Army go to Iraq, but not come here? We *want* you to come and free us, sir."

Of course, Zimbabwe is a problem for the Commonwealth of Nations, but what's striking in much of Africa is the desire for American involvement that one encounters below the level of bureaucrats and intellectuals still blinded by the ideology of the liberation struggle. The people of sub-Saharan Africa harbor the most pro-American sentiments of any population outside of our own country. Even in francophone Ivory Coast, last autumn's violence resulted in signs, written in English and held aloft by demonstrators, begging Uncle Sam to rescue them from Paris and its support for Islamic insurgents.

One of the many unintended consequences of the 9/11 attacks, as well as of al Qaeda strikes in East Africa, has been the sudden realization in Washington that Africa matters. At present, the focus is heavily on security issues. But, as the Administration is already learning, enduring security is inseparable from development, opportunity, justice, and the rule of law. In the long term, President Bush's journey to Africa could prove of even greater strategic significance than our war-on-terror campaigns in Afghanistan and Iraq.

In an unfortunate symmetry, however, the same terror events that led to a new appreciation of Africa's relevance stopped the President's initiatives to improve relations with Mexico and the rest of Latin America dead in their tracks. The hopes of Mexico's reformist President, Vicente Fox, became unintended victims of 9/11, and recent elections decreased the number of seats in the legislature held by Fox's National Action Party. Fox, whose country may be the most important of all foreign powers for America's security, economy, and society, was forgotten amid the dust and rubble of the World Trade Center towers.

Nonetheless, much of Latin America is on the threshold—or already across the threshold—of genuine reforms and profound cultural changes. For the first time, traditional political parties throughout Latin America are losing the power to resist the popular will—and the popular will wants real democracy, economic opportunity, and an end to the plague of corruption. There are now two generations of Latin American technocrats, almost a critical mass, educated in the United States. Miami is the informal financial and cultural capital of Latin America. Yet, the United States pays more attention to Pakistan than it does to all of the countries south of the Panama Canal. We bribe our enemies, while ignoring our greatest potential friends.

Latin America's family secret is that everybody really wants to be a gringo, though it dare not be said in public. The "Yankee go home" era is over, except for the dwindling revolutionary hardliners who have failed the continent as badly as did their nemeses, the *caudillos*, the strongmen and the land barons. Latin Americans don't want to Latinize the United States—they want to Americanize their own countries by creating responsible governments, lawful economies, and social regimes that respect human rights and human dignity. Yet the United States shows greater respect for Saudi Arabia, a regime founded on the principle of religious intolerance that permits no political dissent, routinely abuses human rights, and denies the most elementary freedoms to its female citizens. It would be hard to design a more counterproductive, nearsighted foreign policy.

* * *

During the buildup to Operation Iraqi Freedom, a fascinating constellation of allies emerged. When President Bush, British Prime Minister Tony Blair, and Spain's Prime Minister Jose Maria Aznar posed in front of the cameras after their mini-summit, an unwitting world got a snapshot of a strategic triumvirate of North Atlantic powers positioned to change the world and their own situations for the better, if only they could continue to work together (both Britain and Spain should be viewed as members of a great Atlantic community, not primarily as European states). Indeed, if Portugal could be persuaded to join the group, you would have the ideal combination of North Atlantic democracies to work with Latin America and Africa in the coming decades.

The linguistic and cultural ties are there, as is a surprising degree of goodwill on the part of previously colonized populations. While the most oppressive and corrupt colonial powers of the 20th century, notably France, watch their influence fade in Africa (President Bush's visit to Senegal was calculated to show the flag in a developing power vacuum), the British legacy has been profoundly different. The French, Belgians, and others left behind a system of corrupt economies in service to statist governments. The British left behind a belief in the rule of law, democracy, and human betterment.

Despite the suffering and tribulations of black Africans in British colonies, the colonized learned to value the colonist's ideals for his own country even as they despised and fought against the colonist himself. The vile Apartheid regime in South Africa and the white-supremacy policies of Ian Smith's Rhodesia could not destroy the legacy of the missionary school's lessons about the Magna Carta, elected parliaments, and fair play. Those colonized by the British kept more than the sport of cricket for themselves. They also kept a belief in constitutions.

The Spanish legacy in Latin America was much harsher, but Spain's rule was cast off almost 200 years ago. The old wounds healed, while the cultural affinities remain. Indeed, in much of the 20th century, it was Spain, slumbering under the Franco regime, that wasn't moving forward. Now, with Spain vibrantly democratic and economically successful (for the first time in four centuries),Madrid has rediscovered its long-lost empire and seeks to engage it in emulation of Britain's Commonwealth.

In Prime Minister Jose Maria Aznar, Spain found a visionary. While his party may suffer because of his unpopular support for the war to depose Saddam Hussein, he did not let opinion polls dictate his actions. Aznar did what he believed to be necessary and right, not only in the sense of ridding the world of a dangerous dictator, but in recognizing that Spain's greatest potential for market expansion and diplomatic influence lies in working constructively with the United States, its fellow Atlantic power, rather than slavishly following the dictates of continental states with profoundly divergent interests. Spanish investors have sunk billions into Latin America, and they are in for the long haul. They want cooperation, not confrontation, with the United States.

Aznar recognizes that the best route to an Atlantic future runs through Washington. While fashionable anti-Americanism in the streets of Spain may limit intense cooperation in the near term, in the longer term ever more Spaniards, chafing under European Union restrictions dictated by Paris and Berlin, will see opportunity to the west, not east. And it is hard to imagine any coalition that would be better for Latin America than a strategic partnership between the United States and Spain.

The Portuguese legacy is the most peculiar under consideration here. Portugal was the first European colonial power and the most enduring. While Lisbon withdrew from Brazil in the mid-19th century, it continued to occupy its African colonies into the 1970s. The prevalent post-colonial model would suggest that Portugal has no role to play for the present, given the degree of alienation manifested by recently liberated colonies. But Portugal's small size and lack of strategic power paradoxically offer it recuperative advantages. Mozambique and Angola, for example, do not fear creeping recolonization from the Iberian Peninsula—they're more concerned about South African "economic imperialism." Portugal has a surprisingly laissez-faire relationship with its former colonies, where its cultural influence is still felt profoundly and welcomed. Should Portugal recognize its future where its past greatness lay, in Africa and South America, it could serve as an essential bridge between its former colonies and other states in the Atlantic strategic network.

The United States, however, offers the model of success others wish to emulate. While the empty hubris of much of the Arab world leads it to anathematize all things American, the populations of the South Atlantic continents admire the social and economic success of the United States, our cultural totems, and our political values.

Certainly, a significant—though shrinking—number of leftists and populists in Latin America cling to yesterday's image of a ruthless, interventionist Uncle Sam bringing his guns to bear on behalf of the United Fruit Company. But the average citizen yearns for his or her voice to be heard as the voices of citizens are heard in the United States. They want a fair shake, economically and legally. They hate the corruption that torments their lives and robs them of their potential. They despise their inheritance of nepotism and a rigid class system. And, thanks to the information revolution and increased economic migration, they now know that things are better elsewhere.

Centuries of Latin American awareness that things were wrong were not enough. The people of Latin America also needed to know that change was possible, that things truly could be different. Now they know. And we will see decades of heady change south of the Rio Grande.

The people of Latin America do not want another Juan Peron or Fidel Castro. They want their FDR and JFK.

*   *   *

In sub-Saharan Africa, the reluctance to embrace the United States and its ideals is generational. The leaders and intellectuals who waged Africa's long independence struggle were shaped by the decades in which socialist solutions and communist rhetoric seemed indispensable tools of liberation. Now, even though statist socialism has collapsed or turned capitalist everywhere else, many of those aging heroes of the independence movement—even giants such as Nelson Mandela—cannot fully overcome the prejudices of their youth. And with sadly few exceptions, most notably Mandela, the old maxim that successful revolutionaries fail at governing certainly has been proven by the African experience.

The first European conquest of Africa was accomplished with guns. The second European conquest was achieved through the inspiring rhetoric and practical folly of Marxism-Leninism and related theories of "rational" social organization. Today, Africans must achieve a third conquest of their continent by themselves, a liberation from the poisonous cant of their liberators. The progress some African countries have made in just the last ten years in embracing practical, humane solutions to societal problems has been remarkable. But vicious wars and genocide make headlines, while African initiatives that slowly improve economies, gradually increase literacy, limit the spread of AIDS, or battle against corruption do not. Journalists flock to scoundrels, not to dull, dutiful bureaucrats.

In much of Africa, the transition from the revolutionary generation and its tainted protégé generation is already underway. Africa has been allowed to fall so far that progress will be slow and wildly uneven, but the willingness to embrace the rule-of-law and market economics is there, impeded only by the corrupt political class in far too many sub-Saharan countries. And the old, automatic anti-Americanism is passing from the scene where it has not already disappeared entirely.

Instead, younger Africans increasingly see the United States as a model of a racially integrated society in which blacks are accorded opportunity and dignity. It is impossible to overstate the contrast in African eyes between uniformly white European politicians on state visits to Africa and the arrival of Colin Powell or the sight of Condoleezza Rice standing beside the American President.

Where can sub-Saharan Africans turn for models, for support, for friends? To the north, the Islamic world is profoundly bigoted against them, religiously and racially. Muslims were the original slave traders, the worst exploiters, and, except for the Belgians, the most savage oppressors of sub-Saharan Africa. Today, the collision between North African Islam and black African Christianity is not only a matter of daily violence, from Nigeria to Sudan, but of growing confrontation and conflict. Indeed, the new "church militant" is emerging in Africa, and the struggle with expansionist Islam may lead to the most savage religious wars of our century. This is the dynamic that should most concern us about the continent's future, since Africa's religious fault line is largely a racial divide, as well—a combination that, historically, has made for especially virulent hatreds and merciless wars. The African deserts, grasslands, and cities where Christianity and Islam collide already offer a textbook example of Samuel Huntington's theory of the "clash of civilizations."

If the Islamic world's North African crusaders are viewed as implacable enemies of Christian Africa, neither can the populations of sub-Saharan Africa turn to Europe and their former colonial masters for social or political models. Even Britain, which has an enormous, positive role to play in Africa's future, remains a racist, stratified society, despite much progress since the 1960s. On the continent, states such as France and Germany are rabidly racist, and despite protestations to the contrary from Paris and Berlin, the people of Africa know it. (A recent, severe miscalculation by President Chirac of France occurred when he insisted on hosting Zimbabwe's dictator Robert Mugabe in Paris, even though the European Union had imposed a travel ban on Mugabe. The visit was so deeply resented by the half-starved population of Zimbabwe that it guaranteed the French will not be welcome between the Zambezi and the Limpopo for a long time to come.)

Indeed, one of the key lessons Africans have drawn from comparing foreign societies is that, while anyone can become an American, no one can be- come French, or German, or Swedish. Of course, the global popularity of black American sports and entertainment figures helps, too. But they do not play the primary role we often imagine for them. The people of Africa don't just want good music and jump shots. They want good government. And jobs. And justice. The Statue of Liberty is still a better draw than Beyonce Knowles.

We don't think of Latin America and Africa as similar, despite their cultural ties and geographic proximity. Yet, the identical dreams of the average residents of Monrovia or Mexico City are to claim the best of America for themselves.

This vision of affinities and strategic connectivity between the Americas and Africa isn't new. It's the vision Fidel Castro tried—and failed—to apply 30 years ago. Castro simply connected the historical lines on the map. His mistake was to see Havana as the nexus, when the lines actually converge in New York City.

For all his many faults and stubborn cruelty, Castro was one of the great visionaries of our time (and whether we like it or not, he did as much good for Cuba as harm; his great mistake was outliving his virtues). He recognized that the slave trade from Africa to the New World hadn't created a one-way street (or sea lane), but that the chronically underestimated African influence on the Americas paved the way for the development of mutual strategic ties. Culture opened the door for power and influence.

Castro had the vision, but lacked the resources to implement it successfully —although his forces repeatedly defeated the Apartheid-era South Africans in Angola. The United States had the resources, but, blinded by the prejudices and priorities of the Cold War, failed to grasp the vision.We saw only an attempt to spread communism with a Cuban accent, while Castro was trying to build strategic bridges across the seas that once carried slave ships.

Indeed, for all the oppression and problems of Cuban society, it offers the best example of racial integration outside of the United States; by some practical measures, integration is even more advanced in Cuba. Castro understood that he could offer a model no one else was advertising (and 30 years ago, integration certainly had not progressed as far in the United States as it has today). He didn't just offer soldiers and doctors to Africa. Castro tried to offer a model of empowerment. His was, perhaps, the greatest strategic dream of the last half century. His failure must be bitter to him.

Now we have inherited Castro's dream of trans-Atlantic peoples bound together by culture, common interests, and mutual aspirations. Americans have the resources to do what Castro and his expeditionary forces could not achieve. But will we have even half the vision of that aging revolutionary in fatigues?

Whenever Africa comes up in a Washington conversation, eyes roll, shoulders shrug, and an entire continent is dismissed with a few phrases about AIDS, civil wars, genocide, and corruption. The unspoken message is that Africa is hopeless, that it's "just the way those people are."

But it's *not* just the way "those people" are. Africa is the way brutal colonization, fatal borders, the struggles of the Cold War, foreign ideologies, and, finally, utter neglect have made it. Few of the arms used in those wars or tribal massacres were made in Africa. European governments—most notably France again— not only didn't fight corruption in their former colonies, they fostered it as a tool for continuing their control. French presidents and prime ministers have a long tradition of mutually profitable, personal relationships with African dictators. Indeed, corruption as a form of exploitation may have done even more damage to post-independence Africa than any other cata-strophe prior to the advent of AIDS.

And what about AIDS? Has the disease doomed Africa to failure and backwardness? Considering the scope of the human devastation, with HIV infection rates that may range as high as 60 percent in some populations, unrestrained pessimism may, indeed, be in order. Tens of millions of Africans have died or will die, leaving millions of orphans behind. Professionals, the educated, and skilled workers are especially hard hit, since they have the disposable income to acquire more sexual partners. Military establishments are being gutted by AIDS.

Yet the effects of catastrophes are rarely linear. On the contrary, human collectives react unexpectedly to disasters, and the greater the scope of the loss, the more nonlinear the ultimate reaction may be. AIDS is, unquestionably, so great a tragedy for today's Africa that its devastation cannot be measured simply in the number of deaths. But that does not mean that the reverberations in tomorrow's Africa will necessarily take negative forms.

Consider a historical event that may have been even more lethal to a continental population: The Black Death, which reached the edges of Europe in 1346, is believed to have killed between one-third and two-thirds of the continent's inhabitants. Nothing known to human history killed so high a proportion of victims with such speed. A linear extrapolation would have predicted Europe's economic collapse, a faltering culture, and, at best, centuries of slow recovery.

The real results were decidedly nonlinear. Despite recurrent bouts of the plague, modern Europe was born in the disease's shadow. The epidemic fatally weakened the feudal system, opened Europe's cities to fresh blood, undercut Rome's religious monopoly, challenged the tradition of static, Aristotelian knowledge, and led to a flowering of the arts. The labor shortage created by the Black Death laid the foundations for collective bargaining and put talent at a new, far higher premium.

Instead of triggering a European collapse, the Black Death exploded the established order and was followed by the Renaissance, Europe's voyages of discovery, the Reformation, foreign colonization, the scientific revolution, and the rise of the West to centuries of global domination.

*   *   *

This observation is not intended to make light of the vast misery caused by AIDS in Africa (or elsewhere), but only to warn that those who assume that disaster can only lead to further disasters are wrong. Catastrophe, paradoxically, unleashes human creativity and great energies. Out of the many imaginable post-AIDS scenarios for Africa, one certainly would be economic and governmental failure. But an alternative scenario could see an Africa reborn.We simply do not know. But the smart money will always bet on human ingenuity, innovation, and will.

AIDS could lead to militarized societies based along tribal lines, or to the breakdown of tribal control, to the rise of violent millenarian sects, or to more egalitarian societies, to an opening of markets or their collapse. The results simply are not predictable at this point. But it is fair to observe that our continued insistence that Africa can only fail runs the risk of becoming a self-fulfilling prophecy.

Saints, con-men, politicians, and smart investors see opportunity in disaster. The correct question isn't whether or not there are opportunities in Africa, but which of the many opportunities Africa offers its people and the world are the most promising. In the Arab world, we play down the negatives. In Africa, we ignore the positives. As a nation proud of our rationality,we are behaving very irrationally, indeed.

Consider, briefly, the most promising major country on the continent— South Africa. If you only read the statistics from afar—HIV-infection rate, 30 percent or higher; unemployment rate, 40 percent or higher; up to three million AIDS orphans; low levels of literacy; astronomical crime rates—you would conclude that South Africa is on the brink of becoming a failed state. The visitor, on the other hand, sees a coalescing multiracial society that has done an astonishing (if still imperfect) job of overcoming historical hatreds. Much of the infrastructure is world-class. The government is serious about fighting corruption, improving living conditions for the poor, and expanding educational opportunities. South African boardrooms are no longer populated only by white faces, and South African firms invest in the rest of the continent and beyond (earlier this year, for example, South African Breweries bought Miller Breweries in the United States, and SAB-Miller also has extensive investments in China). Elsewhere, some Africans fear South African "economic imperialism." And the infamous "white flight" of the early days of majority rule has reversed itself, with emigres returning to South Africa from abroad.

Despite many grave challenges, South Africa appears programmed for success on a continental scale. Events still could derail the country's future, but it now appears that South Africa, not Nigeria, is destined to become the continent's leader and moral beacon. Indeed, any Africa policy that does not strive for close relations with South Africa as a fundamental objective could achieve only partial, localized successes.

As noted above, the liberation generation and its protégés continue to suspect the United States of all sorts of deviousness, too often breaking out into ludicrous public accusations. But those men and their rhetoric will pass. We need to lay the groundwork now to work with the practical men and women who will succeed to government posts and positions of leadership in business across the next generation. What is especially striking to an American visitor to South Africa is how similar our two countries are, in so many respects, from a multi-ethnic society, to a can-do frontier spirit, to the varieties of landscape. We share elementary values, an English constitutional heritage, and a belief in the future (as opposed to Europe's fixation on the status quo). We are natural allies.

Elsewhere on the continent, the United States has already established a military presence in the northeast, on the Horn of Africa, in formerly French-occupied Djibouti. If we are both wise and humane, we will assist Liberia on Africa's west coast, considering—if the people of Liberia approve—the establishment of a permanent naval and Marine base in the country. In the continent's southern third, however, we need to allow South Africa to take the lead, to continue its effort to build regional military cooperation among democratic states, while we explore ways in which we can work more closely with Angola on the Atlantic coast and Mozambique, Tanzania, and Kenya on the eastern coast. In the north, more and more former French colonies will turn toward us, especially those that are black and majority-Christian. Through a strategy of "triangulation," of positive engagement (with a limited permanent presence) in converging spheres of influence on Africa's west coast, east coast, and in the southern cone, we and our allies would be well-positioned to help Africa and thereby help ourselves throughout this century.

This is not a recommendation for trying to do everything, but a suggestion that we have neglected even the minimum commitments that could bring us enormous strategic advantages. After all, seen from one perspective, the United States is simply the most successful African country.

*   *   *

Less need be said here about Latin America, since so much has been written elsewhere on the subject, at least in comparison to our neglect of Africa. But the same admonition applies: The routine Washington response to the mention of Latin America, as with Africa, suggests that "those people" just can't put all the pieces together. While many arguments might be made about the complex history of Latin America—multiple histories, really—what matters is the here-and now and the future. And, despite setbacks, much of Latin America has begun to change, profoundly, over the past generation.

Mexicans have gone from blaming the United States for everything that goes wrong to blaming their own political leaders and their own society. One gets the feeling from Chile that its opinion leaders believe all parties concerned would be better off if Chile could swap places with California. In Colombia, the elite finally has begun to take responsibility for the country's internal war with its narco-guerrillas and paramilitaries (in the past, the poor were drafted to die, the lower-middle-class supplied the combat leaders, and the elite decamped to their mansions in greater Miami).

The election of a labor leader Washington feared as Brazil's head of state resulted in increased dialog, responsible economic policies, and a surprising personal rapport between the leaders of our two nations. After their turn-of the- millennium economic collapse, Argentines don't want another demagogue. They want fair, transparent government, and they just might get it. Venezuela is led by a populist who yearns to be Fidel Castro, but the democratic system that put him in office also restrains his most authoritarian impulses—the repeated street crises in Caracas are a rough form of democracy in action. And Mexico, which defined itself through much of the last century as the anti-US, now recognizes the criticality of working constructively with Washington on multiple fronts, from fighting crime to economic immigration to fostering democracy elsewhere in the Western hemisphere. Unfortunately, Washington's attentions are elsewhere.

We have much to repair in our relations with Latin America. Some of the errors that long plagued our relationship have been theirs, but not a few have been our own. Arrogance and condescension toward our southern neighbors need to be banished from our diplomatic fashion show. We need to begin to build a serious, long-term partnership of equals—not yet equal in wealth, or in quality of government, or in raw power, but equal in our human dignity and our popular aspirations. Working together, we can develop our mutual potential far more efficiently and rapidly than by continuing along our far-too-separate paths.

Imperial Spain looked to Latin America for the silver in its mountains. We must look toward Latin America for the gold in its population. In a century when Europe's populations are aging toward fiscal and societal crises (the truly old Europe) and our ties with East Asia may become more limited, rather than expanding, even America's progressive immigration system will not be able to supply all the human power needed to fuel our continued economic expansion. It will not be a matter of "exporting American jobs," but of creating new jobs elsewhere that generate wealth for both host states and the United States.

For the next several decades, Africa will need its talent to focus primarily on internal development, but the better-educated, more urbane pools of talent in Latin America are the natural resource to which we can turn. Especially given the deepening cultural impact of American Latinos on our own society, we will have in place human bridges that no other country will be able to match. Even Spain, which will play an ever-greater role in much of Latin America, will have only a shared language and heritage in common with local populations, while we will have their relatives—carrying American passports.

As with Africa, if we look only for problems in Latin America, we will have no difficulty in finding so many that we might easily convince ourselves to stay home. But the current trend in the wake of Operation Iraqi Freedom to downplay our recent differences with France, Germany, and other European powers is wrongheaded. Increasingly, continental Europe's interests, values, and aspirations diverge from our own. Certainly, we will continue to work together productively in many spheres. But the United States and Europe are growing apart, not converging.

The future—our future—lies elsewhere, in those long-neglected realms where human wastage has been blithely dismissed and every local misfortune was seized upon as proof that "they" simply weren't in our league. We have been seduced into playing 19th-century European great-power politics in the 21st century; indeed, considering our current involvement in the Middle East, one is tempted to claim that we're playing 12th-century European power politics.

To the extent strategic requirements allow, we need to reduce our commitments to Europe, as well as combating our psychological dependence on the Eurocentric worldview. We are the children of Mark Twain, not of Proust. Like Huck Finn, we need to avoid Aunt Polly's attempts to put too many table manners on us. We always need to light out for new frontiers. And the human frontiers of the 21st century are in our own country, in Latin America, and in Africa.

Try a simple experiment. Lay out a map of the world. With a pencil and ruler, connect the United Kingdom, Spain, and Portugal with all the countries in the Americas or in Africa to which they have historical or cultural ties. Next, connect the countries of Africa to those states of the Western Hemisphere to which they have ethnic and cultural ties. Now connect the United States to the countries in Latin America and Africa to which we have ties of population and culture. You have just drawn the most promising strategic network of this century.

It is time for the United States to begin making Castro's dream a reality, leaving behind his socialist baggage and replacing it with respect for the popular will, individual rights, and truly free markets. We need to begin to bind together North America, Latin America, Africa, and the Atlantic powers on Europe's western frontier in a mutually beneficial, ocean-spanning network of rule-of-law democracies. Our history laid the foundation. Now we need to build the Atlantic Century.

Part VIII
Should Foreign Policy Be Moral?

In his prescriptions to rulers in *The Prince,* Machiavelli said the ruler should "know how to resort to evil." Does that mean the ruler should always be evil?

Around 400 B.C., during the Peloponnesian Wars between democratic Athens and oligarchic Sparta to consider how morality & ethics affects a state's foreign policy in the *Mytlinean Debate.* In this debate, two Athenians—Cleon & Diodotus—vehemently debate before the Athenian Assembly what should be done about an ally that revolted against Athens—death or mercy. Closely read Diodotus' reasons for showing mercy to the revolting city—is he a Liberal or Realist?

The concepts that Cleon & Diodotus can still be seen today as the US engages in a Global War on Terror—why or how can the US fight morally when its opponent does not? Anthony Arend explores that question in *Terrorism & Just War Doctrine.* Arend begins by summarizing classical (state-centric) *jus ad bello* and *jus in bello* doctrine and then provides a set of recommendations on how to adapt those state-centric "rules" to fighting a non-state actor (terrorism).

The Mytilenian Debate[1]

Thucides

When Salaethus and the other prisoners reached Athens, the Athenians immediately put Salaethus to death in spite of the fact that he undertook, among other things, to have the Peloponnesians withdrawn from Plataea, which was still being besieged. They then discussed what was to be done with the other prisoners and, in their angry mood, decided to put to death not only those now in their hands but also the entire adult male population of Mytilene, and to make slaves of the women and children. What they held against Mytilene was the fact that it had revolted even though it was not a subject state, like the others, and the bitterness of their feelings was considerably increased by the fact that the Peloponnesian fleet had actually dared to cross over to Ionia to support the revolt. This, it was thought, could never have happened unless the revolt had been long premeditated. So they sent a trireme to Paches to inform him of what had been decided, with orders to put the Mytilenians to death immediately.

Next day, however, there was a sudden change of feeling and people began to think how cruel and how unprecedented such a decision was—to destroy not only the guilty, but the entire population of a state. Observing this, the deputation from Mytilene which was in Athens and the Athenians who were supporting them approached the authorities with a view to having the question debated again. They won their point the more easily because the authorities themselves saw clearly that most of the citizens were wanting someone to give them a chance of reconsidering the matter. So an assembly was called at once. Various opinions were expressed on both sides, and Cleon, the son of Cleaenetus, spoke again. It was he who had been responsible for passing the original motion for putting the Mytilenians to death. He was remarkable among the Athenians for the violence of his character, and at this time he exercised far the greatest influence over the people.[2] He spoke as follows:

'Personally I have had occasion often enough already to observe that a democracy is incapable of governing others, and I am all the more convinced of this when I see how you are now changing your minds about the Mytilenians. Because fear and conspiracy play no part in your daily relations with each other, you imagine that the same thing is true of your allies, and you fail to see that when you allow them to persuade you to make a mistaken decision and when you give way to your own feelings of compassion you are being guilty of a kind of weakness which is dangerous to you and which will not make them love you any more. What you do not realize is that your empire is a tyranny exercised over subjects who do not like it and who are always plotting against you; you will not make them obey you by injuring your own interests in order to do them a favour; your leadership depends on superior strength and not on any goodwill of theirs. And this is the very worst thing—to pass measures and then not to abide by them. We should realize that a city is better off with bad laws, so long as they remain fixed, than with good laws that are constantly being altered, that lack of learning combined with sound common sense is more helpful than the kind of cleverness that gets out of hand, and that as a general rule states are better governed by the man in the street than by intellectuals.

These are the sort of people who want to appear wiser than the laws, who want to get their own way in every general discussion, because they feel that they cannot show off their intelligence in matters of greater importance, and who, as a result, very often bring ruin on their country. But the other kind—the people who are not so confidence in their own intelligence—are prepared to admit that the laws are wiser than they are and that they lack the ability to pull to pieces a speech made by a good speaker; they are unbiased judges, and not people taking part in some kind of a competition; so things usually go well when they are in control. We statesmen, too, should try to be like them, instead of being carried away by mere cleverness and a desire to show off our intelligence and so giving you, the people, advice which we do not really believe in ourselves.

'As for me, I have not altered my opinion, and I am amazed at those who have proposed a reconsideration of the question of Mytilene, thus causing a delay which is all to the advantage of the guilty party. After a lapse of time the injured party will lose the edge of his anger when he comes to act against those who have wronged him; whereas the best punishment and the one most fitted to the crime is when reprisals follow immediately. I shall be amazed, too, if anyone contradicts me and attempts to prove that the harm done to us by Mytilene is really a good thing for us, or that when we suffer ourselves we are somehow doing harm to our allies. It is obvious that anyone who is going to say this must either have such confidence in his powers as an orator that he will struggle to persuade you that what has been finally settled was, on the contrary, not decided at all, or else he must have been bribed to put together some elaborate speech with which he will try to lead you out of the right track. But in competitions of this sort the prizes go to others and the state takes all the danger for herself. The blame is yours, for stupidly instituting these competitive displays. You have become regular speech-goers, and as for action, you merely listen to accounts of it; if something is to be done in the future you estimate the possibilities by hearing a good speech on the subject, and as for the past you rely not so much on the facts which you have seen with your own eyes as on what you have heard about them in some clever piece of verbal criticism. Any novelty in an argument deceives you at once, but when the argument is tried and proved you become unwilling to follow it; you look with suspicion on what is normal and are the slaves of every paradox that comes your way. The chief wish of each one of you is to be able to make a speech himself, and, if you cannot do that, the next best thing is to compete with those who can make this sort of speech by not looking as though you were at all out of your depth while you listen to the views put forward, by applauding a good point even before it is made, and by being as quick at seeing how an argument is going to be developed as you are slow at understanding what in the end it will lead to. What you are looking for all the time is something that is, I should say, outside the range of ordinary experience, and yet you cannot even think straight about the facts of life that are before you. You are simply victims of your own pleasure in listening, and are more like an audience sitting at the feet of a professional lecturer than a parliament discussing matters of state.

'I am trying to stop you behaving like this, and I say that no single city has ever done you the harm that Mytilene has done. Personally I can make allowances for those who revolt because they find your rule intolerable or because they have been forced into it by enemy action. Here, however, we have the case of people living on an island, behind their own fortifications, with nothing to fear from our enemies except an attack by sea against which they were adequately protected by their own force of triremes; they had their own independent government and they were treated by us with the greatest consideration. Now, to act as they acted is not what I should call a revolt (for people only revolt when they have been badly treated); it is a case of calculated aggression, of deliberately taking sides with our bitterest enemies in order to destroy us. And this is far worse than if they had made war against us simply to increase their own power. They learned nothing from the fate of those of their neighbours who had already revolted and been subdued; the prosperity which they enjoyed did not make them hesitate before running into danger; confident in the future, they declared war on us, with hopes that indeed extended beyond their means, though still fell short of their desires. They made up their minds to put might first and right second, choosing the moment when they thought they would win, and then making their unprovoked attack upon us.

'The fact is that when great prosperity comes suddenly and unexpectedly to a state, it usually breeds arrogance; in most cases it is safer for people to enjoy an average amount of success rather than something which is out of all proportion; and it is easier, I should say, to ward off hardship than to maintain happiness. What we should have done long ago with the Mytilenians was to treat them in exactly the same way as all the rest; then they would never have grown so arrogant; for it is a general rule of human nature that people despise those who treat them well and look up to those who make no concessions. Let them now therefore have the punishment which their crime deserves. Do not put the blame on the aristocracy and say that the people were innocent. The fact is that the whole lot of them attacked you together, although the people might have come over to us and, if they had, would now be back again in control of their city. Yet, instead of doing this, they thought it safer to share the dangers, and join in the revolt of the aristocracy.

'Now think of your allies. If you are going to give the same punishment to those who are forced to revolt by your enemies and those who do so of their own accord, can you not see that they will all revolt upon the slightest pretext, when success means freedom and failure brings no very dreadful consequences? Meanwhile we shall have to spend our money and risk our lives against state after state; if our efforts are successful, we shall recover a city that is in ruins, and so lose the future revenue from it, on which our strength is based; and if we fail to subdue it, we shall have more enemies to deal with in addition to those we have already, and we shall spend the time which ought to be used in resisting our present foes in making war on our own allies.

'Let there be no hope, therefore, held out to the Mytilenians that we, either as a result of a good speech or a large bribe, are likely to forgive them on the grounds that it is only human to make mistakes. There was nothing involuntary about the harm they did us; they knew what they were about and they planned it all beforehand; and one only forgives actions that were not deliberate. As for me, just as I was at first, so I am now, and I shall continue to impress on you the importance of not altering your previous decisions. To feel pity, to be carried away by the pleasure of hearing a clever argument, to listen to the claims of decency are three things that are entirely against the interests of an imperial power. Do not be guilty of them. As for compassion, it is proper to feel it in the case of people who are like ourselves and who will pity us in their turn, not in the case of those who, so far from having the same feelings towards us, must always and inevitably be our enemies. As for the speech-makers who give such pleasure by their arguments, they should hold their competitions on subjects which are less important, and not on a question where the state may have to pay a heavy penalty for its light pleasure, while the speakers themselves will no doubt be enjoying splendid rewards for their splendid arguments. And a sense of decency is only felt towards those who are going to be our friends in future, not towards those who remain just as they were and as much our enemies as they ever have been.

'Let me sum the whole thing up. I say that, if you follow my advice, you will be doing the right thing as far as Mytilene is concerned and at the same time will be acting in your own interests; if you decide differently, you will not win them over, but you will be passing judgement on yourselves. For if they were justified in revolting, you must be wrong in holding power. If, however, whatever the rights or wrongs of it may be, you propose to hold power all the same, then your interest demands that these too, rightly or wrongly, must be punished. The only alternative is to surrender your empire, so that you can afford to go in for philanthropy. Make up your minds, therefore, to pay them back in their own coin, and do not make it look as though you who escaped their machinations are less quick to react than they who started them. Remember how they would have been likely to have treated you, if they had won, especially as they were the aggressors. Those who do wrong to a neighbour when there is no reason to do so are the ones who persevere to the point of destroying him, since they see the danger involved in allowing their enemy to survive. For he who has suffered for no good reason is a more dangerous enemy, if he escapes, than the one who has both done and suffered injury.

'I urge you, therefore, not to be traitors to your own selves. Place yourselves in imagination at the moment when you first suffered and remember how then you would have given anything to have them in your power. Now pay them back for it, and do not grow soft just at this present moment, forgetting meanwhile the danger that hung over your heads then. Punish them as they deserve, and make an example of them to your other allies, plainly showing that revolt will be punished by death. Once they realize this, you will not have so often to neglect the war with your enemies because you are fighting with your own allies.'

So Cleon spoke. After him Diodotus, the son of Eucrates, who in the previous assembly also had vigorously opposed the motion to put the Mytilenians to death, came forward again on this occasion and spoke as follows:

'I do not blame those who have proposed a new debate on the subject of Mytilene, and I do not share the view which we have heard expressed, that it is a bad thing to have frequent discussions on matters of importance. Haste and anger are, to my mind, the two greatest obstacles to wise counsel–haste, that usually goes with folly, anger, that is the mark of primitive and narrow minds. And anyone who maintains that words cannot be a guide to action must be either a fool or one with some personal interest at stake; he is a fool, if he imagines that it is possible to deal with the uncertainties of the future by any other medium, and he is personally interested if his aim is to persuade you into some disgraceful action, and, knowing that he cannot make a good speech in a bad cause, he tries to frighten his opponents and his hearers by some good-sized pieces of misrepresentation. Then still more intolerable are those who go further and accuse a speaker of making a kind of exhibition of himself, because he is paid for it. If it was only ignorance with which he was being charged, a speaker who failed to win his case could retire from the debate and still be thought an honest man, if not a very intelligent one. But when corruption is imputed, he will be suspect if he wins his case, and if he loses it, will be regarded as dishonest and stupid at the same time. This sort of thing does the city no good; her counselors will be afraid to speak and she will be deprived of their services. Though certainly it would be the best possible thing for the city if these gentlemen whom I have been describing lacked the power to express themselves; we should not then be persuaded into making so many mistakes.

'The good citizen, instead of trying to terrify the opposition, ought to prove his case in fair argument; and a wise state, without giving special honours to its best counsellors, with certainly not deprive them of the honour they already enjoy; and when a man's advice is not taken, he should not even be disgraced, far less penalized. In this way successful speakers will be less likely to pursue further honours by speaking against their own convictions in order to make themselves popular, and unsuccessful speakers, too, will not struggle to win over the people by the same acts of flattery. What we do here, however, is exactly the opposite. Then, too, if a man gives the best possible advice but is under the slightest suspicion of being influenced by his own private profit, we are so embittered by the idea (a wholly unproved one) of this profit of his, that we do not allow the state to receive the certain benefit of his good advice. So a state of affairs has been reached where a good proposal honestly put forward is just as suspect as something thoroughly bad, and the result is that just as the speaker who advocates some monstrous measure has to win over the people by deceiving them, so also a man with good advice to give has to tell lies if he expects to be believed. And because of this refinement in intellectuality, the state is put into a unique position; it is only she to whom no one can ever do a good turn openly and without deception. For if one openly performs a patriotic action, the reward for one's pains is to be thought to have made something oneself on the side. Yet in spite of all this we are discussing matters of the greatest importance, and we who give you our advice ought to be resolved to look rather further into things than you whose attention is occupied only with the surface—especially as we can be held to account for the advice we give, while you are not accountable for the way in which you receive it. For indeed you would take rather more care over your decisions, if the proposer of a motion and those who voted for it were all subject to the same penalties. As it is, on the occasions when some emotional impulse on your part has led you into disaster, you turn upon the one man who made the original proposal and you let yourself off, in spite of the fact that you are many and in spite of the fact that you were just as wrong as he was.

'However, I have not come forward to speak about Mytilene in any spirit of contradiction or with any wish to accuse anyone. If we are sensible people, we shall see that the question is not so much whether they are guilty as whether we are making the right decision for ourselves. I might prove that they are the most guilty people in the world, but it does not follow that I shall propose the death penalty, unless that is in your interests; I might argue that they deserve to be forgiven, but should not recommend forgiveness unless that seemed to me the best thing for the state.

'In my view our discussion concerns the future rather than the present. One of Cleon's chief points is that to inflict the death penalty will be useful to us in the future as a means for deterring other cities from revolt; but I, who am just as concerned as he is with the future, am quite convinced that this is not so. And I ask you not to reject what is useful in my speech for the sake of what is specious in his. You may well find his speech attractive, because it fits in better with your present angry feelings about the Mytilenians; but this is not a law-court, where we have to consider what is fit and just; it is a political assembly, and the question is how Mytilene can be most useful to Athens.

'Now, in human societies the death penalty has been laid down for many offences less serious than this one. Yet people still take risks when they feel sufficiently confident. No one has ever yet risked committing a crime which he thought he could not carry out successfully. The same is true of states. None has ever yet rebelled in the belief that it had insufficient resources, either in itself or from its allies, to make the attempt. Cities and individuals alike, all are by nature disposed to do wrong, and there is no law that will prevent it, as is shown by the fact that men have tried every kind of punishment, constantly adding to the list, in the attempt to find greater security from criminals. It is likely that in early times the punishments even for the greatest crimes were not as severe as they are now, but the laws were still broken, and in the course of time the death penalty became generally introduced. Yet even with this, the laws are still broken. Either, therefore, we must discover some fear more potent that the fear of death, or we must admit that here certainly we have not got an adequate deterrent. So long as poverty forced men to be bold, so long as the insolence and pride of wealth nourish their ambitions, and in the other accidents of life they are continually dominated by some incurable master passion or another, so long will their impulses continue to drive them into danger. Hope and desire persist throughout and cause the greatest calamities—one leading and the other following, one conceiving the enterprise, and the other suggesting that it will be successful—invisible factors, but more powerful than the terrors that are obvious to our eyes. Then too, the idea that fortune will be on one's side plays as big a part as anything else in creating a mood of over-confidence; for sometimes she does come unexpectedly to one's aid, and so she tempts men to run risks for which they are inadequately prepared. And this is particularly true in the case of whole peoples, because they are playing for the highest stakes—either for their own freedom or for the power to control others—and each individual, when acting as part of a community, has the irrational opinion that his own powers are greater than in fact they are. In a word it is impossible (and only the most simple-minded will deny this) for human nature, when once seriously set upon a certain course, to be prevented from following that course by the force of law or by any other means of intimidation whatever.

'We must not, therefore, come to the wrong conclusions through having too much confidence in the effectiveness of capital punishment, and we must not make the condition of rebels desperate by depriving them of the possibility of repentance, and of a chance of atoning as quickly as they can for what they did. Consider this now: at the moment, if a city has revolted and realizes that the revolt cannot succeed, it will come to terms while it is still capable of paying an indemnity and continuing to pay tribute afterwards. But if Cleon's method is adopted, can you not see that every city will not only make much more careful preparations for revolt, but will also hold out against siege to the very end, since to surrender early or late means just the same thing? This is, unquestionably, against our interests—to spend money on a siege because of the impossibility of coming to terms, and, if we capture the place, to take over a city that is in ruins so that we lose the future revenue from it. And it is just on this revenue that our strength in war depends.

'Our business, therefore, is not to injure ourselves by acting like a judge who strictly examines a criminal; instead we should be looking for a method by which, employing moderation in our punishments, we can in future secure for ourselves the full use of those cities which bring us important contributions. And we should recognize that the proper basis of our security is in good administration rather than in the fear of legal penalties. As it is, we do just the opposite: when we subdue a free city, which was held down by force and has, as we might have expected, tried to assert its independence by revolting, we think that we ought to punish it with the utmost severity. But the right way to deal with free people is this—not to inflict tremendous punishments on them after they have revolted, but to take tremendous care of them before this point is reached, to prevent them even contemplating the idea of revolt, and, if we do not have to use force with them, to hold as few as possible of them responsible for this.

'Consider what a mistake you would be making on this very point, if you took Cleon's advice. As things are now, in all the cities the democracy is friendly to you; either it does not join in with the oligarchies in revolting, or, if it is forced to do so, it remains all the time hostile to the rebels, so that when you go to war with them, you have the people on your side. But if you destroy the democratic party at Mytilene, who never took any hand in the revolt and who, as soon as they got arms, voluntarily gave the city up to you, you will first of all be guilty of killing those who have helped you, and, secondly, you will be doing exactly what the reactionary classes want most. For now, when they start a revolt, they will have the people on their side from the beginning, because you have already made it clear that the same punishment is laid down both for the guilty and the innocent. In fact, however, even if they were guilty, you should pretend that they were not, in order to keep on your side the one element that is still not opposed to you. It is far more useful to us, I think, in preserving our empire, that we should voluntarily put up with injustice than that we should justly put to death the wrong people. As for Cleon's point—that in this act of vengeance both justice and self-interest are combined—this is not a case where such a combination is at all possible.

'I call upon you, therefore, to accept my proposal as the better one. Do not be swayed too much by pity or by ordinary decent feelings. I, no more than Cleon, wish you to be influenced by such emotions. It is simply on the basis of argument which you have heard that I ask you to be guided by me, to try at your leisure the men whom Paches has considered guilty and sent to Athens, and allow the rest to live in their own city. In following this course you will be acting wisely for the future and will be doing something which will make your enemies fear you now. For those who make wise decisions are more formidable to their enemies than those who rush madly into strong action.'

This was the speech of Diodotus. And now, when these two motions, each so opposed to each, had been put forward, the Athenians, in spite of the recent change of feeling, still held conflicting opinions, and at the show of hands the votes were nearly equal. However, the motion of Diodotus was passed.

Immediately another trireme was sent out in all haste, since they feared that, unless it overtook the first trireme, they would find on their arrival that the city had been destroyed. The first trireme had a start of about twenty-four hours. The ambassadors from Mytilene provided wine and barley for the crew and promised great rewards if they arrived in time, and so the men made such speed on the voyage that they kept on rowing while they took their food (which was barley mixed with oil and wine) and rowed continually, taking it in turn to sleep. Luckily they had no wind against them, and as the first ship was not hurrying on its distasteful mission, while they were pressing on with such speed, what happened was that the first ship arrived so little ahead of them that Paches had just had time to read the decree and to prepare to put it into force, when the second ship put into the harbour and prevented the massacre. So narrow had been the escape of Mytilene.

The other Mytilenians whom Paches had sent to Athens as being the ones chiefly responsible for the revolt were, on the motion of Cleon, put to death by the Athenians. There were rather more than 1,000 of them. The Athenians also destroyed the fortifications of Mytilene and took over their navy. Afterwards, instead of imposing a tribute on Lesbos, they divided all the land, except that belonging to the Methymnians, into 3,000 holdings, 300 of which were set apart as sacred for the gods, while the remainder was distributed by lot to Athenian shareholders, who were sent out to Lesbos. The Lesbians agreed with these shareholders to pay a yearly rent of two minae for each holding, and cultivated the land themselves. The Athenians also took over all the towns on the mainland that had been under the control of Mytilene. So for the future the Mytilenians became subjects of Athens. This completes the account of what took place is Lesbos.

NOTES

1. See the Introduction, pp. 27.

2. This wording is echoed by Thucydides in VI, 35 when he introduces the Syracusan 'demagogue' Athenagoras.

Terrorism and Just War Doctrine

Anthony Clark Arend

When classic just war theory developed, the world consisted of a variety of political entities—kingdoms, principalities, empires, and the like. With the passage of time, however, the territorial state emerged as the primary political unit, and writers in this tradition began to apply just war doctrine exclusively to the behavior of states. Today, the vast corpus of just war writings deals with questions about the permissibility of the recourse to force *by states* (the principles of *ius ad bellum*) and the conduct of hostilities *by states* (the principles of *ius in bello*).[1]

Since the Second World War, however, the world has witnessed the emergence of a number of non-state actors on the international stage. Among these actors are terrorist groups. Over the last several decades, the Palestine Liberation Organization [PLO], the Hezbollah, the Irish Republican Army [IRA], the Abu Nidal Group, the Red Brigade, the Red Army, and numerous other groups have used force against a variety of state and non-state targets. Their activities have elicited forcible responses by states—the United States and Israel, in particular.[2] Yet because these groups are not states and operate quite differently from states, it is unclear just how the principles of contemporary just war doctrine would apply to states attempting to counter these terrorist groups.

My purpose here is to attempt to find out—that is, to apply contemporary just war doctrine to state efforts to respond to terrorist actions. Parts one and two will explore the traditional *ius ad bellum* and *ius in bello* principles in relation to terrorism, and part three will offer several recommendations for making just war doctrine more applicable to the terrorist threat.

IUS AD BELLUM AND TERRORISM

Classic just war doctrine was most concerned about when a political entity could justly undertake the use of force.[3] Plato and Aristotle, Augustine and Aquinas, and others searched for specific criteria that could be used to determine when war was justly entered into, and modern just war theorists have continued to use and refine these criteria. Today, while there is no single set that all just war theorists use, six elements figure in most contemporary discussions of *ius ad bellum*; competent authority, just cause, right intention, last resort, probability of success, and proportionality.

Anthony Clark Arend is an associate professor of government at Georgetown University and adjunct professor at the Georgetown University Law Center. His main research and teaching interests are in the areas of international law, international organization, and constitutional law of U.S. foreign relations; he is especially interested in international law relating to the use of force and international legal theory. He is the author of several books and numerous articles. Among his recent publications is the book *Legal Rules and International Society* (1999).

1. Competent Authority

To be justly undertaken, a war or other use of force must be initiated by a legitimate authority. As Aquinas explained, "[a] private individual may not declare war...."[4] Instead, "since responsibility for public affairs is entrusted to the rul[ers], it is they who are charged with the defence of the city, realm, or province."[5] In the world of today, the notion of competent authority has generally been understood to mean that *states* can declare or otherwise initiate hostilities. Whether any entity other than a state has the authority to do so is less clear. Given the historic support within the just war tradition for "just revolution," there seems to be reason to think that certain *revolutionary groups* may constitute competent authority.[6] But just what criteria such a group would need to meet remains unclear.[7] It would also seem logical to conclude that *the United Nations* can be considered a competent authority, given the authority vested in it by states. As states ratified the United Nations Charter, they did so with the understanding that the Charter empowered the Security Council to authorize the use of force when the Council determined that there was a threat to the peace, breach of the peace, or act of aggression.[8]

When the concept of competent authority is applied to the use of force against terrorists, on the surface it seems to provide no particular difficulty. Clearly, states are the entities that respond to terrorists, and states are the competent authorities *par excellence*. On closer examination, however, the situation is a bit murkier. In recent discussions of competent authority, scholars have explored precisely who or what body within a state is empowered to authorize the use of force. Can the American president do so alone? Or must Congress, which under the Constitution has the authority to "declare war," be involved in the decision? Virtually all scholars would argue that when the United States is under direct attack, the president can use force without the consent of Congress. But beyond that, scholars and public officials differ considerably on the circumstances under which the president can use force without congressional approval.

This problem is especially acute with respect to terrorism and its unconventional methods of warfare. Terrorists do not generally wear military uniforms and engage in overt attacks across international borders. It is not to be expected that a terrorist group will march across the U.S.–Mexican border with flags flying. Instead, terrorists will attack military and diplomatic installations abroad, take hostages, and kill civilians. Under American constitutional law, it is not clear whether the president has the authority to respond forcibly without the consent of Congress. The War Powers Resolution provides that the president can introduce troops into hostilities only "pursuant to (1) a declaration of war, (2) specific statutory authorization, or (3) a national emergency created by attack upon the United States, its territories or possessions, or its armed forces."[9] It does not provide for the use of force in response to actions against U.S. nationals abroad. Yet, presidents have certainly asserted such a right. In 1985, for example, Ronald Reagan unilaterally authorized force to bring down an Egyptian aircraft carrying terrorists allegedly involved in the *Achille Lauro* hijacking.[10]

2. Just Cause

The second criterion, just cause, can be divided into (a) the substance of the cause and (b) comparative justice.

a. The Substance of the Cause. Every just war theorist—from the most ancient to the most recent—has asserted that for war to be properly undertaken, there must be a substantive just cause, some legitimate reason for going to war. A state cannot simply declare war. Underlying this concept is a critical element of just war doctrine: there is always a presumption against the recourse to force. As the National Conference of Catholic Bishops has observed, "just-war teaching has evolved... as an effort to prevent war; only if war cannot be rationally avoided, does the teaching then seek to restrict and reduce its horrors."[11] It does this, they explain, "by establishing a set of rigorous conditions which must be met if the decision to go to war is to be morally permissible."[12] Especially today, they continue, "such decision... requires extraordinarily strong reasons for overriding the presumption *in favor of peace and against war.*"[13]

But while just war theorists agree that there must be a just cause, they do not agree on exactly what qualifies as a substantive just cause. Augustine wrote in the broadest of terms, explaining that "those wars are generally defined as just which avenge some wrong, when a nation or a state is to be punished for having failed to make amends for the wrong done, or to restore what has been taken unjustly."[14] More recently, James Childress has refined this concept of substantive just cause by narrowing it to three circumstances: "to protect the innocent from unjust attack," "to restore rights wrongfully denied," and "to re-establish a just order."[15]

Regarding the first of these circumstances there is universal agreement. All just war theorists would assert that a state can use force in the event of an armed attack. Indeed, Article 51 of the United Nations Charter guarantees states a *legal* right to "individual or collective self-defense if an armed attack occurs."[16] But the precise meaning of "armed attack" is unclear, especially in regard to terrorism. When does a terrorist action constitute an armed attack? Must it occur in the territory of the aggrieved state? Must it be of a particular intensity? Would an isolated terrorist action amount to an armed attack, or would it have to be part of an ongoing effort? Would the *threat* of an armed attack be sufficient? In other words, could a state justly engage in preemptive or anticipatory self-defense?

More problems arise with the second category of Childress's understanding of substantive just cause, the use of force "to restore rights wrongfully denied." In general just war discussions, scholars would probably take this to mean that force can be used in the face of genocide or other massive human-rights violations. With respect to state actions, a government that engages in genocide or other systematic abuses of the rights of its citizens may be liable to forcible intervention. Indeed, a growing body of literature discusses circumstances under which a "humanitarian" intervention can be justly undertaken.[17] But how the concept of humanitarian intervention would translate to terrorist activity is uncertain. If terrorists were killing or torturing innocents on a massive scale or taking large numbers of people hostage, that action would probably be equivalent to genocide by a state. But what if a terrorist group were causing a group of people to live in great fear for their lives, without actually doing physical harm on a large scale—could such a "reign of terror" give rise to a just intervention? Could a state argue that the mere presence of some terrorist groups poses such a threat to the indigenous population that a forcible action would be justified?

Finally, there are also difficulties with Childress's third category, that force can be justly undertaken "to re-establish a just order." What is a "just order," and when would terrorists violate it? Over the past several years, non-state actors of a variety of sorts have caused a tremendous degree of instability in states. In Lebanon, Somalia, the former Yugoslavia, Liberia, and Sierra Leone, for example, such actors have prevented the centralized government from exercising effective control over large portions of the state's territory. Would such a cast justify intervention? Could it be argued that force is necessary "to preserve," in the words of the U.S. Catholic bishops, "conditions necessary for decent human existence"?[18]

b. Comparative Justice. It is not enough that a state have a substantive just cause for force: it must also satisfy the requirement of comparative justice. While scholars differ on its meaning, this requirement seems to acknowledge that while all parties to a dispute may have substantive just causes, not all such causes justify the resort to force. As the American bishops conceive of comparative justice, the issue is two-fold: "which side is sufficiently 'right' in a dispute, and are the values at stake critical enough to override the presumption against war?"[19] In other words, for a state to use force, its "just cause" should be better than its opponent's and must be worth the "violence, destruction, suffering, and death"[20] caused by war.

Here I will take the first aspect of the bishops' definition of comparative justice— which side is sufficiently "right"?—to reflect a proper understanding of that concept. The latter aspect—is the just cause worth the evil to be produced in the war?—can, I believe, be subsumed under the concept of proportionality and will be discussed later.

To apply the requirement of comparative justice to terrorism may seem at first to produce an extremely undesirable result. Typically, terrorist groups are motivated by legitimate causes. The Irish Republican Army has fought against the British for its "unjust occupation" of Northern Ireland. For years, the PLO challenged Israeli possession of the West Bank, the Golan Heights, and other territories. An observer might be inclined to conclude that comparative justice was indeed on the side of these groups. But terrorism introduces another factor into the calculation. What is abhorrent about terrorism is not the cause for which it is acting but the nature of the act. While certain terrorist groups may indeed have legitimate reasons for desiring change in the status quo, the methods of terrorism are in and of themselves impermissible. Targeting innocent civilians and other non-combatants, taking hostages, killing and torturing prisoners of war—these are completely unacceptable violations of the concept of *ius in bello*.

This aspect of terrorism introduces an important challenge to just war doctrine. How can we evaluate the comparative-justice requirement when the methods of one party are clearly unjust from the perspective of *ius in bello*?

3. Right Intention

Aristotle, one of the earliest proponents of the notion of the just war, explained that the ultimate purpose of war must be to establish peace. Just wars are to be fought out of a desire for charity and peace.[21] The purpose is not to obliterate an enemy but to end the aberrant behavior that has breached the peace. As Augustine noted, "the desire to hurt, the cruelty of vendetta, the stern and implacable spirit, arrogance in victory, the thirst for power, and all that is similar, all these are justly condemned in war."[22] Accordingly, revenge, hatred, and the demonization of the enemy have no place in a just war.[23]

This requirement of *ius ad bellum* is one of the most difficult in a conventional war.[24] It is a rare war in which the enemy is not portrayed as evil and the notion of revenge is not present—think of the American propaganda about the Germans and the Japanese during the Second World War. And for terrorist actions, the problem is even greater. Given the tactics of terrorist groups and their often fanatic ideology, it is quite easy to vilify them beyond reason. Moreover, because their deeds engender international outrage, the desire for punishment or revenge sometimes seems to be the main motivation for forcible response.

4. Last Resort

Hostilities should commence only after peaceful alternatives have been explored. There is, however, some disagreement among just war commentators as to how much effort should be expended on exploring these other methods of dispute resolution. The American bishops, for example, state that "all peaceful alternatives must have been exhausted,"[25] while William V. O'Brien notes that "all reasonable efforts to avoid it [war] while protecting the just cause should be tried."[26] The latter approach, requiring all "reasonable" efforts at avoidance, seems to make the most sense. In any conflict, an observer could always argue that there was "one more" alternative that had not been explored.

But even if we understand this criterion as requiring that we exhaust all reasonably peaceful remedies, terrorism raises special difficulties. In conventional international conflict, there are established diplomatic channels and international organizations that have states as parties. Such institutions provide clear methods for pursuing peaceful settlement and non-violent sanctions. Before the Gulf War, for example, the United States and its allies pursued traditional diplomacy and various multilateral methods available through the United Nations. Such methods are not formally available with terrorist groups. They do not have diplomatic missions in the traditional sense and are normally not members of international organizations, and they are not readily susceptible to economic sanctions and other non-violent pressures. As a consequence, it is unclear how a state could reasonably be said to have exhausted peaceful methods of dispute resolution in dealing with terrorists. Furthermore, efforts to establish any form of official contact may be seen as granting a legitimacy to the terrorist group that would help its cause. Israel's reluctance to negotiate with the PLO stemmed in part from this fear.

5. Probability of Success

A state should engage in the use of force only if the action is likely to succeed. As the American bishops note, the purpose of this requirement "is to prevent irrational resort to force or hopeless resistance when the outcome of either will clearly be disproportionate or futile."[27] But, they continue, "the determination includes a recognition that at times defense of key values, even against great odds, may be a 'proportionate' witness."[28]

But how is success defined when this criterion is applied to terrorism? In a standard war, success means the aggression is ended, or the territory is returned, or the status quo ante is reestablished. But does success against terrorism mean the ending of a particular series of terrorist acts? The capture or death of all the terrorists? Because of the tenacity of terrorists, success can often be elusive. How many years should a state fight against a PLO or an IRA?

6. Proportionality

While this criterion is also present in *ius in bello* calculations, as a *ius ad bellum* category proportionality means that "the damage to be inflicted and the costs incurred by war must be proportionate to the good expected by taking up arms."[29] Are the just causes sufficient to outweigh the injustices of war? Needless to say, this can be a perplexing calculation. It is difficult to anticipate the full consequences of a war. The tragedy far outstretches the number of persons killed or injured and the amount of property damage. War can destroy entire cultures and break the spirit of nations.[30]

In regard to terrorist actions, the requirement of proportionality does not seem to pose any more problems that it does in conventional international conflict; it may even present fewer. First, since terrorist groups do not have full authority and control over a territory, it could be contended that force against them would have less significant long-term consequences than force against a state. Second, it also seems logical to assume that the type of force used against terrorists is likely to be less destructive than the force necessary to combat state actions.

IUS IN BELLO AND TERRORISM

Once a state has properly undertaken to use force, once it has satisfied the requirements of *ius ad bellum*, the conflict must then meet the *ius in bello* requirements in order to be considered just.[31] Over the years, two *in bello* criteria have emerged: proportionality and discrimination.

1. Proportionality

Here the requirement is that the means used in war be proportionate to the ends to be achieved. This means two things. First, any given use of force must be proportionate to the military end sought in that particular case. For example, if the military objective in a battle can be achieved by destroying the communications center of a particular unit, then only the amount of force necessary to accomplish that task should be used. Anything beyond that would be considered disproportionate and, thus, impermissible. Second, proportionality means that, as William V. O'Brien puts it, a military action "must be proportionate in the context of the grand strategic and moral ends of the war."[32] In his book on Israeli's conflict with the PLO, O'Brien notes that "an action might be justified in purely military terms at the tactical or strategic level, but not justified as part of a total pattern of behavior when viewed from the standpoint of the grand strategic ends of the war."[33] Specific uses of force must be proportionate not only in context but also to the overall goals of the general conflict.

Proportionality seems more difficult to apply at the tactical level of terrorism than at the grand strategic level. This is because at the specific case level, proportionality has frequently been understood to mean that the response to a specific terrorist act must be at roughly the same level of force as the act itself.[34] Oscar Schachter, for example, has observed that from a legal perspective, "the U.N. Security Council in several cases, most involving Israel, has judged proportionality by comparing the response on a quantitative basis to the single attack which preceded it."[35] This approach has been called "tit-for-tat proportionality."[36] The difficulty with it is that it could lead to a vicious cycle of terrorist acts and equivalent responses without any real progress toward ending the series of acts.

When the problem of terrorism is viewed through the lens of the broader goals, however, another approach to proportionality becomes plausible. This is what has been called the "eye-for-a-tooth" approach or "deterrent proportionality."[37] As O'Brien has explained, "counter-terror measures should be proportionate to the purposes of counter-terror and defense, viewed in the total context of hostilities as well as the broader political-military strategic context."[38] Accordingly, "the referent of proportionality" is "the overall pattern of past and projected acts."[39] Under this approach, a state responding to a terrorist act would be able to use force not just proportionate to that single act but proportionate to the terrorists' accumulated past acts and anticipated future acts. This approach makes a great deal of sense in light of the peculiar problem of terrorism; yet it is not universally accepted.

2. Discrimination

The principle of discrimination "prohibits direct intentional attacks on noncombatants and nonmilitary targets."[40] Needless to say, all these terms—"direct intentional attack," "noncombatants," and "nonmilitary targets"—have inspired debate.[41] This is especially true with regard to nuclear-weapons use and targeting.[42] Leaving aside these general debates, let us consider difficulties that the principle of discrimination presents for counterterrorism efforts.

A basic element of discrimination is that innocent civilians are not to be attacked or targeted. In a conventional war, military personnel are clearly identifiable. They wear uniforms, use military vehicles, and stay in military installations. Terrorists are not nearly so easy to identify. They do not necessarily wear uniforms or live in military compounds. They are, in fact, civilians. But they are not innocent civilians. Hence, one of the greatest difficulties is figuring out exactly who the guilty parties are. The matter becomes even more complicated because terrorists frequently use innocent civilians and normally immune targets—such as hospitals and churches—as covers. A terrorist group may have its headquarters in the middle of a crowded city, where innocent people go about their daily activities. How can any targeting policy that complies with the requirement of discrimination be established in such conditions?

TERRORISM AND JUST WAR: RECOMMENDATIONS

Given the particular difficulties that terrorism poses for contemporary just war doctrine, I would like to make some recommendations regarding application of the *ius ad bellum* and *ius in bello* principles. These recommendations seek to preserve the spirit of just war thinking while responding to the specific challenges that terrorism presents.

The Principles of Ius ad Bellum

1. Competent Authority. The real question here is whether under domestic constitutional arrangements it should be easier to use force against terrorists than to engage in conventional war. My recommendation is that more freedom should be given to the executive of a state—the president of the United States in particular—to respond to terrorism. Short, quick actions against terrorist targets should be permitted. Without this type of accommodation, it could be very difficult to intervene in a timely fashion to prevent future terrorism.

2. Just Cause. First, regarding *substantive just cause*: Under traditional just war doctrine, *self-defense* is the most obvious just cause. But how this applies to terrorism is somewhat unclear. I suggest that terrorist actions be regarded as an armed attack, engendering the right of self-defense, under the following circumstances.[43] First, a terrorist attack against targets within a particular state should be considered tantamount to an armed attack. If, for example, terrorists blew up New York's World Trade Center, that would constitute an attack upon the United States. Second, a terrorist attack against state targets abroad—such as embassies and military bases—should be regarded as an armed attack. If terrorist groups attacked an American military base in Germany, the United States could use force in self-defense to respond to that act. Third, significant attacks upon the citizens of a state who are outside that state's territory should be regarded as an attack upon that state. This is harder to specify. Certainly, an isolated action against a few citizens abroad is tragic, but does it amount to an armed attack that would engender the right of forcible response? My own sense is that only when such acts are of significant proportion should they be considered an armed attack. Of course, "significant" is open to varying interpretations; but I believe that this criterion can be a starting point.

Must a state experience an act of terrorism before using force, or can it act preemptively to prevent such an act? Many scholars hold that under contemporary international law, states maintain a right of *anticipatory self-defense*.[44] Traditionally, however, the right can be asserted only if the state (1) can show necessity and (2) responds proportionately. In other words, the state must first demonstrate that if it does not respond immediately an attack will occur, and its response must be proportionate to the threatened attack.

I believe that these same criteria can be applied to anticipatory self-defense to preempt terrorist actions. If a state can show that an armed attack, as defined above, is imminent, and if it responds proportionately, such actions should be considered permissible.

As for *terrorist "genocide"*: Most just war theorists would assert that if a state engages in genocide or similar massive violations of human rights, another state can intervene justly to prevent further human suffering. I strongly suggest that this concept of "humanitarian intervention" be applied to terrorist actions. If a terrorist group is involved in wide-scale killings and terrorizing, an outside state should be able to intervene justly even if it or its citizens are not directly affected. If, for example, a terrorist group in the Sudan is murdering hundreds of innocent civilians, the United States would have a substantive just cause to intervene.

Concerning the second category of just cause, *comparative justice*: While it is clear that terrorists may indeed have just motivation for their actions, their methods are fundamentally unjust. I recommend that the methods employed by the terrorist be part of the comparative-justice calculation. Even if a group is pursuing a valid cause, if it uses indiscriminate killings, torture, hostage-taking, and other such abhorrent methods, those actions should tip the balance against the terrorists.

3. Right Intention. Any use of force—even for a just cause—tends to be accompanied with a vilification of the enemy and a desire for revenge. This tendency is especially strong in response to actions by terrorists. I believe, however, that the same strict standard of right intention must also be applied to terrorists. While it is always proper to acknowledge an evil deed as evil, terrorists are human beings who must be dealt with out of charity. The purpose of using force against them must be to end their abhorrent actions, not to exact revenge. While it is of course impossible to change the hearts of decisionmakers who respond to terrorists, at the very least just war theorists should condemn rhetoric that savors of revenge.

4. Last Resort. This *ius ad bellum* requirement poses a particular problem for counterterrorist actions because the normal diplomatic channels available to states do not exist for terrorist groups. While states understandably wish not to legitimize the terrorist group through negotiations, the presumption against the use of force requires a good-faith exploration of peaceful alternatives. I am not suggesting that compromises should be struck with terrorists that would be fundamentally unjust, or that states should engage in negotiations if to do so would enhance the terrorists' status. Rather, I am suggesting that states should not immediately assume that only forcible methods exist. They should make an effort to determine if any other methods would secure a just result. It may very well be that in virtually all cases, the problems of attempting to pursue such alternatives would greatly outweigh the cost of forcible action. Nonetheless, the examination of these non-forcible options should still be undertaken. It is a fundamental tenet of just war thinking that force is not to be chosen without an exploration of other options.

5. Probability of Success. Another difficulty with counterterror actions is how to define success. What would be a successful forcible action against terrorists? I recommend that success be defined as the elimination of the terrorist threat. This may not mean the capture of all members of a particular terrorist group, but rather the effective ending of the terrorist actions.

This goal is unlikely to be achieved by force alone, since force does not deal with the underlying causes of the terrorism—a desire for territory, a desire to participate in the political system, and the like. While states should not accede to terrorist "demands," they must give some consideration to addressing the underlying causes if they are to succeed in eradicating the terrorist threat.

The Principles of Ius in Bello

1. Proportionality. Some would argue that each specific forcible response to terrorists must be directly proportionate to the proximate terrorist act. Given the nature of terrorism, however, I recommend adoption of the "deterrent proportionality" approach discussed above, according to which a state may respond in a manner proportionate to the accumulated past acts of the terrorists and their anticipated future acts. While this approach clearly introduces a greater element of subjectivity than the "tit-for-tat" approach, it is more suited to prevention of further terrorist actions.

2. Discrimination. Once a determination has been made that it is permissible to use force to respond to terrorism, against what targets can a state act? This is a very difficult question, given the differences between terrorists and conventional warriors. In keeping with the importance of the principle of discrimination, I offer a couple of recommendations, aware that the precise targets will vary depending upon circumstances.[45] First, a clearly identifiable terrorist camp or training facility would be a legitimate target. Second, if the terrorists are being supported by another state, military assets in that state would be legitimate targets. Thus, if it were clearly established that Libya was providing a great deal of support to a particular terrorist group, Libyan weapons and military installations would be legitimate targets.

To conclude: While the nature of terrorists and terrorist actions raises a number of critical challenges for just war doctrine, that doctrine offers a great deal of guidance for counterterror operations. It is my hope that the observations presented here will help to illuminate this guidance.

NOTES

1. Among the most important works on the just war tradition are: Paul Ramsey, *The Just War: Force and Political Responsibility* (1968); James Turner Johnson, *Ideology, Reason, and the Limitation of War* (1975); and *Just War Tradition and the Restraint of War: A Moral and Historical Inquiry* (1981); Michael Walzer, *Just and Unjust Wars* (1977); William V. O'Brien, *The Conduct of Just and Limited War* (1981) and, earlier, *War and/or Survival* (1969).

2. See Robert J. Beck and Anthony Clark Arend, "Don't Tread on Us: International Law and Forcible State Responses to Terrorism." *Wisconsin International Law Journal* 12 (1994): 153–219, for an examination of recent forcible responses to terrorism.

3. This is a point made by William V. O'Brien in *Law and Morality in Israel's War with the PLO* (1991), 275.

4. St. Thomas Aquinas, *Summa Theologies, Secunda Secundae.* 15 Q. 40 (Art. 1) cited in O'Brien, *The Conduct of Just and Limited War*, 17.

5. Ibid.

6. See National Conference of Catholic Bishops (NCCB), *The Challenge of Peace: God's Promise and Our Response* (1983), 28–29.

7. O'Brien, *The Conduct of Just and Limited War*, 18–19.

8. U.N. Charter, Arts. 39–51.

9. War Powers Resolution, sec. 2(c).

10. Beck and Arend, "Don't Tread on Us," 175–76.

11. NCCB, *The Challenge of Peace*, 27.

12. Ibid.

13. Ibid.

14. St. Augustine, Book LXLLIII, *Super Josue*, gu. X; cited in O'Brien, *The Conduct of Just and Limited War*, 20.

15. James A. Childress, "Just-War Criteria," in Thomas A. Shannon, ed., *War or Peace: The Search for New Answers*, 46; cited in O'Brien, *The Conduct of Just and Limited War*, 20.

16. U.N. Charter, Art. 51.

17. See, for example, Richard B. Lillich, ed., *Humanitarian Intervention and the United Nations* (1973); Natalino Ronzitti, *Rescuing Nationals Abroad Through Military Coercion and Intervention on the Grounds of Humanity* (1985); Fernando Teson, *Humanitarian Intervention* (1988).

18. NCCB, *The Challenge of Peace*, 28.

19. Ibid., 29.

20. Ibid.

21. As Professor O'Brien observes, "right intention insists that charity and love exist even among enemies." O'Brien, *The Conduct of Just and Limited War*, 34.

22. Augustine, *Contra Faustum* (LXXIV); cited in O'Brien, *The Conduct of Just and Limited War*, 33–34.

23. See John Foster Dulles, *War, Peace and Change* (1939), for a fascinating discussion of this dilemma.

24. See O'Brien, *The Conduct of Just and Limited War*, 34–35.

25. NCCB, *The Challenge of Peace*, 30.

26. O'Brien, *Law and Morality in Israel's War with the PLO*, 280.

27. NCCB, *The Challenge of Peace*, 30.

28. Ibid.

29. Ibid, 31.

30. See Anthony Clark Arend and Robert J. Beck, *International Law and the Use of Force* (London: Routledge, 1993).

31. NCCB, *The Challenge of Peace*, 31.

32. O'Brien, *Law and Morality in Israel's War with the PLO*, 281.

33. Ibid.

34. See Beck and Arend, "Don't Tread on Us," 206–9, for a discussion of different legal interpretations of proportionality.

35. Oscar Schachter, "The Extra-Territorial Use of Force Against Terrorist Bases," *Houston Journal of International Law* 11:215, 315 (emphasis added).

36. Beck and Arend, "Don't Tread on Us," 207.

37. Ibid.

38. William V. O'Brien, "Reprisal, Deterrence and Self-Defense in Counterterror Operations," *Virginia Journal of International Law*, 30: 462, 477.

39. Ibid., 472.

40. O'Brien, *The Conduct of Just and Limited War*, 42.

41. Ibid.

42. See NCCB, *The Challenge of Peace*, 31–34.

43. This draws upon recommendations that Robert Beck and I presented in "Don't Tread on Us," 216–19.

44. See Beck and Arend, *International Law and the Use of Force*, 71–79, for a discussion of anticipatory self-defense under international law.

45. These recommendations also draw upon Beck and Arend, "Don't Tread on Us," 218–19.

Part IX
Defining, Understanding, and Confronting Terrorism

We then present a number of articles on terrorism that focus on: 1) defining terrorism; 2) asking why terrorism occurs—what motivates terrorist groups; and 3) asks how can the US fight terrorism.

In the UIR, Hoffman's article on *Defining Terrorism* addresses some of the challenges in identifying what and who terrorist are. The first two articles in this book by Jason Burke and Timothy Thomas describe *al Queda* and its use of technology, especially the internet, in "cyber-planning" its operations.

The next three articles look at *why* terrorism occurs. Audrey Cronin argues that globalization is both a cause and facilitator of global terrorism. Mark Juergensmeyer examines the religious roots of some terror groups. And Matthew Morgan looks at cultural, political & organizational, and technological factors that can lead to terrorism

Our last three articles discuss how the United States can fight a non-state, transnational actor such as *al Queda*. Russell Howard argues that, based on the threat to the survival of the lives of United States citizens, "pre-emptive" military doctrine is essential. Base don in-depth analysis of *al Queda's* motivations, capabilities and limitations, Brian Jenkins offers a very clear policy/political aim regarding *al Queda* by using a multi-pronged strategy—using many more elements of national force than just the military. The last article by Robert Tomes is focused on our soon to be commissioned cadets that could find themselves fighting insurgents in Afghanistan and Iraq shortly after graduation.

Think Again: Al Qaeda

Jason Burke

The mere mention of al Qaeda conjures images of an efficient terrorist network guided by a powerful criminal mastermind. Yet al Qaeda is more lethal as an ideology than as an organization. "Al Qaedaism" will continue to attract supporters in the years to come—whether Osama bin Laden is around to lead them or not.

"AL QAEDA IS A GLOBAL TERRORIST ORGANIZATION"

No. It is less an organization than an ideology. The Arabic word *qaeda* can be translated as a "base of operation" or "foundation," or alternatively as a "precept" or "method." Islamic militants always understood the term in the latter sense. In 1987, Abdullah Azzam, the leading ideologue for modern Sunni Muslim radical activists, called for al-qaeda al-sulbah (a vanguard of the strong). He envisaged men who, acting independently, would set an example for the rest of the Islamic world and thus galvanize the *umma* (global community of believers) against its oppressors. It was the FBI—during its investigation of the 1998 U.S. Embassy bombings in East Africa—which dubbed the loosely linked group of activists that Osama bin Laden and his aides had formed as "al Qaeda." This decision was partly due to institutional conservatism and partly because the FBI had to apply conventional antiterrorism laws to an adversary that was in no sense a traditional terrorist or criminal organization.

Although bin Laden and his partners were able to create a structure in Afghanistan that attracted new recruits and forged links among preexisting Islamic militant groups, they never created a coherent terrorist network in the way commonly conceived. Instead, al Qaeda functioned like a venture capital firm—providing funding, contacts, and expert advice to many different militant groups and individuals from all over the Islamic world.

Today, the structure that was built in Afghanistan has been destroyed, and bin Laden and his associates have scattered or been arrested or killed. There is no longer a central hub for Islamic militancy. But the al Qaeda worldview, or "al Qaedaism," is growing stronger every day. This radical internationalist ideology—sustained by anti-Western, anti-Zionist, and anti-Semitic rhetoric—has adherents among many individuals and groups, few of whom are currently linked in any substantial way to bin Laden or those around him. They merely follow his precepts, models, and methods. They act

May/June 2004

Jason Burke is chief reporter for Britain's Observer and author of *Al-Qaeda: Casting a Shadow of Terror* (New York: I.B. Tauris, 2003)

in the style of al Qaeda, but they are only part of al Qaeda in the very loosest sense. That's why Israeli intelligence services now prefer the term "jihadi international" instead of "al Qaeda."

"CAPTURING OR KILLING BIN LADEN WILL DEAL A SEVERE BLOW TO AL QAEDA"

Wrong. Even for militants with identifiable ties to bin Laden, the death of the "sheik" will make little difference in their ability to recruit people. U.S. Secretary of Defense Donald Rumsfeld recently acknowledged as much when he questioned in an internal Pentagon memo whether it was possible to kill militants faster than radical clerics and religious schools could create them. In practical terms, bin Laden now has only a very limited ability to commission acts of terror, and his involvement is restricted to the broad strategic direction of largely autonomous cells and groups. Most intelligence analysts now consider him largely peripheral.

This turn of events should surprise no one. Islamic militancy predates bin Laden's activities. He was barely involved in the Islamic violence of the early 1990s in Algeria, Egypt, Bosnia, and Kashmir. His links to the 1993 World Trade Center attack were tangential. There were no al Qaeda training camps during the early 1990s, although camps run by other groups churned out thousands of highly trained fanatics. Even when bin Laden was based in Afghanistan in the late 1990s, it was often Islamic groups and individuals who sought him out for help in finding resources for preconceived attacks, not vice versa. These days, Islamic groups can go to other individuals, such as Jordanian activist Abu Musab al-Zarqawi, who set up his al Tauhid group in competition with bin Laden (rather than, as is frequently claimed, in alliance with him) to obtain funds, expertise, or other logistical assistance.

Bin Laden still plays a significant role in the movement as a propagandist who effectively exploits modern mass communications. It is likely that the United States will eventually apprehend bin Laden and that this demonstration of U.S. power will demoralize many militants. However, much depends on the manner in which he is captured or killed. If, like deposed Iraqi President Saddam Hussein, he surrenders without a fight, which is very unlikely, many followers will be deeply disillusioned. If he achieves martyrdom in a way that his cohorts can spin as heroic, he will be an inspiration for generations to come. Either way, bin Laden's removal from the scene will not stop Islamic militancy.

"THE MILITANTS SEEK TO DESTROY THE WEST SO THEY CAN IMPOSE A GLOBAL ISLAMIC STATE"

False. Islamic militants' main objective is not conquest, but to beat back what they perceive as an aggressive West that is supposedly trying to complete the project begun during the Crusades and colonial periods of denigrating, dividing, and humiliating Islam. The militants' secondary goal is the establishment of the caliphate, or single Islamic state, in the lands roughly corresponding to the furthest extent of the Islamic empire of the late first and early second centuries. Today, this state would encompass the Middle East, the Maghreb (North Africa bordering the Mediterranean), Andalusia in southern Spain, Central Asia, parts of the Balkans, and possibly some Islamic territories in the Far East. Precisely how this utopian caliphate would function is vague. The militants believe that if all Muslims act according to a literal interpretation of the Islamic holy texts, an almost mystical transformation to a just and perfect society will follow.

The radical Islamists seek to weaken the United States and the West because they are both impediments to this end. During the 1990s, militants in countries such as Egypt, Saudi Arabia, and

Algeria began turning their attention abroad as they grew frustrated by their failure to change the status quo at home. The militants felt that striking at the Arab regimes' Western sponsors (the "far enemy" as opposed to the "near enemy") would be the best means to improve local conditions. This strategy, which bin Laden and those around him aggressively advocate, remains contentious among Islamic radicals, especially in Egypt.

Yet, as the March 11, 2004, terrorist bombings in Madrid revealed, attacks on the "far enemy" can still be employed with great effect. By striking Spain just before its elections, the militants sent a message to Western governments that their presence in the Middle East would exact a heavy political and human toll.

"THE MILITANTS REJECT MODERN IDEAS IN FAVOR OF TRADITIONAL MUSLIM THEOLOGY"

No. Although Islamic hard-liners long to return to an idealized seventh-century existence, they have little compunction about embracing the tools that modernity provides. Their purported medievalism has not deterred militants from effectively using the Internet and videocassettes to mobilize the faithful.

At the ideological level, prominent thinkers such as Sayyid Qutb and Abu Ala Maududi have borrowed heavily from the organizational tactics of secular leftist and anarchist revolutionaries. Their concept of the vanguard is influenced by Leninist theory. Qutb's most important work, Ma'alim fi'l-tariq (Milestones), reads in part like an Islamicized Communist Manifesto. A commonly used Arabic word in the names of militant groups is Hizb (as in Lebanon's Hizb Allah, or Hezbollah), which means "party"—another modern concept.

In fact, the militants often couch their grievances in Third-Worldist terms familiar to any contemporary antiglobalization activist. One recent document purporting to come from bin Laden berates the United States for failing to ratify the Kyoto agreement on climate change. Egyptian militant leader Ayman al-Zawahiri has decried multinational companies as a major evil. Mohammed Atta, one of the September 11 hijackers, once told a friend how angered he was by a world economic system that meant Egyptian farmers grew cash crops such as strawberries for the West while the country's own people could barely afford bread. In all these cases, the militants are framing modern political concerns, including social justice, within a mythic and religious narrative. They do not reject modernization per se, but they resent their failure to benefit from that modernization.

Also, within the context of Islamic observance, these new Sunni militants are not considered traditionalists, but radical reformers, because they reject the authority of the established clergy and demand the right to interpret doctrine themselves, despite a general lack of academic credentials on the part of leading figures such as bin Laden or Zawahiri.

"SINCE THE RISE OF AL QAEDA, ISLAMIC MODERATES HAVE BEEN MARGINALIZED"

Incorrect. Al Qaeda represents the lunatic fringe of political thought in the Islamic world. While al Qaedaism has made significant inroads in recent years, only a tiny minority of the world's 1.3 billion Muslims adhere to its doctrine. Many sympathize with bin Laden and take satisfaction at his ability to strike the United States, but that does not mean they genuinely want to live in a unified Islamic state governed along strict Koranic lines. Nor does anti-Western sentiment translate into a rejection of Western values. Surveys of public opinion in the Arab world, conducted by organizations such as

Zogby International and the Pew Research Center for the People and the Press, reveal strong support for elected government, personal liberty, educational opportunity, and economic choice.

Even those who believe "Islam is the solution" disagree over precisely what that solution might be and how it might be achieved. Radical militants such as bin Laden want to destroy the state and replace it with something based on a literal reading of the Koran. However, some political Islamists want to appropriate the structures of the state and, in varying degrees, Islamicize them, usually with a view toward promoting greater social justice and outflanking undemocratic and powerful regimes. An example of the latter would be the Pakistani Jamaat-e-Islami (JI) movement, currently led by veteran activist Qazi Hussein Ahmed. JI represents a significant swath of Pakistani popular opinion, and although it is tainted by appalling levels of anti-Semitism, it has taken a stance against bin Laden and the Taliban when politically feasible. Often, as in Iraq, Jordan, and Turkey, such groups are relatively moderate and can serve as useful interlocutors for the West. They should not be rejected out of hand as "Islamists"; refusing to engage them only allows the extremists to dominate the political discourse.

"THE ISRAELI-PALESTINIAN CONFLICT IS CENTRAL TO THE MILITANTS' CAUSE"

Wrong. Televised images of Israeli troops violently repressing Palestinian protesters in the occupied territories certainly reinforce the militants' key message that the lands of Islam are under attack and that all Muslims must rise up and fight. However, although a resolution to the Israeli-Palestinian conflict would help alleviate political tensions in the region, it would not end the threat of militant Islam.

The roots of contemporary Sunni Islamic militancy cannot be reduced to any single, albeit thorny, problem. Militants feel the *umma* is under attack. In their view, Israel is merely the West's most obvious outpost—as it was when it became a Crusader kingdom in the 12th century. If the Jewish state disappeared, the Islamists would still fight in Chechnya, Kashmir, Egypt, Uzbekistan, Indonesia, and Algeria. Their agenda is typically determined by local grievances, often with lengthy histories. For instance, although bin Laden was already calling for a boycott of U.S. goods to protest support for Israel in the late 1980s, he had never been involved in an attack on an Israeli target until recently. His primary focus has always been to topple the regime in his homeland of Saudi Arabia. Likewise, Zawahiri's lengthy 2002 book, Knights Under the Prophet's Banner—part autobiography, part militant manifesto, which first appeared in serial form in 2001—focuses almost exclusively on the author's native Egypt.

Moreover, considerable support for the Islamic cause stems from Muslims' sense of humiliation. A two-state solution to the Israeli-Palestinian conflict, which would still leave the "Zionist entity" intact, would therefore offer little succor to the wounded pride of any committed militant or, more crucial, to the pride of those in the wider community who support and legitimize extremism and violence.

"SORT OUT SAUDI ARABIA AND THE WHOLE PROBLEM WILL DISAPPEAR"

No. Saudi Arabia has contributed significantly to the spread of radicalism through the government-subsidized export of its Wahhabist strand of hard-line Islam. This policy arose from the turmoil of the late 1970s, when outrage over government corruption and the royal family's decadence prompted hundreds of Islamic radicals to occupy the Grand Mosque in Mecca. The 1978-79 Shiite revolution in Iran threatened Saudi leadership in the Muslim world and offered a cautionary tale of the fate that could await the House of Saud. In an effort to appeal to religious conservatives and counter the Iranian regime, the royal family gave the Wahhabi clerics more influence at home and a mandate to expand their ideology abroad.

Since then, Saudi money disbursed through quasi-governmental organizations such as the Muslim World League has built hundreds of mosques throughout the world. The Saudis provide hard-line clerics with stipends and offer financial incentives to those who forsake previous patterns of worship. In Pakistan, money from the Persian Gulf has funded the massive expansion of *madrasas* (Islamic schools) that indoctrinate young students with virulent, anti-Western dogma. This Saudi-funded proselytism has enormously damaged long-standing tolerant and pluralist traditions of Islamic observance in East and West Africa, the Far East, and Central Asia. Wahhabism was virtually unknown in northern Iraq until a massive push by Gulf-based missionaries in the early 1990s. And many of the mosques known for radical activity in Germany, the United Kingdom, and Canada were built with donations from private and state sources in Saudi Arabia.

The inequities of the Saudi system—in which most people are very poor and ruled by a super-rich clique—continues to create a sense of disenfranchisement that allows extremism to flourish. Many of the most militant preachers (and some of the Saudi hijackers who perpetrated the September 11 terrorist attacks) come from marginalized tribes and provinces. A more inclusive style of government and a more just redistribution of resources would undercut the legitimacy of local militants and deny radicals new recruits. Yet, while such reforms might slow the spread of Wahhabism and associated strands outside Saudi Arabia, in much of the world the damage has already been done. As with the Israeli-Palestinian conflict, Saudi Arabia is one of the many causes of modern Islamic militancy, but it has no monopoly on blame.

"IT IS ONLY A MATTER OF TIME BEFORE ISLAMIC MILITANTS USE WEAPONS OF MASS DESTRUCTION"

Calm down. Although Islamic militants (including bin Laden) have attempted to develop a basic chemical or biological arsenal, those efforts have been largely unsuccessful due to the technical difficulty of creating, let alone weaponizing, such materials. As one of the first journalists to enter the research facilities at the Darunta camp in eastern Afghanistan in 2001, I was struck by how crude they were. The Ansar al-Islam terrorist group's alleged chemical weapons factory in northern Iraq, which I inspected the day after its capture in 2003, was even more rudimentary. Alleged attempts by a British group to develop ricin poison, but for the apparent seriousness of the intent, could be dismissed as farcical.

Nor is there any compelling evidence that militants have come close to creating a "dirty bomb" (a conventional explosive packaged with radioactive material). The claim that Jose Padilla, an alleged al Qaeda operative arrested in the United States in 2002, had intended to deploy a dirty bomb has been largely discounted—it was an aspiration rather than a practical plan. Constructing a dirty bomb is more difficult than most imagine. Although the International Atomic Energy Agency warns that more than 100 countries have inadequate control of radioactive material, only a small percentage of that material is lethal enough to cause serious harm. It also requires considerable technical sophistication to build a device that can effectively disperse radioactive material. Some have also voiced the fear that militants might obtain a "prepackaged" working nuclear warhead from Pakistan. However, that would only be a plausible scenario if an Islamic regime came to power, or if high-ranking elements of the Pakistani military developed greater sympathy for the Islamists than currently exists.

The 1995 Aum Shinrikyo sarin gas attack in Japan highlights the difficulties terrorist groups face in deploying weapons of mass destruction. Despite possessing sophisticated research facilities funded by an estimated $1 billion in assets, the group failed nine times to launch a successful attack prior to the incident in the Tokyo subway system. (Even then, the fatalities were mercifully limited to a dozen people.) Confronted with such constraints, Islamic militants are far more likely to use conventional bombs or employ conventional devices in imaginative ways—as was the case with the September 11, 2001, attacks in the United States and the March 11, 2004, train bombings in Spain.

"THE WEST IS WINNING THE WAR ON TERROR"

Unfortunately, no. The military component of the war on terrorism has had some significant success. A high proportion of those who associated with bin Laden between 1996 and 2001 are now either dead or in prison. Bin Laden's own ability to commission and instigate terror attacks has been severely curtailed. Enhanced cooperation between intelligence organizations around the world and increased security budgets have made it much harder for terrorists to move their funds across borders or to successfully organize and execute attacks.

However, if countries are to win the war on terror, they must eradicate enemies without creating new ones. They also need to deny those militants with whom negotiation is impossible the support of local populations. Such support assists and, in the minds of the militants, morally legitimizes their actions. If Western countries are to succeed, they must marry the hard component of military force to the soft component of cultural appeal. There is nothing weak about this approach. As any senior military officer with experience in counterinsurgency warfare will tell you, it makes good sense. The invasion of Iraq, though entirely justifiable from a humanitarian perspective, has made this task more pressing.

Bin Laden is a propagandist, directing his efforts at attracting those Muslims who have hitherto shunned his extremist message. He knows that only through mass participation in his project will he have any chance of success. His worldview is receiving immeasurably more support around the globe than it was two years ago, let alone 15 years ago when he began serious campaigning. The objective of Western countries is to eliminate the threat of terror, or at least to manage it in a way that does not seriously impinge on the daily lives of its citizens. Bin Laden's aim is to radicalize and mobilize. He is closer to achieving his goals than the West is to deterring him.

Al Qaeda and the Internet:
The Danger of "Cyberplanning"

Timothy L. Thomas

We can say with some certainty, al Qaeda loves the Internet. When the latter first appeared, it was hailed as an integrator of cultures and a medium for businesses, consumers, and governments to communicate with one another. It appeared to offer unparalleled opportunities for the creation of a "global village." Today the Internet still offers that promise, but it also has proven in some respects to be a digital menace. Its use by al Qaeda is only one example. It also has provided a virtual battlefield for peacetime hostilities between Taiwan and China, Israel and Palestine, Pakistan and India, and China and the United States (during both the war over Kosovo and in the aftermath of the collision between the Navy EP-3 aircraft and Chinese MiG). In times of actual conflict, the Internet was used as a virtual battleground between NATO's coalition forces and elements of the Serbian population. These real tensions from a virtual interface involved not only nation-states but also non-state individuals and groups either aligned with one side or the other, or acting independently.

Evidence strongly suggests that terrorists used the Internet to plan their operations for 9/11. Computers seized in Afghanistan reportedly revealed that al Qaeda was collecting intelligence on targets and sending encrypted messages via the Internet. As recently as 16 September 2002, al Qaeda cells operating in America reportedly were using Internet-based phone services to communicate with cells overseas. These incidents indicate that the Internet is being used as a "cyberplanning" tool for terrorists. It provides terrorists with anonymity, command and control resources, and a host of other measures to coordinate and integrate attack options.

Cyberplanning may be a more important terrorist Internet tool than the much touted and feared cyberterrorism option—attacks against information and systems resulting in violence against noncombatant targets. The Naval Postgraduate School (NPS) has defined cyberterrorism as the unlawful destruction or disruption of digital property to intimidate or coerce people.[1] Cyberplanning, not defined by NPS or any other source, refers to the digital coordination of an integrated plan stretching across geographical boundaries that may or may not result in bloodshed. It can include cyberterrorism as part of the overall plan. Since 9/11, US sources have monitored several websites linked to al Qaeda that appear to contain elements of cyberplanning:

- alneda.com, which US officials said contained encrypted information to direct al Qaeda members to more secure sites, featured international news on al Qaeda, and published articles, fatwas (decisions on applying Muslim law), and books.

Lieutenant Colonel Timothy L. Thomas, USA Ret., is an analyst at the Foreign Military Studies Office, Fort Leavenworth, Kansas. He has written extensively on information operations, combat in cities, and peacekeeping operations, among other issues, including four previous articles for *Parameters*. During his military career he served in the 82d Airborne Division and was the Department Head of Soviet Military-Political Affairs at the US Army's Russian Institute in Garmisch, Germany.

- assam.com, believed to be linked to al Qaeda (originally hosted by the Scranton company BurstNET Technologies, Inc.), served as a mouthpiece for jihad in Afghanistan, Chechnya, and Palestine.
- almuhrajiroun.com, an al Qaeda site which urged sympathizers to assassinate Pakistani President Musharraf.
- qassam.net, reportedly linked to Hamas.
- jihadunspun.net, which offered a 36-minute video of Osama bin Laden.[2]
- 7hj.7hj.com, which aimed to teach visitors how to conduct computer attacks.[3]
- aloswa.org, which featured quotes from bin Laden tapes, religious legal rulings that "justified" the terrorist attacks, and support for the al Qaeda cause.[4]
- drasat.com, run by the Islamic Studies and Research Center (which some allege is a fake center), and reported to be the most credible of dozens of Islamist sites posting al Qaeda news.
- jehad.net, alsaha.com, and islammemo.com, alleged to have posted al Qaeda statements on their websites.
- mwhoob.net and aljehad.online, alleged to have flashed political religious songs, with pictures of persecuted Muslims, to denounce US policy and Arab leaders, notably Saudi.[5]

While it is prudent to tally the Internet cyberplanning applications that support terrorists, it must be underscored that few if any of these measures are really anything new. Any hacker or legitimate web user can employ many of these same measures for their own purposes, for business, or even for advertising endeavors. The difference, of course, is that most of the people on the net, even if they have the capabilities, do not harbor the intent to do harm as does a terrorist or al Qaeda member.

Highlighting several of the more important applications may help attract attention to terrorist methodologies and enable law enforcement agencies to recognize where and what to look for on the net. Sixteen measures are listed below for consideration. More could be added.

• *The Internet can be used to put together profiles.* Internet user demographics allow terrorists to target users with sympathy toward a cause or issue, and to solicit donations if the right "profile" is found. Usually a front group will perform the fundraising for the terrorist, often unwittingly. E-mail fundraising has the potential to significantly assist a terrorist's publicity objectives and finances simultaneously.[6]

Word searches of online newspapers and journals allow a terrorist to construct a profile of the means designed to counter his actions, or a profile of admitted vulnerabilities in our systems. For example, recent articles reported on attempts to slip contraband items through security checkpoints. One report noted that at Cincinnati's airport, contraband slipped through over 50 percent of the time. A simple Internet search by a terrorist would uncover this shortcoming, and offer the terrorist an embarkation point to consider for his or her next operation. A 16 September report noted that US law enforcement agencies were tracing calls made overseas to al Qaeda cells from phone cards, cell phones, phone booths, or Internet-based phone services. Exposing the targeting techniques of law enforcement agencies allows the terrorist to alter his or her operating procedures. The use of profiles by terrorists to uncover such material greatly assists their command and control of operations. The implication is that in a free society such as the United States, you can publish too much information, and while the information might not be sensitive to us, it might be very useful to a terrorist.

• *Internet access can be controlled or its use directed according to the server configuration, thus creating a true ideological weapon.* In the past, if some report was offensive to a government, the content of the report could be censored or filtered. Governments cannot control the Internet to the same degree they could control newspapers and TV. In fact, the Internet can serve as a terrorist's TV or radio station, or his international newspaper or journal. The web allows an uncensored and unfiltered version of events to be broadcast worldwide. Chat rooms, websites, and bulletin boards are largely uncontrolled, with few filters in place. This climate is perfect for an underfunded group to explain its actions or to offset both internal and international condemnation, especially when using specific servers. The Internet can target fence-sitters as well as true believers with different messages, oriented to the target audience.

In the aftermath of the 9/11 attacks, al Qaeda operatives used the Internet to fight for the hearts and minds of the Islamic faithful worldwide. Several internationally recognized and respected Muslims who questioned the attacks were described as hypocrites by al Qaeda. Al Qaeda ran two websites, alneda.com and drasat.com, to discuss the legality of the attacks on 9/11. Al Qaeda stated that Islam shares no fundamental values with the West and that Muslims are committed to spread Islam by the sword. As a result of such commentary, several Muslim critics of al Qaeda's policies withdrew their prior condemnation.[7] Ideological warfare worked.

• *The Internet can be used anonymously, or as a shell game to hide identities.* Terrorists have access to Internet tools to create anonymity or disguise their identities. Online encryption services offer encryption keys for some services that are very difficult to break. The website spammimic.com offers tools that hide text in "spam," unsolicited bulk commercial e-mail. Speech compression technology allows users to convert a computer into a secure phone device. Network accounts can be deleted or changed as required. For example, Internet users can create Internet accounts with national firms such as America Online (AOL), or can even create an AOL Instant Messenger (AIM) account on a short-term basis. In addition, anonymous logins are possible for many of the thousands of chat rooms on the net. If desired, the user can access cyber cafes, university and library computers, or additional external resources to further hide the source of the messages.[8] An al Qaeda laptop found in Afghanistan had linked with the French Anonymous Society on several occasions. The site offers a two-volume Sabotage Handbook online.

Not only are anonymous methods available for the people who use the Internet, but at times Internet service providers (ISPs) unwittingly participate in serving people or groups for purposes other than legitimate ones. The al Qaeda web site www.alneda.com was originally located in Malaysia until 13 May. It reappeared in Texas at http://66.34.191.223/ until 13 June, and then reappeared on 21 June at www.drasat.com in Michigan. It was shut down on 25 June 2002. The ISPs hosting it apparently knew nothing about the content of the site or even the fact that it was housed on their servers.[9] This shell game with their website enabled the al Qaeda web to remain functional in spite of repeated efforts to shut it down. Cyber deception campaigns will remain a problem for law enforcement personnel for years to come.

• *The Internet produces an atmosphere of virtual fear or virtual life.* People are afraid of things that are invisible and things they don't understand. The virtual threat of computer attacks appears to be one of those things. Cyberfear is generated by the fact that what a computer attack *could* do (bring down airliners, ruin critical infrastructure, destroy the stock market, reveal Pentagon planning secrets, etc.) is too often associated with what *will* happen. News reports would lead one to believe that hundreds or thousands of people are still active in the al Qaeda network on a daily basis just because al Qaeda says so. It is clear that the Internet empowers small groups and makes them appear much more capable than they might actually be, even turning bluster into a type of virtual fear. The net allows terrorists to amplify the consequences of their activities with follow-on messages and threats directly to the population at large, even though the terrorist group may be totally impotent. In effect, the Internet allows a person or group to appear to be larger or more important or threatening than they really are.

The Internet can be used to spread disinformation, frightening personal messages, or horrific images of recent activities (one is reminded of the use of the net to replay the murder of reporter Daniel Pearl by his Pakistani captors). Virtually, it appears as though attacks are well planned and controlled, and capabilities are genuine. Messages are usually one-sided, however, and reflect a particular political slant. There is often little chance to check the story and find out if it is mere bravado or fact. The Internet can thus spread rumors and false reports that many people, until further examination, regard as facts.

Recently, the Arab TV station al-Jazeera has played tape recordings of bin Laden's speeches and displayed a note purportedly signed by him praising attacks on an oil tanker near Yemen, and on US soldiers participating in a war game in Kuwait. These messages were picked up and spread around the Internet, offering virtual proof that bin Laden was alive. Most likely bin Laden was seriously injured (which is why we haven't seen him in over a year), but his image can be manipulated through radio or Internet broadcasts so that he appears confident, even healthy.

• *The Internet can help a poorly funded group to raise money.* Al Qaeda has used Islamic humanitarian "charities" to raise money for jihad against the perceived enemies of Islam. Analysts found al Qaeda and humanitarian relief agencies using the same bank account numbers on numerous occasions. As a result, several US-based Islamic charities were shut down.[10] The Sunni extremist group Hizb al-Tahrir uses an integrated web of Internet sites from Europe to Africa to call for the return of an Islamic caliphate. The website states that it desires to do so by peaceful means. Supporters are encouraged to assist the effort by monetary support, scholarly verdicts, and encouraging others to support jihad. Bank information, including account numbers, is provided on a German site, www.explizit-islam.de.[11] Portals specializing in the anonymous transfer of money, or portals providing services popular with terrorists (such as the issue of new identities and official passports) are also available.[12]

The fighters in the Russian breakaway republic of Chechnya have used the Internet to publicize banks and bank account numbers to which sympathizers can contribute. One of these Chechen bank accounts is located in Sacramento, California, according to a Chechen website known as amina.com.

Of course, there are other ways to obtain money for a cause via the Internet. One of the most common ways is credit card fraud. Jean-Francois Ricard, one of France's top anti-terrorism investigators, noted that many Islamist terror plots in Europe and North America were financed through such criminal activity.[13]

• *The Internet is an outstanding command and control mechanism.* Command and control, from a US military point of view, involves the exercise of authority and direction by a properly designated commander over assigned and attached forces in the accomplishment of the mission. Personnel, equipment, communications, facilities, and procedures accomplish command and control by assisting in planning, directing, coordinating, and controlling forces and operations in the accomplishment of a mission.

Command and control on the Internet is not hindered by geographical distance, or by lack of sophisticated communications equipment. Antigovernment groups present at the G8 conference in Cologne used the Internet to attack computers of financial centers and to coordinate protests from locations as distant as Indonesia and Canada. Terrorists can use their front organizations to coordinate such attacks, to flood a key institution's e-mail service (sometimes as a diversionary tactic for another attack), or to send hidden messages that coordinate and plan future operations.

The average citizen, the antigovernment protester, and the terrorist now have access to command and control means, limited though they may be, to coordinate and plan attacks. Further, there are "cracking" tools available to detect security flaws in systems and try to exploit them. Attaining access to a site allows the hacker or planner to command and control assets (forces or electrons) that are not his. The Internet's potential for command and control can vastly improve an organization's effectiveness if it does not have a dedicated command and control establishment, especially in the propaganda and internal coordination areas. Finally, command and control can be accomplished via the Internet's chat rooms. One website, alneda.com, has supported al Qaeda's effort to disperse its forces and enable them to operate independently, providing leadership via strategic guidance, theological arguments, and moral inspiration. The site also published a list of the names and home phone numbers of 84 al Qaeda fighters captured in Pakistan after escaping from Afghanistan. The aim presumably was to allow sympathizers to contact their families and let them know they were alive.[14]

• *The Internet is a recruiting tool.* The web allows the user complete control over content, and eliminates the need to rely on journalists for publicity. Individuals with sympathy for a cause can be converted by the images and messages of terrorist organizations, and the addition of digital video has reinforced this ability. Images and video clips are tools of empowerment for terrorists. More important, net access to such products provides contact points for men and women to enroll in the cause, whatever it may be.[15] Additionally,

> Current versions of web browsers, including Netscape and Internet Explorer, support JavaScript functions allowing Internet servers to know which language is set as the default for a particular client's computer. Hence, a browser set to use English as the default language can be redirected to a site optimized for publicity aimed at Western audiences, while one set to use Arabic as the default can be redirected to a different site tailored toward Arab or Muslim sensibilities.[16]

This allows recruiting to be audience- and language-specific, enabling the web to serve as a recruiter of talent for a terrorist cause. Recently, the Chechen website qoqaz.net, which used to be aimed strictly against Russian forces operating in Chechnya, changed its address to assam.com, and now includes links to Jihad in Afghanistan, Jihad in Palestine, and Jihad in Chechnya. Such sites give the impression that the entire Islamic world is uniting against the West, when in fact the site may be the work of just a few individuals.

• *The Internet is used to gather information on potential targets.* The website operated by the Muslim Hackers Club reportedly featured links to US sites that purport to disclose sensitive information like code names and radio frequencies used by the US Secret Service. The same website offers tutorials in viruses, hacking stratagems, network "phreaking" and secret codes, as well as links to other militant Islamic and cyberprankster web addresses.[17] Recent targets that terrorists have discussed include the Centers for Disease Control and Prevention in Atlanta; FedWire, the money-movement clearing system maintained by the Federal Reserve Board; and facilities controlling the flow of information over the Internet.[18] Attacks on critical infrastructure control systems would be particularly harmful, especially on a system such as the Supervisory Control and Data Acquisition (SCADA) system. Thus any information on insecure network architectures or non-enforceable security protocols is potentially very damaging.

Terrorists have access, like many Americans, to imaging data on potential targets, as well as maps, diagrams, and other crucial data on important facilities or networks. Imaging data can also allow terrorists to view counterterrorist activities at a target site. One captured al Qaeda computer contained engineering and structural architecture features of a dam, enabling al Qaeda engineers and planners to simulate catastrophic failures.[19]

With regard to gathering information through the Internet, on 15 January 2003 Defense Secretary Donald Rumsfeld observed that an al Qaeda training manual recovered in Afghanistan said, "Using public sources openly and without resorting to illegal means, it is possible to gather at least 80 percent of all information required about the enemy."[20]

• *The Internet puts distance between those planning the attack and their targets.* Terrorists planning attacks on the United States can do so abroad with limited risk, especially if their command and control sites are located in countries other than their own. Tracing the route of their activity is particularly difficult. The net provides terrorists a place to plan without the risks normally associated with cell or satellite phones.

• *The Internet can be used to steal information or manipulate data.* Ronald Dick, Director of the FBI's National Infrastructure Protection Center, considers the theft or manipulation of data by terrorist groups as his worst nightmare, especially if the attacks are integrated with a physical attack such as on a US power grid.[21] Richard Clark, Chairman of the President's Critical Infrastructure Protection Board, said the problem of cybersecurity and data protection had its own 9/11 on 18 September 2001 when the Nimda virus spread through Internet-connected computers around the world, causing billions of dollars of damage. Nimda's creator has never been identified. This virus, hardly noticed in the wake of the airliner attacks and anthrax scares, set off a chain reaction among software companies (including Microsoft) to get very serious about plugging vulnerabilities.[22] In the fall of 2001 a number of unexplained intrusions began occurring against Silicon Valley computers. An FBI investigation traced the intrusions to telecommunication switches in Saudi Arabia, Indonesia, and Pakistan. While none was directly linked to al Qaeda, there remain strong suspicions that the group was somehow involved.[23]

• *The Internet can be used to send hidden messages.* The practice of steganography, which involves hiding messages inside graphic files, is a widespread art among criminal and terrorist elements. Hidden pages or nonsensical phrases can be coded instructions for al Qaeda operatives and supporters. One recent report noted,

> Al Qaeda uses prearranged phrases and symbols to direct its agents. An icon of an AK-47 can appear next to a photo of Osama bin Laden facing one direction one day, and another direction the next. The color of icons can change as well. Messages can be hidden on pages inside sites with no links to them, or placed openly in chat rooms.[24]

In addition, it is possible to buy encryption software for less than $15. Cyberplanners gain an advantage in hiding their messages via encryption. Sometimes the messages are not even hidden in a sophisticated manner. Al-Jazeera television reported that Mohammed Atta's final message (another advantage of the Internet—the impossibility of checking sources) to direct the attacks on the Twin Towers was simple and open. The message purportedly said, "The semester begins in three more weeks. We've obtained 19 confirmations for studies in the faculty of law, the faculty of urban planning, the faculty of fine arts, and the faculty of engineering."[25] The reference to the various faculties was apparently the code for the buildings targeted in the attacks.

• *The Internet allows groups with few resources to offset even some huge propaganda machines in advanced countries.* The web is an attractive device to those looking for a way to attack major powers via the mass media. The "always on" status of the web allows these individuals not only to access sites day and night but also to scold major powers and treat them with disdain in a public forum. The web can be used to counter facts and logic with the logic of the terrorist. There is no need for the terrorist organization to worry about "the truth," because ignoring facts is a standard operating procedure.

Al Qaeda uses polemics on the net not only to offset Western reporting, but also to counter Muslims who don't toe the party line. It defends the conduct of its war against the West and encourages violence. The web is important to al Qaeda because it can be used to enrage people and neutralize moderate opinion. The website of the Center for Islamic Studies and Research (according to one source, a made-up name), for example, has 11 sections, including reports on fighting in Afghanistan, world media coverage of the conflict, books on jihad theology, videos of hijackers' testaments, information about prisoners held in Pakistan and Guantanamo Bay, and jihad poetry.[26]

It does not pay for any major power to lie, as facts can be easily used against them. Even in the war in Chechnya, there were times when the Chechens would report a successful ambush of a Russian convoy, and the Russians would deny the event ever happened. To prove their point, the Chechens would show video footage of the ambush on the Internet, thus offsetting the credibility of the Russian official media and undercutting the power of their massive propaganda machine. Al Qaeda officials are waiting to do the same to Western media reporting if the opportunity presents itself.

• *The Internet can be used to disrupt business.* This tactic requires precise timing and intimate knowledge of the business climate in the target country. It attempts to harm businesses by accusing them of guilt by association.

Hizbullah, for example, has outlined a strategy to cripple Israeli government, military, and business sites with the aim of disrupting normal economic and societal operations. Phase one might be to disable official Israeli government sites; phase two might focus on crashing financial sites such as those on the Israeli stock exchange; phase three might involve knocking out the main Israeli internet servers; and phase four might blitz Israeli e-commerce sites to ensure the loss of hundreds of transactions.[27] A final phase could be to accuse companies that do business with a target government as guilty by association and call for a boycott of the firm's products. Arab terrorists attacked Lucent Technologies in a round of Israeli-Arab cyber skirmishes, for example.[28] All of these plans require insider knowledge in order to carry out the operation in a timely and accurate manner.

• *The Internet can mobilize a group or diaspora, or other hackers to action.* Websites are not only used to disseminate information and propaganda. They also are used to create solidarity and brotherhood among groups. In the case of Islamist terrorist organizations, the Internet substitutes for the loss of bases and territory. In this respect the most important sites are alneda.com, jehad.net, drasat.com, and aloswa.org, which feature quotes from bin Laden tapes, religious legal rulings that justify the terrorist attacks, and support for the al Qaeda cause.[29] In addition, website operators have established a site that is "a kind of database or encyclopedia for the dissemination of computer viruses."[30] The site is 7hj.7hj.com, and it aims to teach Internet users how to conduct computer attacks, purportedly in the service of Islam.[31]

• *The Internet takes advantage of legal norms.* Non-state actors or terrorists using the Internet can ignore Western notions of law and focus instead on cultural or religious norms. At a minimum, they ignore legal protocols on the Internet. In addition, they use the net to break the law (when they hack websites or send out viruses) while at the same time the law protects them (from unlawful surveillance, etc.).

International investigations into such behavior are difficult to conclude due to the slow pace of other nations' investigative mechanisms, and the limited time that data is stored.[32] However, in the aftermath of the events of 9/11 in the United States, the terrorists' actions actually initiated several changes in the US legal system that were not to the terrorists' advantage. For example, in the past, the privacy concerns of Internet users were a paramount consideration by the US government. After 9/11, new legislation was enacted.

The controversial USA Patriot Act of 2001 included new field guidance relating to computer crime and electronic evidence. The Patriot Act is designed to unite and strengthen the United States by providing the appropriate tools required to intercept and obstruct terrorism. It establishes a counterterrorism fund in the Treasury Department, amends federal criminal code that authorizes enhanced surveillance procedures, provides guidelines for investigating money-laundering concerns, removes obstacles to investigating terrorism (granting the FBI authority to investigate fraud and computer-related activity for specific cases), and strengthens criminal laws against terrorism.[33]

The "Field Guidance on New Authorities that Relate to Computer Crime and Electronic Evidence Enacted in the USA Patriot Act of 2001" provides the authority to do several things. Authorizations include: intercepting voice communications in computer hacking investigations; allowing law enforcement to trace communications on the Internet and other computer networks within the pen register and trap and trace statute ("pen/trap" statute); intercepting communications of computer trespassers; writing nationwide search warrants for e-mail; and deterring and preventing cyberterrorism. The latter provision raises the maximum penalty for hackers that damage protected computers (and eliminates minimums); states that hackers need only show intent to cause damage, not a particular consequence or degree of damage; provides for the aggregation of damage caused by a hacker's entire course of conduct; creates a new offense for damaging computers used for national security and criminal justice; expands the definition of a "protected computer" to include computers in foreign countries; counts prior state convictions of computer crime as prior offenses; and defines computer "loss." In addition, the guidance develops and supports cyber-security forensic capabilities.[34]

• *The Internet can be used to divert attention from a real attack scenario.* Al Qaeda can plant threats on the Internet or via cell phones to mislead law enforcement officials. Terrorists study how the United States collects and analyzes information, and thus how we respond to information.

Terrorists know when their Internet "chatter" or use of telecommunications increases, US officials issue warnings. Terrorists can thus introduce false information into a net via routine means, measure the response it garners from the US intelligence community, and then try to figure out where the leaks are in their systems or what type of technology the United States is using to uncover their plans. For example, if terrorists use encrypted messages over cell phones to discuss a fake operation against, say, the Golden Gate Bridge, they can then sit back and watch to see if law enforcement agencies issue warnings regarding that particular landmark. If they do, then the terrorists know their communications are being listened to by US officials.[35]

*   *   *

In conclusion, it should be reiterated that cyberplanning is as important a concept as cyberterrorism, and perhaps even more so. Terrorists won't have an easy time shutting down the Internet. Vulnerabilities are continuously reported and fixed while computers function without serious interference (at least in the United States). One hopes that law enforcement and government officials will focus more efforts on the cyberplanning capabilities of terrorists in order to thwart computer attacks and other terrorist activities. At a minimum, America can use such measures to make terrorist activities much harder to coordinate and control. Paul Eedle, writing in *The Guardian*, summed up the value of the Internet to al Qaeda:

> Whether bin Ladin or al Qaeda's Egyptian theorist Ayman al-Zawahiri and their colleagues are on a mountain in the Hindu Kush or living with their beards shaved off in a suburb of Karachi no longer matters to the organization. They can inspire and guide a worldwide movement without physically meeting their followers— without knowing who they are.[36]

Such is the power and the danger of cyberplanning.

NOTES

1. Patricia Daukantas, "Government Computer News via Infowar.com," 14 December 2001, http://www.infowar.com.

2. Jack Kelley, "Militants WireWeb with Links to Jihad," *USA Today*, 10 July 2002, from *CNO/IO Newsletter*, 8-14 July 2002.

3. Ibid.

4. Yossi Melman, "Virtual Soldiers in a Holy War," *Ha'aretz*, http://www.haaretz.com, 17 September 2002.

5. Habib Trabelsi, "Al-Qaeda Wages Cyber War against US," *Middle East Times*, Dubai, 27 June 2002, rpt. in CNO/IO Newsletter, 1-7 July 2002.

6. Patrick S. Tibbetts, "Terrorist Use of the Internet and Related Information Technologies," unpublished paper, School of Advanced Military Studies, Fort Leavenworth, Kansas, June 2002, p. 20.

7. Paul Eedle, "Al-Qaeda Takes Fight for 'Hearts and Minds' to the Web," *Jane's Intelligence Review*, August 2002, rpt. in CNO/IO Newsletter, 5-11 August 2002.

8. Tibbetts, pp 7, 9.

9. Eedle, "Al-Qaeda Takes Fight."

10. Colin Soloway, Rod Nordland, and Barbie Nadeau, "Hiding (and Seeking) Messages on the Web," *Newsweek*, 17 June 2002, p. 8.

11. "Sunni Extremist Group Hizb al-Tahrir Promotes Ideology on the Internet," FBIS, http://199.221.15.211, 5 February 2002.

12. C. E. Manin, "Terrorism and Information Communication Technology," *La Tribune*, College Interarmees de Defense, April 2002, p. 112.

13. Michael Elliot, "Reeling Them In," *Time*, 23 September 2002, p. 33.

14. Paul Eedle, "Terrorism.com," *The Guardian*, 17 July 2002, downloaded from the FBIS website on 17 July 2002.

15. Tibbetts, p. 37.

16. Ibid., p. 34.

17. Mark Hosenball, "Islamic Cyberterror," *Newsweek*, 20 May 2002

18. Tom Squitieri, "Cyberspace Full of Terror Targets," *USA Today*, 5 June 2002.

19. Barton Gellman, "FBI Fears Al-Qaeda Cyber Attacks," *San Francisco Chronicle*, 28 June 2002, pp. 1, 10.

20. "Citing Al Qaeda Manual, Rumsfeld Re-Emphasizes Web Security," *InsideDefense.com*, http://www.insidedefense.com/, 15 January 2003.

21. Gellman, pp. 1, 10.

22. John Schwartz, "Despite 9/11 Warnings, Cyberspace Still at Risk," *The Post Standard* (Syracuse, N.Y.), 11 September 2002, pp. D-10, 11.

23. Maria T. Welch, "Accumulating Digital Evidence is Difficult," *The Post Standard*, 11 September 2002, pp. D-9, 11.

24. Ibid.; also Soloway, Nordland, and Nadeau.

25. Melman.

26. Eedle, "Terrorism.com."

27. Giles Trendle, "Cyberwars: The Coming Arab E-Jihad," *The Middle East*, No. 322 (April 2002), p. 6.

28. Tim McDonald, "Fanatics with Laptops: The Coming Cyber War," *NewsFactor.com* via *Yahoo! News*, 16 May 2002.

29. Melman.

30. Ibid.

31. Ibid.

32. Manin, p. 112.

33. See "Bill Summary & Status for the 107th Congress," http://thomas.loc.gov/cgi-bin/bdquery/z?d107:HR03162:@@@L&summ2=m&.

34. See "Field Guidance on New Authorities that Relate to Computer Crime and Electronic Evidence Enacted in the USA Patriot Act of 2001," http://www.cybercrime.gov/PatriotAct.htm.

35. John Diamond, "Al-Qaeda Steers Clear of NSA's Ears," *USA Today*, 17 October 2002, *CNO/IO Newsletter*, 23-30 October 2002, pp. 17-18.

36. Eedle, "Terrorism.com."

Behind the Curve:
Globalization and International Terrorism

Audrey Kurth Cronin

The coincidence between the evolving changes of globalization, the inherent weaknesses of the Arab region, and the inadequate American response to both ensures that terrorism will continue to be the most serious threat to U.S. and Western interests in the twenty-first century. There has been little creative thinking, however, about how to confront the growing terrorist backlash that has been unleashed. Terrorism is a complicated, eclectic phenomenon, requiring a sophisticated strategy oriented toward influencing its means and ends over the long term. Few members of the U.S. policymaking and academic communities, however, have the political capital, intellectual background, or inclination to work together to forge an effective, sustained response. Instead, the tendency has been to fall back on established bureaucratic mind-sets and prevailing theoretical paradigms that have little relevance for the changes in international security that became obvious after the terrorist attacks in New York and Washington on September 11, 2001.

The current wave of international terrorism, characterized by unpredictable and unprecedented threats from nonstate actors, not only is a reaction to globalization but is facilitated by it; the U.S. response to this reality has been reactive and anachronistic. The combined focus of the United States on state-centric threats and its attempt to cast twenty-first-century terrorism into familiar strategic terms avoids and often undermines effective responses to this nonstate phenomenon. The increasing threat of globalized terrorism must be met with flexible, multifaceted responses that deliberately and effectively exploit avenues of globalization in return; this, however, is not happening.

As the primary terrorist target, the United Sates should take the lead in fashioning a forward-looking strategy. As the world's predominant military, economic, and political power, it has been able to pursue its interests throughout the globe with unprecedented freedom since the breakup of the Soviet Union more than a decade ago. Even in the wake of the September 11 terrorist attacks on the World Trade Center and the Pentagon, and especially after the U.S. military action in Afghanistan, the threat of terrorism, mostly consisting of underfunded and ad hoc cells motivated by radical fringe

Audrey Kurth Cronin is specialist in international terrorism at the Congressional Research Service at the Library of Congress. The article was written when she was visiting associate professor at the Edmund A. Walsh School of Foreign Service and a research fellow at the Center for Peace and Security Studies, Georgetown University.

I am grateful for helpful comments and criticisms on previous drafts from Robert Art, Patrick Cronin, Timothy Hoyt, James Ludes, and an anonymous reviewer. I have been greatly influenced by conversations and other communications with Martha Crenshaw, to whom I owe a huge debt. None of these people necessarily agrees with everything here. Also beneficial was a research grant from the School of Foreign Service at Georgetown University. My thanks to research assistants Christopher Connell, William Josiger, and Sara Skahill and to the members of my graduate courses on political violence and terrorism. Portions of this article will be published as "Transnational Terrorism and Security: The Terrorist Threat to Globalization," in Michael E. Brown, ed., *Grave New World: Global Dangers in the Twenty-First Century* (Washington, D.C.: Georgetown University Press, forthcoming).

ideas, has seemed unimportant by comparison. U.S. strategic culture has a long tradition of downplaying such atypical concerns in favor of a focus on more conventional state-based military power.[1] On the whole, this has been an effective approach: As was dramatically demonstrated in Afghanistan, the U.S. military knows how to destroy state governments and their armed forces, and the American political leadership and public have a natural bias toward using power to achieve the quickest results. Sometimes it is important to show resolve and respond forcefully.

The United States has been far less impressive, however, in its use of more subtle tools of domestic and international statecraft, such as intelligence, law enforcement, economic sanctions, educational training, financial controls, public diplomacy, coalition building, international law, and foreign aid. In an ironic twist, it is these tools that have become central to the security of the United States and its allies since September 11. In an era of globalized terrorism, the familiar state-centric threats have not disappeared; instead they have been joined by new (or newly threatening) competing political, ideological, economic, and cultural concerns that are only superficially understood, particularly in the West. An examination of the recent evolution of terrorism and a projection of future developments suggest that, in the age of globalized terrorism, old attitudes are not just anachronistic; they are dangerous.

Terrorism as a phenomenon is not new, but for reasons explained below, the threat it now poses is greater than ever before. The current terrorist backlash is manifested in the extremely violent asymmetrical response directed at the United States and other leading powers by terrorist groups associated with or inspired by al-Qaeda. This backlash has the potential to fundamentally threaten the international system. Thus it is not just an American problem. Unless the United States and its allies formulate a more comprehensive response to terrorism, better balanced across the range of policy instruments, the results will be increasing international instability and long-term failure.

The article proceeds in five main sections. First, it provides a discussion of the definition, history, causes, and types of terrorism, placing the events of September 11, 2001, in their modern context. Second, it briefly describes key trends in modern terrorism, explaining how the phenomenon appears to be evolving. Third, it analyzes the implications of these trends for the stability and security of the international community generally, and the United States and its allies more specifically. Fourth, the article outlines the prospects of these trends. It concludes with a range of policy recommendations suggested by the analysis.

DEFINITION, ORIGINS, MOTIVATIONS, AND TYPES OF MODERN TERRORISM

The terrorist phenomenon has a long and varied history, punctuated by lively debates over the meaning of the term. By ignoring this history, the United States runs the risk of repeating the plethora of mistakes made by other major powers that faced similar threats in the past. This section begins with an explanation of the definition of terrorism, then proceeds to an examination of terrorism's origins, major motivations, and predominant types.

Definition of Terrorism

Terrorism is notoriously difficult to define, in part because the term has evolved and in part because it is associated with an activity that is designed to be subjective. Generally speaking, the targets of a terrorist episode are not the victims who are killed or maimed in the attack, but rather the governments, publics, or constituents among whom the terrorists hope to engender a reaction—such as fear, repulsion, intimidation, overreaction, or radicalization. Specialists in the area of terrorism studies have devoted hundreds of pages toward trying to develop an unassailable definition of the term, only to realize the fruitlessness of their efforts: Terrorism is intended to be a matter of perception and is thus seen differently by different observers.[2]

Although individuals can disagree over whether particular actions constitute terrorism, there are certain aspects of the concept that are fundamental. First, terrorism always has a political nature. It involves the commission of outrageous acts designed to precipitate political change.[3] At its root, terrorism is about justice, or at least someone's perception of it, whether man-made or divine. Second, although many other uses of violence are inherently political, including conventional war among states, terrorism is distinguished by its nonstate character—even when terrorists receive military, political, economic, and other means of support from state sources. States obviously employ force for political ends: When state force is used internationally, it is considered an act of war; when it is used domestically, it is called various things, including law enforcement, state terror, oppression, or civil war. Although states can terrorize, they cannot by definition be terrorists. Third, terrorism deliberately targets the innocent, which also distinguishes it from state uses of force that inadvertently kill innocent bystanders. In any given example, the latter may or may not be seen as justified; but again, this use of force is different from terrorism. Hence the fact that precision-guided missiles sometimes go astray and kill innocent civilians is a tragic use of force, but it is not terrorism. Finally, state use of force is subject to international norms and conventions that may be invoked or at least consulted; terrorists do not abide by international laws or norms and, to maximize the psychological effect of an attack, their activities have a deliberately unpredictable quality.[4]

Thus, at a minimum, terrorism has the following characteristics: a fundamentally political nature, the surprise use of violence against seemingly random targets, and the targeting of the innocent by nonstate actors.[5] All of these attributes are illustrated by recent examples of terrorism—from the April 2000 kidnapping of tourists by the Abu Sayyaf group of the Philippines to the various incidents allegedly committed by al-Qaeda, including the 1998 bombings of the U.S. embassies in Kenya and Tanzania and the September 11 attacks. For the purposes of this discussion, the shorthand (and admittedly imperfect) definition of terrorism is the threat or use of seemingly random violence against innocents for political ends by a nonstate actor.

Origins of Terrorism

Terrorism is as old as human history. One of the first reliably documented instances of terrorism, however, occurred in the first century B.C.E. The Zealots-Sicarri, Jewish terrorists dedicated to inciting a revolt against Roman rule in Judea, murdered their victims with daggers in broad daylight in the heart of Jerusalem, eventually creating such anxiety among the population that they generated a mass insurrection.[6] Other early terrorists include the Hindu Thugs and the Muslim Assassins. Modern terrorism, however, is generally considered to have originated with the French Revolution.[7]

The term "terror" was first employed in 1795, when it was coined to refer to a policy systemically used to protect the fledgling French republic government against counterrevolutionaries. Robespierre's practice of using revolutionary tribunals as a means of publicizing a prisoner's fate for broader effect within the population (apart from questions of legal guilt or innocence) can be seen as a nascent example of the much more highly developed, blatant manipulation of media attention by terrorist groups in the mid- to late twentieth century.[8] Modern terrorism is a dynamic concept, from the outset dependent to some degree on the political and historical context within which it has been employed.

Decolonization and Antiglobalization: Drivers of Terrorism?

Although individual terrorist groups have unique characteristics and arise in specific local contexts, an examination of broad historical patterns reveals that the international system within which such groups are spawned does influence their nature and motivations. A distinguishing feature of modern terrorism has been the connection between sweeping political or ideological concepts and increasing levels of terrorist activity internationally. The broad political aim has been against (1) empires, (2) colonial powers, and (3) the U.S.-led international system marked by globalization. Thus it is important to understand the general history of modern terrorism and where the current threat fits within an international context.

David Rapoport has described modern terrorism such as that perpetuated by al-Qaeda as part of a religiously inspired "fourth wave." This wave follows three earlier historical phases in which terrorism was tied to the breakup of empires, decolonization, and leftist anti-Westernism.[9] Rapoport argues that terrorism occurs in consecutive if somewhat overlapping waves. The argument here, however, is that modern terrorism has been a power struggle along a continuum: central power versus local power, big power versus small power, modern power versus traditional power. The key variable is a widespread perception of opportunity, combined with a shift in a particular political or ideological paradigm. Thus, even though the newest international terrorist threat, emanating largely from Muslim countries, has more than a modicum of religious inspiration, it is more accurate to see it as part of a larger phenomenon of antiglobalization and tension between the have and have-not nations, as well as between the elite and underprivileged within those nations. In an era where reforms occur at a pace much slower than is desired, terrorists today, like those before them, aim to exploit the frustrations of the common people (especially in the Arab world).

In the nineteenth century, the unleashing of concepts such as universal suffrage and popular empowerment raised the hopes of people throughout the western world, indirectly resulting in the first phase of modern terrorism. Originating in Russia, as Rapoport argues, it was stimulated not by state repression but by the efforts of the czars to placate demands for economic and political reforms, and the inevitable disappointment of popular expectations that were raised as a result. The goal of terrorists was to engage in attacks on symbolic targets to get the attention of the common people and thus provoke a popular response that would ultimately overturn the prevailing political order. This type of modern terrorism was reflected in the activities of groups such as the Russian Narodnaya Volya (People's Will) and later in the development of a series of movements in the United States and Europe, especially in territories of the former Ottoman Empire.

The dissolution of empires and the search for a new distribution of political power provided an opportunity for terrorism in the nineteenth and twentieth centuries. It climaxed in the assassination of Archduke Franz Ferdinand on June 28, 1914, an event that catalyzed the major powers into taking violent action, not because of the significance of the man himself but because of the suspicion of rival state involvement in the sponsorship of the killing. World War I, the convulsive systemic cataclysm that resulted, ended the first era of modern terrorism, according to Rapoport.[10] But terrorism tied to popular movements seeking greater democratic representation and political power from coercive empires has not ceased. Consider, for example, the Balkans after the downfall of the former state of Yugoslavia. The struggle for power among various Balkan ethnic groups can be seen as the final devolution of power from the former Ottoman Empire. This postimperial scramble is also in evidence elsewhere— for example, in Aceh, Chechnya, and Xinjiang, to mention just a few of the trouble spots within vast (former) empires. The presentation of a target of opportunity, such as a liberalizing state or regime, frequently evokes outrageous terrorist acts.

According to Rapoport, a second, related phase of modern terrorism associated with the concept of national self-determination developed its greatest predominance after World War I. It also continues to the present day. These struggles for power are another facet of terrorism against larger political powers and are specifically designed to win political independence or autonomy. The mid–twentieth-century era of rapid decolonization spawned national movements in territories as diverse as Algeria, Israel, South Africa, and Vietnam.[11] An important by-product was ambivalence toward the phenomenon in the international community, with haggling over the definition of terrorism reaching a fever pitch in the United Nations by the 1970s.

The question of political motivation became important in determining international attitudes toward terrorist attacks, as the post–World War II backlash against the colonial powers and the attractiveness of national independence movements led to the creation of a plethora of new states often born from violence. Arguments over the justice of international causes and the designation of terrorist struggles as "wars of national liberation" predominated, with consequentialist philosophies excusing the killing of innocent people if the cause in the long run was "just." Rapoport sees the U.S. intervention in Vietnam, and especially the subsequent American defeat by the Vietcong, as having catalyzed a "third wave" of modern terrorism; however, the relationship between the Vietnam conflict and other decolonization movements might just as easily be considered part of the same phase. In any case, the victory of the Vietcong excited the imaginations of revolutionaries throughout the world and, according to Rapoport, helped lead to a resurgence in terrorist violence. The Soviet Union underwrote the nationalist and leftist terrorist agendas of some groups, depicting the United States as the new colonial power—an easy task following the Vietnam intervention—and furthering an ideological agenda oriented toward achieving a postcapitalist, international communist utopia. Other groups, especially in Western Europe, rejected both the Soviet and capitalist models and looked admiringly toward nationalist revolutionaries in the developing world.[12] Leftist groups no longer predominate, but the enduring search for national self-determination continues, not only in the areas mentioned above but also in other hot spots such as the Basque region, East Timor, Sri Lanka, and Sudan.

Terrorism achieved a firmly international character during the 1970s and 1980s,[13] evolving in part as a result of technological advances and partly in reaction to the dramatic explosion of international media influence. International links were not new, but their centrality was. Individual, scattered national causes began to develop into international organizations with links and activities increasingly across borders and among differing causes. This development was greatly facilitated by the covert sponsorship of states such as Iran, Libya, and North Korea, and of course the Soviet Union, which found the underwriting of terrorist organizations an attractive tool for accomplishing clandestine goals while avoiding potential retaliation for the terrorist attacks.

The 1970s and 1980s represented the height of state-sponsored terrorism. Sometimes the lowest common denominator among the groups was the concept against which they were reacting—for example, "Western imperialism"—rather than the specific goals they sought. The most important innovation, however, was the increasing commonality of international connections among the groups. After the 1972 Munich Olympics massacre of eleven Israeli athletes, for example, the Palestinian Liberation Organization (PLO) and its associated groups captured the imaginations of young radicals around the world. In Lebanon and elsewhere, the PLO also provided training in the preferred techniques of twentieth-century terrorism such as airline hijacking, hostage taking, and bombing.

Since the September 11 attacks, the world has witnessed the maturation of a new phase of terrorist activity, the jihad era, spawned by the Iranian Revolution of 1979 as well as the Soviet defeat in Afghanistan shortly thereafter. The powerful attraction of religious and spiritual movements has overshadowed the nationalist or leftist revolutionary ethos of earlier terrorist phases (though many of those struggles continue), and it has become the central characteristic of a growing international trend. It is perhaps ironic that, as Rapoport observes, the forces of history seem to be driving international terrorism back to a much earlier time, with echoes of the behavior of "sacred" terrorists such as the Zealots-Sicarii clearly apparent in the terrorist activities of organizations such as al-Qaeda and its associated groups. Religious terrorism is not new; rather it is a continuation of an ongoing modern power struggle between those with power and those without it. Internationally, the main targets of these terrorists are the United States and the U.S.-led global system.

Like other eras of modern terrorism, this latest phase has deep roots. And given the historical patterns, it is likely to last at least a generation, if not longer. The jihad era is animated by widespread alienation combined with elements of religious identity and doctrine—a dangerous mix of forces that resonate deep in the human psyche.

What is different about this phase is the urgent requirement for solutions that deal both with the religious fanatics who are the terrorists and the far more politically motivated states, entities, and people who would support them because they feel powerless and left behind in a globalizing world. Thus if there is a trend in terrorism, it is the existence of a two-level challenge: the hyperreligious motivation of small groups of terrorists and the much broader enabling environment of bad governance, nonexistent social services, and poverty that punctuates much of the developing world. Al-Qaeda, a band driven by religious extremism, is able to do so much harm because of the secondary support and sanctuary it receives in vast areas that have not experienced the political and economic benefits of globalization. Therefore, the prescription for dealing with Osama bin Laden and his followers is not just eradicating a relatively small number of terrorists, but also changing the conditions that allow them to acquire so much power. Leaving aside for the moment the enabling environment, it is useful to focus on the chief motivations of the terrorists themselves, especially the contrasting secular and spiritual motivations of terrorism.

Leftist, Rightist, Ethnonationalist/Separatist, and "Sacred" Terrorism

There are four types of terrorist organizations currently operating around the world, categorized mainly by their source of motivation: left-wing terrorists, right-wing terrorists, ethnonationalist/separatist terrorists, and religious or "sacred" terrorists. All four types have enjoyed periods of relative prominence in the modern era, with left-wing terrorism intertwined with the Communist movement,[14] right-wing terrorism drawing its inspiration from Fascism,[15] and the bulk of ethnonationalist/separatist terrorism accompanying the wave of decolonization especially in the immediate post–World War II years. Currently, "sacred" terrorism is becoming more significant.[16] Although groups in all categories continue to exist today, left-wing and right-wing terrorist groups were more numerous in earlier decades. Of course, these categories are not perfect, as many groups have a mix of motivating ideologies—some ethnonationalist groups, for example, have religious characteristics or agendas[17]—but usually one ideology or motivation dominates.

Categories are useful not simply because classifying the groups gives scholars a more orderly field to study (admittedly an advantage), but also because different motivations have sometimes led to differing styles and modes of behavior. Understanding the type of terrorist group involved can provide insight into the likeliest manifestations of its violence and the most typical patterns of its development. At the risk of generalizing, left-wing terrorist organizations, driven by liberal or idealist political concepts, tend to prefer revolutionary, antiauthoritarian, antimaterialistic agendas. (Here it is useful to distinguish between the idealism of individual terrorists and the frequently contradictory motivations of their sponsors.) In line with these preferences, left-wing organizations often engage in brutal criminal-type behavior such as kidnapping, murder, bombing, and arson, often directed at elite targets that symbolize authority. They have difficulty, however, agreeing on their long-term objectives.[18] Most left-wing organizations in twentieth-century Western Europe, for example, were brutal but relatively ephemeral. Of course, right-wing terrorists can be ruthless, but in their most recent manifestations they have tended to be less cohesive and more impetuous in their violence than leftist terrorist groups. Their targets are often chosen according to race but also ethnicity, religion, or immigrant status, and in recent decades at least, have been more opportunistic than calculated.[19] This makes them potentially explosive but difficult to track.[20] Ethnonationalist/separatist terrorists are the most conventional, usually having a clear political or territorial aim that is rational and potentially negotiable, if not always justifiable in any given case. They can be astoundingly violent, over lengthy periods. At the same time, it can be difficult to distinguish between goals based on ethnic identity and those rooted in the control of a piece of land. With their focus on gains to be made in the traditional state-oriented international system, ethnonationalist/separatist terrorists often transition in and out of more traditional paramilitary structures, depending on how the cause is going. In addition, they typically have sources of support among the local populace of the same ethnicity with whom their separatist goals (or appeals to blood links) may resonate. That broader popular support is usually the key to the greater average longevity of ethnonationalist/ separatist groups in the modern era.[21]

All four types of terrorist organizations are capable of egregious acts of barbarism. But religious terrorists may be especially dangerous to international security for at least five reasons.

First, religious terrorists often feel engaged in a Manichaean struggle of good against evil, implying an open-ended set of human targets: Anyone who is not a member of their religion or religious sect may be "evil" and thus fair game. Although indiscriminate attacks are not unique to religious terrorists, the exclusivity of their faith may lead them to dehumanize their victims even more than most terrorist groups do, because they consider nonmembers to be infidels or apostates—as perhaps, for instance, al-Qaeda operatives may have viewed Muslims killed in the World Trade Center.

Second, religious terrorists engage in violent behavior directly or indirectly to please the perceived commands of a deity. This has a number of worrisome implications: The whims of the deity may be less than obvious to those who are not members of the religion, so the actions of violent religious organizations can be especially unpredictable. Moreover, religious terrorists may not be as constrained in their behavior by concerns about the reactions of their human constituents. (Their audience lies elsewhere.)

Third, religious terrorists consider themselves to be unconstrained by secular values or laws. Indeed the very target of the attacks may be the law-based secular society that is embodied in most modern states. The driving motivation, therefore, is to overturn the current post-Westphalian state system—a much more fundamental threat than is, say, ethnonationalist terrorism purporting to carve out a new secular state or autonomous territory.

Fourth, and related, religious terrorists often display a complete sense of alienation from the existing social system. They are not trying to correct the system, making it more just, more perfect, and more egalitarian. Rather they are trying to replace it. In some groups, apocalyptic images of destruction are seen as a necessity—even a purifying regimen—and this makes them uniquely dangerous, as was painfully learned on September 11.[22]

Fifth, religious terrorism is especially worrisome because of its dispersed popular support in civil society. On the one hand, for example, groups such as al-Qaeda are able to find support from some Muslim nongovernmental foundations throughout the world,[23] making it truly a global network. On the other hand, in the process of trying to distinguish between the relatively few providers of serious support from the majority of genuinely philanthropic groups, there is the real risk of igniting the very holy war that the terrorists may be seeking in the first instance.

In sum, there are both enduring and new aspects to modern terrorism. The enduring features center on the common political struggles that have characterized major acts of international terrorism. The newest and perhaps most alarming aspect is the increasingly religious nature of modern terrorist groups. Against this historical background, the unique elements in the patterns of terrorist activity surrounding September 11 appear starkly.

KEY TRENDS IN MODERN TERRORISM

By the late 1990s, four trends in modern terrorism were becoming apparent: an increase in the incidence of religiously motivated attacks, a decrease in the overall number of attacks, an increase in the lethality per attack, and the growing targeting of Americans.

Statistics show that, even before the September 11 attacks, religiously motivated terrorist organizations were becoming more common. The acceleration of this trend has been dramatic: According to the RAND–St. Andrews University Chronology of International Terrorism,[24] in 1968 none of the identified international terrorist organizations could be classified as "religious"; in 1980, in the aftermath of the Iranian Revolution, there were 2 (out of 64), and that number had expanded to 25 (out of 58) by 1995.[25]

Careful analysis of terrorism data compiled by the U.S. Department of State reveals other important trends regarding the frequency and lethality of terrorist attacks. The good news was that there were fewer such attacks in the 1990s than in the 1980s: Internationally, the number of terrorist attacks in the 1990s averaged 382 per year, whereas in the 1980s the number per year averaged 543.[26] But even before September 11, the absolute number of casualties of international terrorism had increased, from a low of 344 in 1991 to a high of 6,693 in 1998.[27] The jump in deaths and injuries can be partly explained by a few high-profile incidents, including the bombing of the U.S. embassies in Nairobi and Dar-es-Salaam in 1998;[28] but it is significant that more people became victims of terrorism as the decade proceeded. More worrisome, the number of people killed per incident rose significantly, from 102 killed in 565 incidents in 1991 to 741 killed in 274 incidents in 1998.[29] Thus, even though the number of terrorist attacks declined in the 1990s, the number of people killed in each one increased.

Another important trend relates to terrorist attacks involving U.S. targets. The number of such attacks increased in the 1990s, from a low of 66 in 1994 to a high of 200 in the year 2000.[30] This is a long-established problem: U.S. nationals consistently have been the most targeted since 1968.[31] But the percentage of international attacks against U.S. targets or U.S. citizens rose dramatically over the 1990s, from about 20 percent in 1993–95 to almost 50 percent in 2000.[32] This is perhaps a consequence of the increased role and profile of the United States in the world, but the degree of increase is nonetheless troubling.

The increasing lethality of terrorist attacks was already being noticed in the late 1990s, with many terrorism experts arguing that the tendency toward more casualties per incident had important implications. First it meant that, as had been feared, religious or "sacred" terrorism was apparently more dangerous than the types of terrorism that had predominated earlier in the twentieth century. The world was facing the resurgence of a far more malignant type of terrorism, whose lethality was borne out in the larger death toll from incidents that increasingly involved a religious motivation.[33] Second, with an apparent premium now apparently placed on causing more casualties per incident, the incentives for terrorist organizations to use chemical, biological, nuclear, or radiological (CBNR) weapons would multiply. The breakup of the Soviet Union and the resulting increased availability of Soviet chemical, biological, and nuclear weapons caused experts to argue that terrorist groups, seeking more dramatic and deadly results, would be more drawn to these weapons.[34] The 1995 sarin gas attack by the Japanese cult Aum Shinrikyo in the Tokyo subway system seemed to confirm that worry. More recently, an examination of evidence taken from Afghanistan and Pakistan reveals al-Qaeda's interest in chemical, biological, and nuclear weapons.[35]

In addition to the evolving motivation and character of terrorist attacks, there has been a notable dispersal in the geography of terrorist acts—a trend that is likely to continue. Although the Middle East continues to be the locus of most terrorist activity, Central and South Asia, the Balkans, and the Transcaucasus have been growing in significance over the past decade. International connections themselves are not new: International terrorist organizations inspired by common revolutionary principles date to the early nineteenth century; clandestine state use of foreign terrorist organizations occurred as early as the 1920s (e.g., the Mussolini government in Italy aided the Croat Ustasha); and complex mazes of funding, arms, and other state support for international terrorist organizations were in place especially in the 1970s and 1980s.[36] During the Cold War, terrorism was seen as a form of surrogate warfare and seemed almost palatable to some, at least compared to the potential prospect of major war or nuclear cataclysm.[37] What has changed is the self-generating nature of international terrorism, with its diverse economic means of support allowing terrorists to carry out attacks sometimes far from the organization's base. As a result, there is an important and growing distinction between where a terrorist organization is spawned and where an attack is launched, making the attacks difficult to trace to their source.

Reflecting all of these trends, al-Qaeda and its associated groups[38] (and individuals) are harbingers of a new type of terrorist organization. Even if al-Qaeda ceases to exist (which is unlikely), the dramatic attacks of September 2001, and their political and economic effects, will continue to inspire similarly motivated groups—particularly if the United States and its allies fail to develop broad-based, effective counterterrorist policies over the long term. Moreover, there is significant evidence that the global links and activities that al-Qaeda and its associated groups perpetuated are not short term or anomalous. Indeed they are changing the nature of the terrorist threat as we move further into the twenty-first century. The resulting intersection between the United States, globalization, and international terrorism will define the major challenges to international security.

THE UNITED STATES, GLOBALIZATION, AND INTERNATIONAL TERRORISM

Whether deliberately intending to or not, the United States is projecting uncoordinated economic, social, and political power even more sweepingly than it is in military terms. Globalization,[39] in forms including Westernization, secularization, democratization, consumerism, and the growth of market capitalism, represents an onslaught to less privileged people in conservative cultures repelled by the fundamental changes that these forces are bringing—or angered by the distortions and uneven distributions of benefits that result.[40] This is especially true of the Arab world. Yet the current U.S. approach to this growing repulsion is colored by a kind of cultural naïveté, an unwillingness to recognize —let alone appreciate or take responsibility for—the influence of U.S. power except in its military dimension. Even doing nothing in the economic, social, and political policy realms is still doing something, because the United States is blamed by disadvantaged and alienated populations for the powerful Western-led forces of globalization that are proceeding apace, despite the absence of a focused, coordinated U.S. policy. And those penetrating mechanisms of globalization, such as the internet, the media, and the increasing flows of goods and peoples, are exploited in return. Both the means and ends of terrorism are being reformulated in the current environment.

The Means

Important changes in terrorist methods are apparent in the use of new technologies, the movement of terrorist groups across international boundaries, and changes in sources of support. Like globalization itself, these phenomena are all intertwined and overlapping but, for ease of argument, they are dealt with consecutively here.

First, the use of information technologies such as the internet, mobile phones, and instant messaging has extended the global reach of many terrorist groups. Increased access to these technologies has so far not resulted in their widely feared use in a major cyberterrorist attack: In Dorothy Denning's words, terrorists "still prefer bombs to bytes."[41] Activists and terrorist groups have increasingly turned to "hacktivism"—attacks on internet sites, including web defacements, hijackings of websites, web sit-ins, denial-of-service attacks, and automated email "bombings"—attacks that may not kill anyone but do attract media attention, provide a means of operating anonymously, and are easy to coordinate internationally.[42] So far, however, these types of attacks are more an expense and a nuisance than an existential threat.

Instead the tools of the global information age have led to enhanced efficiency in many terrorist-related activities, including administrative tasks, coordination of operations, recruitment of potential members, communication among adherents, and attraction of sympathizers.[43] Before the September 11 attacks, for example, members of al-Qaeda communicated through Yahoo email;

Mohammed Atta, the presumed leader of the attacks, made his reservations online; and cell members went online to do research on subjects such as the chemical-dispersing powers of crop dusters. Although not as dramatic as shutting down a power grid or taking over an air traffic control system, this practical use of technology has significantly contributed to the effectiveness of terrorist groups and the expansion of their range.[44] Consider, for example, the lethal impact of the synchronized attacks on the U.S. embassies in 1998 and on New York andWashington in 2001, neither of which would have been possible without the revolution in information technology. When he was arrested in 1995, Ramzi Yousef, mastermind of the 1993 World Trade Center attack, was planning the simultaneous destruction of eleven airliners.[45]

The internet has become an important tool for perpetuating terrorist groups, both openly and clandestinely. Many of them employ elaborate list serves, collect money from witting or unwitting donors, and distribute savvy political messages to a broad audience online.[46] Groups as diverse as Aum Shinrikyo, Israel's Kahane Chai, the Popular Front for the Liberation of Palestine, the Kurdistan Workers' Party, and Peru's Shining Path maintain user-friendly official or unofficial websites, and almost all are accessible in English.[47] Clandestine methods include passing encrypted messages, embedding invisible graphic codes using steganography,[48] employing the internet to send death threats, and hiring hackers to collect intelligence such as the names and addresses of law enforcement officers from online databases.[49] All of these measures help to expand and perpetuate trends in terrorism that have already been observed: For example, higher casualties are brought about by simultaneous attacks, a diffusion in terrorist locations is made possible by internet communications, and extremist religious ideologies are spread through websites and videotapes accessible throughout the world.

More ominous, globalization makes CBNR weapons increasingly available to terrorist groups.[50] Information needed to build these weapons has become ubiquitous, especially through the internet. Among the groups interested in acquiring CBNR (besides al-Qaeda) are the PLO, the Red Army Faction, Hezbollah, the Kurdistan Workers' Party, German neo-Nazis, and the Chechens.[51]

Second, globalization has enabled terrorist organizations to reach across international borders, in the same way (and often through the same channels) that commerce and business interests are linked. The dropping of barriers through the North American Free Trade Area and the European Union, for instance, has facilitated the smooth flow of many things, good and bad, among countries. This has allowed terrorist organizations as diverse as Hezbollah, al- Qaeda, and the Egyptian al-Gama'at al-Islamiyya to move about freely and establish cells around the world.[52] Movement across borders can obviously enable terrorists to carry out attacks and potentially evade capture, but it also complicates prosecution if they are apprehended, with a complex maze of extradition laws varying greatly from state to state. The increased permeability of the international system has also enhanced the ability of nonstate terrorist organizations to collect intelligence (not to mention evade it); states are not the only actors interested in collecting, disseminating, and/or acting on such information. In a sense, then, terrorism is in many ways becoming like any other international enterprise—an ominous development indeed.

Third, terrorist organizations are broadening their reach in gathering financial resources to fund their operations. This is not just an al-Qaeda phenomenon, although bin Laden's organization—especially its numerous business interests—figures prominently among the most innovative and wealthy pseudocorporations in the international terrorist network. The list of groups with global financing networks is long and includes most of the groups identified by the U.S. government as foreign terrorist organizations, notably Aum Shinrikyo, Hamas, Hezbollah, and the Tamil Tigers. Sources of financing include legal enterprises such as nonprofit organizations and charities (whose illicit activities may be a small or large proportion of overall finances, known or unknown to donors); legitimate companies that divert profits to illegal activities (such as bin Laden's large network of construction companies); and illegal enterprises such as drug smuggling and production (e.g., the Revolutionary Armed Forces of Colombia—FARC), bank robbery, fraud, extortion, and kidnapping (e.g., the Abu

Sayyaf group, Colombia's National Liberation Army, and FARC).[53] Websites are also important vehicles for raising funds. Although no comprehensive data are publicly available on how lucrative this avenue is, the proliferation of terrorist websites with links or addresses for contributions is at least circumstantial evidence of their usefulness.

The fluid movement of terrorists' financial resources demonstrates the growing informal connections that are countering the local fragmentation caused elsewhere by globalization. The transit of bars of gold and bundles of dollars across the border between Afghanistan and Pakistan as U.S. and allied forces were closing in on the Taliban's major strongholds is a perfect example. Collected by shopkeepers and small businessmen, the money was moved by operatives across the border to Karachi, where it was transferred in the millions of dollars through the informal *hawala* or *hundi* banking system to the United Arab Emirates.[54] There it was converted into gold bullion and scattered around the world before any government could intervene. In this way, al-Qaeda preserved and dispersed a proportion of its financial resources.[55] In addition to gold, money was transferred into other commodities—such as diamonds in Sierra Leone and the Democratic Republic of Congo, and tanzanite from Tanzania —all while hiding the assets and often making a profit,[56] and all without interference from the sovereign governments that at the time were at war with al-Qaeda and the Taliban.[57]

As this example illustrates, globalization does not necessarily require the use of high technology: It often takes the form of traditional practices used in innovative ways across increasingly permeable physical and commercial borders. Terrorist groups, whose assets comparatively represent only a small fraction of the amount of money that is moved by organized crime groups and are thus much more difficult to track, use everything from direct currency transport (by couriers) to reliance on traditional banks, Islamic banks, money changers (using accounts at legitimate institutions), and informal exchange (the *hawala* or *hundi* system).

This is by no means a comprehensive presentation of global interpenetration of terrorist means, and some of the connections described above have existed for some time and in other contexts. The broad strategic picture, however, is of an increasing ability of terrorist organizations to exploit the same avenues of communication, coordination, and cooperation as other international actors, including states, multinational corporations, nongovernmental organizations, and even individuals. It would be naïve to assume that what is good for international commerce and international communication is not also good for international terrorists[58]—who are increasingly becoming opportunistic entrepreneurs whose "product" (often quite consciously "sold") is violence against innocent targets for a political end.

The Ends

The objectives of international terrorism have also changed as a result of globalization. Foreign intrusions and growing awareness of shrinking global space have created incentives to use the ideal asymmetrical weapon, terrorism, for more ambitious purposes.

The political incentives to attack major targets such as the United States with powerful weapons have greatly increased. The perceived corruption of indigenous customs, religions, languages, economies, and so on, are blamed on an international system often unconsciously molded by American behavior. The accompanying distortions in local communities as a result of exposure to the global marketplace of goods and ideas are increasingly blamed on U.S.-sponsored modernization and those who support it. The advancement of technology, however, is not the driving force behind the terrorist threat to the United States and its allies, despite what some have assumed.[59] Instead, at the heart of this threat are frustrated populations and international movements that are increasingly inclined to lash out against U.S.-led globalization.

As Christopher Coker observes, globalization is reducing tendencies toward instrumental violence (i.e., violence between states and even between communities), but it is enhancing incentives for expressive violence (or violence that is ritualistic, symbolic, and communicative).[60] The new international terrorism is increasingly engendered by a need to assert identity or meaning against forces of homogeneity, especially on the part of cultures that are threatened by, or left behind by, the secular future that Western-led globalization brings.

According to a report recently published by the United Nations Development Programme, the region of greatest deficit in measures of human development—the Arab world—is also the heart of the most threatening religiously inspired terrorism.[61] Much more work needs to be done on the significance of this correlation, but increasingly sources of political discontent are arising from disenfranchised areas in the Arab world that feel left behind by the promise of globalization and its assurances of broader freedom, prosperity, and access to knowledge. The results are dashed expectations, heightened resentment of the perceived U.S.-led hegemonic system, and a shift of focus away from more proximate targets within the region.

Of course, the motivations behind this threat should not be oversimplified: Anti-American terrorism is spurred in part by a desire to change U.S. policy in the Middle East and Persian Gulf regions as well as by growing antipathy in the developing world vis-à-vis the forces of globalization. It is also crucial to distinguish between the motivations of leaders such as Osama bin Laden and their followers. The former seem to be more driven by calculated strategic decisions to shift the locus of attack away from repressive indigenous governments to the more attractive and media-rich target of the United States. The latter appear to be more driven by religious concepts cleverly distorted to arouse anger and passion in societies full of pent-up frustration. To some degree, terrorism is directed against the United States because of its engagement and policies in various regions.[62] Anti-Americanism is closely related to antiglobalization, because (intentionally or not) the primary driver of the powerful forces resulting in globalization is the United States.

Analyzing terrorism as something separate from globalization is misleading and potentially dangerous. Indeed globalization and terrorism are intricately intertwined forces characterizing international security in the twenty-first century. The main question is whether terrorism will succeed in disrupting the promise of improved livelihoods for millions of people on Earth. Globalization is not an inevitable, linear development, and it can be disrupted by such unconventional means as international terrorism. Conversely, modern international terrorism is especially dangerous because of the power that it potentially derives from globalization—whether through access to CBNR weapons, global media outreach, or a diverse network of financial and information resources.

PROSPECTS FOR THE FUTURE

Long after the focus on Osama bin Laden has receded and U.S. troops have quit their mission in Afghanistan, terrorism will be a serious threat to the world community and especially to the United States. The relative preponderance of U.S. military power virtually guarantees an impulse to respond asymmetrically. The lagging of the Arab region behind the rest of the world is impelling a violent redirection of antiglobalization and antimodernization forces toward available targets, particularly the United States, whose scope and policies are engendering rage. Al-Qaeda will eventually be replaced or redefined, but its successors' reach may continue to grow via the same globalized channels and to direct their attacks against U.S. and Western targets. The current trajectory is discouraging, because as things currently stand, the wellspring of terrorism's means and ends is likely to be renewed: Arab governments will probably not reform peacefully, and existing Western governments and their supporting academic and professional institutions are disinclined to understand or analyze in depth the sources, patterns, and history of terrorism.

Terrorism is a by-product of broader historical shifts in the international distribution of power in all of its forms—political, economic, military, ideological, and cultural. These are the same forms of power that characterize the forces of Western-led globalization. At times of dramatic international change, human beings (especially those not benefiting from the change—or not benefiting as much or as rapidly from the change) grasp for alternative means to control and understand their environments. If current trends continue, widening global disparities, coupled with burgeoning information and connectivity, are likely to accelerate—unless the terrorist backlash, which is increasingly taking its inspiration from misoneistic religious or pseudoreligious concepts, successfully counters these trends. Because of globalization, terrorists have access to more powerful technologies, more targets, more territory, more means of recruitment, and more exploitable sources of rage than ever before. The West's twentieth-century approach to terrorism is highly unlikely to mitigate any of these long-term trends.

From a Manichean perspective, the ad hoc and purportedly benign intentions of the preponderant, secular West do not seem benign at all to those ill served by globalization. To frustrated people in the Arab and Muslim world, adherence to radical religious philosophies and practices may seem a rational response to the perceived assault, especially when no feasible alternative for progress is offered by their own governments. This is not to suggest that terrorists should be excused because of environmental factors or conditions. Instead, Western governments must recognize that the tiny proportion of the population that ends up in terrorist cells cannot exist without the availability of broader sources of active or passive sympathy, resources, and support. Those avenues of sustenance are where the center of gravity for an effective response to the terrorist threat must reside. The response to transnational terrorism must deal with the question of whether the broader enabling environment will increase or decrease over time, and the answer will be strongly influenced by the policy choices that the United States and its allies make in the near future.

CONCLUSIONS AND POLICY PRESCRIPTIONS

The characteristics and causes of the current threat can only be analyzed within the context of the deadly collision occurring between U.S. power, globalization, and the evolution of international terrorism. The U.S. government is still thinking in outdated terms, little changed since the end of the Cold War. It continues to look at terrorism as a peripheral threat, with the focus remaining on states that in many cases are not the greatest threat. The means and the ends of terrorism are changing in fundamental, important ways; but the means and the ends of the strategy being crafted in response are not.

Terrorism that threatens international stability, and particularly U.S. global leadership, is centered on power-based political causes that are enduring: the weak against the strong, the disenfranchised against the establishment, and the revolutionary against the status quo. Oversimplified generalizations about poverty and terrorism, or any other single variable, are caricatures of a serious argument.[63] The rise in political and material expectations as a result of the information revolution is not necessarily helpful to stability, in the same way that rising expectations led terrorists to take up arms against the czar in Russia a century ago. Indeed the fact that so many people in so many nations are being left behind has given new ammunition to terrorist groups; produced more sympathy for those willing to take on the United States; and spurred Islamic radical movements to recruit, propagandize, and support terrorism throughout many parts of the Muslim world. The al-Qaeda network is an extremist religious terrorist organization, its Taliban puppet regime was filled with religious zealots, and its suicide recruits were convinced that they were waging a just holy war. But the driving forces of twenty-first-century terrorism are power and frustration, not the pursuit of religious principle. To dismiss the broad enabling environment would be to focus more on the symptoms than the causes of modern terrorism.

The prescriptions for countering and preventing terrorism should be twofold: First, the United States and other members of the international community concerned about this threat need to use a balanced assortment of instruments to address the immediate challenges of the terrorists themselves. Terrorism is a complex phenomenon; it must be met with short-term military action, informed by in-depth, long-term, sophisticated analysis. Thus far, the response has been virtually all the former and little of the latter. Second, the United States and its counterterrorist allies must employ a much broader array of longer-term policy tools to reshape the international environment, which enables terrorist networks to breed and become robust. The mechanisms of globalization need to be exploited to thwart the globalization of terrorism.

In the short term, the United States must continue to rely on capable military forces that can sustain punishing air strikes against terrorists and those who harbor them with an even greater capacity for special operations on the ground. This requires not only improved stealthy, long-range power projection capabilities but also agile, highly trained, and lethal ground forces, backed up with greater intelligence, including human intelligence supported by individuals with language skills and cultural training. The use of military force continues to be important as one means of responding to terrorist violence against the West, and there is no question that it effectively preempts and disrupts some international terrorist activity, especially in the short term.[64]

Over time, however, the more effective instruments of policy are likely to remain the nonmilitary ones. Indeed the United States needs to expand and deepen its nonmilitary instruments of power such as intelligence, public diplomacy, cooperation with allies, international legal instruments, and economic assistance and sanctions. George Kennan, in his 1947 description of containment, put forth the same fundamental argument, albeit against an extremely different enemy.[65] The strongest response that the United States can muster to a serious threat has to include political, economic, and military capabilities—in that order; yet, the U.S. government consistently structures its policies and devotes its resources in the reverse sequence.

The economic and political roots of terrorism are complex, increasingly worrisome, and demanding of as much breadth and subtlety in response as they display in their genesis. The United States must therefore be strategic in its response: An effective grand strategy against terrorism involves planning a global campaign with the most effective means available, not just the most measurable, obvious, or gratifying. It must also include plans for shaping the global environment after the so-called war on terrorism has ended—or after the current political momentum has subsided.

The United States, working with other major donor nations, needs to create an effective incentive structure that rewards "good performers"—those countries with good governance, inclusive education programs, and adequate social programs—and works around "bad performers" and intervenes to assist so-called failed states. Also for the longer term, the United States and its allies need to project a vision of sustainable development—of economic growth, equal access to basic social needs such as education and health, and good governance—for the developing world. This is particularly true in mostly Muslim countries whose populations are angry with the United States over a perceived double standard regarding its long-standing support for Israel at the expense of Palestinians, policies against the regime of Saddam Hussein at the expense of some Iraqi people, and a general abundance of American power, including the U.S. military presence throughout the Middle East. Whether these policies are right or wrong is irrelevant here; the point is that just as the definition of terrorism can be subjective and value laden, so too can the response to terrorism take into account perceptions of reality. In an attempt to craft an immediate military response, the U.S. government is failing to put into place an effective long-term grand strategy.

This is not just a problem for the U.S. government. The inability to develop a strategy with a deep-rooted, intellectually grounded understanding of the history, patterns, motivations, and types of terrorism is reflective of the paucity of understanding of the terrorist phenomenon in the academic community. Terrorism is considered too policy-oriented an area of research in political science,[66] and it operates in an uncomfortable intersection between disciplines unaccustomed to working together, including psychology, sociology, theology, economics, anthropology, history, law, political science, and international relations. In political science, terrorism does not fit neatly into either the realist or liberal paradigms, so it has been largely ignored.[67] There are a few outstanding, well-established senior scholars in the terrorism studies community— people such as Martha Crenshaw, David Rapoport, and Paul Wilkinson—but in the United States, most of the publicly available work is being done in policy-oriented research institutes or think tanks that are sometimes limited by the narrow interests and short time frames of the government contracts on which they depend. Some of that research is quite good,[68] but it is not widely known within the academy. The situation for graduate students who wish to study terrorism is worse: A principal interest in terrorism virtually guarantees exclusion from consideration for most academic positions. This would not necessarily be a problem if the bureaucracy were more flexible and creative than the academy is, but as we know from the analysis of the behavior of U.S. agencies shortly before September 11, it is not. In the United States, academe is no more strategic in its understanding of terrorism than is the U.S. government.

The globalization of terrorism is perhaps the leading threat to long-term stability in the twenty-first century. But the benefit of globalization is that the international response to terrorist networks has also begun to be increasingly global, with international cooperation on law enforcement, intelligence, and especially financial controls being areas of notable recent innovation.[69] If globalization is to continue—and there is nothing foreordained that it will—then the tools of globalization, including especially international norms, the rule of law, and international economic power, must be fully employed against the terrorist backlash. There must be a deliberate effort to move beyond the current episodic interest in this phenomenon: Superficial arguments and short attention spans will continue to result in event-driven policies and ultimately more attacks. Terrorism is an unprecedented, powerful nonstate threat to the international system that no single state, regardless of how powerful it may be in traditional terms, can defeat alone, especially in the absence of long-term, serious scholarship engaged in by its most creative minds.

NOTES

1. The issue of U.S. strategic culture and its importance in the response to international terrorism is explored in more depth in Audrey Kurth Cronin, "Rethinking Sovereignty: American Strategy in the Age of Terror," *Survival*, Vol. 44, No. 2 (Summer 2002), pp. 119–139.

2. On the difficulty of defining terrorism, see, for example, Omar Malik, *Enough of the Definition of Terrorism!* Royal Institute of International Affairs (London: RIIA, 2001); and Alex P. Schmid, *Political Terrorism: A Research Guide* (New Brunswick, N.J.: Transaction Books, 1984). Schmid spends more than 100 pages grappling with the question of a definition, only to conclude that none is universally accepted.

3. Saying that terrorism is a political act is not the same as arguing that the political ends toward which it is directed are necessarily negotiable. If violent acts do not have a political aim, then they are by definition criminal acts.

4. The diabolical nature of terrorism has given resonance to Robert Kaplan's view that the world is a "grim landscape" littered with "evildoers" and requiring Western leaders to adopt a "pagan ethos." But such conclusions deserve more scrutiny than space allows here. See Steven Mufson, "The Way Bush Sees the World," *Washington Post*, Outlook section, February 17, 2002, p. B1.

5. R.G. Frey and Christopher W. Morris, "Violence, Terrorism, and Justice," in Frey and Morris, eds., *Violence, Terrorism, and Justice* (Cambridge: Cambridge University Press, 1991), p. 3.

6. Walter Laqueur, *Terrorism* (London: Weidenfeld and Nicolson, 1977, reprinted in 1978), pp. 7– 8; and David C. Rapoport, "Fear and Trembling: Terrorism in Three Religious Traditions," *American Political Science Review*, Vol. 78, No. 3 (September 1984), pp. 658–677.

7. David C. Rapoport, "The Fourth Wave: September 11 in the History of Terrorism," *Current History*, December 2001, pp. 419–424; and David C. Rapoport, "Terrorism," *Encyclopedia of Violence, Peace, and Conflict* (New York: Academic Press, 1999).

8. Ironically, Robespierre's tactics during the Reign of Terror would not be included in this article's definition of terrorism, because it was state terror.

9. Rapoport, "The Fourth Wave."

10. Ibid., pp. 419–420.

11. Ibid., p. 420.

12. Adrian Gulke, *The Age of Terrorism and the International Political System* (London: I.B. Tauris, 1995), pp. 56–63.

13. This is not to imply that terrorism lacked international links before the 1970s. There were important international ties between anarchist groups of the late nineteenth century, for example. See David C. Rapoport, "The Four Waves of Modern Terrorism," in Audrey Kurth Cronin and James Ludes, eds., *The Campaign against International Terrorism* (Washington, D.C.: Georgetown University Press, forthcoming).

14. Groups such as the Second of June Movement, the Baader-Meinhof Gang, the Red Brigades, the Weathermen, and the Symbionese Liberation Army belong in this category.

15. Among right-wing groups would be other neo-Nazi organizations (in the United States and Europe) and some members of American militia movements such as the Christian Patriots and the Ku Klux Klan.

16. The list here would be extremely long, including groups as different as the Tamil Tigers of Sri Lanka, the Basque separatist party, the PLO, and the Irish Republican Army (IRA) and its various splinter groups.

17. Bruce Hoffman notes that secular terrorist groups that have a strong religious element include the Provisional IRA, Armenian factions, and perhaps the PLO; however, the political/separatist aspect is the predominant characteristic of these groups. Hoffman, "Terrorist Targeting: Tactics, Trends, and Potentialities," *Technology and Terrorism* (London: Frank Cass, 1993), p. 25.

18. An interesting example is France's Action Directe, which revised its raison d'être several times, often altering it to reflect domestic issues in France—anarchism and Maoism, dissatisfaction with NATO and the Americanization of Europe, and general anticapitalism. See Michael Dartnell, "France's Action Directe: Terrorists in Search of a Revolution," *Terrorism and Political Violence*, Vol. 2, No. 4 (Winter 1990), pp. 457–488.

19. For example, in the 1990s Germany and several other European countries experienced a rash of random arson attacks against guest houses and offices that provided services to immigrants, many of whom were Middle Eastern in origin. Other examples include the violence associated with groups such as Europe's "football hooligans." A possible American example of the opportunistic nature of right-wing terrorism may be the anthrax letter campaign conducted in October 2001. See Susan Schmidt, "Anthrax Letter Suspect Profiled: FBI Says Author Likely Is Male Loner; Ties to Bin Laden Are Doubted," *Washington Post*, November 11, 2001, p. A1; and Steve Fainaru, "Officials Continue to Doubt Hijackers' Link to Anthrax: Fla. Doctor Says He Treated One for Skin Form of Disease," *Washington Post*, March 24, 2002, p. A23.

20. It is interesting to note that, according to Christopher C. Harmon, in Germany, 1991 was the first year that the number of indigenous rightist radicals exceeded that of leftists. Harmon, *Terrorism Today* (London: Frank Cass, 2000), p. 3.

21. For example, in discussing the longevity of terrorist groups, Martha Crenshaw notes only three significant terrorist groups with ethnonationalist ideologies that ceased to exist within ten years of their formation (one of these, EOKA, disbanded because its goal—the liberation of Cyprus —was attained). By contrast, a majority of the terrorist groups she lists as having existed for ten years or longer have recognizable ethnonationalist ideologies, including the IRA (in its many forms), Sikh separatist groups, Euskadi Ta Askatasuna, the various Palestinian nationalist groups, and the Corsican National Liberation Front. See Crenshaw, "How Terrorism Declines," *Terrorism and Political Violence*, Vol. 3, No. 1 (Spring 1991), pp. 69–87.

22. On the characteristics of modern religious terrorist groups, see Bruce Hoffman, *Inside Terrorism* (New York: Columbia University Press, 1998), especially pp. 94–95; and Bruce Hoffman, "Terrorism Trends and Prospects," in Ian O. Lesser, Bruce Hoffman, John Arguilla, Michelle Zanini, and David Ronfeldt, eds., *Countering the New Terrorism* (Santa Monica, Calif.: RAND, 1999), especially pp. 19–20. On the peculiar twists of one apocalyptic vision, see Robert Jay Lifton, *Destroying the World to Save It: Aum Shinrikyo, Apocalyptic Violence, and the New Global Terrorism* (New York: Henry Holt, 1999).

23. There is a long list of people and organizations sanctioned under Executive Order 13224, signed on September 23, 2001. Designated charitable organizations include the Benevolence International Foundation and the Global Relief Foundation. The list is available at http:// www.treas.gov/offices/enforcement/ofac/sanctions/t11ter.pdf (accessed November 26, 2002).

24. The RAND–St. Andrews University Chronology of International Terrorism is a databank of terrorist incidents that begins in 1968 and has been maintained since 1972 at St. Andrews University, Scotland, and the RAND Corporation, Santa Monica, California.

25. Hoffman, *Inside Terrorism*, pp. 90–91; and Nadine Gurr and Benjamin Cole, *The New Face of Terrorism: Threats from Weapons of Mass Destruction* (London: I.B. Tauris, 2000), pp. 28–29.

26. Statistics compiled from data in U.S. Department of State, *Patterns of Global Terrorism*, published annually by the Office of the Coordinator for Counterterrorism, U.S. Department of State.

27. Ibid. For a graphical depiction of this information, created on the basis of annual data from *Patterns of Global Terrorism*, see Cronin, "Rethinking Sovereignty," p. 126.

28. In the 1998 embassy bombings alone, for example, 224 people were killed (with 12 Americans among them), and 4,574 were injured (including 15 Americans). U.S. Department of State, *Patterns of Global Terrorism, 1998*.

29. Ibid. For a graphical depiction of deaths per incident, created on the basis of annual data from *Patterns of Global Terrorism*, see Cronin, "Rethinking Sovereignty," p. 128.

30. Ibid.

31. Hoffman, "Terrorist Targeting," p. 24.

32. U.S. Department of State, *Patterns of Global Terrorism*, various years.

33. Examples include Bruce Hoffman, *"Holy Terror": The Implications of Terrorism Motivated by a Religious Imperative*, RAND Paper P-7834 (Santa Monica, Calif.: RAND, 1993); and Mark Juergensmeyer, "Terror Mandated by God," *Terrorism and Political Violence*, Vol. 9, No. 2 (Summer 1997), pp. 16–23.

34. See, for example, Steven Simon and Daniel Benjamin, "America and the New Terrorism," *Survival*, Vol. 42, No. 1 (Spring 2000), pp. 59–75, as well as the responses in the subsequent issue, "America and the New Terrorism: An Exchange," *Survival*, Vol. 42, No. 2 (Summer 2000), pp. 156– 172; and Hoffman, "Terrorism Trends and Prospects," pp. 7–38.

35. See Peter Finn and Sarah Delaney, "Al-Qaeda's Tracks Deepen in Europe," *Washington Post*, October 22, 2001, p. A1; Kamran Khan and Molly Moore, "2 Nuclear Experts Briefed Bin Laden, Pakistanis Say," *Washington Post*, December, 12, 2001, p. A1; James Risen and Judith Miller, "A Nation Challenged: Chemical Weapons—Al Qaeda Sites Point to Tests of Chemicals," *New York Times*, November 11, 2001, p. B1; Douglas Frantz and David Rohde, "A Nation Challenged: Biological Terror—2 Pakistanis Linked to Papers on Anthrax Weapons," *New York Times*, November 28, 2001; and David Rohde, "A Nation Challenged: The Evidence— Germ Weapons Plans Found at a Scientist's House in Kabul," *New York Times*, December 1, 2001.

36. Laqueur, *Terrorism*, pp. 112–116.

37. Ibid., pp. 115–116.

38. Groups with known or alleged connections to al-Qaeda include Jemaah Islamiyah (Indonesia, Malaysia, and Singapore), the Abu Sayyaf group (Philippines), al-Gama'a al-Islamiyya (Egypt), Harakat ul-Mujahidin (Pakistan), the Islamic Movement of Uzbekistan (Central Asia), Jaish-e-Mohammed (India and Pakistan), and al-Jihad (Egypt).

39. For the purposes of this article, globalization is a gradually expanding process of interpenetration in the economic, political, social, and security realms, uncontrolled by (or apart from) traditional notions of state sovereignty. Victor D. Cha, "Globalization and the Study of International Security," *Journal of Peace Research*, Vol. 37, No. 3 (March 2000), pp. 391–393.

40. With respect to the Islamic world, there are numerous books and articles that point to the phenomenon of antipathy with the Western world, either because of broad cultural incompatibility or a specific conflict between Western consumerism and religious fundamentalism. Among the earliest and most notable are Samuel P. Huntington, "The Clash of Civilizations?" *Foreign Affairs*, Vol. 72, No. 3 (Summer 1993); Benjamin R. Barber, *Jihad vs. McWorld: Terrorism's Challenge to Democracy* (New York: Random House, 1995); and Samuel P. Huntington, *The Clash of Civilizations and the Remaking of World Order* (New York: Simon and Schuster, 1996).

41. For more on cyberterrorism, see Dorothy Denning, "Activism, Hacktivism, and Cyberterrorism: The Internet as a Tool for Influencing Foreign Policy," paper presented at Internet and International Systems: Information Technology and American Foreign Policy Decision-making Workshop at Georgetown University, http://www.nautilus.org/info-policy/workshop/papers/ denning.html (accessed January 5, 2003); Dorothy Denning, "Cyberterrorism," testimony before the U.S. House Committee on Armed Services, Special Oversight Panel on Terrorism, 107th Cong., 1st sess., May 23, 2001, available on the Terrorism Research Center website, http://www.cs.georgetown.edu/?denning/infosec/cyberterror.html (accessed January 5, 2003); Jerold Post, Kevin Ruby, and Eric Shaw, "From Car Bombs to Logic Bombs: The Growing Threat of Information Terrorism," *Terrorism and Political Violence*, Vol. 12, No. 2 (Summer 2000), pp. 97–122; and Tom Regan, "When Terrorists Turn to the Internet," *Christian Science Monitor*, July 1, 1999, http://www.csmonitor.com (accessed January 5, 2003).

42. Ibid. Dorothy Denning cites numerous examples, among them: In 1989, hackers released a computer worm into the NASA Space Physics Analysis Network in an attempt to stop a shuttle launch; during Palestinian riots in October

2000, pro-Israeli hackers defaced the Hezbollah website; and in 1999, following the mistaken U.S. bombing of the Chinese embassy in Belgrade during the war in Kosovo, Chinese hackers attacked the websites of the U.S. Department of the Interior, showing images of the three journalists killed during the bombing.

43. Paul R. Pillar, *Terrorism and U.S. Foreign Policy* (Washington, D.C.: Brookings, 2001), p. 47.

44. Ibid.

45. Simon Reeve, *The New Jackals: Ramzi Yousef, Osama bin Laden, and the Future of Terrorism* (Boston: Northeastern University Press, 1999), p. 260.

46. Dorothy Denning, "Cyberwarriors: Activists and Terrorists Turn to Cyberspace," *Harvard International Review*, Vol. 23, No. 2 (Summer 2001), pp. 70–75. See also Brian J. Miller, "Terror.org: An Assessment of Terrorist Internet Sites," Georgetown University, December 6, 2000.

47. Miller, "Terror.org," pp. 9, 12.

48. Steganography is the embedding of messages usually in pictures, where the messages are disguised so that they cannot be seen with the naked eye. See Denning, "Cyberwarriors."

49. I am indebted to Dorothy Denning for all of this information. The Provisional IRA hired contract hackers to find the addresses of British intelligence and law enforcement officers. See Denning, "Cyberterrorism"; and Denning, "Cyberwarriors."

50. There are many recent sources on CBNR. Among the best are Jonathan B. Tucker, ed., *Toxic Terror: Assessing Terrorist Use of Chemical and Biological Weapons* (Cambridge, Mass.: MIT Press, 2000); Joshua Lederberg, *Biological Weapons: Limiting the Threat* (Cambridge, Mass.: MIT Press, 1999); Richard A. Falkenrath, Robert D. Newman, and Bradley A. Thayer, *America's Achilles' Heel: Nuclear, Biological, and Chemical Terrorism and Covert Attack* (Cambridge, Mass.: MIT Press, 1998); Gurr and Cole, *The New Face of Terrorism*; Jessica Stern, *The Ultimate Terrorists* (Cambridge, Mass.: Harvard University Press, 1999); and Brad Roberts, ed., *Terrorism with Chemical and Biological Weapons: Calibrating Risks and Responses* (Alexandria, Va.: Chemical and Biological Arms Control Institute, 1997).

51. See Falkenrath, Newman, and Thayer, *America's Achilles' Heel*, pp. 31–46.

52. A clear example of this phenomenon was the uncovering in December 2001 of a multinational plot in Singapore by the international terrorist group Jemaah Islamiyah to blow up severalWestern targets, including the U.S. embassy. A videotape of the intended targets (including a description of the plans in Arabic) was discovered in Afghanistan after al-Qaeda members fled. Thus there are clear connections between these organizations, as well as evidence of cooperation and coordination of attacks. See, for example, Dan Murphy, "'Activated' Asian Terror Web Busted," *Christian Science Monitor*, January 23, 2002, http://www.csmonitor.com (accessed January 23, 2002); and Rajiv Chandrasekaran, "Al Qaeda's Southeast Asian Reach," *Washington Post*, February 3, 2002, p. A1.

53. Rensselaer Lee and Raphael Perl, "Terrorism, the Future, and U.S. Foreign Policy," issue brief for Congress, received through the Congressional Research Service website, order code IB95112, Congressional Research Service, Library of Congress, July 10, 2002, p. CRS-6.

54. Roger G. Weiner, "The Financing of International Terrorism," Terrorism and Violence Crime Section, Criminal Division, U.S. Department of Justice, October 2001, p. 3. According toWeiner, the *hawala* (or *hundi*) system "relies entirely on trust that currency left with a particular service provider or merchant will be paid from bank accounts he controls overseas to the recipient specified by the party originating the transfer." Ibid. See also Douglas Frantz, "Ancient Secret System Moves Money Globally," *New York Times*, October 3, 2001, http:// www.nytimes.com (accessed October 3, 2001).

55. International efforts to freeze bank accounts and block transactions between suspected terrorists have hindered, at least to some degree, al-Qaeda's ability to finance attacks; however, a proportion remains unaccounted for. "Cash Moves a Sign Al-Qaeda Is Regrouping," *Straits Times*, March 18, 2002, http://www.straitstimes.asia1.com.sg (accessed March 18, 2002).

56. U.S. Department of State, *Patterns of Global Terrorism, 2001*. According to the U.S. Department of State, Hezbollah also may have transferred resources by selling millions of dollars' worth of Congolese diamonds to finance operations in the Middle East.

57. Douglas Farah, "Al Qaeda's Road Paved with Gold," *Washington Post*, February 17, 2002, pp. A1, A32.

58. Pillar, *Terrorism and U.S. Foreign Policy*, p. 48.

59. Many in the United States focus on the technologies of terrorism, with a much less developed interest in the motivations of terrorists. Brian M. Jenkins, "Understanding the Link between Motives and Methods," in Roberts, *Terrorism with Chemical and Biological Weapons*, pp. 43– 51. An example of a study that focuses on weapons and not motives is Sidney D. Drell, Abraham D. Sofaer, and George W. Wilson, eds., *The New Terror: Facing the Threat of Biological and Chemical Weapons* (Stanford, Calif.: Hoover Institution, 1999).

60. Christopher Coker, *Globalisation and Insecurity in the Twenty-first Century: NATO and the Management of Risk*, Adelphi Paper 345 (London: International Institute for Strategic Studies, June 2002), p. 40.

61. The indicators studied included respect for human rights and human freedoms, the empowerment of women, and broad access to and utilization of knowledge. See United Nations Development Programme, Arab Fund for Economic and Social Development, *Arab Human Development Report, 2002: Creating Opportunities for Future Generations* (New York: United Nations Development Programme, 2002).

62. Martha Crenshaw, "Why America? The Globalization of Civil War," *Current History*, December 2001, pp. 425–432.

63. A number of recent arguments have been put forth about the relationship between poverty and terrorism. See, for example, Anatol Lieven, "The Roots of Terrorism, and a Strategy against It," Prospect (London), October 2001, http://www.ceip.org/files/Publications/lieventerrorism.asp? from=pubdate (accessed November 17, 2002); and Daniel Pipes, "God and Mammon: Does Poverty Cause Militant Islam?" *National Interest*, No. 66 (Winter 2001/02), pp. 14–21. This is an extremely complex question, however, and much work remains to be done. On the origins of the new religious terrorism, see Hoffman, *Inside Terrorism*; and Mark Juergensmeyer, *Terror in the Mind of God: The Global Rise of Religious Violence* (Berkeley: University of California Press, 2000). Important earlier studies on the sources of terrorism include Martha Crenshaw, "The Causes of Terrorism," *Comparative Politics*, July 1981, pp. 379–399; Martha Crenshaw, *Terrorism in Context* (University Park: Pennsylvania State University Press, 1995); and Walter Reich, ed., *Origins of Terrorism: Psychologies, Ideologies, Theologies, States of Mind*, 2d ed. (Washington, D.C.: Woodrow Wilson Center for International Scholars, 1998).

64. For more discussion on the traditional elements of U.S. grand strategy, especially military strategy, see Barry R. Posen, "The Struggle against Terrorism: Grand Strategy, Strategy, and Tactics," *International Security*, Vol. 26, No. 3 (Winter 2001/02), pp. 39–55.

65. George F. Kennan, "The Sources of Soviet Conduct," *Foreign Affairs*, Vol. 25, No. 4 (July 1947), pp. 575–576.

66. See the extremely insightful article by Bruce W. Jentleson, "The Need for Praxis: Bringing Policy Relevance Back In," *International Security*, Vol. 26, No. 4 (Spring 2002), pp. 169–183.

67. I am indebted to Fiona Adamson for this observation.

68. Important terrorism scholars in the think tank community include Walter Laqueur (Center for Strategic and International Studies), Brian Jenkins (RAND), Bruce Hoffman (RAND) and, from the intelligence community, Paul Pillar. This list is illustrative, not comprehensive.

69. On these issues, see Cronin and Ludes, *The Campaign against International Terrorism*.

Holy Orders:
Religious Opposition to Modern States

Mark Juergensmeyer

No one who watched in horror as the towers of the World Trade Center crumbled into dust on September 11, 2001, could doubt that the real target of the terrorist assault was US global power. Those involved in similar attacks and in similar groups have said as much. Mahmood Abouhalima, one of the Al Qaeda-linked activists convicted for his role in the 1993 attack on the World Trade Center, told me in a prison interview that buildings such as these were chosen to dramatically demonstrate that "the government is the enemy." While the US government and its allies have been frequent targets of recent terrorist acts, religious leaders and groups are seldom targeted. An anomaly in this regard was the assault on the Shi'a shrine in the Iraqi city of Najaf on August 29, 2003, which killed more than 80 people including the venerable Ayatollah Mohammad Baqir al Hakim. The Al Qaeda activists who allegedly perpetrated this act were likely more incensed over the Ayatollah's implicit support for the US-backed Iraqi Governing Council than they were jealous of his popularity with Shi'a Muslims. Since the United Nations has also indirectly supported the US occupation of Iraq and Afghanistan, it too has been subject to Osama bin Laden's rage. This may well be the reason why the UN office in Baghdad was the target of the devastating assault on August 19, 2003, which killed the distinguished UN envoy Sergio Vieira de Mello. Despite the seeming diversity of the targets, the object of most recent acts of religious terror is an old foe of religion: the secular state.

Secular governments have been the objects of terrorism in virtually every religious tradition—not just Islam. A Christian terrorist, Timothy McVeigh, bombed the Oklahoma City Federal Building on April 19, 1995. A Jewish activist, Yigal Amir, assassinated Israel's Prime Minister Yitzhak Rabin. A Buddhist follower, Shoko Asahara, orchestrated the nerve gas attacks in the Tokyo subways near the Japanese parliament buildings. Hindu and Sikh militants have targeted government offices and political leaders in India. In addition to government offices and leaders, symbols of decadent secular life have also been targets of religious terror. In August 2003, the Marriott Hotel in Jakarta, frequented by Westerners and Westernized Indonesians, was struck by a car bomb. The event resembled the December 2002 attacks on Bali nightclubs, whose main patrons were college-age Australians. In the United States, abortion clinics and gay bars have been targeted. The 2003 bombings in Morocco were aimed at clubs popular with tourists from Spain, Belgium, and Israel. Two questions arise regarding this spate of vicious religious assaults on secular government and secular life around the world. Why is religion the basis for opposition to the state? And why is this happening now?

Mark Juergensmeyer is Professor of Sociology and Director of Global and International Studies at the University of California, Santa Barbara.

WHY RELIGION?

Religious activists are puzzling anomalies in the secular world. Most religious people and their organizations either firmly support the secular state or quiescently tolerate it. Bin Laden's Al Qaeda, like most of the new religious activist groups, is a small group at the extreme end of a hostile subculture that is itself a small minority within the larger Muslim world. Bin Laden is no more representative of Islam than McVeigh is of Christianity or Asahara of Buddhism.

Still, it is undeniable that the ideals of activists like bin Laden are authentically and thoroughly religious. Moreover, even though their network consists of only a few thousand members, they have enjoyed an increase in popularity in the Muslim world after September 11, 2001, especially after the US-led occupations of Afghanistan and Iraq. The authority of religion has given bin Laden's cadres the moral legitimacy to employ violence in assaulting symbols of global economic and political power. Religion has also provided them the metaphor of cosmic war, an image of spiritual struggle that every religion contains within its repository of symbols, seen as the fight between good and bad, truth and evil. In this sense, attacks such as those on the World Trade Center and UN headquarters in Baghdad were very religious. They were meant to be catastrophic acts of biblical proportions.

FROM WORLDLY STRUGGLES TO SACRED BATTLES

Although recent acts of religious terrorism such as the attacks on the World Trade Center and United Nations had no obvious military goal, they were intended to make an impact on the public consciousness. They are a kind of perverse performance of power meant to ennoble the perpetrators' views of the world while drawing viewers into their notions of cosmic war. In my 2003 study of the global rise of religious violence, Terror in the Mind of God, I found a strikingly familiar pattern. In almost every recent case of religious violence, concepts of cosmic war have been accompanied by claims of moral justification. It is not so much that religion has become politicized but that politics has become religionized. Through enduring absolutism, worldly struggles have been lifted into the high proscenium of sacred battle.

This is what makes religious warfare so difficult to address. Enemies become satanized, and thus compromise and negotiation become difficult. The rewards for those who fight for the cause are transtemporal, and the timelines of their struggles are vast. Most social and political struggles look for conclusions within the lifetimes of their participants, but religious struggles can take generations to succeed.

I once had the opportunity to point out the futility—in secular military terms—of the radical Islamic struggle in Palestine to Dr. Abdul Aziz Rantisi, the head of the political wing of the Hamas movement. It seemed to me that Israel's military force was strong enough that a Palestinian military effort could never succeed. Dr. Rantisi assured me that "Palestine was occupied before, for two hundred years." He explained that he and his Palestinian comrades "can wait again—at least that long." In his calculation, the struggles of God can endure for eons before their ultimate victory.

Insofar as the US public and its leaders embraced the image of war following the September 11 attacks, the US view of the war was also prone to religionization. "God Bless America" became the country's unofficial national anthem. US President George Bush spoke of defending America's "righteous cause" and of the "absolute evil" of its enemies. However, the US military engagement in the months following September 11 was primarily a secular commitment to a definable goal and largely restricted to objectives in which civil liberties and moral rules of engagement still applied.

In purely religious battles waged in divine time and with heavenly rewards, there is no need to compromise goals. There is also no need to contend with society's laws and limitations when one is obeying a higher authority. In spiritualizing violence, religion gives the act of violence remarkable power.

Ironically, the reverse is also true: terrorism can empower religion. Although sporadic acts of terrorism do not lead to the establishment of new religious states, they make the political potency of religious ideology impossible to ignore. The first wave of religious activism, from the Islamic revolution in Iran in 1978 to the emergence of Hamas during the Palestinian intifada in the early 1990s, focused on religious nationalism and the vision of individual religious states. Now religious activism has an increasingly global vision. The Christian militia, the Japanese Aum Shinrikyo, and the Al Qaeda network all target what they regard as a repressive and secular form of global culture and control.

Part of the attraction of religious ideologies is that they are so personal. They impart a sense of redemption and dignity to those who uphold them, often men who feel marginalized from public life. One can view their efforts to demonize their enemies and embrace ideas of cosmic war as attempts at ennoblement and empowerment. Such efforts would be poignant if they were not so horribly destructive.

Yet they are not just personal acts. These violent efforts of symbolic empowerment have an effect beyond whatever personal satisfaction and feelings of potency they impart to those who support and conduct them. The very act of killing on behalf of a moral code is a political statement. Such acts break the state's monopoly on morally sanctioned killing. By putting the right to take life in their own hands, the perpetrators of religious violence make a daring claim of power on behalf of the powerless—a basis of legitimacy for public order other than that on which the secular state relies.

COINCIDENCE OF GLOBALIZATION AND MODERNIZATION

These recent acts of religious violence are occurring in a way different from the various forms of holy warfare that have occurred throughout history. They are responses to a contemporary theme in the world's political and social life: globalization. The World Trade Center symbolized bin Laden's hatred of two aspects of secular government—a certain kind of modernization and a certain kind of globalization— even though the Al Qaeda network was itself both modern and transnational. Its members were often highly sophisticated and technically skilled professionals, and its organization was composed of followers of various nationalities who moved effortlessly from place to place with no obvious nationalist agenda or allegiance. In a sense, they were not opposed to modernity and globalization, so long as it fit their own design. But they loathed the Western-style modernity that they perceived secular globalization was forcing upon them.

Some 23 years earlier, during the Islamic revolution in Iran, Ayatollah Khomeini rallied the masses with the similar notion that the United States was forcing its economic exploitation, political institutions, and secular culture on an unknowing Islamic society. The Ayatollah accused urban Iranians of having succumbed to "Westoxification"—an inebriation with Western culture and ideas. The many strident movements of religious nationalism that have erupted around the world in the more than two decades following the Iranian revolution have echoed this cry. This anti-Westernism has at heart an opposition to a certain kind of modernism that is secular, individualistic, and skeptical. Yet, in a curious way, by accepting the modern notion of the nation-state and adopting the technological and financial instruments of modern society, many of these movements of religious nationalism have claimed a kind of modernity on their own behalf.

Religious politics could be regarded as an opportunistic infection that has set in at the present weakened stage of the secular nation-state. Globalization has crippled secular nationalism and the nation-state in several ways. It has weakened them economically, not only through the global reach of transnational businesses, but also by the transnational nature of their labor supply, currency, and financial instruments. Globalization has eroded their sense of national identity and unity through the expansion of media and communications, technology, and popular culture, and through the unchallenged military power of the United States. Some of the most intense movements for ethnic and religious nationalism have arisen in states where local leaders have felt exploited by the global economy, unable to gain military leverage against what they regard as corrupt leaders promoted by the United States, and invaded by images of US popular culture on television, the Internet, and motion pictures.

Other aspects of globalization—the emergence of multicultural societies through global diasporas of peoples and cultures and the suggestion that global military and political control might fashion a "new world order"—has also elicited fear. Bin Laden and other Islamic activists have exploited this specter, and it has caused many concerned citizens in the Islamic world to see the US military response to the September 11 attacks as an imperialistic venture and a bully's crusade, rather than the righteous wrath of an injured victim. When US leaders included the invasion and occupation of Iraq as part of its "war against terror," the operation was commonly portrayed in the Muslim world as a ploy for the United States to expand its global reach.

This image of a sinister US role in creating a new world order of globalization is also feared in some quarters of the West. Within the United States, for example, the Christian Identity movement and Christian militia organizations have been alarmed over what they imagine to be a massive global conspiracy of liberal US politicians and the United Nations to control the world. Timothy McVeigh's favorite book, *The Turner Diaries*, is based on the premise that the United States has already unwittingly succumbed to a conspiracy of global control from which it needs to be liberated through terrorist actions and guerrilla bands. In Japan, a similar conspiracy theory motivated leaders of the Aum Shinrikyo religious movement to predict a catastrophic World War III, and attempted to simulate Armageddon with their 1995 nerve gas attack in a Tokyo subway train.

IDENTITY AND CONTROL

As far-fetched as the idea of a "new world order" of global control may be, there is some truth to the notion that the integration of societies and the globalization of culture have brought the world closer together. Although it is unlikely that a cartel of malicious schemers designed this global trend, the effect of globalization on local societies and national identities has nonetheless been profound. It has undermined the modern idea of the state by providing non-national and transnational forms of economic, social, and cultural interaction. The global economic and social ties of the inhabitants of contemporary global cities are intertwined in a way that supercedes the idea of a national social contract—the Enlightenment notion that peoples in particular regions are naturally linked together in a specific country. In a global world, it is hard to say where particular regions begin and end. For that matter, in multicultural societies, it is hard to say how the "people" of a particular nation should be defined.

This is where religion and ethnicity step in to redefine public communities The decay of the nation-state and disillusionment with old forms of secular nationalism have produced both the opportunity and the need for nationalisms. The opportunity has arisen because the old orders seem so weak, yet the need for national identity persists because no single alternative form of social cohesion and affiliation has yet appeared to dominate public life the way the nation-state did in the 20th century. In a curious way, traditional forms of social identity have helped to rescue one of Western modernity's central themes: the idea of nationhood. In the increasing absence of any other demarcation of national loyalty and commitment, these old staples—religion, ethnicity, and traditional culture—have become resources for national identification.

Consequently, religious and ethnic nationalism has provided a solution in the contemporary political climate to the perceived insufficiencies of Western-style secular politics. As secular ties have begun to unravel in the post- Soviet and post-colonial era, local leaders have searched for new anchors with which to ground their social identities and political loyalties. What is significant about these ethno-religious movements is their creativity—not just their use of technology and mass media, but also their appropriation of national and global networks. Although many of the framers of the new nationalisms have reached back into history for ancient images and concepts that will give them credibility, theirs are not simply efforts to resuscitate old ideas from the past. These are contemporary ideologies that meet present-day social and political needs.

In the context of Western modernism, the notion that indigenous culture can provide the basis for new political institutions, including resuscitated forms of the nation-state, is revolutionary. Movements that support ethno-religious nationalism are therefore often confrontational and sometimes violent. They reject the intervention of outsiders and their ideologies and, at the risk of being intolerant, pander to their indigenous cultural bases and enforce traditional social boundaries. It is thus no surprise that they clash with each other and with defenders of the secular state. Yet even such conflicts serve a purpose for the movements: they help define who they are as a people and who they are not. They are not, for instance, secular modernists.

Understandably, then, these movements of anti-Western modernism are ambivalent about modernity, unsure whether it is necessarily Western and always evil. They are also ambivalent about globalization, the most recent stage of modernity. On one hand, these political movements of anti-modernity are reactions to the globalization of Western culture. They are responses to the insufficiencies of what is often touted as the world's global standard: the elements of secular, Westernized urban society that are found not only in the West but in many parts of the former Third World, seen by their detractors as vestiges of colonialism. On the other hand, these new ethno-religious identities are alternative modernities with international and supernational aspects of their own. This means that in the future, some forms of anti-modernism will be global, some will be virulently antiglobal, and yet others will be content with creating their own alternative modernities in ethno-religious nation-states.

Each of these forms of religious anti-modernism contains a paradoxical relationship between forms of globalization and emerging religious and ethnic nationalisms. One of history's ironies is that the globalism of culture and the emergence of transnational political and economic institutions enhance the need for local identities. They also promote a more localized form of authority and social accountability.

The crucial problems in an era of globalization are identity and control. The two are linked in that a loss of a sense of belonging leads to a feeling of powerlessness. At the same time, what has been perceived as a loss of faith in secular nationalism is experienced as a loss of agency as well as selfhood. For these reasons, the assertion of traditional forms of religious identities are linked to attempts to reclaim personal and cultural power. The vicious outbreaks of antimodernist religious terrorism in the first few years of the 21st century can be seen as tragic attempts to regain social control through acts of violence. Until there is a surer sense of citizenship in a global order, religious visions of moral order will continue to appear as attractive, though often disruptive, solutions to the problems of authority, identity, and belonging in a globalized world.

The Origins of the New Terrorism

Matthew J. Morgan

The suicidal collision of hijacked commercial airliners into the World Trade Center and the Pentagon on 11 September 2001 was the most destructive terrorist attack in world history. Before the deaths of approximately 3,000 people in those attacks, the most devastating single terrorist attack had claimed the lives of about 380 people. The 2001 disaster took place at a time when experts had been defining a new form of terrorism focused on millennial visions of apocalypse and mass casualties. The catastrophic attacks confirmed their fears.

The State Department's *Patterns of Global Terrorism*, published in early 2002, revealed that terrorist attacks have scaled back in number in recent years, even though more casualties have occurred.[1] The late 1980s were a high point for the number of terrorist attacks, with the incidence of attacks exceeding 600 annually in the years 1985-88.With the exception of 1991, the number of terrorist attacks after 1988 decreased to fewer than 450 every year, reaching their recent low point in the years 1996-98, when the number of attacks was about 300. The number of attacks has increased slightly since 1998, when there were 274 attacks, but the level has not reached the number realized in any of the years of the 1980s. This report is not a linear progression from a large number to a small number of attacks, but the trend revealed is one of a decreasing incidence. Yet even if the frequency has decreased, the danger has not.

Osama bin Laden and the al Qaeda network of international terrorists are the prime examples of the new terrorism, but Islamic radicalism is not the only form of apocalyptic, catastrophic terrorism. Aum Shinrikyo, the Japanese religious cult, executed the first major terrorist attack using chemical weapons on a Tokyo subway in 1995. The bombing of the Murrah Federal Building in Oklahoma revealed similar extremism by American right-wing militants. Other plots by Christian Identity terrorists have shown similar mass-casualty proclivities.

Nadine Gurr and Benjamin Cole labeled nuclear-biological-chemical (NBC) terrorism as the "third wave of vulnerability" experienced by the United States beginning in 1995. (The first two waves were the Soviet test of the atomic bomb in 1949 and the escalating nuclear arms race that followed.[2]) David Rapoport made a similar assessment that religiously motivated modern terrorism is the "fourth wave" in the evolution of terrorism, having been preceded by terrorism focused on the breakup of empires, decolonialization, and anti-Westernism.[3]

The National Commission on Terrorism found that fanaticism rather than political interests is more often the motivation now, and that terrorists are more unrestrained than ever before in their methods.[4] Other scholarly sources have reached similar conclusions. Terrorism is increasingly based

---

Captain Matthew J. Morgan is the Commander of the Headquarters and Headquarters Operations Company (HHOC), 125th Military Intelligence Battalion, at Schofield Barracks, Hawaii. Following command, Captain Morgan will deploy to Operation Enduring Freedom in Afghanistan on the Joint Task Force intelligence staff.

on religious fanaticism.[5] Warnings about the dangers of nontraditional terrorism were raised frequently in pre-2001 literature.[6] For instance, Ashton Carter, John Deutch, and Philip Zelikow declared in the pages of *Foreign Affairs* in 1998 that a new threat of catastrophic terrorism had emerged.[7] Earlier concerns about alienating people from supporting the cause are no longer important to many terrorist organizations. Rather than focusing on conventional goals of political or religious movements, today's terrorists seek destruction and chaos as ends in themselves. Yossef Bodansky's *Bin Laden* quotes from S. K. Malik's *The Quranic Concept of War*:

> Terror struck into the hearts of the enemies is not only a means, it is in the end in itself. Once a condition of terror into the opponent's heart is obtained, hardly anything is left to be achieved. It is the point where the means and the ends meet and merge. Terror is not a means of imposing decision upon the enemy; it is the decision we wish to impose upon him.[8]

Today's terrorists are ultimately more apocalyptic in their perspective and methods. For many violent and radical organizations, terror has evolved from being a means to an end, to becoming the end in itself. The National Commission on Terrorism quoted R. James Woolsey: "Today's terrorists don't want a seat at the table, they want to destroy the table and everyone sitting at it."[9]

Some analysts argue that the evolution of terrorism represents continuity rather than change, that mass-casualty bombings have long been characteristic of terrorist methods, and that radical extremism has always dominated terrorist motivations.[10] Walter Laqueur's most recent book warns against trying to categorize or define terrorism at all because there are "many terrorisms," and he emphasizes the particularities of various terrorist movements and approaches.[11] (Laqueur, however, recognizes some evolving strains of terrorism, especially the Islamist variant.) Bruce Hoffman discussed the definition of terrorism at length in his 1998 book, *Inside Terrorism*, and his final definition includes "political change" as the desired end-state of terrorist activity.[12] This would be more consistent with traditional means-end constructions of terrorism. Richard Falkenrath pointed out in a pre-9/11 article that mass-casualty terrorism is still an aberrant occurrence.[13] A recent survey of terrorism suggests historical and intellectual links between the fascism of fanatical Islamist terrorism today and the totalitarian movements of the 20th century, further emphasizing continuity rather than change.[14]

Most recent scholarship, however, has taken the perspective that contemporary terrorism represents a significant departure from the past. Various factors have led to the development of this new type of terrorism. Paul Wilkinson pondered the increase in indiscriminateness among terrorists, and he posited several possible reasons accounting for this upsurge.[15] First, the saturation of the media with images of terrorist atrocity has raised the bar on the level of destruction that will attract headline attention. Second, terrorists have realized that civilian soft targets involve lower risk to themselves. Finally, there has been a shift from the politically-minded terrorist to the vengeful and hardline fanatic.

While Wilkinson's factors accurately describe developments in terrorist strategy and tactics, there are more fundamental forces at work. The world has undergone a variety of changes on several levels. While it is impossible to link all social changes to terrorism today, it is possible to track several distinct factors that have converged to evolve a form of terrorism that is unprecedented in the level of threat it poses around the world. This article will explore these factors from cultural, political, and technological perspectives.

CULTURAL FACTORS

Islamic radicalism is the most notorious form of the new culture of terrorism, but it is far from the only variety of cultural trends motivating terrorist activity. Numerous cults, whose emergence in many cases has been synchronized with the turn of the new millennium, have also posed an in- creasing threat. Finally, the American religious right has been active with escalating and destructive objectives, although law enforcement presence has restrained these groups.

It is important to distinguish religious terrorists from those terrorists with religious components, but whose primary goals are political. Religiously motivated terrorist groups grew sixfold from 1980 to 1992 and continued to increase in the 1990s. Hoffman asserted that "the religious imperative for terrorism is the most important characteristic of terrorist activity today."[16] This may not be as much an entirely new phenomenon as a cyclic return to earlier motivations for terror. Until the emergence of political motives such as nationalism, anarchism, and Marxism, "religion provided the only acceptable justifications for terror."[17] However, terrorism in modern times has not, until recent years, been so dominated by religious overtones. At the time when modern international terrorism first appeared, of the 11 identifiable terrorist groups, none could be classified as religious.[18]

Today's terrorists increasingly look at their acts of death and destruction as sacramental or transcendental on a spiritual or eschatological level. The pragmatic reservations of secular terrorists[19] do not hold back religious terrorists. Secular terrorists may view indiscriminate violence as immoral. For religious terrorists, however, indiscriminate violence may not be only morally justified, but constitute a righteous and necessary advancement of their religious cause. In addition, the goals of secular terrorists are much more attuned to public opinion, so senseless violence would be counterproductive to their cause, and hence not palatable to them. As Hoffman observed, the constituency itself differs between religious and secular terrorists. Secular terrorists seek to defend or promote some disenfranchised population and to appeal to sympathizers or prospective sympathizers. Religious terrorists are often their own constituency, having no external audience for their acts of destruction.[20]

Aum Shinrikyo has been included in typologies of terrorism that include radical Islamists as part of a group of religiously motivated organizations that attack symbols of the modern state.[21] In many ways, the dynamics of cultist followings make groups such as AumShinrikyo (also known as Aleph) more dangerous than religious terrorists rooted in conventional and broadly based religious traditions or denominations. There is no constituency of more moderate adherents to share common beliefs with the radical group while at the same time posing a restraining influence. For the fundamentalist Islamic or Christian radical, authoritative figures from either of those religions can condemn violence and de-legitimize the terrorist, at least in the eyes of the average faithful.

Another feature of religious cults that makes them incredibly dangerous is the personality-driven nature of these groups. Cultist devotion to one leader leaves followers less able to make their own moral decisions or to consult other sources of reasoning. If that leader is emotionally or mentally unstable, the ramifications can be catastrophic. The more dangerous religious terrorist groups from traditional faiths may often share this feature of the cult: a charismatic leader who exerts a powerful influence over the members of the group.

According to many analysts, Aum Shinrikyo demonstrated its comparatively more threatening potential in its sarin attack in the Tokyo subway. As D.W. Brackett wrote, "A horrible bell had tolled in the Tokyo subway. . . . Terrorists do not follow rules of engagement in their operations but they do absorb the lessons to be learned from successful acts of violence."[22] If for no other reason than providing an example to others, Aum Shinrikyo has gained notoriety as one of the more dangerous terrorist elements. Despite setbacks such as the incarceration of key leadership figures, the group continues to pose future threats. The ability of Aum Shinrikyo to recruit individuals with a high level of education and technical knowledge also has been a significant aspect of the threat posed by the cult.[23]

In the past, cults were not viewed as national security threats; they were more dangerous to unwary individuals who might succumb to the cult's influence. Even the emergence of cultist mass suicides did not alter this perception. However, the recent appearance of cults willing and able to adopt destructive political goals has revised the more benign view of the cult phenomenon. Since cults are often fundamentally based on the violence of coercion, they can be accustomed to the mindset necessary to adopt terrorist methods. Although cults more often practice a mental violence with psychological control and extreme invasions of privacy, they do occasionally engage in physical abuse. The most dangerous cults are also fascinated by visions of the end of the world—which, like radicals from more mainstream religions, cultists often believe that they are instrumental in bringing about. The nature of the cult's mythical figure can also be indicative of the level of threat. A vengeful deity is more threatening than a suffering savior. This sign is somewhat unpredictable, however, because cults can switch their principal myths as circumstances change.[24] In summary, cults are a particularly dangerous form of religious terrorism because they can appear quickly without warning, have no rational goals, and can become agitated due to the apprehension and hostility with which they are viewed by the society at large.

Whether initiated by cultists or by extremists from more established religions, the violence of religious terrorists can be particularly threatening in comparison with that of the political terrorists of earlier years. As Hoffman notes, "For the religious terrorist, violence is a divine duty . . . executed in direct response to some theological demand . . . and justified by scripture."[25] Religion can be a legitimizing force that not only sanctions but compels large-scale violence on possibly open-ended categories of opponents.[26] Terrorist violence can be seen as a divinely inspired end in itself. One explanation that has been proffered to account for violent Islamic extremism views revenge as the principal goal of the terrorists.[27] This reasoning makes political change or conventional political objectives irrelevant, and it is consistent with observations that violence is itself the objective. Fundamentalist Islam "cannot conceive of either coexistence or political compromise. To the exponents of Holy Terror, Islam must either dominate or be dominated."[28] A recent study that traced the Islamic theological doctrine to the Middle Ages noted recent philosophical developments that explain the preponderance of religious mass-casualty terrorism coming from adherents of Islam.[29] Remarkably, a recent analysis of bin Laden's fatwa, published in *Studies of Conflict and Terrorism*, found that the content of the fatwa was "neither revolutionary nor unique, as it encapsulates broad sentiments in the Muslim world, especially that of Islam's being on the defensive against foreign secular forces and modernization."[30] However, some of the content of the fatwa does fall directly within the paradigm of contemporary religious terrorism. Consider the following excerpts:

> Praise be to God, who revealed the book, controls the clouds, defeats factionalism, and says in his book: "But when the forbidden months are past, then fight and slay the pagans wherever ye find them. . . ."

> On that basis, and in compliance with God's order, we issue the following fatwa to all Muslims:

> The ruling to kill the Americans and their allies—civilians and military—is an individual duty for every Muslim who can do it in any country in which it is possible to do it.[31]

In an article published shortly after 9/11, Steven Simon and David Benjamin noted that many al Qaeda attacks, including the major planning phase of the 9/11 attacks, took place during favorable times for the Palestinians in the Middle East peace process, and that no foreign policy changes by the US government could possibly have appeased the bin Ladenist radical.[32]

While Islamic terrorists are the most notorious of today's violent radicals, others such as right-wing Christian extremists also exhibit many characteristics of the new terrorism. Mark Juergensmeyer, in his book *Terror in the Mind of God: The Global Rise of Religious Violence*, identified three elements that Islamists, radical Christians, and other religious terrorists share: They perceive their objective as a defense of basic identity and dignity; losing the struggle would be unthinkable; and the struggle is in deadlock and cannot be won in real time or in real terms.[33]

In the past, right-wing Christian terrorists conducted racially motivated or religiously motivated acts of violence discriminately against chosen victims, and confrontation with the state was limited to instances when the state interfered with the political or religious agenda of the terrorist groups.[34]

Today, some such groups are directly hostile to the government, which adherents believe is engaged in a widespread conspiracy threatening the existence of the "white Christian way of life." A recent FBI strategic assessment of the potential for domestic terrorism in the United States focused on such groups as Christian Identity and other ultraconservative movements associated with Christian fundamentalism.[35] The most extreme of these fanatics attribute a subhuman status to people of color, which in their eyes mitigates any moral compunction to avoid harming such individuals. In addition, they view themselves in a perpetual battle with the forces of evil (as manifested through non-white races and a powerful, sinister government) that must culminate in the apocalyptic crisis predicted by the Book of Revelations. The Christian terrorists view it as their duty to hasten the realization of this divine plan, which permits and even exhorts them to greater levels of violence. That violence is directed against existing social structures and governments, which are viewed to be hopelessly entangled with such "dark forces" as Jewry, enormous financial conglomerates, and international institutions trying to form an ominous "new world order."

While Christian violence in the United States has been discriminately focused for decades against racial minorities and "immoral" targets, it recently has expanded into attempted bombings and poisoning municipal water supplies. [36] These indiscriminate attacks demonstrate a willingness to tolerate greater levels of collateral damage in efforts to generate mass levels of casualties. The bombing of the Murrah Federal Building in Oklahoma City was the pinnacle of this trend, and although Timothy McVeigh accepted responsibility for that attack, some speculate that there was additional involvement by other conservative militia or Christian terrorists.[37] Effective domestic law enforcement in the United States has largely prevented these groups from achieving widespread violence on the level of Oklahoma City, making that incident a tragic exception among a larger number of foiled plots.

While there is certainly no cooperation between foreign Islamist and US-domestic Christian radicals, there is a disquieting similarity in their views. August Kreis of the paramilitary group Posse Comitatus responded to the collapse of the World Trade Center towers with this disconcerting rant: "Hallelu-Yahweh! May the WAR be started! DEATH to His enemies, may the World Trade Center BURN TO THE GROUND!"[38] Jessica Stern's recent book, *Terror in the Name of God: Why Religious Militants Kill*, which compiles interviews with international terrorists conducted over five years, does not begin with an example from the Guantanamo Bay detention facility or the streets of the Middle East.[39] Her introductory example is a former Christian terrorist in a Texas trailer park. While Islamic terrorism is the most salient threat to the United States, it is not the only danger posed by the new trend of a culture of religious violence and extremism.

A cluster of several cultural features among new international terrorist groups indicates the high level of threat. These aspects include a conception of righteous killing-as-healing, the necessity of total social destruction as part of a process of ultimate purification, a preoccupation with weapons of mass destruction, and a cult of personality where one leader dominates his followers who seek to become perfect clones.[40] These aspects taken together represent a significant departure from the culture of earlier terrorist groups, and the organizations that these characteristics describe represent a serious threat to the civilized world.

POLITICAL AND ORGANIZATIONAL FACTORS

A number of developments on the international scene have created conditions ripe for mass-casualty terrorism. Gross inequalities in economic resources and standards of living between different parts of the world are a popular reason given for the ardency and viciousness of contemporary terrorists,[41] although governmental collapse in "failed states" as a breeding ground for terrorists presents a more convincing variation on this logic.[42] However, there is no "comprehensive explanation in print for how poverty causes terror," nor is there a "demonstrated correlation between the two."[43] The intrusion of Western values and institutions into the Islamic world through the process of free- market globalization is an alternative explanation for the growth of terrorism, which is the weaker party's method of choice to strike back.[44] The process of globalization, which involves the technological, political, economic, and cultural diminution of boundaries between countries across the world, has insinuated a self-interested, inexorable, corrupting market culture into traditional communities. Many see these forces as threatening their way of life. At the same time that globalization has provided a motivation for terrorism, it has also facilitated methods for it.

One of the major consequences of globalization has been a deterioration of the power of the state.[45] The exponential expansion of non-governmental organizations (NGOs), regional alliances, and international organizations has solidified this trend. Although certainly not a conventional humanitarian-based NGO-like the Red Cross or Doctors without Borders, al Qaeda has distinguished itself as among the most "successful" of non-governmental organizations in pursuing its privately-funded global agenda. The trend among terrorists to eschew direct connections with state sponsors has had several advantages for the enterprising extremist. Terrorist groups are more likely to maintain support from "amorphous constituencies," so extreme methods are more acceptable because such methods can be used without fear of alienating political support.[46] Harvey Kushner described this development as a growth of "amateur" groups as direct state sponsorship has declined.[47] Lawrence Freedman pointed out that the Taliban-ruled Afghanistan was not so much a state sponsor of terrorism as it was a "terrorist-sponsored state."[48]

Terrorists do, however, continue to enjoy the benefits of indirect state sponsorship. Although the opportunity for state sponsorship has arguably diminished as a result of the Bush Administration's war on terror that has been prosecuted in the aftermath of the 9/11 attacks, state sponsorship remains widespread. In fact, developments in counterterrorist measures may propagate some dangerous trends of modern terrorism. When terrorists cannot rely on direct state sponsorship, they may become less accountable and harder to track. States must conceal their involvement by exercising less control and thus maintain less-comprehensive intelligence of radical terrorist organizations. Many states have been on the US government list of state sponsors for more than a decade, including Cuba, Iran, Iraq, North Korea, Libya, and Syria. More recently, Sudan and Afghanistan became government sponsors of terrorism. Many state sponsors cooperate with one another to promote terrorist violence, making terrorist activity further disconnected from the foreign policy of any single state. Iran has funded training camps in Sudan, and the Palestinian Islamic Jihad has received support from both Iran and Syria.[49]

Further exacerbating the problem is the method of funding, which often has no measures for accountability. Iran's support for terrorist organizations can include no particular target selection, and it occasionally results, with the funds disappearing, in no terrorist attacks.[50] This unpredictability is tolerated by state sponsors because of the occasional destructive payoff and the obfuscation of evidence connecting the state to the terrorist. Iran has consciously created a decentralized command structure because of these advantages.[51] A further advantage of maintaining arm's length from extremist operatives is for self-protection. The government intelligence organization of Sudan evidently monitored Osama bin Laden while he lived in that country, apparently to prevent his activists from eventually doing harm to even that extremist government.[52]

While the American operations in Afghanistan and Iraq have diluted the threat from those states, other sponsors have possibly been left off official lists for political reasons. (It has been frequently argued that inclusion of a state on the list of state sponsors of terrorism reflects its relationship with the United States.[53]) Pakistani intelligence reportedly has been involved in sponsoring violent terrorists, both in Afghanistan and in the contentious Kashmir. Additionally, the Kingdom of Saudi Arabia has been at the center of controversy over sponsorship and proliferation of radicalism and violence. Laurent Murawiec, an analyst at the RAND Corporation, attracted public attention by pointing out the dangers of Saudi support for radical Islamists and specifically Osama bin Laden in a briefing to the Defense Policy Board in 2002. While no official publication of the RAND Corporation documents this analysis, Murawiec highlighted evidence of Saudi support for the Islamist agenda through Islamic educational venues and financial backing.

So while globalization has helped remove many of the restraints that state sponsorship once imposed, terrorists can still enjoy the funding and protection that sponsorship provides. Another factor of globalization that benefits terrorism is targeting: "In today's globalizing world, terrorists can reach their targets more easily, their targets are exposed in more places, and news and ideas that inflame people to resort to terrorism spread more widely and rapidly than in the past."[54] Among the factors that contribute to this are the easing of border controls and the development of globe-circling infrastructures, which support recruitment, fund-raising, movement of materiel, and other logistical functions.

In addition to international political changes, developments in organizational practice have enhanced the lethality of terrorists. As corporations have evolved organizationally, so have terrorist organizations. Terrorist groups have evolved from hierarchical, vertical organizational structures, to more horizontal, less command-driven groups. John Arquilla, David Ronfeldt, and Michele Zanini note that terrorist leadership is derived from a "set of principles [that] can set boundaries and provide guidelines for decisions and actions so that members do not have to resort to a hierarchy—'they know what they have to do.'" The authors describe organizational designs that may "sometimes appear acephalous (headless), and at other times polycephalous (Hydra-headed)."[55] Paul Smith observed that the multi-cellular structure of al Qaeda gave the organization agility and cover and has been one of its key strengths.[56] This flexibility has allowed al Qaeda to establish bases using indigenous personnel all over the world. It has infiltrated Islamic nongovernmental organizations in order to conceal operations.[57] Jessica Stern recently commented on al Qaeda's ability to maintain operations in the face of an unprecedented onslaught:

> The answer lies in the organization's remarkably protean nature. Over its life span, al Qaeda has constantly evolved and shown a surprising willingness to adapt its mission. This capacity for change has consistently made the group more appealing to recruits, attracted surprising new allies, and—most worrisome from a Western perspective—made it harder to detect and destroy.[58]

TECHNOLOGICAL FACTORS

In addition to the cultural and religious motivations of terrorists and the political and organizational enabling factors, technology has evolved in ways that provide unprecedented opportunities for terrorists. The collapse of the Soviet Union and the possibility of proliferation of nuclear weapons to non-state users is the primary factor that has significantly increased the danger of nuclear terrorism.[59] However, nonnuclear weapons of mass destruction and information technology also have created opportunities for terrorists that are in many ways more threatening than radiological terrorism because these alternatives are more probable.

Some theorists have argued that weapons of mass destruction do not represent a weapon of choice for most terrorists, even in these changing times. Stern writes that "most terrorists will continue to avoid weapons of mass destruction (WMD) for a variety of reasons," preferring the "gun and the bomb."[60] Brian Jenkins agreed that most terrorist organizations are technologically conservative, but he also noted that the self-imposed moral restraints which once governed terrorist actions are fading away.[61] As the trends in the preceding sections reach fullness, increasing the proclivity toward mass-casualty terrorism, terrorists may turn more to these weapons that will better fit their objectives and moralities.

Walter Laqueur's *New Terrorism* emphasizes the availability of very powerful weapons of mass destruction as the major current danger facing the industrialized world.[62] Aside from the nuclear variety of WMD, biological and chemical weapons pose serious dangers. Biological weapons are limited because human contact is required to spread the effects, but as the Asian brush with Severe Acute Respiratory Syndrome (SARS) demonstrated, the associated panic and uncertainty can take a large economic and political toll—not to mention the cost in human suffering for those exposed to the pathogen, perhaps without knowing how or even whether they have been infected. Biological weapons can come in a variety of forms, including viruses, bacteria, and rickettsia (bacteria that can live inside host cells like viruses).

Chemical toxins differ from biological weapons in that they are nonliving pathogens and require direct infection and contact with the victim. This negates the continual spread of the weapon, but it entails more direct and possibly more damaging effects. Chemical agents appear in several types: choking agents that damage lung tissue, blood agents that cause vital organs to shut down, blister agents (also known as vesicants) that damage the skin, and—most lethal—nerve agents. Various methods allow the agent to infect its victim, including inhalation, skin absorption, and ingestion into the digestive tract. Exacerbating the danger is the fact that many deadly chemicals, or their components, are commercially available.

The State Department's annual report on terrorism asserted that the events of 11 September 2001 confirmed the intent and capability of terrorist organizations to plan and execute mass-casualty attacks. The report also stated that these unprecedented attacks may lead to an escalation of the scope of terrorism in terms of chemical, biological, radiological, or nuclear methods. [63] The report further cited evidence discovered in military raids of Afghan terrorist facilities, the use of poison by Hamas to coat shrapnel in improvised explosives, and an unnamed group arrested in Italy with maps of the US embassy and possessing a compound capable of producing hydrogen cyanide. Activities of cults such as Aum Shinrikyo and American terrorist plans to poison municipal water facilities provide further evidence of the WMD threat.

Another key development is recent advances in communications and information technology. This technology provides both assistance to the terrorists and an opportunity for targeting as industrialized societies place greater reliance on information infrastructures. Terrorists will likely avoid dismantling the internet because they need the technology for their own communication and propaganda activities. Accordingly, terrorists may be more interested in "systemic disruption" rather than the total destruction of information networks.[64] While the consequences of a major disruption of American or global information infrastructures could be catastrophic financially or socially, terrorists have not shown the inclination or capability to undertake massive strikes in this area. There have been limited attacks along these lines, but the major use of information technology has been as an aid for terrorists rather than as a target of their activity. The reported use of the internet and e-mail by al Qaeda to coordinate the strikes on the World Trade Center and the Pentagon provides a dramatic example of this sort of coordination. As Paul Pillar noted, "Information technology's biggest impact on terrorists has involved the everyday tasks of organizing and communicating, rather than their methods of attack."[65]

Technology also has increased the ability of terrorists to conduct mass-casualty attacks. As noted earlier, the worst single terrorist attack before 9/11 claimed the lives of about 380 people. The yield of contemporary radiological, chemical, and biological weapons could dwarf that number, given the goals of today's terrorists as exemplified by the World Trade Center and Pentagon attacks, the Oklahoma City bombing, the sarin gas attack on the Tokyo subway, and other, less-successful attacks of the past decade. Technological developments and their availability as spread by the globalized market economy have unavoidably expanded the dangers of terrorism in the new century.

CONCLUSIONS

The practice of terrorism has undergone dramatic changes in recent years. The categorical fanaticism that is apparent in terrorist organizations across a spectrum of belief systems is a major part of this change. In the past, terrorists were more likely to be dominated by pragmatic considerations of political and social change, public opinion, and other such factors. Today, a phenomenon that was a minute rarity in the past—terrorists bent on death and destruction for its own sake—is more commonplace than ever. In addition, the statelessness of today's terrorists removes crucial restraints that once held the most extreme terrorists in check or prevented them from reaching the highest levels in their organizations. Terrorists can still enjoy the funding and shelter that only a national economy can mobilize, but they are on their own to a greater degree in greater numbers than in the past. Organizationally, terrorists are using the non-hierarchical structures and systems that have emerged in recent years. Finally, the potential availability of nuclear, chemical, and biological WMD technology provides the prospect that these trends could result in unprecedented human disasters.

Terrorism has quantitatively and qualitatively changed from previous years. Whether it is Gurr and Coleman's "third wave of vulnerability" or Rapoport's "fourth wave of terrorism," contemporary terrorism is a significant departure from the phenomenon even as recently as during the Cold War. The US *National Security Strategy* has recognized terrorism, in the memorable phrase "the crossroads of radicalism and technology," as the predominant security threat in the post-Cold War world. The cataclysmic impact of 9/11 on both the American strategic consciousness and the international security environment can scarcely be overstated. Those attacks resulted from a combination of cultural, political, and technological factors and were a revelation to the world of the emergence of the new terrorism.

NOTES

1. US Department of State, *Patterns of Global Terrorism 2001* (Washington: GPO, May 2002), p. 171. The statistical review in the State Department's report does not cover total casualties; it tracks only Americans, and the casualty reporting is not as longitudinal as the number of attacks. The casualties of terrorist incidents are tracked for the previous five years versus the previous 20 years.

2. Nadine Gurr and Benjamin Cole, *The New Face of Terrorism: Threats from Weapons of Mass Destruction* (New York: I. B. Tauris, 2002).

3. David C. Rapoport, "The Fourth Wave: September 11 and the History of Terrorism," *Current History*, December 2001, pp. 419-24.

4. National Commission on Terrorism, *Countering the Changing Threat of International Terrorism: Report of the National Commission on Terrorism* (Washington: GPO, 2000).

5. Walter Laqueur, "Terror's New Face," *Harvard International Review*, 20 (Fall 1998), 48-51.

6. Richard A. Falkenrath, Robert D. Newman, and Bradley A. Thayer, *America's Achilles' Heel: Nuclear, Biological, and Chemical Terrorism and Covert Attack* (Cambridge, Mass.: MIT Press, 1998); Philip B. Heymann, *Terrorism and America: A Commonsense Strategy for a Democratic Society* (Cambridge, Mass.: MIT Press, 1998); Bruce Hoffman, *Inside Terrorism* (New York: Columbia Univ. Press, 1998); Brad Roberts, ed., *Terrorism with Chemical and Biological Weapons: Calibrating Risks and Responses* (Alexandria, Va.: Chemical and Biological Arms Control Institute, 1997); and Jessica Stern, *The Ultimate Terrorists* (Cambridge, Mass.: Harvard Univ. Press, 1999).

7. Ashton Carter, John Deutch, and Philip Zelikow, "Catastrophic Terrorism," *Foreign Affairs*, 77 (November/ December 1998), 80-94.

8. S. K. Malik, *The Quranic Concept of War* (Lahore, India: wajidalis, 1979), quoted in Yossef Bodansky, *Bin Laden* (Roosevelt, Calif.: Prima Publishing, 1999), p. xv.

9. National Commission on Terrorism, *Countering the Changing Threat*, p. 2.

10. Chris Quillen, "A Historical Analysis of Mass Casualty Bombers," *Studies in Conflict and Terrorism*, 25 (September/October 2002), 279-92.

11. Walter Laqueur, *No End to War: Terrorism in the Twenty-First Century* (New York: Continuum, 2003).

12. Bruce Hoffman, *Inside Terrorism* (New York: Columbia Univ. Press, 1998).

13. Richard Falkenrath, "Confronting Nuclear, Biological and Chemical Terrorism," *Survival*, 40 (Autumn 1998), 52.

14. Paul Beuman, *Terror and Liberalism* (New York: W. W. Norton, 2003).

15. Paul Wilkinson, *Terrorist Targets and Tactics: New Risks to World Order*, Conflict Study 236 (Washington: Research Institute for the Study of Conflict and Terrorism, December 1990), p. 7.

16. Hoffman, *Inside Terrorism*.

17. David C. Rapoport, "Fear and Trembling: Terrorism in Three Religious Traditions," *American Political Science Review*, 78 (September 1984), 668-72.

18. Bruce Hoffman, "'Holy Terror': The Implications of Terrorism Motivated by a Religious Imperative," *Studies in Conflict and Terrorism*, 18 (October-December 1995), 271-84.

19. Brian M. Jenkins, *The Likelihood of Nuclear Terrorism*, P-7119 (Santa Monica, Calif.: RAND, July 1985).

20. Hoffman, "'Holy Terror,'" p. 273.

21. Mark Juergensmeyer, "Terror Mandated by God," *Terrorism and Political Violence*, 9 (Summer 1997), 16-23.

22. D. W. Brackett, *Holy Terror: Armageddon in Tokyo* (New York: Weatherhill, 1996), pp. 5-7.

23. David Kaplan and Andrew Marshall, *The Cult at the End of the World* (New York: Crown Publishers, 1996), p. 74.

24. Stern, *The Ultimate Terrorists*, p. 72.

25. Hoffman, *Inside Terrorism*, p. 20.

26. Hoffman, "'Holy Terror,'" p. 280.

27. Gavin Cameron, *Nuclear Terrorism* (Basingstoke, Eng.: Macmillan, 1999), p. 139.

28. Amir Taheri, *Holy Terror: The Inside Story of Islamic Terrorism* (London: Hutchinson, 1987), p. 192.

29. Daniel Benjamin and Steven Simon, *The Age of Sacred Terror* (New York: Random House, 2002).

30. Magnus Ranstorp, *Studies in Conflict & Terrorism*, 21 (October-December 1998), 321-32.

31. Shaikh Osama Bin Muhammad Bin Laden, Ayman al Zawahiri, Abu-Yasir Rifa'I Abroad Taha, Shaikh Mir Hamzah, and Fazlul Rahman, "the World Islamic Front's Statement Urging Jihad Against Jews and Crusaders," *London al-Quds al-Arabi*, 23 February 1998.

32. Steven Simon and Daniel Benjamin, "The Terror," *Survival*, 43 (Winter 2001), 12.

33. Mark Juergensmeyer, *Terror in the Mind of God: The Global Rise of Religious Violence* (Berkeley: Univ. of California Press, 2000).

34. Gurr and Cole, *The New Face of Terrorism*, p. 144.

35. Federal Bureau of Investigation, *Project Megiddo* (Washington: GPO, 20 October 1999), http://permanent.access.gpo.gov/lps3578/www.fbi.gov/library/megiddo/megiddo.pdf.

36. Gurr and Cole, *The New Face of Terrorism*.

37. See Gore Vidal, *Perpetual War for Perpetual Peace: How We Got to Be So Hated* (New York: Verso, 2002) for an exposition of the point of view that the Murrah Federal Building bombing could not have possibly occurred without a larger support structure.

38. Daniel Levitas, *The Terrorist Next Door: The Militia Movement and the Radical Right* (New York: Thomas Dunne Books, 2002).

39. Jessica Stern, *Terror in the Name of God: Why Religious Militants Kill* (New York: HarperCollins, 2003).

40. Robert J. Lifton, *Destroying the World to Save It: Aum Shinrikyo, Apocalyptic Violence, and the New Global Terrorism* (New York: Metropolitan Books, 1999).

41. James D.Wolfensohn, "Making the World a Better and Safer Place: The Time for Action is Now," *Politics*, 22 (May 2002), 118-23; Andrew S. Furber, "Don't Drink the Water . . ." *British Medical Journal*, 326 (22 March 2003), 667; Jan Nederveen Pieterse, "Global Inequality: Bringing Politics Back In, *Third World Quarterly*, 23 (December 2002), 1023-46.

42. Karin von Hippel, "The Roots of Terrorism: Probing the Myths," *Political Quarterly*, 73 (August 2002), 25-39.

43. Michael Mousseau, "Market Civilization and Its Clash With Terror," *International Security*, 27 (Winter 2003), 6.

44. Mousseau, "Market Civilization"; Audrey Kurth Cronin, "Behind the Curve: Globalization and International Terrorism," *International Security*, 27 (Winter 2003), 30-58.

45. Charles W. Kegley, Jr., and Gregory A. Raymond, *Exorcising the Ghost of Westphalia: Building World Order in the New Millennium* (Upper Saddle River, N.J.: Prentice Hall, 2002).

46. Stern, *The Ultimate Terrorists*.

47. Harvey W. Kushner, ed., *The Future of Terrorism: Violence in the New Millennium* (Thousand Oaks, Calif.: Sage Publications, 1998).

48. Lawrence Freedman, "The Third World War?" *Survival*, 43 (Winter 2001), 61-88.

49. James Adams, *The New Spies* (London: Hutchinson, 1994), pp.180, 184.

50. Ibid., p. 180.

51. Taheri, *Holy Terror*, pp. 100-01.

52. Frank Smyth, "Culture Clash, bin Laden, Khartoum and the War Against the West," *Jane's Intelligence Review*, October 1998, p. 22.

53. Adrian Guelke, *The Age of Terrorism* (London: I. B. Tauris, 1998), p. 148.

54. Paul R. Pillar, "Terrorism Goes Global: Extremist Groups Extend their Reach Worldwide," *The Brookings Review*, 19 (Fall 2001), 34-37.

55. John Arquilla, David Ronfeldt, and Michele Zanini, "Networks, Netwar, and Information-Age Terrorism," in *Countering the New Terrorism*, ed. Ian O. Lesser et al., MR-989-AF (Santa Monica, Calif.: RAND, 1999), p. 51.

56. Paul J. Smith, "Transnational Terrorism and the al Qaeda Model: Confronting New Realities," *Parameters*, 32 (Summer 2002), 37.

57. Ibid., p. 37.

58. Jessica Stern, "The Protean Enemy," *Foreign Affairs*, 82 (July/August 2003).

59. Brian M. Jenkins, "Will Terrorists Go Nuclear? A Reappraisal," in Kushner, *The Future of Terrorism*, pp. 225-49.

60. Stern, *The Ultimate Terrorist*, p. 70.

61. Jenkins, "Will Terrorists Go Nuclear?"

62. Walter Laqueur, *The New Terrorism: Fanaticism and the Arms of Mass Destruction* (New York: Oxford Press, 2000).

63. US Department of State, *Patterns of Global Terrorism*, p. 66.

64. Arquilla, Ronfeldt, and Zanini, "Networks, Netwar, and Information-Age Terrorism."

65. Pillar, "Terrorism Goes Global."

Preemptive Military Doctrine:
No Other Choice Against Transnational,
Non-State Actors

Russell D. Howard, 2003

In a speech delivered June 1, 2002, to graduating cadets at the U.S. Military Academy at West Point, President George W. Bush asserted his administration's intention to carry out preemptive military attacks if necessary to protect American interests.[1]

The implications of the speech signaled a historic shift from the long-accepted Cold War applications of the use of force. "For much of the last century," the president said, "America's defense relied on the Cold War doctrines of deterrence and containment. In some cases, those strategies still apply." However, the president contended, "new threats also require new thinking."

> Deterrence—the promise of massive retaliation against nations—means nothing against shadowy terrorist networks with no nation or citizens to defend. Containment is not possible when unbalanced dictators with weapons of mass destruction can deliver those weapons on missiles or secretly provide them to terrorist allies.[2]

More recently, President Bush reinforced his use-of-force-position in the "The National Security Act of the United States of America." According to the document, deterrence and containment, the previous foundations of U.S. strategy, are no longer valid. According to the president, the United States must instead identify and destroy the terrorist threat before it reaches our borders," and, if necessary, act alone and use preemptive force.[3]

This paper agrees with the president's assertion that a preemptive strategy is necessary in a post–Cold War security environment, in which America's most dangerous adversaries are transnational, non-state actors who have access to weapons of mass destruction and intend to use them. I argue that the United States must have a preemption doctrine that enables decision-makers to face the unique security threat posed by transnational, non-state actors such as al Qaeda. This paper does not engage in the debate regarding the use of military preemption or "preventive war" against sovereign states. Military preemption against a sovereign state may be an acceptable tactic in certain situations, particularly if the state is threatening the use of weapons of mass destruction. However, in addition to preemption, other military means such as defense, deterrence, and coercion can be used to influence an adversarial state's behavior. Better yet, non-military means of persuasion such as diplomacy and economic pressure can

---

Colonel Russell D. Howard is professor and head of the Department of Social Sciences at the United States Military Academy at West Point. He is a career Special Forces officer, who has served at every level of unit command in Special Forces, including command of the 1st Special Forces Group from 1994 to 1996.

also be used. Unfortunately, at least in my opinion, these more acceptable means of persuasion are not viable when dealing with a hostile, non-state actor, such as al Qaeda.

During the Cold War, most international terrorism was part of the East versus West, left versus right confrontation—a small but dangerous side show to the greater, bipolar, Cold War drama. Terrorism in this era was almost always the province of groups of militants that had the backing of political forces and states hostile to American interests. What is new today is the emergence of terrorism that is not ideological in a political sense. Instead, it is inspired by religious extremists and ethnic separatist elements. These elements might be individuals akin to the Unabomber or other like-minded people working in cells, small groups, or larger coalitions.[4] They do not answer completely to any government, they operate across national borders, and they have access to funding and advanced technology.[5]

These new terrorist groups are not bound by the same constraints or motivated by the same goals as nation-states. Religious extremists, ethnic separatists, and lone Unabombers are not responsive to traditional diplomacy or military deterrence because there is no state to negotiate with or to retaliate against.

Today's terrorists are not concerned about limiting casualties. Under the old rules, as Brian Jenkins first noted, terrorists wanted a lot of people watching, not a lot of people dead.[6] They did not want large body counts because they wanted converts and they also wanted a seat at the table. Today's terrorists are not particularly concerned about converts, and rather than wanting a seat at the table, "they want to destroy the table and everyone sitting at it."[7] In fact, religious terrorists such as al Qaeda, in particular, want casualties—lots of them.[8]

Today's terrorism is not an ideological "ism" like communism or capitalism, with values that can be debated in the classroom or decided at the polls. Rather, it is the fanatical misuse of an ancient tactic and instrument of conflict. The only difference between modern terrorism and its ancient roots is that the "new terrorism" is better financed and has a global reach that it did not have before the advent of globalization and the information revolution. The new terrorism can ride the back of the Web and use advanced communications systems to move vast financial sums from Sudan to the Philippines or virtually any place on earth. And for $28.50, any Internet surfer, including terrorists, can purchase the book *Bacteriological Warfare: A Major Threat to North America,* which explains how to grow deadly bacteria that could be used in a weapon of mass destruction (WMD).

TERRORISTS AND WMD

The prospect of terrorists using WMD (nuclear, biological, and chemical) weapons to attack the United States is the main reason the president has little choice but to add preemption to his menu of potential military power options. About this, the president has been very clear:

> When the spread of chemical and biological and nuclear weapons, along with ballistic missile technology occurs, even weak states and small groups could attain a catastrophic power to strike great nations. Our enemies have declared this very intention, and have been caught seeking these terrible weapons. They want the capability to blackmail us, or to harm us, or to harm our friends—and we will oppose them with all our power.[9]

Indeed, al Qaeda has threatened the United States with WMD. Recent discoveries in Afghanistan have confirmed that al Qaeda and other terrorist groups are actively pursuing the capability of using biological agents against United States and its allies.[10] According to David Kaye, this should not be a surprise:

Only a blind, deaf and dumb terrorist group could have survived the last five years and not been exposed at least to the possibility of the use of WMD, while the more discerning terrorists would have found some tactically brilliant possibilities already laid out on the public record.[11]

Steven Miller, director of the International Security Program at the John F. Kennedy School of Government at Harvard University, agrees that policy makers should be concerned about terrorist access to nuclear weapons, too. Presently, Miller believes the opportunities for well-organized and well-financed terrorists to infiltrate a Russian nuclear storage facility are greater than ever.[12]

Miller further believes there have been more than two-dozen thefts of weapons-usable materials in the former Soviet Union in recent years. According to Miller, several suspects have been arrested in undercover sting operations, leaving doubt about those who may have gotten away.[13] It almost happened in 1994, says Miller, "when 350 grams of plutonium were smuggled on board a Lufthansa flight from Moscow to Munich. Fortunately, SWAT teams confiscated the material as soon as it arrived."[14]

Given the known goals of terrorists, the United States can no longer rely solely on a reactive, crisis-response military posture as it has in the past. The inability to deter a potential attacker, the immediacy of today's threats, and the catastrophic consequences of a WMD attack do not permit that option. The United States simply cannot allow its enemies to strike first with nuclear, radiological, biological, or chemical weapons.[15]

ARMS CONTROL PROTOCOLS AND WESTPHALIAN RULES NO LONGER APPLY

The inability of the United States to negotiate with non-state actors and its over-reliance on treaties and conventions limit the usefulness of diplomacy in reducing the likelihood of WMD attacks. For example, U.S. policy states that it will not negotiate with terrorists.[16] The rationale behind this policy is clear: Giving in to terrorist demands will prompt more terrorist activity. This is especially true in hostage situations because negotiations with terrorists could potentially force the U.S. to risk having to meet certain demands for ransom or safe passage.

However, it would be very beneficial to have a mechanism—most likely secret—that could enable an opportunity to dialogue with terrorists. This would be especially important in regard to transnational, non-state actors who have no formal diplomatic voice. The manner in which this dialogue might take place would depend on the situation. Discussions could be held in secret or through surrogates. Preferably, a dialogue—not necessarily negotiations—with terrorists could be established before an attack and prevent it from happening, thus avoiding the necessity of preemption. In addition to the aforementioned possibility, opening a dialogue is important if for no other reason than because understanding what is really on a terrorist's mind has intelligence value. More importantly, a terrorist who understands what our response to a hostile act will be has deterrent value.

Nuclear arms control and reduction treaties promulgated during the Cold War were, and still are, valuable assets for preventing conflict. They provided baseline agreements that fostered cooperation between the powers and led to greater transparency and confidence-building measures that still exist today. Unfortunately, treaties meant to control and reduce the number of chemical and biological weapons have not been as effective.

The Chemical Weapons Convention (CWC) entered into force on April 29, 1997. It has been signed by 120 states, and bans chemical weapons production and storage as well as use. The strength of the convention is that it calls for unprecedented and highly intrusive inspection provisions, including routine and challenge inspection mechanisms. The weakness of the convention is that several countries that pose concerns about chemical proliferation have not joined the CWC regime. These include Iraq, Libya, North Korea, and Syria.[17]

Biological weapons are also prohibited by a treaty, the Biological and Toxin Weapons Convention (BWC), which entered into force in 1975 and now comprises some 140 member states. The strength of the BWC is that it bans an entire class of weapons, prohibiting the development, production, stockpiling, or acquisition of biological agents or toxins of any type or quantity that do not have protective, medical, or other peaceful purposes. "The major shortfall of the BWC is its lack of any on-site verification mechanism."[18]

The chemical warfare and biological warfare conventions and nuclear arms control and reduction treaties only affect state behavior. They have no impact on the behavior of transnational and other non-state actors that might possess and use chemical, biological, or nuclear weapons, or on rogue states that are not signatories to the conventions.

The major problems the United States has in addressing international WMD threats are outdated military doctrine and the traditional way the U.S. employs military force. The traditional uses of military force are defense, deterrence, compellence, and presence. Defense against terrorist use of WMD is extremely difficult, especially in a democracy. Without compromising civil liberties in draconian ways—a goal of terrorists—no defense regime could come close to guaranteeing security against a terrorist intent on attacking the United States with WMD. Or, as Secretary of Defense Donald Rumsfeld reflected in a speech at the National Defense University in January 2002, "It is not possible to defend against every conceivable kind of attack in every conceivable location at every minute of the day or night. The best, and in some cases, the only defense is a good offense."

Deterrence against non-governmental actors would be also be extremely difficult to implement. For example, where exactly do you nuke Osama bin Laden if he launches a biological attack?

> Deterrence generally does not work against terrorists. Stateless and usually spread over wide regions or even among continents, terrorists do not present a viable target for retaliation. The death and destruction that can be visited upon a terrorist organization in a retaliatory attack is greatly exceeded by the damage even a small terrorist cell can inflict on civilian society.[19]

Presence would certainly help get U.S. forces to a crisis area more rapidly, but U.S. military presence overseas—other than those already committed to combat or peace enforcement roles—is declining, as is the number of military personnel in the United States who can be deployed. Therefore, using military force to stop adversaries before they act has more utility in the post–Cold War world.

Historically, the United States has employed its military to compel enemies to change their behavior after a crisis has occurred. In the past, the United States could take a massive blow such as Pearl Harbor, retreat, accept some risk while re-arming and building up power, then counterattack, defeat the enemy, declare victory, and demobilize. This was "the American way of war." Today, the risk and the opportunity to attack are before the blow, not afterward. After the blow today—from a dirty nuke, biological or chemical agent, or something worse like a super strain of flu that is resistant to all antibodies—what gets mobilized if there is anything left to mobilize? Who gets counterattacked, if the attacker is unknown? What defines victory?

PREEMPTION—NOT FIGHTING FAIR?

The use of military force preemptively is a difficult concept for many Americans to accept. It defies American's sense of fairness and proportionality as well as the rules of warfare, as Brad Roberts points out:

> Moral philosophy establishes that wars of self-defense are just, whereas wars of aggression are not. But there has long been a healthy debate about precisely what constitutes a war of self-defense.

A mid-sixteenth-century scholar of just war wrote, "There is a single and only just cause for commencing a war… namely, wrong received." In our day Michael Walzer has argued, "Nothing but aggression can justify war…. There must actually have been a wrong, and it must actually have been received (or its receipt must be, as it were, only minutes away)."[20]

However, this view has not been held by all. In 1625, Hugo Grotius wrote, "The first just cause of war… is an injury, which even though not actually committed, threatens our persons or our property."[21] Grotius emphasized that to safeguard against wars of aggression, it was essential to be certain about the enemy's intent to attack.

In 1914, Elihu Root said that international law did not require the aggrieved state to wait before using force in self-defense "until it is too late to protect itself."[22] Interestingly, in his book _Just Wars_, Michael Walzer seems to contradict earlier statements referenced by Brad Roberts by arguing that, "states can rightfully defend themselves against violence that is imminent but not actual."

Roberts contends, and I agree, that there can be, "no blanket reply to the question, is there a moral case for preemption? Some acts of preemption will be deemed just, others unjust." In the case of preemption against WMD threats, Roberts further argues that the strongest moral case for U.S. strategy of preemption exists under the following conditions:

(1) an aggressor has actually threatened to use his WMD weapons, has taken steps to ready the means to do so, and has specifically threatened the United States (including its territory, citizens, or military forces); (2) those WMD weapons have been built in violation of international law; (3) the aggressor's threatened actions invoke larger questions about the credibility of security guarantees or the balance of power within a region; (4) the president has secured the approval of the U.S. Congress; and (5) the United States has secured the backing of the U.N. Security Council and any relevant regional organization. The prudential tests of last resort, proportionality, and reasonable chance of success must also be met.[23]

I agree with the first four tenets of Roberts's argument but not with the last. The backing of the UN and regional organizations would strengthen the moral argument for preemption, but may be impossible to obtain given China's reluctance to violate sovereignty under any circumstances and Russia's recurring, post-Kosovo intervention habit of siding with rogue states like Iraq and Iran. Also, the United States must never forgo the option to act unilaterally.

DOMESTIC POLITICAL SUPPORT

The commonly held view that Americans disapprove of preemption is simply not true. A good example of this is the 1998 bombing of a Sudanese chemical plant that was suspected of having ties to Osama bin laden. After the attack, even when it was revealed that the plant was probably making nothing sinister, U.S. public opinion was still strongly in favor of the attacks.[24] In fact, two-thirds of Americans approved of the military strike, while only 19 percent were opposed.[25]

More recent data show that Congress is in favor of preemption under certain conditions, particularly when conducted against non-state actors intent on harming the United States. Dr. Scott Silverstone, a professor and researcher at the United States Military Academy, has categorized data from congressional hearings, memos, media articles, and personal statements that show that members of the Senate and House are nearly unanimous in their support for preemption as a strategy. In fact, Silverstone's 2002–2003 data show that 90 percent of the Senate favored a preemption strategy against non-state actors. The figure in the House was 81 percent. Interestingly, not one elected official in the House or Senate explicitly rejected the notion of preemptive warfare directed against non-state actors.[26]

PREEMPTION AND INTERNATIONAL LAW

According to Anthony Clark Arend, "Under the regime of customary international law that developed long before the UN Charter was adopted, it was generally accepted that preemptive force was permissible in self-defense."[27] If a state could demonstrate necessity—that another state was about to engage in armed attack—and act proportionately, preemptive self-defense was an acceptable, and legal, action.[28]

In the post–UN Charter world, Article 2(4) stipulates that states were to refrain from the threat or use of force against another state unless—as stipulated in Article 39—the Security Council authorizes the use of force against offending states due to a threat to peace, breach of the peace, or an act of aggression. However, Article 51 confirms that the Charter will not impair the inherent right of individual or collective self-defense if an armed attack occurs against a UN member.[29]

Two divergent interpretations of Article 51 prevent the UN from wholly accepting the preemptive use of force as an acceptable national strategy. Restrictionists interpret Article 51 to mean that a state can only respond if attacked, while counter-restrictionists believe states can use anticipatory self-defense, for many of the same reasons that self-defense was acceptable prior to the UN Charter.

My view is that neither "customary" nor "post–UN Charter" international law addresses the issue of preemptive self-defense against transnational, non-state actors with access to weapons of mass destruction who are intent on committing acts of terrorism. Therefore, preemption as defined by President Bush is as valid as any other interpretation of "preemptive self-defense."

CONCLUSION

I was on the dais at West Point when President Bush gave his "preemption speech" and was taken with one of his statements, which I include as part of my concluding remarks. He told the audience that "The gravest danger to freedom lies at the perilous crossroads of radicalism and technology. When the spread of chemical and biological and nuclear weapons, along with ballistic missile technology... when that occurs, even weak states and small groups could attain a catastrophic power to strike great nations.... Our enemies have declared this very intention, and have been caught seeking these terrible weapons. They want the capability to blackmail us, or to harm us, or to harm our friends—and we will oppose them with all our power."

In my view, "opposing them with all our power," must include the preemptive use of force to defeat terrorists before they can inflict pain on the United States.

Traditional applications of American power—economic, political, diplomatic, and military—used to leverage and influence states in the past are not effective against non-state actors. Whom do you sanction or embargo? With whom do you negotiate? How do you defend against or deter Osama bin Laden? You don't. The only effective way to influence the Osama bin Ladens of the world is to preempt them before they can act.

NOTES

1. President George W. Bush, June 1, 2002, West Point, New York.

2. Ibid.

3. Karen DeYoung and Mike Allen, "Bush Shifts Strategy From Deterrence to Dominance," *Washington Post*, September 21, 2002, P. A01.

4. Stephen A. Cambone, *A New Structure for National Security Policy Planning*, Washington D.C.: Government Printing Office, 1996, p. 43.

5. Gideon Rose, "It Could Happen Here—Facing the New Terrorism," *Foreign Affairs*, March– April 1999, p. 1.

6. Frequently quoted remark made by Brian Jenkins in 1974.

7. Quote attributed to James Woolsey, 1994.

8. Bruce Hoffman, *Inside Terrorism*, New York: Columbia University Press, 1998, p. 205.

9. George W. Bush, June 1, 2002.

10. Judith Miller, "Lab Suggests Qaeda Planned to Build Arms, Officials Say," *New York Times*, September 14, 2002, p. 1.

11. David Kay, "WMD Terrorism: Hype or Reality," in James M. Smith and William C. Thomas, ed., *The Terrorism Threat and U.S. Government Response: Operational and Organizational Factors* (U.S. Air Force Academy: INSS Book Series, 2001), p. 12.

12. Doug Gavel, "Can Nuclear Weapons Be Put Beyond the Reach of Terrorists," *Kennedy School of Government Bulletin*, Autumn 2002, p. 43.

13. Ibid., p. 45.

14. Ibid., p. 48.

15. See the National Security Strategy of the United States.

16. Stansfield Turner, *Terrorism and Democracy*, (Boston: Houghton Mifflin, 1991), p. xii. Actually Admiral Turner makes the argument that the United States will negotiate with terrorists. See Chapter 26, *We Will Make Deals*.

17. "Weapons of Mass Destruction," *Great Decisions*, 1999, p. 51.

18. Ibid., p. 52.

19. James Wirtz and James A. Russell, "U.S. Policy on Preventive War and Preemption," *The Nonproliferation Review*, vol. 10, number 1, Spring 2003, p. 116.

20. Brad Roberts, "NBC-Armed Rogues: Is there a Moral Case for Preemption?" *Close Calls: Intervention, Terrorism, Missile Defense, and 'Just War' Today*, Ed. Elliott Abrams, (EPPC-March, 1998), p. 11.

21. Hugo Grotius, *The Law of War and Peace*, book 2, chapter 1, section 2.

22. Elihu Root, "The Real Monroe Doctrine," *American Journal of International Law* 35 (1914), p. 427.

23. Roberts, p. 13.

24. "Excerpts: U.S. Editorials Assess Impact of Anti-Terrorist Strikes," *USIS Washington File*, www.fas.org/man/dod-101/ops/docs/98082307_tpo.html, June 14, 2000, p. 1–6.

25. John Diamond, "U.S. Strikes Tougher Stance Against Terrorism," *Cnews*, www.canoe.ca/ CNEWSStrikeAtTerrorism/aug20_us.html, August 21, 1998.

26. Multiple conversations with Dr. Scott Silverstone.

27. Anthony Clark Arend, "International Law and Preemptive Use of Military Force," *Washington Quarterly*, Spring 2003, p, 90.

28. Ibid., p. 91.

29. Ibid.

Countering Al Qaeda

Brian Michael Jenkins, 2002

SUMMARY

Since the terrorist attacks of September 11, 2001, the United States has achieved significant successes in its war on terrorism. Removing the Taliban government in Afghanistan, thereby eliminating al Qaeda's sanctuary and training camps, has broken an important link in the process that once provided al Qaeda's leadership with a continuing flow of recruits. Toppling the Taliban also demonstrated American resolve and international support, and it underscored the considerable risk run by governments that provide assistance to terrorists.

Having achieved its initial goals in Afghanistan, the United States is now in a second, more complex phase of the war, where it must continue its efforts to destroy al Qaeda and at the same time attempt to combat terrorism as a mode of conflict. Al Qaeda, along with its associates and its successors, will fight on, drawing upon a deep reservoir of hatred and a desire for revenge. It must be presumed that al Qaeda will exploit all of its ability to cause catastrophic death and destruction—there will be no self-imposed limits to its violence. It can also be presumed that the organization will continue its efforts to acquire and use weapons of mass destruction (WMD); that it will attack U.S. targets abroad where possible; and that it will attempt to mount attacks within the United States. Al Qaeda constitutes the most serious immediate threat to the security of the United States.

Although some measure of success has been achieved in uncovering terrorist plots, the ability of U.S. agencies to detect and prevent future terrorist attacks is limited. Al Qaeda, however, must now operate in a less-permissive environment. If al Qaeda can be kept on the run, the numbers it can train will decline. And declining numbers eventually will result in a corresponding qualitative decline in terrorist operations. However, it is possible that al Qaeda will adapt to the more difficult post–September 11 operational environment by morphing into an even looser network, devolving more initiative and resources to local operatives.

The greatest challenge in the second phase of the campaign against terrorism is that as military operations move beyond a single theater, the more complex tasks will be dispersed among numerous departments, agencies, and offices, and the focus on the overall U.S. strategy will be lost, along with the nation's ability to coordinate operations. The American campaign must continue to emphasize the following central elements:

Brian Michael Jenkins has devoted the last 25 years to an in-depth study of terrorism and international crime. Appointed in 1996 by President Clinton, Mr. Jenkins served on the White House Commission on Aviation Safety and Security. In 2000 he became a member of the U.S. Comptroller General's Advisory Board. He wrote his first monograph on the topic of terrorism in 1974. In addition, he has written several books and articles; over 100 articles have appeared in the RAND reports.

- The destruction of al Qaeda remains the primary aim.
- The pursuit of al Qaeda must be single-minded and unrelenting.
- The campaign against terrorism will take time, possibly decades.
- The fight in Afghanistan must be continued as long as al Qaeda operatives remain in the country.
- Pakistan must be kept on the side of the allies in efforts to destroy the remnants of al Qaeda and the Taliban and dilute Islamic extremism.
- New networks must be created to exploit intelligence across frontiers.
- The goals of the war on terrorism cannot be accomplished unilaterally —international cooperation is a prerequisite for success.
- This is a war against specific terrorists, the larger goal of which is to combat terrorism.
- The strategy should include political warfare, aimed at reducing the appeal of extremists, encouraging alternative views, and discouraging terrorists' use of WMD.
- Deterrent strategies may be appropriate for dealing with the terrorists' support structures.
- It must be made clear that terrorist use of WMD will bring extraordinary responses.
- Homeland security strategies must be developed that are both effective and efficient.
- The war against the terrorists at home and abroad must be conducted in a way that is consistent with American values.

Finally, it is necessary to be determinedly pragmatic. America's goal is not revenge for the September 11 attacks. The goal is not even bringing individual terrorists to justice. It is the destruction of a terrorist enterprise that threatens American security and, by extension, the security of the world.

INTRODUCTION

Since the terrorist attacks of September 11, 2001, the United States has achieved significant successes in its war on terrorism. Removing the Taliban government in Afghanistan, thereby eliminating al Qaeda's sanctuary and training camps, has broken an important link in the process that once provided al Qaeda's leadership with a continuing flow of recruits. Toppling the Taliban also demonstrated American resolve and international support, and it underscored the considerable risk run by governments that provide assistance to terrorists.

The United States has avoided portraying its campaign against al Qaeda and the Taliban as a crusade against Islam (an accusation made by al Qaeda's leaders), and it has successfully brought about a fundamental change in Pakistan's policy. Once a Taliban supporter, Pakistan has become an ally in the campaign against Islamic extremism. U.S. diplomacy has also turned the international outrage and concern prompted by the September 11 attacks into a global commitment to combat terrorism, confirmed in United Nations Resolution 1373. Through its military presence in Uzbekistan, its diplomatic intervention in the confrontation between Pakistan and India over Kashmir, and its direct military assistance to the Philippines and Georgia, the United States has limited al Qaeda's ability to exploit other conflicts and develop new bases.

Despite these successes, the United States still faces a serious terrorist threat. Public warnings of possible attacks continue to rattle nerves and impede economic recovery, and September 11 signaled a fundamental and permanent change in the security environment. But while Americans are apprehensive, still in shock over the attacks on the World Trade Center and the Pentagon, they appear reluctant to accept that this was not a one-time anomaly. Despite the continuing issuance of new warnings, Americans are capable of lapsing into a dangerous complacency.

The tasks of reorganizing government, investigating perceived failures in intelligence, implementing new security measures, dealing with new crises abroad, and addressing important domestic matters inevitably distract government and public attention from the very real threat posed by al Qaeda. In this environment, one can understand the relentless determination of the otherwise unappealing ancient Roman Senator Cato, who reportedly concluded every speech with the reminder that "Carthage must be destroyed."

Having achieved its initial goals in Afghanistan, the United States is now in a second, more complex phase of the war, where it must continue its efforts to destroy al Qaeda and at the same time attempt to combat terrorism as a mode of conflict. This will require the orchestration of intelligence collection, the pursuit of traditional criminal investigations leading to trials, the imposition of financial controls and economic sanctions as well as offers of material reward, the application of conventional military power, the use of covert and special operations, the provision of military assistance, and psychological warfare to disrupt terrorist operations and destroy terrorist groups. Greater international coordination will be required. Without a clear exposition of strategy, the focus of the campaign could easily be lost.

UNDERSTANDING THE ENEMY

The Emergence of al Qaeda

Al Qaeda was a product of the struggle to eject the Soviet Union from Afghanistan. Portrayed as a holy war, that campaign brought together volunteers and financial contributors from throughout the Islamic world. Muslims from Algeria, Egypt, Saudi Arabia, Southeast Asia, and beyond fought side by side, forging relationships and creating a cadre of veterans who shared a powerful life experience, a more global view, and a heady sense of confidence underscored by the Soviet Union's ultimate withdrawal and subsequent collapse, for which they assumed credit. Instead of being welcomed home as heroes, however, the returning veterans of the Afghan campaign were watched by suspicious regimes who worried that the religious fervor of the fighters posed a political threat. Isolated at home, they became ready recruits for new campaigns.

There were ample reasons and opportunities to continue the fight: the Gulf War and the consequent arrival of American troops in Saudi Arabia; the continued repression of Islamic challenges to local regimes; armed struggles in Algeria, Egypt, the newly independent Muslim republics of the former Soviet Union, Kashmir, the Philippines, and Bosnia; the forces of globalization that seemed threatening to all local cultures; and the continuing civil war in Afghanistan. Organizational survival, the natural desire to continue in meaningful activity, and the rewards of status and an inflated self-image contributed powerful incentives to continue the fight. The subsequent victories of a like-minded Taliban guaranteed safe haven for the militants and their training camps, which graduated thousands of additional volunteers.

What Osama bin Laden and his associates contributed to this potent but unfocused force was a sense of vision, mission, and strategy that combined twentieth century theory of a unified Islamic polity with restoration of the Islamic Caliphate that, at its height, stretched from Spain to India. This vision had operational utility. It recast the numerous local conflicts into a single struggle between an authentic Islam and a host of corrupt satraps who would collapse without the backing of the West—the United States in particular. It thereby provided a single, easily agreed-upon enemy, whose fate, when confronted with a unified Islamic struggle, would be the same as that of the Soviet Union. By erasing the boundaries between individual countries and their conflicts, al Qaeda could draw upon a much larger reservoir of human resources for the larger battle. In addition to the

thousands of veterans of the war against the Soviet Union, al Qaeda now had thousands of new recruits to train.

Quantity ultimately translates into quality. It enables organizers to identify and exploit specialized talent that would be scarce or not available in a smaller enterprise. This is key to al Qaeda's operational capabilities. Amply funded, protected in Afghanistan, supported by Pakistan, motivated by a
powerful vision, al Qaeda became the banner carrier of Islam's response to past defeats, frustration,
humiliation, resentment, and fear. Al Qaeda's spectacular terrorist blows against the United States in
Africa and the Middle East and America's feeble response, despite its vigorous denunciations, made
Osama bin Laden a heroic leader. Everything seemed to confirm al Qaeda's calculations.

Process, Planning, and Mission

Al Qaeda is more than just an organization; it is also a process, and its principal resource is its human
capital. Al Qaeda's future ability to grow and continue operations depends most strongly on its ability to gather new recruits.

On the basis of what we know about the September 11 attackers and the limited testimony of captured al Qaeda operatives, al Qaeda appears to function like many cults. Frustrated immigrants in Europe
and America, drifters living on the margins of society, seekers of absolute truth or greater meaning in
their lives, lonely souls with varying levels of education show up—on their own or invited by friends—
at mosques and prayer groups, a few of which offer radical interpretations of faith. Fiery sermons identify common enemies, the obstacles to political and personal achievement. Recruiters watch for resonance and select promising acolytes for more intense indoctrination and training.

Prior to September 11, the training camps in Afghanistan provided a way of testing commitment. In Afghanistan, volunteers faced hardship and sacrifice, as well as opportunities for combat.
With practical training came further indoctrination. The recruits became part of a secret international brotherhood that superseded all other affiliations and loyalties.

Fulfillment of the radical Islamic vision of heroic deeds leading to the restoration of a utopian
Islamic empire on earth—or, if God wills, eternal reward in the hereafter—requires embracing an
aggressive interpretation of jihad. Exhortations to kill in quantity underscore the teaching that there
are no innocents in this war. The most intelligent and dedicated volunteers receive further training
and indoctrination, and they return to the world with a sense of mission and power. Of course, not
all are Mohammed Attas, fanatics capable of planning and executing complex operations. Some are
"acorns," buried at random to be dug up when needed for an operation.

Most of the proposals for terrorist operations appear to come from the operatives in the field,
rather than from the center. Approval from above, however, brings resources that elevate such plans
to a deadlier realm. The provision of technical advice, money, documents, and additional manpower
to the self-selected warriors suggests the existence of an underground bureaucracy—al Qaeda has middle management. Some operations seem to receive little central support, but a plan for an attack on
the scale of September 11 would certainly have significant central control and could well have been
initiated by al Qaeda's command.

An attack that carries the al Qaeda brand, duly credited in the news media to Osama bin Laden,
thus enhances his reputation. Each attack becomes a recruiting poster, demonstrating the power of al
Qaeda's interpretation of Islam, attracting more recruits.

Changed Perceptions of the Terrorist Threat

The September 11 attack destroyed America's sense of invulnerability and illustrated the limits of its intelligence infrastructure. It demonstrated that foreign terrorists were capable of mounting major attacks on
U.S. soil without being detected. Preparations for earlier terrorist attacks, including the 1996 bombing of

Khobar Towers in Saudi Arabia, the bombings of the American embassies in Kenya and Tanzania, and the attack on the U.S.S. *Cole*, had also gone undetected, but those incidents took place in areas where U.S. authorities had limited opportunities to obtain intelligence firsthand. Preparations for the 1993 bombing of the World Trade Center and the 1995 bombing of the federal building in Oklahoma City had also gone undetected, but these were the work of small domestic conspiracies (although there was some foreign participation in the 1993 World Trade Center bombing). The fact that at least 20 operatives from a terrorist organization that was already being closely watched by American intelligence services could enter the United States, remain in the country for months while training to carry out multiple terrorist attacks of unprecedented scale, receive instructions and hundreds of thousands of dollars from abroad, even travel out of the country and return, all without being detected by the authorities, raised questions about the adequacy of American intelligence that are still being debated.

September 11 also raised the lethality of terrorism to a new level. The terrorists clearly were determined to cause catastrophic casualties—tens of thousands of casualties— confirming a long-term trend toward increasingly large-scale, indiscriminate attacks. Tens died in the worst incidents of terrorism in the 1970s, hundreds in the 1980s and 1990s, but thousands died on September 11. The September 11 attacks involved an imaginative plan (although no exotic weapons), and they indicated a mindset that would not preclude the use of weapons of mass destruction (WMD) if the terrorists could somehow acquire them. Subsequent discoveries in al Qaeda's training camps showed that the use of chemical, biological, and nuclear weapons certainly was an aspiration, even if the organization lacked the actual capabilities.

Fears of bioterrorism increased when a still unidentified perpetrator sent letters contaminated with anthrax to target recipients in the news media and government. No evidence directly connects the anthrax attacks to al Qaeda's September 11 attack, but the coincidence in timing led to a convergence of concerns. Regardless of who was responsible for the anthrax attacks, bioterrorism had become a deadly and disruptive reality.

The Aftermath of September 11: Al Qaeda's View

From the terrorists' perspective, the September 11 attacks dealt a massive blow to the most prominent symbols of American economic and military might, a dramatic demonstration of what could be achieved through commitment to the Islamic extremists' vision of jihad. Al Qaeda's leadership probably anticipated that the attack would provoke a major military response, which it could then portray as an assault on Islam. This would inspire thousands of additional volunteers and could provoke the entire Islamic world to rise up against the West. Governments that opposed the people's wrath, quislings to Western imperialism, would fall. The West would be destroyed.

If this was al Qaeda's rapture, it repeated the folly of terrorists past. The strategy of carrying out spectacular attacks to deliberately provoke an overreaction by government authorities which, in turn, would provoke a popular uprising has seldom worked, and it didn't work this time either. To be sure, the attacks on the World Trade Center and the Pentagon were popular on Arab streets, where they were met with spontaneous celebrations and reportedly made Osama a popular name for new babies. But when the United States launched its attack on Afghanistan, careful not to portray it as an assault on Islam despite bin Laden's efforts to do so, there were no visible rivers of recruits streaming toward al Qaeda's banner, nor were there any uprisings or organized resistance.

More than nine months after the attacks, the Taliban have been removed from government, although not eliminated from Afghanistan entirely, and al Qaeda has lost its sanctuary and training camps. The "business continuity" plans that al Qaeda probably had in place before September 11 may have permitted many of its leaders and operatives to escape, but some have been killed, others have been captured, and the rest are on the run. Pakistan, once a source of support and recruits, has reversed its policy and cracked down on Taliban and al Qaeda sympathizers. Other governments in the Middle East and beyond have rounded up al Qaeda suspects and have committed themselves to cooperation in combating terrorism, although they still cannot agree on a definition of what terrorism is. Whatever appreciation Palestinians might have owed Osama bin Laden for opportunistically including their cause on his broader agenda has been offset by the vicissitudes of their own struggle. Its operatives forced deeper underground and its financial supporters forced to be more circumspect, al Qaeda's balance sheet does not look so favorable. However, we have not seen the last of al Qaeda.

Al Qaeda will not quit. Terrorist groups seldom quit, and al Qaeda did not retire on September 12. Growing evidence acquired since September 11 suggests that in addition to taking steps to protect its finances, instructing some of its key operatives to disappear, and making preparations to protect its leadership, al Qaeda has vowed to carry out further attacks. And indeed, terrorist attacks have occurred in Pakistan, Tunisia, and Saudi Arabia, and other terrorist plots have been discovered before they could be carried out. Some of the plots originated prior to September 11, but others were set in motion afterwards. Not all of the plots are directly linked to al Qaeda, although some clearly are. Some of the attacks may have simply been provoked by America's war on terrorism and Pakistan's decision to support it, as well as by other events in the Middle East.

Al Qaeda's leaders may have underestimated the American response, just as they may have overestimated the readiness of their sympathizers to rise up against the West. They now must adapt their organization and strategy to this new reality, but they will continue their campaign.

Religious conviction gives them strength, but the armed struggle is what holds them together. Violence is their *raison d'être*. The enterprise of terrorism provides status, power, and psychological satisfaction. It attracts new recruits. It demonstrates their devotion and gives them historical importance. Without terrorism, al Qaeda would collapse into just another exotic sect.

Terrorists understand when they suffer setbacks, but they operate in a clandestine world, a closed universe cut off from normal discourse and competing views. They measure success differently: They define death and destruction as achievements in themselves. Terrorists do not feel that it is necessary to translate these into political progress, and they have a high tolerance for cognitive dissonance. Adversity is seen as a test of their commitment. Compromise equals apostasy, so leaders counseling restraint risk accusations of betrayal. In an association of extremists, it is perilous to be less than the most extreme. Successes are seen to derive from violence, and setbacks thus call for greater violence. Individual terrorists may become disillusioned, but there is no easy way for them to leave the organization. A few groups have officially suspended their campaigns of violence, but their leaders were denounced, while splinter and rival groups vowed to fight on.

Other groups have faded with the death or capture of charismatic and effective leaders (e.g., Peru's Shining Path and Turkey's PKK), the loss of state sponsors or the imposition of state control that left their tongues but removed their teeth (the Palestinian rejectionists currently residing in Damascus), or the drying up of their reservoir of support (America's Weathermen Underground). In some cases, circumstances changed, making the terrorists' struggle less relevant (e.g., Germany's Red Army Faction). Other groups have disappeared when a generation passed without successors. The evolution of terrorist organizations is a long process, measured in decades.

Sources of al Qaeda's strength. Although al Qaeda has been damaged by the American-led campaign, it continues to benefit from its image as a powerful Islamic force that is capable of inflicting devastating blows on its foes. Osama bin Laden's mystique survives, even if his personal fate is in doubt. Al Qaeda's key figures remain at large, and there may be others who have not yet been identified.

It is more difficult to assess the capability of al Qaeda's global network. We know that as of September 11, 2001, it was extensive, reportedly in place in at least 60 countries. More than 2,000 suspected al Qaeda operatives have been captured or arrested, but others have disappeared underground. Since September 11, terrorist attacks carried out or thwarted in Singapore, Pakistan, Saudi Arabia,

Lebanon, Tunisia, Morocco, Macedonia, Bosnia, Italy, France, and the United States indicate that al Qaeda's operational capability still exists. It is able to communicate, reconnoiter targets, plan operations, travel, meet clandestinely, and obtain finances.

Al Qaeda also still benefits from a large reservoir of recruits. While many have been dispersed or perhaps temporarily demoralized, at least some fighters remain dedicated and willing to carry out attacks, including suicide missions. That some attacks have been prevented by intelligence, alert police, or simply good luck is fortunate. At the same time, there remains the nagging fear that another catastrophic attack is being prepared somewhere and that it will be revealed only when it occurs, days, months, or years from now.

Terrorist organizations benefit from having virtually unlimited targets, as homeland defense planners are discovering. Al Qaeda's strategy playbook, however, shows certain preferences. Commercial aviation, diplomatic facilities, and American (or allied) servicemen recur as targets. Naval vessels in port (or in narrow straits), government buildings, monuments, and symbolic landmarks also figure prominently. Finally, al Qaeda enjoys a large constituency that accepts and applauds extreme violence against the West in general and the United States in particular.

Operating environment. While al Qaeda clearly continues to benefit from certain strengths, it must now operate in a less-permissive environment. The loss of the supportive Taliban government, its easily accessible safe haven, and its training camps may not be felt immediately, as al Qaeda will be able to draw upon its reserves for some time while it tries to establish new centers. But these are likely to be smaller and less accessible. Moreover, the pilgrimage to Afghanistan, the experience in the training camps, and participation in Afghanistan's armed conflict served an important role in attracting and indoctrinating volunteers to the cause and in providing future terrorist operatives. Televised videotapes and virtual realms on the Internet may not suffice to maintain a high level of devotion. If al Qaeda can be kept on the run, the numbers it can train will decline. And declining numbers eventually will result in a corresponding qualitative decline in terrorist operations.

Pakistan's withdrawal of support for the Taliban and its promised crackdown on the extremist religious schools that supplied volunteers for al Qaeda's training camps will also reduce the flow of recruits. Poorly educated Pakistani youth were never likely to become sophisticated international operatives. On the other hand, they will pose a continuing danger within Pakistan.

Financial contributors may also be constrained by international efforts to limit terrorist finances. The new measures will not prevent the financing of terrorist operations, which require relatively small amounts, but they could reduce al Qaeda's welfare and proselytizing efforts. The new laws also provide additional sources of intelligence about terrorist organizations.

Finally, increased surveillance and intelligence gathered from captured al Qaeda members and documents will further increase al Qaeda's risks.

Adapting to new circumstances. The greatest threat posed by al Qaeda is that it will attempt another attack as catastrophic as the September 11 attacks or even more so. None of the terrorist plots uncovered since then have been that ambitious, but we know now that the planning for the September 11 attacks was under way for several years, overlapping planning for other major attacks and undetected by the authorities.

An attack on the scale of September 11 could have profound political, social, and economic consequences for the United States. It could inspire widespread anxiety, anger at the government for failing in its primary mission of providing security, and popular demand for draconian measures that could shake the American political system and fundamentally alter the American lifestyle. The economic effects of such an attack, the subsequent disruption, and the need for even greater security measures could be devastating to the economy. But that level of destruction can be achieved only with coordinated conventional attacks, multidimensional assaults calculated to magnify the disruption, or the use of chemical, biological, or nuclear weapons. These, in turn, are likely to need the kind of organization that requires some participation on the part of al Qaeda's central command. We are uncertain whether al Qaeda's key leaders are still alive or able to "do" strategy. Wild-eyed recruits may be plentiful. Brains are precious. Thus, the immediate goal of the war on terrorism must be to destroy al Qaeda's ability to operate at this level.

It is also possible that al Qaeda will adapt to the more difficult post–September 11 operational environment by morphing into an even looser network, devolving more initiative and resources to local operatives. This does not appear to be inconsistent with al Qaeda's current operational philosophy, which seems to invite local initiative. A looser al Qaeda network would be better able to survive the intense worldwide surveillance of authorities, but it might not be able to operate at the level required for a catastrophic attack. The failed attempt to sabotage an American airliner last December might be characteristic of this level of organization.

Continuing, but uncoordinated, acts of terrorism may be waged by al Qaeda cells, unconnected supporters, and even individuals, inspired by al Qaeda's call or provoked by America's war on terrorism. It may be difficult to distinguish these from isolated acts of violence unconnected with any terrorist organization. Such attacks could be lethal and capable of inspiring terror among an already apprehensive population, but they are likely to remain sporadic events. The anthrax letters and the recent bombings in Pakistan are characteristic of this level of terrorism.

Prospects for the use of weapons of mass destruction. Much of the concern about the current terrorist threat relates to the possible employment of WMD. These include chemical and biological weapons, radioactive dispersal devices, and, potentially, stolen nuclear weapons or improvised nuclear devices. Such concerns are not new; they have been debated at least since the early 1970s.[1] Participants in that debate could appropriately be described in theological terms, since the arguments reflected beliefs more than evidence. "Apocalyptians" believed that terrorist escalation to mass destruction was inevitable, while disbelievers pointed to the absence of any evidence indicating that terrorists were moving in this direction. In the middle were "prudent agnostics," who remained uncertain about whether chemical, biological, or nuclear terrorism was inevitable but nonetheless argued for increased security.

Skeptics found support in the fact that terrorists at that time clearly did not operate at the upper limits of their capabilities if mayhem was their goal. Terrorists who did not understand technically challenging chemical, biological, or nuclear weapons certainly knew how to build large conventional bombs, which they could have set off in public areas to kill far more people than they did. The fact that they did not do so, therefore, had to indicate that they operated under self-imposed constraints. Subsequent research showed that terrorists argued about the proper level of violence. Some believed that wanton killing could jeopardize group cohesion. They also did not want to alienate their perceived legions of supporters. Terrorists wanted publicity and to create alarm; they did not necessarily want to provoke public backlashes that would support government crackdowns that the terrorists themselves might not survive.

In the 1980s, the constraints appeared to erode as terrorists escalated their violence, especially in the Middle East. By the 1990s, terrorists turned to large-scale, indiscriminate attacks calculated to kill in quantity. Part—but only part—of the reason could be found in the changing motives that drove conflict in the final decade of the twentieth century. Whereas terrorism in the 1970s and 1980s had been driven mostly by political ideology— terrorists had secular motives, political agendas, and therefore constituents, real or imaginary, on whose behalf they fought—terrorism in the 1990s was increasingly driven by ideologies that exploited religion. The conviction that they had God's sanction freed religious fanatics from ordinary political or moral constraints. But the religious angle should not be overstated, as some of the most deadly terrorist attacks, in terms of fatalities, were carried out by agents of Libya, who sabotaged PanAm and UTA flights in 1988 and 1989, or North Koreans, who brought down a Korean airliner in 1987. Nor should the frequency of large-scale attacks be overestimated. According to RAND's chronology of international terrorism, between 1968 and September 11, 2001, only 14 of more than 10,000 international terrorist incidents resulted in 100 or more fatalities, although there appear to have been more attempts to kill in quantity.

At the same time the terrorists seemed to be escalating their violence, the fall of the Soviet Union raised concerns about the security of the Soviet weapons research program and its vast nuclear arsenal. In an environment of poverty, increasing corruption, and growing organized crime, would Soviet weapons remain secure? Would impoverished Soviet weapons designers and builders find employment in the clandestine weapons research programs of would-be proliferators or state sponsors of terrorism? Might Russia or other republics of the former Soviet Union, desperate for hard currency, willingly provide the materiel and expertise that could accelerate nuclear weapons development by terrorist organizations? Further anxiety derived from the realization that Iraq was further along in developing WMD than had been imagined.

The 1995 sarin attack on Tokyo's subways seemed to confirm the darker view of the apocalyptians. At the direction of their very human god, Aum Shinrikyo's members fit the pattern of religious fanatics willing to kill thousands. This attack reminded us that organizations other than identified terrorist groups could carry out significant acts of terrorism. It showed that a group was capable of clandestinely acquiring and experimenting with both chemical and biological weapons for years without detection, despite numerous suspicious incidents. But the attack also demonstrated the difficulties of developing and deploying biological or chemical devices. Although it had months of experimentation and an ample budget, the Aum Shinrikyo cult developed only a crude version of nerve gas, which it dispersed in a primitive manner that reduced its effectiveness so that casualties were limited. Within weeks of the attack, Aum Shinrikyo was destroyed, its leaders under arrest. More than seven years later, no terrorist organization has yet tried to duplicate the attack.

There is no inexorable escalation from truck bombs or even suicide air attacks to WMD. Nonetheless, terrorist desires to use WMD cannot be discounted. On September 11, al Qaeda terrorists were trying to kill tens of thousands. They succeeded in killing thousands. Captured documents and interrogations of captured al Qaeda members have revealed the organization's aspirations to acquire chemical, biological, and nuclear capabilities, although there is no indication that it has such capabilities today. If it had those capabilities, al Qaeda would undoubtedly be willing to use them.

There is distance between ambition and achievement. Chemical, biological, and radiological weapons will not necessarily cause mass destruction—worst-case scenarios are planning vehicles, not forecasts. In the most plausible scenarios, the psychological effects of chemical, biological, or radiological attacks are likely to vastly exceed the actual death and destruction, but we are on the frontier of a new, more dangerous domain.

Some Realistic Assumptions

Strategy must be based upon realistic assumptions about the current situation. Al Qaeda, its associates, and its successors will fight on. It draws upon a deep reservoir of hatred and a desire for revenge, and U.S. efforts have reduced, not eliminated, its ability to mount significant terrorist operations.

It must be presumed that al Qaeda will exploit all of its ability to cause catastrophic death and destruction—there will be no self-imposed limits to its violence. Attempts to cause massive death and destruction using conventional or unconventional weapons are likely. It can also be presumed that al Qaeda will continue its efforts to acquire and use WMD; that it will attack U.S. targets abroad where possible; and that it will attempt to mount attacks within the United States. Al Qaeda constitutes the most serious immediate threat to the security of the United States.

Although some measure of success has been achieved in uncovering terrorist plots, the ability of U.S. agencies to detect and prevent future terrorist attacks is limited. There will not be sufficient intelligence to provide adequate warning in every case, and while security is being increased around likely targets of terrorist attack, terrorists can attack anything, anywhere, anytime, while it is not possible to protect everything, everywhere, all the time. Some attacks will occur.

STRATEGY FOR THE SECOND PHASE OF THE WAR ON TERRORISM

The United States has formulated and carried out a coherent first-phase strategy in the war on terrorism. But what next? The campaign has now entered a more difficult phase. The greatest challenge is that as military operations move beyond a single theater, the more complex tasks will be dispersed among numerous departments, agencies, and offices, and the focus on the overall U.S. strategy will be lost, along with the nation's ability to coordinate operations. That strategy must continue to emphasize the key elements outlined below.

The destruction of al Qaeda must remain the primary aim of the American campaign. Al Qaeda will adapt to new circumstances; it may disperse, change names, merge with other entities, or be absorbed into its own successors, but as long as its leadership, structure, operatives, relationships, financing, and ability to recruit survive in any form, it will seek to repair damage, reestablish connections, issue instructions, and mobilize resources to support further terrorist operations. The al Qaeda enterprise itself cannot easily be deterred. It can be disabled only by permanently disrupting the process that provides it with human and material resources. Further terrorist attacks must be kept within the level of tolerable tragedy; another catastrophe on the scale of September 11 must not be allowed to occur.

The pursuit of al Qaeda must be single-minded and unrelenting. The episodic nature of terrorism (long periods of time elapse between major attacks), the heavy burden of security, and the public's impatience for closure can tempt the United States into dangerous complacency. Distracting events, including the conflict between Israel and the Palestinians, the confrontation between India and Pakistan over Kashmir, and America's determination to deal with other threats to national security must be addressed in the context of the immediate and continuing threat posed by al Qaeda.

The United States cannot inflict upon its dispersed and amorphous terrorist foe the immediate destruction that would serve as a deterrent to other terrorist entities contemplating alliance with it or replication of its war on America. However, assured destruction can be pursued over time—years, if necessary—without letup, without amnesty, as an ongoing reminder to others of the consequences of provoking the United States.

The campaign against terrorism will take time. Wars against terrorists throughout history have been long, even when the terrorists operate on the national territory of the government they oppose and are accessible to its authorities. Italy's Red Brigades fought from the late 1960s to the early 1980s, and after years of quiet, they may now be reemerging. Germany's Red Army Faction survived from the early 1970s to the 1990s. The Provisional Wing of the Irish Republican Army emerged in the late 1960s and laid down its arms only at the end of the 1990s. Spain's ETA is approaching its fifth decade in the field. Colombia's guerrillas can find their origins in armed struggles that began more than a half-century ago.

Al Qaeda itself represents more than a decade of organizational development built upon relationships that were first established in the 1980s. Its active planning for a terrorist war on the United

States began not later than the mid-1990s, and its planning for September 11 began three or possibly four years before the actual attack, starting with plots elaborated in the first half of the 1990s. The thoroughness of al Qaeda's planning suggests that it has prepared for a long campaign, one that inevitably will involve setbacks. It is probably prepared to lie low indefinitely. The battle against al Qaeda could last decades.

The fight in Afghanistan must be continued as long as al Qaeda operatives remain in the country. There may be differences within al Qaeda between those who wish to make their last stand in Afghanistan (and have no other options) and those who would disperse to reconstitute new versions of the organization elsewhere. Although some analysts argue that the United States has only complicated its task by chasing al Qaeda out of Afghanistan, I believe that it is preferable to destroy al Qaeda operatives in Afghanistan rather than hunting for them elsewhere. Continued pressure in Afghanistan will consume al Qaeda's resources and distract its leadership. Premature withdrawal—historically, the American tendency—would be dangerous. Only when al Qaeda is completely destroyed or when the new Afghan government can effectively exercise authority throughout its territory can withdrawal be risked.

Long-term operations in Afghanistan will require carefully controlling the application of violence in order to avoid the errors and collateral damage that will fuel Afghan hostility and pressure to depart. If Americans accept the commitment to remain in Afghanistan for a very long haul, the mode of operations can be altered to reduce the risks of counterproductive incidents. It may be prudent to place more emphasis on Special Forces operations, longer tours of duty, and the creation of specially trained combined Afghan-American hunter units. It may also be necessary to tighten the rules governing the use of American air power. With time, it will be increasingly beneficial to ensure that military successes are seen as those of Afghan warriors rather than American air power.

The continued U.S. presence in Afghanistan must not be seen as an occupation by foreign predators. Positive benefits of America's involvement —the reconstruction of infrastructure, assistance for health care and education, the restoration and preservation of Afghanistan's cultural heritage—can temper the country's natural resistance to outsiders.

Pakistan must be kept on the side of the allies in efforts to destroy the remnants of al Qaeda and the Taliban and dilute Islamic extremism. The government of Pervez Musharraf faces a potential coalition of Taliban supporters, militant Muslim groups committed to a continuation of the war in Kashmir, and Sunni extremists who for years have waged terrorist campaigns against Shi'ites and political opponents, principally in Karachi. The loss of Pakistan's support could reverse America's victory in Afghanistan. It could provide al Qaeda with a new sanctuary in the turbulent tribal frontier areas that border Afghanistan, leaving the United States and its allies with the dismal prospect of large-scale military operations in Pakistan. If a new Pakistani government were hostile to the West, the United States could find itself faced with military action against Pakistan itself. The most likely successor to the present government is not a more liberal, democratic, pro-Western regime, but one that is at the very least less accommodating. A more radical Islamic Pakistan could emerge, one that is more sympathetic to the extremists, more belligerent on the issue of Kashmir, and in possession of nuclear weapons.

The United States must be firm in ensuring that President Musharraf fulfills his pledges, especially those that involve constraining the activities of the extremists and halting infiltration into Kashmir, which could provoke a dangerous war with India. This will demand much of a weak government: that it check the activities of extremists in Pakistan and Kashmir; shut down the religious academies that feed recruits to extremist groups; cooperate with the allies in rooting out and running down al Qaeda operatives; and implement political reforms that ultimately will deliver democracy, while confronting religious extremism, sectarian violence, separatist sentiments, and hostile neighbors. The United States needs to provide political and economic support that will enable the Pakistani government to demonstrate the positive benefits of the alliance while checking popular bellicose sentiments in Kashmir. Without destabilizing the country, the United States should also try to nudge Pakistan toward the political reforms that are prerequisite to democracy and development.

New networks must be created to exploit intelligence across frontiers. Suspected al Qaeda operatives arrested worldwide since September 11 are providing some information about the terrorist network. The capture of documents found at al Qaeda safe houses and training camps will add to the picture, but this material must be effectively exploited to support the continued identification and pursuit of al Qaeda's remaining cells and the successful prosecution of those arrested. Rapid and accurate translation, analysis, and dissemination to investigators and prosecutors in the United States and abroad will require an unprecedented level of multinational coordination between intelligence services and justice departments. Magistrates and prosecutors abroad must receive intelligence in a form that is both useful and legally admissible within their varying systems of law. And the United States must understand the legal and political concerns of each of its allies and adapt its strategy accordingly. Not every suspected terrorist need be in U.S. custody, nor can information flow only in the direction of Washington.

U.S. agencies still have great difficulty sharing intelligence among themselves, although the situation is improving. Only recently have intelligence efforts and criminal investigations been orchestrated to enable successful prosecution of foreign terrorists. Achieving even better cooperation and coordination internationally will require structures that exist today only in embryonic form. It may require the creation of a U.S. task force dedicated to the coordination, collection, and dissemination of vital material to justice departments and intelligence services abroad. It may require the creation of bilateral and multilateral task forces focused on dismantling the al Qaeda network and the deployment of liaison personnel abroad for the duration of the campaign.

The crucial second phase of the war on terrorism cannot be accomplished unilaterally— international cooperation is a prerequisite for success. Full cooperation will be limited to a few governments. The British, with whom some of the mechanisms for close intelligence cooperation are already in place, will continue to be America's closest allies. NATO and other traditional allies also can be expected to cooperate closely. The cooperation of the French is especially important, although it brings with it a unique set of challenges. France has global intelligence resources, vast area knowledge, and valuable historical experience in dealing with the threat posed by terrorists operating in North Africa and the Middle East.

Russian cooperation is also important, for both political and technical reasons. Although Russian intelligence today may not match the capabilities of the Soviet intelligence infrastructure during the Cold War, and the Russian leadership tends to see terrorism exclusively through the lens of its conflict in Chechnya, Russia nonetheless has valuable knowledge and experience in Central and South Asia and can be a major contributor to ongoing international efforts to combat terrorism. Although they have significant differences in approach, Russia and the United States are natural allies on this issue.

Israel, America's closest ally in the Middle East, has vast knowledge and a strong political agenda. Historically, intelligence cooperation is close and will continue to be so, even as the two countries occasionally have differences on how to address the Palestinian issue.

Moderate Arab regimes will also contribute to the intelligence pool. Diplomacy can create new coalitions that extend beyond those of traditional allies. The United States should be flexible enough to exploit opportunities for cooperation among governments it previously has penalized for their support of terrorism. Both Libya and Sudan are anxious to normalize relations, and Sudan has offered outright cooperation in the fight against bin Laden. The United States need not seek the political endorsement of those countries on every issue, but it could be operationally and politically useful to have strong nationalist governments—even those critical of the United States— seen to be cooperating against al Qaeda's terrorism.

It is not natural for intelligence agencies to share. The CIA, with more experience in the give and take of international intelligence collection and diplomacy, is better at it than the FBI, whose organizational culture derives from the prosecution of crime. Sharing intelligence with foreign services is never easy, but unlike the Cold War era when there were understandable concerns about Soviet penetration, there is far less concern today that al Qaeda or other terrorists have burrowed into the intelligence services of America's traditional allies, and no one is concerned about keeping the terrorists' secrets. Except as intelligence-sharing is limited by the requirement to protect sources, methods, and ongoing operations, exposure rather than withholding should be the aim.

This is a war against specific terrorists—the goal is to combat terrorism. The president has said that we are at war, and the Congress has passed a joint resolution authorizing military action against al Qaeda and the Taliban as well as future actions against other nations, organizations, or persons found to have participated in the September 11 attacks. Although it may still fall short of a declaration of war, this formal expression of belligerency against terrorists and those who assist them enables the United States to more easily keep the initiative. Previous uses of military force against terrorists were limited to the framework of retaliation, although U.S. officials shunned that specific term. The United States on occasion struck back against terrorists and their state sponsors to disrupt or discourage further attacks, but the initiative remained in the hands of the terrorists. Moreover, retaliatory strikes had to be timely and seen as proportionate to the attacks that provoked them. While it might have been hoped that terrorists would fear that the United States would attack them a second time, this never happened. The president's declaration and subsequent Congressional resolution clearly signal an intent to attack terrorists whenever, wherever, and with whatever methods the United States chooses. It facilitates covert operations, and it creates a requirement for a specific plan of action.

The use of the term *war* does not carry any recognition of terrorist outlaws as *privileged combatants* entitled to treatment as prisoners of war, although, of course, the United States will not mistreat captives. It does not end American efforts to bring terrorists to justice through the legal system, either the American system or that of other countries with capable authorities who are willing to enforce the law. In countries without such authorities, the United States may take appropriate measures to defend itself. Such a declaration does not oblige the United States to run down every terrorist or attack every nation identified as a state sponsor of terrorism. Sensible diplomacy will prevail.

President Bush has correctly portrayed the war on terrorism as likely to be a long war, but it has finite aims: the removal of the Taliban government; the destruction of al Qaeda's training bases in Afghanistan; putting Osama bin Laden and his associates on the run; and rounding up al Qaeda's operatives around the world. The United States is not going to destroy every terrorist group or pursue every terrorist in the world, but as a matter of self-defense, it will wage war against terrorists capable of causing casualties on the scale of September 11. The targets are specific.

But America is not "at war" with terrorism, which is a phenomenon, not a foe. It is trying to *combat* terrorism. To make terrorism an unattractive mode of conflict, the United States will collect and exchange intelligence with allies. It will conduct criminal investigations. It will seek to expand international conventions and cooperation. It will assist in resolving conflicts that may produce terrorism and will address the causes of the deep hatred that terrorists are able to exploit. This is consistent with U.S. actions for the 30 years since the creation in 1972 of the Cabinet Committee to Combat Terrorism.

The distinction between *war* on terrorism and *combating* terrorism may also be useful in dealing with allies who attempt to enlist the United States in their wars. As counterterrorism becomes a new basis for American foreign policy, local conflicts are being presented or relabeled to enlist American political and material support. In some cases, the United States may go along in order to gain the support of other nations for its own efforts. But America is not at war with everyone's terrorists, and not all nations need be front-line participants in America's war against al Qaeda. Nevertheless, all nations should cooperate in combating terrorism, an obligation that has been formally recognized in United Nations Resolution 1373. Efforts to deal with root causes of terrorism fall under the rubric of combating terrorism, not the war against al Qaeda. Dealing with terrorist events below the threshold of catastrophe falls within the realm of combating terrorism; events above that threshold provoke war. For the foreseeable future, the United States will be dealing with both.

The current U.S. strategy should be amended to include political warfare.   There appears to be a curious bias in America: The nation endorses death to terrorists but is loath to use influence. This bias has been perpetuated in bureaucratic in-fighting and deliberate misrepresentation. But it is not sufficient to merely outgun the terrorists. The enemy here is an ideology, a set of attitudes, a belief system organized into a recruiting network that will continue to replace terrorist losses unless defeated politically. At a tactical level, the campaign should include efforts to discredit al Qaeda, create discord, provoke distrust among its operatives, demoralize volunteers, and discourage recruits. At a strategic level, political warfare should be aimed at reducing the appeal of extremists, encouraging alternative views that are currently silenced by fear and hostile policy, and discouraging terrorists' use of WMD. The United States invested a great deal in this type of activity in the early years of the Cold War with some success, but its growing military superiority has led to this vital component of warfare being discarded. Changes in public attitudes and in communications technology will not permit a return to the sometimes brilliant but often risky operations of a half-century ago, nor would this be desirable. But political warfare is an arena of battle that should be subjected to rational inquiry.

Deterrent strategies may be appropriate for dealing with the terrorists' support structures.   The very nature of the terrorist enterprise makes the traditional strategy of deterrence difficult to apply to terrorist groups. In traditional deterrence, the adversaries do not exceed mutually understood limits and will not employ certain weapons, although their continued existence is accepted. Deterrence worked in the Cold War, where central decisionmakers were in charge and in control on both sides. The limits and the consequences were mutually understood. Coexistence was acceptable. Deterrence regulated the conflict; it did not end the struggle.

Deterring terrorism is an entirely different matter. Here, there are diverse foes, not a single enemy with different goals and values. Terrorist leaders are not always in complete control, and they often have difficulty constraining their own followers. Coexistence is not a goal, on either side. Would the United States accept the existence of al Qaeda and any form of freedom for its current leaders, even with credible promises that they will suspend operations against this country? As individual "repentants" ready to cooperate in the destruction of the organization, perhaps; as leaders of al Qaeda, never. Nor are there any acceptable limits to continued terrorist violence.

Still, the notion of deterrence should not be too hastily abandoned. The existence of self-imposed constraints in the past—and for most groups, today—suggests decisionmaking that calculates risks and costs. Al Qaeda's unwillingness to attack Saudi targets despite its denunciation of the ruling family suggests that even bin Laden's lieutenants make political calculations. We do not know what these are or how they are weighted by the decisionmakers. Al Qaeda may be reluctant to kill fellow Arabs; or if attacked, the ruling Saudi family might push its Wahabi religious allies to denounce bin Laden—and the Saudi government does have clout in the worldwide Islamic community. Moreover, al Qaeda may deem attacking an Arab country to be inconsistent with its vision of focusing its violence on the United States. If any of these speculations is correct, then Saudi Arabia has achieved a level of deterrence. The United States may not be able (or may not want) to duplicate this situation with al Qaeda. It may prefer to demonstrate that large-scale attacks will bring unrelenting pursuit and ultimate destruction in order to deter future terrorist groups.

Deterrence might also be employed in targeting terrorists' support systems. Economic sanctions, although blunt instruments, have had some effect in modifying state behavior. The fate of the Taliban serves as a warning to state supporters of terrorism.

Financial contributors to terrorist fronts may also be deterred by threats of negative publicity, blocked investments, asset seizures, exposure to lawsuits, or merely increased scrutiny of their financial activities. Institutions that assist or tolerate terrorist recruiting may be deterred by the prospect of all members or participants coming under close surveillance. Communities supporting terrorists might be deterred by the threat of expulsions, deportations, selective suspensions of immigration and visa applications, or increased controls on remittances.

Stings may also be used as a deterrent to terrorists seeking WMD. Bogus offers of materials or expertise can be set up to identify and eliminate would-be buyers or middlemen, divert terrorists' financial resources, and provoke uncertainty in terrorists' acquisition efforts.

It must be made clear that terrorist use of WMD will bring extraordinary responses. As terrorists escalate their violence, it is necessary to create a firebreak that signals a different set of responses to terrorist attempts to use WMD. The term *weapons of mass destruction* is used deliberately, to distinguish these weapons from chemical, biological, radiological, or nuclear devices, which collectively may be referred to as *unconventional weapons*. Conventional weapons (from explosives to fully fueled airliners) may be used to create mass destruction—thousands of deaths—whereas chemical, biological, or radiological weapons may cause far less than mass destruction—12 people died in the 1995 Tokyo sarin attack, and the anthrax letters killed five people. The intent here is to focus on *mass destruction*, not *unconventional weapons*, although some ambiguity might not be unwelcome.

Even if attacks involving unconventional weapons do not result in mass casualties, their use could still cause widespread panic with enormous social and economic disruption. This would be true of radiological attacks and almost any deliberate release of a contagious disease. It is, therefore, appropriate to speak of weapons of mass effect as well as weapons of mass destruction. For purposes of response, the United States may decide to treat them as the same.

I have argued since 1977 that it should be a well-understood article of American policy that to prevent terrorist acquisition or use of WMD, the United States will take whatever measures it deems appropriate, including unilateral preemptive military action. In his speech at West Point on June 1, 2002, President Bush warned that "if we wait for threats to fully materialize, we will have waited too long." He went on to declare that the United States would take "preemptive action when necessary."

The United States may reassure its allies that preemptive action is unlikely in circumstances where local authorities have the capability of taking action themselves and can be depended upon to do so, but it is not necessary to precisely outline the circumstances in which U.S. action would be precluded. If preemptive military action is required, the government should be prepared to make a compelling public case *after the event* that such action was justified. The United States failed to do this after the American attack on Sudan in 1998. In the event of such an attack, the United States will be inclined to presume, or may choose to presume, state involvement. In a response to any terrorist attack involving WMD, all weapons may be considered legitimate.

Obviously, these warnings apply more to states than to autonomous terrorist groups who may acquire a WMD capability on their own and may find threats of possible unilateral preemption, unrelenting pursuit, and the possible use of any weapon in the U.S. arsenal to be unpersuasive. The warnings, however, may dissuade states, even hostile ones, from offering expertise or material support to terrorists moving toward WMD; such states may instead be persuaded to take steps to ensure that terrorist actions do not expose them to the danger of preemptive action or retaliation.

Another possible deterrent, perhaps more compelling to the terrorists' supporters and sympathizers than to the terrorists themselves, would be to widely publicize the fact that a major bioterrorism attack involving a highly contagious disease such as smallpox would almost certainly result in a pandemic that would spread beyond U.S. borders. Despite some weaknesses in its public health system, the United States, with its vast medical resources, would be able to cope with an outbreak, as would Europe. But with weak public health institutions and limited medical capabilities, the world's poorer nations would suffer enormously, perhaps losing significant portions of their populations. And if terrorists were to unleash some diabolically designed bug that even the United States could not cope with, the world would be doomed. This grim realization may not stop the most determined fanatic, but it may cause populations that currently find comfort in the illusion that only arrogant Americans will suffer from bioterrorism to come to the view that taboos against certain weapons are necessary to protect all.

Homeland security strategies must be developed that are both effective and efficient. The form future attacks by al Qaeda might take is impossible to predict, and areas of vulnerability both within the United States and abroad are infinite. Commercial aviation remains a preferred target for terrorists seeking high body counts; public surface transportation offers easy access and concentrations of people in contained environments; cargo containers have been identified as a means by which terrorists might clandestinely deliver weapons. Because of its size and complexity, the critical infrastructure of the United States is hard to protect; then again, terrorists have seldom attacked it, preferring instead to go after targets offering high symbolic value or killing fields. Blowing up bridges, pylons, and rail lines is more consistent with guerrilla and civil wars. Still, that does not mean that terrorists will not seek to carry out traditional sabotage in the future.

Security is costly and can be disruptive. A serious terrorist threat to the U.S. homeland may persist for years and indeed may become a fact of life in the twenty-first century; therefore, the security measures that are taken now will likely have to remain in place for a very long time. Terrorists are aware of the cascading economic effects of the September 11 attacks and may conclude that terrorism is an effective way of crippling America's economy.

Terrorists have learned to think strategically rather than tactically, to study and exploit specific vulnerabilities rather than to simply blast away until their opponent yields. If al Qaeda terrorists are allowed to successfully implement a strategy of economic disruption, America will lose the war. It can win only by removing the threat. But at the same time, the U.S. defense must be efficient.

It is therefore necessary not only to increase security but also to reduce the disruption that can be caused by future attacks, as well as the disruptive effects of the security measures themselves. America has just begun to formulate a homeland defense strategy. The current "castles and cops" approach may prove to be costly and disruptive. Priorities must be set. Instead of trying to protect every conceivable target against every imaginable form of attack, policymakers must explore strategies that accept a higher level of risk but offer greater strength or resiliency. The aging infrastructure may be replaced with more powerfully constructed facilities (a feature of some Cold War architecture) or with multiple facilities that provide continued service even if one goes down. This is not a new approach— terrorism simply has become a new ingredient in architecture and system design. There is ample room for research here.

The war against the terrorists at home and abroad must be conducted in a way that is consistent with American values. America cannot expect the world's applause for every action it takes in pursuit of terrorists abroad, but it is important not to squander the international support upon which the United States unavoidably will depend if it is to win the war. Military force is at times justified, but the violence should never be wanton, even if future attacks provoke American rage. The monument to those killed on September 11 and to those who may die in future terrorist attacks cannot be a mountain of innocent dead in some distant land.

At home, it is imperative that America play by the rules, although those rules may be changed. Every liberal democracy confronting terrorism has been obliged to modify rules governing intelligence collection, police powers, preventive detention, access to lawyers, or trial procedures. The United States has attempted to kill enemy commanders during times of war—the prohibition against assassination is a presidential directive, not a law. Captured terrorists may be tried in civilian courts or before military tribunals, but in either case, rules of evidence and the right to representation should apply. It is appropriate that any suspension of such rules be clearly set forth, widely discussed, and endorsed by legislation with time limits or renewal requirements to ensure that it does not become a permanent feature of the landscape. Measures that appear *ad hoc* and arbitrary should be avoided.

Finally, it is necessary to be determinedly pragmatic. America's goal is not revenge for the September 11 attacks. The goal is not even bringing individual terrorists to justice. It is the destruction of a terrorist enterprise that threatens American security.

NOTE

1. I wrote my first monograph on the topic in 1974 (see Brian Michael Jenkins, *Will Terrorists Go Nuclear?* Santa Monica, CA: RAND, P-5541, 1975).

Relearning Counterinsurgency Warfare

Robert R. Tomes

Thirty years after the signing of the January 1973 Paris peace agreement ending the Vietnam War, the United States finds itself leading a broad coalition of military forces engaged in peacemaking, nation-building, and now counterinsurgency warfare in Iraq. A turning point appeared in mid-October 2003 when US Secretary of Defense Donald Rumsfeld's memo on the future of Iraqi operations surfaced. His musings about whether US forces were ready for protracted guerrilla warfare sparked widespread debate about US planning for counterinsurgency operations.

Little attention has been paid to the theory and practice of counterinsurgency warfare in mainstream strategic studies journals. Discussions of the so-called revolution in military affairs (RMA) and RMA-associated technologies for battlefield surveillance and precision targeting dominated defense planning discourse in the 1990s. Nation-building and peacekeeping discussions rarely addressed counterinsurgency warfare, perhaps because nation-building operations during the 1990s did not confront a determined, violent insurgency. Meanwhile, with knowledge about counterinsurgency warfare waning among policymakers, resurgent terrorism scholarship and counterterrorism policy initiatives avoided the issue of a strategic terrorist campaign to destabilize nation-building. More recently, vague historical references and misplaced analogies to Vietnam have muddled discussions of the Iraqi counterinsurgency effort.

Lessons and insights from past low-intensity wars deserve revisiting. They provide perspective as well as context for what may be a defining period for the American war on terrorism. What lessons from past counterinsurgencies can inform current efforts? What theoretical and operational issues are available to aid Coalition activities?

This exploration of why counterinsurgencies fail avoids the American experience in Vietnam, a subject that continues to evoke images and arguments that could possibly overshadow the central purpose—that is, discussing the lessons of previous counterinsurgencies and their applicability to US strategy in Iraq. Avoiding the US experience in Vietnam also shifts attention to historical cases that may be more applicable to Iraq than was the US war in Southeast Asia.

REVISITING MODERN WAR

Those seeking historical insights into counterinsurgency warfare will find Roger Trinquier's classic *Modern Warfare: A French View of Counterinsurgency* disturbingly current. First published in 1961 and one

Robert Tomes is Senior Advisor to the NGA Technical Director, National Geospatial-Intelligence Agency (NGA), a doctoral candidate at the University of Maryland, and a member of the Council for Emerging National Security Affairs. His work has appeared in *Policy Review, National Security Studies Quarterly,* and the *Naval War College Review,* and is forthcoming in *Joint Force Quarterly, Armed Forces and Society,* and *Defence Studies.*

of the best-selling post-World War II books in France, Trinquier influenced a generation of counterinsurgency scholarship. He succeeded in describing the true face of what current observers also label "modern war." Nearly 40 years later, for example, Mark Bowden subtitled his bestseller *Black Hawk Down*, the story of a US Special Forces operation in Somalia gone awry, *A Story of Modern War*.[1] Despite important differences between Somalia and the colonial independence conflicts Trinquier participated in, ongoing operations in Afghanistan and Iraq reflect many of the nonlinear, unconventional elements of what Trinquier labeled modern war to distinguish between armored battles between nation-states and counterinsurgencies pitting nation-builders against organizations using terrorist tactics.

Trinquier was introduced to counterinsurgency warfare in Indochina before being assigned to Algeria in 1957 as a Lieutenant Colonel with the French 10th Parachute Division. Decades of service conditioned his views. Algeria inspired his writings on modern war, including a penetrating testimony to the central tenet of counterinsurgency: winning the allegiance of the indigenous population. A systematic approach is needed. Counterinsurgencies require "an interlocking system of actions—political, economic, psychological, military—that aims at the [insurgents' intended] overthrow of the established authority in a country and its replacement by another regime."[2]

As military theory, Trinquier's "modern war" parallels a prominent theme in post-Cold War military thought, one documented by Israeli military historian Martin Van Creveld's 1991 book, *The Transformation of War*.[3] Trinquier preceded Van Creveld and other post-Cold War military theorists in arguing that nuclear weapons would lead to a decline in traditional armored warfare and a rise in modern warfare in its many variants: guerrilla warfare, insurgency, terrorism, and subversion. As do current military analysts, Trinquier approached the problem of countering modern warfare by assessing differences between linear clashes of armies and the tactics, goals, methods, and norms of the insurgent or guerrilla.

Pitting a traditional combined armed force trained and equipped to defeat similar military organizations against insurgents "reminds one of a pile driver attempting to crush a fly, indefatigably persisting in repeating its efforts."[4] In Indochina, for example, the French "tried to drive the Vietminh into a classic pitched battle, the only kind [they] knew how to fight, in hope that superiority in material would allow an easy victory."[5] The only way to avoid similar pitfalls, according to Trinquier, is to fight the "specially adapted organization" that is common to almost all subversive, violent movements seeking to overthrow the status quo.[6] In October 2003 it appeared the United States was creating its own special organization to combat Iraqi insurgents: Task Force 121, a new joint strike unit reportedly composed of American Special Forces units and Army Rangers.[7]

Presumably steeped in counterinsurgency warfare, Task Force 121 and other units operating against Iraqi resistance have learned the lessons of past modern wars. They will not simply sweep towns. This won't defeat an organized insurgency. Instead, the enemy's organization must be targeted to defeat the clandestine organization attempting to impose its will on the Iraqi people. Four elements typically encompass an insurgency: cell-networks that maintain secrecy; terror used to foster insecurity among the population and drive them to the movement for protection; multifaceted attempts to cultivate support in the general population, often by undermining the new regime; and attacks against the government. Only by identifying and destroying the infrastructure of the subversive organization can the fledgling government persevere. Stated another way, just as the traditional war is not fought with the individual soldier or platoon in mind but rather the state's capacity and will to continue hostilities, modern war seeks to destroy the organization as a whole and not simply its violent arm or peripheral organs.

After comparing the relative resources of the insurgent and government forces, Trinquier concludes "that the guerrilla's greatest advantages are his perfect knowledge of an area (which he himself has chosen) and its potential, and the support given him by the inhabitants."[8] To turn this defeat into a victory, the counterinsurgent must recognize that "this total dependence upon terrain and population is also the guerrilla's weak point."[9] Toward this end, he suggests three simple principles: separate the guerrilla from the population that supports him; occupy the zones that the guerrillas previously operated from, making them dangerous for him and turning the people against the guerrilla movement; and coordinate actions over a wide area and for a long enough time that the guerrilla is denied access to the population centers that could support him.

This requires an extremely capable intelligence infrastructure endowed with human sources and deep cultural knowledge. Indeed, intelligence is key. As the Commander of the US Army's 1st Armored Division in Iraq, Major General Martin Dempsey, observed in November 2003, "Fundamentally, here in Baghdad we do two things: We're either fighting for intelligence or we're fighting based on that intelligence."[10] Despite unparalleled improvements in military intelligence, the United States does not seem to have the depth and breadth required in human intelligence (humint) and cultural intelligence arenas. Arabic linguists are lacking. Undersecretary of Defense for Intelligence Stephen Cambone, discussing intelligence shortcomings documented in an internal report, might have understated the problem, admitting, "We're a little short on the humint side; there's no denying it."[11] For Trinquier, intelligence was one of several crucial enablers for defeating an insurgent. Others included a secure area to operate from, sources in the general population and government, maintaining the initiative, and careful management of propaganda.

Acritical step in any counterinsurgency campaign is the creation of a "tight organization" to counter the enemy's organizational advantages. Created from the bottom up, based on a full appreciation for the tactical situation, a successful counterinsurgency organization must depart from its standard operational approach to warfare. For example, campaign planning should include a system to account for every citizen, coordination with the political effort to designate a hierarchical network of groups headed by pro-government chiefs, and a system to monitor the activities of guerrilla sympathizers. This entails a census, the issuing of photo-identification cards, and a countrywide intelligence system. The ultimate goal is to separate the fish from the sea, leaving it exposed to the state's spear.

In Iraq it is clearly difficult to weed out insurgents while protecting the Coalition's ability to win the trust of the Iraqi people and downplay its image as an occupying force. Whenever the commoner feels threatened or afraid, the guerrilla has the upper hand. Protecting basic liberties must be balanced with weeding out subversive elements and threats to stability. Some means and methods are historically ineffective. Routine patrols, isolated ambushes, large-scale sweeps, and even outposts tend to be wasted activities. Of these, outposts are useful when they keep roads and lines of communication open. But none of these activities establishes lines of battle. In previous counterinsurgencies, success required long occupation, something requiring a degree of political will that the current Coalition in Iraq may not have.

Trinquier suggests an organizational structure to wage this counterguerrilla campaign and elaborates a "gridding" system that divides territory into sectors in which methods are applied to sweep them clear of subversive elements. Again, the use of a census is important, as is the recording of vehicles, animals, and any other assets that may be exploited by the antigovernment forces. During these operations entire towns are to be detained and interrogated, a process that should yield valuable intelligence but may also alienate the population. At times, warns Trinquier, it is vital to take the war to the enemy by going beyond one's borders. Allowing safe havens for subversive elements may negate the successes of previous operations.

RELEARNING THE THEORY AND PRACTICE OF COUNTERINSURGENCY WARFARE

Counterinsurgency Warfare: Theory and Practice, penned by David Galula in 1964, provides a systematic discussion of how to defeat the insurgent —and the pitfalls along the way.[12] Bernard Fall, author of

Component	Insurgent	Counterinsurgent
Resource asymmetry	Limited resources/power	Preponderance of resources/power
Objective = population	Solicit government oppression	Show that insurgency is destabilizing
Political nature of war	Wage war for minds of population	Wage war for same, and to keep legitimacy
Gradual transition to war	Use time to develop cause	Always in reactive mode
Protracted nature of war	Disperse; use limited violence widely	Maintain vigilance; sustain will
Cost	High return for investment	Sustained operations carry high political/economic burden
Role of ideology	Sole asset at beginning is cause or idea	Defeat root of cause or idea

Figure 1. Galula's differences between insurgents and counterinsurgents.

the acclaimed *Street Without Joy*, considered Galula's work the best "how-to" guide to counterinsurgency warfare. Experience in China, Greece, Southeast Asia, and Algeria as a French military officer and attaché led Galula to consider the "need for a compass," and prompted him to "define the laws of counterinsurgency warfare, to deduce from them its principles, and to outline the corresponding strategy and tactics."[13]

A simple theoretical construct underlies the theory and practice of counterinsurgency warfare. It is the essence of what today's theorists and strategists term asymmetric warfare: although an asymmetric distribution of resources and abilities actually favors counterinsurgent forces, they are often inappropriately wielded. The conflict is asymmetric because there is a "disproportion of strength between the opponents at the outset, and from the difference in essence between their assets and liabilities."[14] At the conceptual level, the insurgent is endowed with the "ideological power of a cause on which to base his actions" and the counterinsurgent laden with a "heavy liability—he is responsible for maintaining order throughout the country" without undermining the ideals on which the new government is making its pleas for support.[15]

Figure 1, above, shows the differences that Galula saw between insurgents and counterinsurgents. Exploring the practical implications of those dyadic relationships is the underlying theme of Galula's writings, which reinforce the image of counterinsurgency as one "where most of the rules applicable to one side do not work for the other."[16]

This is a critical point for discussions of Iraqi counterinsurgency operations. Press accounts too frequently criticize an apparent inability of US forces to defeat insurgents without addressing the more complex, diverging objectives of the Coalition. Part of the Coalition's sociological mission is instantiating important concepts into the Iraqi collective conscious, including mercy, restraint, proportional force, and just war.

One cannot understand the theory and practice of counterinsurgency warfare without understanding the socio-political-economic intricacies of the "cause" which insurgents use to mobilize support. Without a cause, the insurgency cannot persuade the population to join or assist in the campaign. Qualities of causes include: a large part of the population must be able to identify with the cause; the counterinsurgent cannot be able to use the same cause or espouse it; the essential social mobilization base remains the same while the cause changes over time as the insurgency adapts. With the right cause, the insurgent can mobilize recruits. Combined with an intermixing of attacks on those aiding the new regime, a successful cause increases insurgent power while blunting the counterinsurgency's intelligence capabilities. Over time, as the new regime appears powerless to prevent terrorism and restore stability, the mobilization potential of the cause increases when propaganda arms of the insurgency identify the new regime as the root of instability.

Arguably, the Iraqi counterinsurgency has entered this stage. Arab media may in fact be aiding the insurgency. Reports of staggering numbers of new Iraqi satellite television dishes suggest that foreign media broadcasts, many of them colored with anti-American bias, are competing with Coalition media services in the battle to shape Iraqi perceptions.

Causes are not static. They change as the insurgency adapts. The basic "strategic criteria" of a cause—and the necessary ingredient of any "best cause" at any moment in the struggle—is that it "can attract the largest number of supporters and repel the minimum of opponents."[17] Once a problem is selected, the insurgent attempts to exacerbate the problem in order to increase the chasm between the government and the people. Political, social, economic, racial, religious, or even artificially created issues can be folded into a cause. In the case of the artificial or concocted cause, the insurgent must work to make the underlying premise appear to be fact. This is possible through "efficient propaganda" or other means to "turn an artificial problem into a real one."[18] Mistakes made in the process of waging a counterinsurgency war often reinforce an insurgent's propaganda. For example, accidental shootings, deaths during interrogations, misdirected raids, and inappropriate behavior by new police organizations fuel insurgent claims that the new regime is corrupt or unable to protect the population.

The ability to switch causes and manipulate them to the detriment of the government is based on a fundamental characteristic of the war where "idealism and a sense of ethics weigh in favor of a consistent stand [but] tactics pull toward opportunism."[19] An asymmetric resource distribution leaves the insurgent few options in his fight against the government institutions opposing him. As the war widens and the population is forced to take sides, the insurgency need not devote as much time and effort in cultivating the cause. By this time, the war has engulfed the country and exposed the weaknesses of the government as well as providing evidence as to the growing power of the movement. The coming months in Afghanistan and Iraq will see insurgency movements adapting their mobilization strategies as they intensify attacks meant to reinforce the argument that new, American-backed regimes cannot protect the population.

What can be done? How can US military planners attack the intangible, political elements of the insurgency? Galula offers several routes to making "a body politic resistant to infection."[20] First is continuously reassessing the nature, scope, and degree of problems around the country. Anticipating problems and proactively addressing them leaves the insurgent without causes to exploit. Second, increase solidarity for the regime. Bring additional propaganda efforts to bear, including Arabic television broadcasts, that promote the new regime as something worth supporting and defending. Third, counterinsurgency leadership must maintain a high level of vigilance and support against the movement. Many times insurgencies will take strategic pauses to adapt, regroup, and develop new mobilization strategies. Too often a new regime will interpret this as victory and focus resources on regime-building. Counterinsurgencies are protracted struggles. Fourth, as Trinquier argued, intelligence and deep knowledge of the enemy are critical. Bringing new sources and methods to bear throughout the effort must be a priority. Too often, commanders consider their intelligence capabilities and tools as fixed resources across the insurgency. Today, there are countless remote sensing, information fusion, and surveillance capabilities available for incorporation into the toolbox. Many are ideally suited to the urban fight and can bolster human intelligence assets.

Intelligence tools, furthermore, must be attuned to geographic conditions, which remain a factor in the ability of the regime to defeat the insurgent. This is an area where US forces should be seeking out and applying new capabilities. Geospatial intelligence capabilities, including integration of demographic information, play an overriding role in insurgency warfare. Insurgents tend to use geography against the new government, including the exploitation of active borders to receive outside support.

A confluence of military and nonmilitary operations defeats the insurgent. This requires an organization vested with the power to coordinate political, social, economic, and military elements. This was, presumably, the goal of a recent US National Security Council decision to reorganize the management of Iraq operations. For Galula, counterinsurgency efforts require unified command, a single source of direction. This means a "tight" organization, to borrow from Trinquier, directing "the operation from the beginning to the end."[21] The military, moreover, cannot be allowed a free hand in the overall direction of the war. At the operational level, "It is better to entrust civilian tasks to civilians." [22] That is, "military action is secondary to the political one, its primary purpose being to afford the political power enough freedom to work safely with the population."[23]

Galula's discussion of command and control problems, which must be settled prior to engaging the enemy, exposes structural and conceptual elements of the counterinsurgency process. Once the decision to engage the enemy has been made and an area selected for operations, a systematic process is initiated in the first, and each consecutive, area where the insurgent is active. The first step involves selecting an area to win back from the enemy. Sufficient troops are massed in the area and moved into contact with the enemy in order to destroy or expel them. "This operation is not an end in itself, for guerrillas, like the heads of the legendary hydra, have the special ability to grow again if not all destroyed at the same time. The real purpose of the operation," Galula continues, "is to prepare the stage for the further development of the counterinsurgent action."[24]

After an area has been cleared of guerrillas, the "over-all operation is finally broken down into several small-scale ones" and "all of the forces work on what is left of the guerrillas after the . . . earlier sweeps."[25] This is predominantly a military activity. As such, there is likely to be some destruction of physical structures, crops, and damage to other local assets. As a result, the insurgent is likely to initiate a propaganda campaign using damaged assets as evidence that the government is unconcerned with, perhaps even antagonistic to, the local peasants or villagers. No easy solution exists for this problem. Preventative steps are concerned mainly with limiting the destruction and imposing constraints on the use of force. "Any damage done should be immediately compensated without red tape."[26]

Counterinsurgents direct propaganda operations at the population with a limited goal of obtaining their neutrality. The underlying message? "Stay neutral and peace will return soon to the area. Help the insurgent, and we will be obliged to carry on more military operations and thus inflict more destruction."[27]

The construction of barracks and other housing should be avoided and the troops forced to live like the population. Psychologically, if the troops live in their own housing which is distinct from that of the locals, they will develop a cognitive distance from the population. Similarly, if the troops live in housing that differs from the locals' housing, they will appear to be outsiders and thus make it more difficult for the people to accept them. This is currently a problem for Coalition forces in Iraq. As insurgents succeeded in attacks, Coalition forces moved into more isolated, secure billeting. Although this is prudent in the short term, in the long run it reinforces the perception of US forces as an occupying power.

LOW-INTENSITY OPERATIONS

A decade after Trinquier's book was published in France, Frank Kitson's *Low Intensity Operations: Subversion, Insurgency and Peacekeeping* rolled of the press across the English Channel. By then, Britain had participated—usually with unsatisfactory performance—in more than 30 low-intensity conflicts that involved elements of subversion.[28] Kitson's book, notes military historian General Sir Michael Carver, was "written for the soldier of today to help him prepare for the operations of tomorrow," an observation that still holds true in the 2000s.[29] Of course, no one, including Kitson, would claim that military engagements during counterinsurgency conflicts are really "low-intensity." All combat is intense.

Like Trinquier and Galula, Kitson observes that the realm of counterinsurgency involves combat with an enemy "likely to be employing a combination of political, economic, psychological, and military measures."[30] He also identifies a viable intelligence organization as critical.

Kitson departs from Trinquier and Galula in his discussion of the proper use of force. After warning against abuses, he discusses "military difficulties about using too little force and about delaying its application for too long."[31] Kitson advocates fighting fire with fire, stressing "that wars of subversion and counter-subversion are fought, in the last resort, in the minds of the people."[32] The soldier cannot become fixated with engaging the guerrilla, nor can he become desensitized to the power of ideas to influence other men. One only has to recognize the importance of waging war in the mind "for the importance of a good psychological operations organization to become apparent."[33] And once this becomes apparent, then the importance of intelligence is elevated.

To clarify the use of intelligence, Kitson distinguishes between information needed in "normal" times and "that which it will have to get after subversion has started."[34] He proposes two kinds of intelligence, political and operational. The former is collected and analyzed before, during, and after the subversion rises and falls; the latter is unique to the fight against the enemy organization and "will cease to be required once the enemy is fully defeated, because it is concerned with information about the enemy's forces and committees which will have ceased to exist by that time."[35]

The move from political intelligence gathering to operational intelligence gathering and the guiding of forces into contact with the enemy involves more than merely expanding the intelligence organization. As discussed above, it requires adapting to the enemy and "developing new methods" to deal with problems as they arise.[36] In simpler terms this means maintaining flexibility, seizing the initiative whenever possible, and effectively coordinating the military, political, economic, and social aspects of the conflict. The army must be involved in the intelligence gathering and analysis aspects of the counterinsurgency effort from the beginning, Kitson argues, "because in the later stages of the campaign when [the army's] units are deployed, it will rely very greatly on the information provided by the intelligence organization for the success of its operations."[37] One facet of building a successful intelligence organization is the use of local assets, which becomes especially true when establishing a psychological-operations organization.

How can the new regime's counterinsurgency forces be educated? First, they must become attuned to the environment, both the cognitive as well as the physical. Second, commanders must learn to optimize resources for each phase in the campaign, including the integration of civil and military activities. Third, commanders must know how to direct and coordinate all resources under their command. Finally, education and training must reach all levels of the organization.[38]

Students of ongoing efforts in Iraq will benefit from Kitson's comparison of counterinsurgencies and peacekeeping. Fundamentally, the two share "a surprising similarity in the outward forms of many of the techniques involved."[39] Both require the combination and efficient integration of military and nonmilitary resources, although peacekeeping arguably requires greater attention to the political aspects of the operation. While the use of force is typical of a campaign against insurgents, there are advantages in avoiding the use of force in peacekeeping operations and focusing on political means. Kitson suggests that the peacekeeper must develop an image of being an honest broker, which enhances the ability of the peacekeeper to negotiate and if necessary mediate between belligerents. A unique attribute of the peacekeeper's mission is the gathering and employment of intelligence within a different set of ethical guidelines, a product of the "peaceful" nature of the mission. To avoid infringing upon the privacy of the population, Kitson suggests the exploitation of open sources and the development of human contacts on both sides of the conflict. Despite the need to remain neutral, however, Kitson does relate experiences where forces intercepted communications, exposing again the need to deploy intelligence assets with the operational force.

CONCLUSION

Trinquier, Galula, and Kitson are certainly not the only authors providing useful insights into the nature and conduct of counterinsurgencies. They are, however, among the best sources of insight from a generation of soldiers with experience fighting modern wars. A number of common lessons or themes from the above discussion apply to the current situation in Iraq.

All three works discuss the asymmetric relationship between the insurgent and the counterinsurgent. This is true not only in terms of the cause, where the insurgent is likely to have the only dynamic one, but extends to the material realm also. Optimizing available counterinsurgency resources is crucial. Education and reeducation of soldiers is one way of sustaining focus and adapting efforts. During and after combat actions, the political nature of the contest must be reinforced. Because transitioning from a combat soldier to a political one is a delicate process, it is important for troop rotations to be aligned with progress in legitimating new political institutions.

Intelligence is the critical enabler. The tactical use of information, which is the responsibility of the operational commander, is the only way to identify the enemy. Background information must be gathered and analyzed at all times, with operational intelligence used to bring forces into contact with the enemy. The operational intelligence effort must remain flexible, adapting to the situation as it develops, and retain the wherewithal to innovate and seize the initiative away from the enemy. Ground commanders must develop and retain a capacity to actively gather information and avoid situations where they are dependent on other organizations for critical operational intelligence. This aids identification and neutralization of causes and concerns before their exploitation for guerrilla mobilization.

Insurgency causes, their mobilization resource, are not static. The movement will manipulate, even create, causes as the war progresses; initial causes often decline in importance as the struggle escalates. Counterinsurgencies must engage in reform, adaptation, or innovation activities to counter the political appeal of evolving causes. Counter-mobilization is a critical, strategic process in the campaign. In Iraq, we are now seeing the shifting of insurgent mobilization appeals from supporting the old regime to defending against foreign occupation to appealing to local tribal elements seeking preservation of paternal social norms. Counterinsurgency efforts must respond accordingly.

Concurrent with the development of a viable intelligence organization is the need to recognize the interdependence of economic, political, psychological, and military factors. The successful counterinsurgency campaign will have an organization which aggregates these factors into one unified command able to adapt and utilize resources efficiently. The efforts of elements within the organization should not be allowed to "cut across each other," and the commander should be aware of their actions at all times.

Finally, the counterinsurgent must possess the training, capability, and will to fight on *cognitive terrain*. Toward this end he must develop and deploy psychological operations units, propaganda operations, and social service units that foster the impression that the government is addressing underlying socio-economic problems. Additionally, the insurgent must be exposed as preventing the government from solving these problems.

In discussing success criteria, counterinsurgents need success as early as possible to demonstrate the will, the means, and the ability to defeat the insurgency. Counterinsurgents, moreover, need to avoid negotiations until they are in a position of strength. Potential supporters will flock to the insurgent's side out of fear of retaliation if the movement considers them disloyal. A negotiated solution to the conflict before the new government possesses a preponderance of power will lead to the undermining of the settlement and the negation of gains.

The above review does not suggest such works can resolve current problems or that concerns can be resolved merely be dusting off and reading counterinsurgency books from the Cold War. However, "studying the past," to borrow from John Lewis Gaddis, "has a way of introducing humility—a first stage toward gaining detachment—because it suggests the continuity of the problems we confront, and the unoriginality of most of our solutions for them. It is a good way of putting things in perspective, of stepping back to take in a wider view."[40]

NOTES

1. Mark Bowden, *Black Hawk Down: A Story of Modern War* (New York: Atlantic Monthly Press, 1999).

2. Roger Trinquier, *Modern Warfare: A French View of Counterinsurgency*, trans. Daniel Lee, with an introduction by Bernard B. Fall (New York: Praeger, 1964), p. 6.

3. Martin Van Creveld, *The Transformation of War* (New York: The Free Press, 1991).

4. Trinquier, p. 4.

5. Ibid., p. 3.

6. Ibid., p. 8.

7. Thom Shanker and Eric Schmitt, "Pentagon Says a Covert Force Hunts Hussein," *The New York Times*, 7 November 2003, p. 1.

8. Ibid.

9. Trinquier, p. 63.

10. Cited in Matt Kelley, "U.S. Intelligence Effort Lacking in Specialists," *San Diego Union-Tribune*, 22 November 2003, p. 1.

11. Ibid.

12. David Galula, *Counterinsurgency Warfare: Theory and Practice* (New York: Praeger, 1964).

13. Ibid., pp. xii-xiii.

14. Ibid., p. 6.

15. Ibid., p. 7.

16. Ibid., p. xi.

17. Ibid., pp. 19-20.

18. Ibid., pp. 21-22.

19. Ibid., pp. 24-25.

20. Ibid., p. 26.

21. Ibid., p. 87.

22. Ibid., p. 88.

23. Ibid.

24. Ibid., p. 107.

25. Ibid., p. 108.

26. Ibid., p. 109.

27. Ibid.

28. Frank Kitson, *Low Intensity Operations: Subversion, Insurgency, Peace-keeping* (London: Faber, 1971), p. xi.

29. Ibid.

30. Ibid.

31. Ibid., p. 70.

32. Ibid., p. 78.

33. Ibid., p. 72.

34. Ibid.

35. Ibid.

36. Ibid.

37. Ibid., p. 73.

38. Ibid., pp. 165-67.

39. Ibid., p. 144.

40. John Lewis Gaddis, *The United States and the End of the Cold War: Implications, Reconstructions, Provocations* (New York: Oxford Univ. Press, 1992), p. 3.

Part X
References

At the end of the book, you can find copies of the:

1. The 1776 Declaration of Independence. A document explaining the British colonies rationale for revolt in very, for the time period, radical terms— the concepts of civil, political & economic liberalism
2. The 1945 United Nations Charter
3. The 1945 Statute of the International Court of Justice
4. The 1949 Washington Treaty (leading to the formation of NATO

The Declaration of Independence of the Thirteen Colonies

In Congress

July 4, 1776

The unanimous Declaration of the thirteen united States of America,

When in the Course of human events, it becomes necessary for one people to dissolve the political bands which have connected them with another, and to assume among the powers of the earth, the separate and equal station to which the Laws of Nature and of Nature's God entitle them, a decent respect to the opinions of mankind requires that they should declare the causes which impel them to the separation.

We hold these truths to be self-evident, that all men are created equal, that they are endowed by their Creator with certain unalienable Rights, that among these are Life, Liberty and the pursuit of Happiness. —That to secure these rights, Governments are instituted among Men, deriving their just powers from the consent of the governed, —That whenever any Form of Government becomes destructive of these ends, it is the Right of the People to alter or to abolish it, and to institute new Government, laying its foundation on such principles and organizing its powers in such form, as to them shall seem most likely to effect their Safety and Happiness. Prudence, indeed, will dictate that Governments long established should not be changed for light and transient causes; and accordingly all experience hath shewn, that mankind are more disposed to suffer, while evils are sufferable, than to right themselves by abolishing the forms to which they are accustomed. But when a long train of abuses and usurpations, pursuing invariably the same Object evinces a design to reduce them under absolute Despotism, it is their right, it is their duty, to throw off such Government, and to provide new Guards for their future security. —Such has been the patient sufferance of these Colonies; and such is now the necessity which constrains them to alter their former Systems of Government. The history of the present King of Great Britain [George III] is a history of repeated injuries and usurpations, all having in direct object the establishment of an absolute Tyranny over these States. To prove this, let Facts be submitted to a candid world.

He has refused his Assent to Laws, the most wholesome and necessary for the public good.

He has forbidden his Governors to pass Laws of immediate and pressing importance, unless suspended in their operation till his Assent should be obtained; and when so suspended, he has utterly neglected to attend to them.

He has refused to pass other Laws for the accommodation of large districts of people, unless those people would relinquish the right of Representation in the Legislature, a right inestimable to them and formidable to tyrants only.

He has called together legislative bodies at places unusual, uncomfortable, and distant from the depository of their public Records, for the sole purpose of fatiguing them into compliance with his measures.

He has dissolved Representative Houses repeatedly, for opposing with manly firmness his invasions on the rights of the people.

He has refused for a long time, after such dissolutions, to cause others to be elected; whereby the Legislative powers, incapable of Annihilation, have returned to the People at large for their exercise; the State remaining in the mean time exposed to all the dangers of invasion from without, and convulsions within.

He has endeavoured to prevent the population of these States; for that purpose obstructing the Laws for Naturalization of Foreigners; refusing to pass others to encourage their migrations hither, and raising the conditions of new Appropriations of Lands.

He has obstructed the Administration of Justice, by refusing his Assent to Laws for establishing Judiciary powers.

He has made Judges dependent on his Will alone, for the tenure of their offices, and the amount and payment of their salaries.

He has erected a multitude of New Offices, and sent hither swarms of Officers to harass our people, and eat out their substance.

He has kept among us, in times of peace, Standing Armies without the consent of our legislatures.

He has affected to render the Military independent of and superior to the Civil power.

He has combined with others to subject us to a jurisdiction foreign to our constitution and unacknowledged by our laws; giving his Assent to their Acts of pretended Legislation:

For Quartering large bodies of armed troops among us:

For protecting them, by a mock Trial, from punishment for any Murders which they should commit on the Inhabitants of these States:

For cutting off our Trade with all parts of the world:

For imposing Taxes on us without our Consent:

For depriving us, in many cases, of the benefits of Trial by Jury:

For transporting us beyond Seas to be tried for pretended offences:

For abolishing the free System of English Laws in a neighbouring Province, establishing therein an Arbitrary government, and enlarging its Boundaries so as to render it at once an example and fit instrument for introducing the same absolute rule into these Colonies:

For taking away our Charters, abolishing our most valuable Laws, and altering fundamentally the Forms of our Governments:

For suspending our own Legislatures, and declaring themselves invested with power to legislate for us in all cases whatsoever.

He has abdicated Government here, by declaring us out of his Protection and waging War against us.

He has plundered our seas, ravaged our Coasts, burnt our towns, and destroyed the lives of our people.

He is at this time transporting large Armies of foreign Mercenaries to compleat the works of death, desolation and tyranny, already begun with circumstances of Cruelty and perfidy scarcely paralleled in the most barbarous ages, and totally unworthy the Head of a civilized nation.

He has constrained our fellow Citizens taken Captive on the high Seas to bear Arms against their Country, to become the executioners of their friends and Brethren, or to fall themselves by their Hands.

He has excited domestic insurrections amongst us, and has endeavoured to bring on the inhabitants of our frontiers, the merciless Indian Savages, whose known rule of warfare, is an undistinguished destruction of all ages, sexes and conditions.

In every stage of these Oppressions We have Petitioned for Redress in the most humble terms: Our repeated Petitions have been answered only by repeated injury. A Prince whose character is thus marked by every act which may define a Tyrant, is unfit to be the ruler of a free people.

Nor have We been wanting in attentions to our British brethren. We have warned them from time to time of attempts by their legislature to extend an unwarrantable jurisdiction over us. We have reminded them of the circumstances of our emigration and settlement here. We have appealed to their native justice and magnanimity, and we have conjured them by the ties of our common kindred to disavow these usurpations, which, would inevitably interrupt our connections and correspondence. They too have been deaf to the voice of justice and of consanguinity. We must, therefore, acquiesce in the necessity, which denounces our Separation, and hold them, as we hold the rest of mankind, Enemies in War, in Peace Friends.

We, therefore, the Representatives of the united States of America, in General Congress, Assembled, appealing to the Supreme Judge of the world for the rectitude of our intentions, do, in the Name, and by the Authority of the good People of these Colonies, solemnly publish and declare, That these United Colonies are, and of Right ought to be Free and Independent States; that they are Absolved from all Allegiance to the British Crown, and that all political connection between them and the State of Great Britain, is and ought to be totally dissolved; and that as Free and Independent States, they have full Power to levy War, conclude Peace, contract Alliances, establish Commerce, and to do all other Acts and Things which Independent States may of right do. And for the support of this Declaration, with a firm reliance on the protection of divine Providence, we mutually pledge to each other our Lives, our Fortunes and our sacred Honor.

THE SIGNERS OF THE DECLARATION REPRESENTED THE NEW STATES AS FOLLOWS:

New Hampshire:
Josiah Bartlett, William Whipple, Matthew Thornton

Massachusetts:
John Hancock, Samual Adams, John Adams, Robert Treat Paine, Elbridge Gerry

Rhode Island:
Stephen Hopkins, William Ellery

Connecticut:
Roger Sherman, Samuel Huntington, William Williams, Oliver Wolcott

New York:
William Floyd, Philip Livingston, Francis Lewis, Lewis Morris

New Jersey:
Richard Stockton, John Witherspoon, Francis Hopkinson, John Hart, Abraham Clark

Pennsylvania:
Robert Morris, Benjamin Rush, Benjamin Franklin, John Morton, George Clymer, James Smith, George Taylor, James Wilson, George Ross

Delaware:
Caesar Rodney, George Read, Thomas McKean

Maryland:
Samuel Chase, William Paca, Thomas Stone, Charles Carroll of Carrollton

Virginia:
George Wythe, Richard Henry Lee, Thomas Jefferson, Benjamin Harrison, Thomas Nelson, Jr., Francis Lightfoot Lee, Carter Braxton

North Carolina:
William Hooper, Joseph Hewes, John Penn

South Carolina:
Edward Rutledge, Thomas Heyward, Jr., Thomas Lynch, Jr., Arthur Middleton

Georgia:
Button Gwinnett, Lyman Hall, George Walton

Charter of the United Nations

We the Peoples of the United Nations . . . United for a Better World

INTRODUCTORY NOTE

The Charter of the United Nations was signed on 26 June 1945, in San Francisco, at the conclusion of the United Nations Conference on International Organization, and came into force on 24 October 1945. The Statute of the International Court of Justice is an integral part of the Charter.

Amendments to Articles 23, 27 and 61 of the Charter were adopted by the General Assembly on 17 December 1963 and came into force on 31 August 1965. A further amendment to Article 61 was adopted by the General Assembly on 20 December 1971, and came into force on 24 September 1973. An amendment to Article 109, adopted by the General Assembly on 20 December 1965, came into force on 12 June 1968.

The amendment to Article 23 enlarges the membership of the Security Council from eleven to fifteen. The amended Article 27 provides that decisions of the Security Council on procedural matters shall be made by an affirmative vote of nine members (formerly seven) and on all other matters by an affirmative vote of nine members (formerly seven), including the concurring votes of the five permanent members of the Security Council.

The amendment to Article 61, which entered into force on 31 August 1965, enlarged the membership of the Economic and Social Council from eighteen to twenty-seven. The subsequent amendment to that Article, which entered into force on 24 September 1973, further increased the membership of the Council from twenty-seven to fifty-four.

The amendment to Article 109, which relates to the first paragraph of that Article, provides that a General Conference of Member States for the purpose of reviewing the Charter may be held at a date and place to be fixed by a two-thirds vote of the members of the General Assembly and by a vote of any nine members (formerly seven) of the Security Council. Paragraph 3 of Article 109, which deals with the consideration of a possible review conference during the tenth regular session of the General Assembly, has been retained in its original form in its reference to a "vote, of any seven members of the Security Council", the paragraph having been acted upon in 1955 by the General Assembly, at its tenth regular session, and by the Security Council.

PREAMBLE

We the Peoples of the United Nations Determined
- to save succeeding generations from the scourge of war, which twice in our lifetime has brought untold sorrow to mankind, and
- to reaffirm faith in fundamental human rights, in the dignity and worth of the human person, in the equal rights of men and women and of nations large and small, and
- to establish conditions under which justice and respect for the obligations arising from treaties and other sources of international law can be maintained, and
- to promote social progress and better standards of life in larger freedom,

And For These Ends
- to practice tolerance and live together in peace with one another as good neighbours, and
- to unite our strength to maintain international peace and security, and
- to ensure, by the acceptance of principles and the institution of methods, that armed force shall not be used, save in the common interest, and
- to employ international machinery for the promotion of the economic and social advancement of all peoples,

Have Resolved to Combine Our Efforts to Accomplish these Aims
Accordingly, our respective Governments, through representatives assembled in the city of San Francisco, who have exhibited their full powers found to be in good and due form, have agreed to the present Charter of the United Nations and do hereby establish an international organization to be known as the United Nations.

CHAPTER I. PURPOSES AND PRINCIPLES

Article 1
The **Purposes** of the United Nations are:
1. To maintain international peace and security, and to that end: to take effective collective measures for the prevention and removal of threats to the peace, and for the suppression of acts of aggression or other breaches of the peace, and to bring about by peaceful means, and in conformity with the principles of justice and international law, adjustment or settlement of international disputes or situations which might lead to a breach of the peace;
2. To develop friendly relations among nations based on respect for the principle of equal rights and self-determination of peoples, and to take other appropriate measures to strengthen universal peace;
3. To achieve international co-operation in solving international problems of an economic, social, cultural, or humanitarian character, and in promoting and encouraging respect for human rights and for fundamental freedoms for all without distinction as to race, sex, language, or religion; and
4. To be a centre for harmonizing the actions of nations in the attainment of these common ends.

Article 2
The Organization and its Members, in pursuit of the Purposes stated in Article 1, shall act in accordance with the following **Principles**.

1. The Organization is based on the principle of the sovereign equality of all its Members.
2. All Members, in order to ensure to all of them the rights and benefits resulting from membership, shall fulfil in good faith the obligations assumed by them in accordance with the present Charter.
3. All Members shall settle their international disputes by peaceful means in such a manner that international peace and security, and justice, are not endangered.
4. All Members shall refrain in their international relations from the threat or use of force against the territorial integrity or political independence of any state, or in any other manner inconsistent with the Purposes of the United Nations.
5. All Members shall give the United Nations every assistance in any action it takes in accordance with the present Charter, and shall refrain from giving assistance to any state against which the United Nations is taking preventive or enforcement action.
6. The Organization shall ensure that states which are not Members of the United Nations act in accordance with these Principles so far as may be necessary for the maintenance of international peace and security.
7. Nothing contained in the present Charter shall authorize the United Nations to intervene in matters which are essentially within the domestic jurisdiction of any state or shall require the Members to submit such matters to settlement under the present Charter; but this principle shall not prejudice the application of enforcement measures under Chapter VII.

CHAPTER II. MEMBERSHIP

Article 3
The original Members of the United Nations shall be the states which, having participated in the United Nations Conference on International Organization at San Francisco, or having previously signed the Declaration by United Nations of 1 January 1942, sign the present Charter and ratify it in accordance with Article 110.

Article 4
1. Membership in the United Nations is open to all other peace-loving states which accept the obligations contained in the present Charter and, in the judgment of the Organization, are able and willing to carry out these obligations.
2. The admission of any such state to membership in the United Nations will be effected by a decision of the General Assembly upon the recommendation of the Security Council.

Article 5
A Member of the United Nations against which preventive or enforcement action has been taken by the Security Council may be suspended from the exercise of the rights and privileges of membership by the General Assembly upon the recommendation of the Security Council. The exercise of these rights and privileges may be restored by the Security Council.

Article 6
A Member of the United Nations which has persistently violated the Principles contained in the present Charter may be expelled from the Organization by the General Assembly upon the recommendation of the Security Council.

CHAPTER III. ORGANS

Article 7
1. There are established as the **principal organs** of the United Nations:
   a **General Assembly**
   a **Security Council**
   an **Economic and Social Council**
   a **Trusteeship Council**
   an **International Court of Justice**
   and a **Secretariat.**

2. Such subsidiary organs as may be found necessary may be established in accordance with the present Charter.

Article 8
The United Nations shall place no restrictions on the eligibility of men and women to participate in any capacity and under conditions of equality in its principal and subsidiary organs.

CHAPTER IV. THE GENERAL ASSEMBLY

Composition

Article 9
1. The General Assembly shall consist of all the Members of the United Nations.
2. Each Member shall have not more than five representatives in the General Assembly.

Functions and Powers

Article 10
The General Assembly may discuss any questions or any matters within the scope of the present Charter or relating to the powers and functions of any organs provided for in the present Charter, and, except as provided in Article 12, may make recommendations to the Members of the United Nations or to the Security Council or to both on any such questions or matters.

Article 11
1. The General Assembly may consider the general principles of co-operation in the mainte-nance of international peace and security, including the principles governing disarmament and the regulation of armaments, and may make recommendations with regard to such prin-ciples to the Members or to the Security Council or to both.
2. The General Assembly may discuss any questions relating to the maintenance of international peace and security brought before it by any Member of the United Nations, or by the Security Council, or by a state which is not a Member of the United Nations in accordance with Article 35, paragraph 2, and, except as provided in Article 12, may make recommendations with regard to any such questions to the state or states concerned or to the Security Council or to both. Any such question on which action is necessary shall be referred to the Security Council by the General Assembly either before or after discussion.

3. The General Assembly may call the attention of the Security Council to situations which are likely to endanger international peace and security.
4. The powers of the General Assembly set forth in this Article shall not limit the general scope of Article 10.

Article 12

1. While the Security Council is exercising in respect of any dispute or situation the functions assigned to it in the present Charter, the General Assembly shall not make any recommendation with regard to that dispute or situation unless the Security Council so requests.
2. The Secretary-General, with the consent of the Security Council, shall notify the General Assembly at each session of any matters relative to the maintenance of international peace and security which are being dealt with by the Security Council and shall similarly notify the General Assembly, or the Members of the United Nations if the General Assembly is not in session, immediately the Security Council ceases to deal with such matters.

Article 13

1. The General Assembly shall initiate studies and make recommendations for the purpose of:
   a. promoting international co-operation in the political field and encouraging the progressive development of international law and its codification;
   b. promoting international co-operation in the economic, social, cultural, educational, and health fields, and assisting in the realization of human rights and fundamental freedoms for all without distinction as to race, sex, language, or religion.
2. The further responsibilities, functions and powers of the General Assembly with respect to matters mentioned in paragraph 1 (b) above are set forth in Chapters IX and X.

Article 14

Subject to the provisions of Article 12, the General Assembly may recommend measures for the peaceful adjustment of any situation, regardless of origin, which it deems likely to impair the general welfare or friendly relations among nations, including situations resulting from a violation of the provisions of the present Charter setting forth the Purposes and Principles of the United Nations.

Article 15

1. The General Assembly shall receive and consider annual and special reports from the Security Council; these reports shall include an account of the measures that the Security Council has decided upon or taken to maintain international peace and security.
2. The General Assembly shall receive and consider reports from the other organs of the United Nations.

Article 16

The General Assembly shall perform such functions with respect to the international trusteeship system as are assigned to it under Chapters XII and XIII, including the approval of the trusteeship agreements for areas not designated as strategic.

Article 17

1. The General Assembly shall consider and approve the budget of the Organization.
2. The expenses of the Organization shall be borne by the Members as apportioned by the General Assembly.
3. The General Assembly shall consider and approve any financial and budgetary arrangements with specialized agencies referred to in Article 57 and shall examine the administrative bud-

gets of such specialized agencies with a view to making recommendations to the agencies concerned.

Voting

Article 18

    1. Each member of the General Assembly shall have one vote.

       Decisions of the General Assembly on important questions shall be made by a twothirds majority of the members present and voting. These questions shall include: recommendations with respect to the maintenance of international peace and security, the election of the non-permanent members of the Security Council, the election of the members of the Economic and Social Council, the election of members of the Trusteeship Council in accordance with paragraph 1 (c) of Article 86, the admission of new Members to the United Nations, the suspension of the rights and privileges of membership, the expulsion of Members, questions relating to the operation of the trusteeship system, and budgetary questions.

    2. Decisions on other questions, including the determination of additional categories of questions to be decided by a two-thirds majority, shall be made by a majority of the members present and voting.

Article 19

A Member of the United Nations which is in arrears in the payment of its financial contributions to the Organization shall have no vote in the General Assembly if the amount of its arrears equals or exceeds the amount of the contributions due from it for the preceding two full years. The General Assembly may, nevertheless, permit such a Member to vote if it is satisfied that the failure to pay is due to conditions beyond the control of the Member.

Procedure

Article 20

The General Assembly shall meet in regular annual sessions and in such special sessions as occasion may require. Special sessions shall be convoked by the Secretary-General at the request of the Security Council or of a majority of the Members of the United Nations.

Article 21

The General Assembly shall adopt its own rules of procedure. It shall elect its President for each session.

Article 22

The General Assembly may establish such subsidiary organs as it deems necessary for the performance of its functions.

CHAPTER V. THE SECURITY COUNCIL

Composition

Article 23

    1. The Security Council shall consist of fifteen Members of the United Nations. The Republic of China, France, the Union of Soviet Socialist Republics, the United Kingdom of Great Britain

and Northern Ireland, and the United States of America shall be permanent members of the Security Council. The General Assembly shall elect ten other Members of the United Nations to be non-permanent members of the Security Council, due regard being specially paid, in the first instance to the contribution of Members of the United Nations to the maintenance of international peace and security and to the other purposes of the Organization, and also to equitable geographical distribution.

2. The non-permanent members of the Security Council shall be elected for a term of two years. In the first election of the non-permanent members after the increase of the membership of the Security Council from eleven to fifteen, two of the four additional members shall be chosen for a term of one year. A retiring member shall not be eligible for immediate re-election.
3. Each member of the Security Council shall have one representative.

Functions and Powers

Article 24

1. In order to ensure prompt and effective action by the United Nations, its Members confer on the Security Council primary responsibility for the maintenance of international peace and security, and agree that in carrying out its duties under this responsibility the Security Council acts on their behalf.
2. In discharging these duties the Security Council shall act in accordance with the Purposes and Principles of the United Nations. The specific powers granted to the Security Council for the discharge of these duties are laid down in Chapters VI, VII, VIII, and XII.
3. The Security Council shall submit annual and, when necessary, special reports to the General Assembly for its consideration.

Article 25
The Members of the United Nations agree to accept and carry out the decisions of the Security Council in accordance with the present Charter.

Article 26
In order to promote the establishment and maintenance of international peace and security with the least diversion for armaments of the world's human and economic resources, the Security Council shall be responsible for formulating, with the assistance of the Military Staff Committee referred to in Article 47, plans to be submitted to the Members of the United Nations for the establishment of a system for the regulation of armaments.

Voting

Article 27
1. Each member of the Security Council shall have one vote.
2. Decisions of the Security Council on procedural matters shall be made by an affirmative vote of nine members.
3. Decisions of the Security Council on all other matters shall be made by an affirmative vote of nine members including the concurring votes of the permanent members; provided that, in decisions under Chapter VI, and under paragraph 3 of Article 52, a party to a dispute shall abstain from voting.

Procedure

Article 28

1. The Security Council shall be so organized as to be able to function continuously. Each member of the Security Council shall for this purpose be represented at all times at the seat of the Organization.
2. The Security Council shall hold periodic meetings at which each of its members may, if it so desires, be represented by a member of the government or by some other specially designated representative.
3. The Security Council may hold meetings at such places other than the seat of the Organization as in its judgment will best facilitate its work.

Article 29

The Security Council may establish such subsidiary organs as it deems necessary for the performance of its functions.

Article 30

The Security Council shall adopt its own rules of procedure, including the method of selecting its President.

Article 31

Any Member of the United Nations which is not a member of the Security Council may participate, without vote, in the discussion of any question brought before the Security Council whenever the latter considers that the interests of that Member are specially affected.

Article 32

Any Member of the United Nations which is not a member of the Security Council or any state which is not a Member of the United Nations, if it is a party to a dispute under consideration by the Security Council, shall be invited to participate, without vote, in the discussion relating to the dispute. The Security Council shall lay down such conditions as it deems just for the participation of a state which is not a Member of the United Nations.

CHAPTER VI. PACIFIC SETTLEMENT OF DISPUTES

Article 33

1. The parties to any dispute, the continuance of which is likely to endanger the maintenance of international peace and security, shall, first of all, seek a solution by negotiation, enquiry, mediation, conciliation, arbitration, judicial settlement, resort to regional agencies or arrangements, or other peaceful means of their own choice.
2. The Security Council shall, when it deems necessary, call upon the parties to settle their dispute by such means.

Article 34

The Security Council may investigate any dispute, or any situation which might lead to international friction or give rise to a dispute, in order to determine whether the continuance of the dispute or situation is likely to endanger the maintenance of international peace and security.

Article 35

1. Any Member of the United Nations may bring any dispute, or any situation of the nature referred to in Article 34, to the attention of the Security Council or of the General Assembly.
2. A state which is not a Member of the United Nations may bring to the attention of the Security Council or of the General Assembly any dispute to which it is a party if it accepts in advance, for the purposes of the dispute, the obligations of pacific settlement provided in the present Charter.
3. The proceedings of the General Assembly in respect of matters brought to its attention under this Article will be subject to the provisions of Articles 11 and 12.

Article 36

1. The Security Council may, at any stage of a dispute of the nature referred to in Article 33 or of a situation of like nature, recommend appropriate procedures or methods of adjustment.
2. The Security Council should take into consideration any procedures for the settlement of the dispute which have already been adopted by the parties.
3. In making recommendations under this Article the Security Council should also take into consideration that legal disputes should as a general rule be referred by the parties to the International Court of Justice in accordance with the provisions of the Statute of the Court.

Article 37

1. Should the parties to a dispute of the nature referred to in Article 33 fail to settle it by the means indicated in that Article, they shall refer it to the Security Council.
2. If the Security Council deems that the continuance of the dispute is in fact likely to endanger the maintenance of international peace and security, it shall decide whether to take action under Article 36 or to recommend such terms of settlement as it may consider appropriate.

Article 38

Without prejudice to the provisions of Articles 33 to 37, the Security Council may, if all the parties to any dispute so request, make recommendations to the parties with a view to a pacific settlement of the dispute.

CHAPTER VII. ACTION WITH RESPECT TO THREATS TO THE PEACE, BREACHES

OF the Peace, and Acts of Aggression

Article 39

The Security Council shall determine the existence of any threat to the peace, breach of the peace, or act of aggression and shall make recommendations, or decide what measures shall be taken in accordance with Articles 41 and 42, to maintain or restore international peace and security.

Article 40

In order to prevent an aggravation of the situation, the Security Council may, before making the recommendations or deciding upon the measures provided for in Article 39, call upon the parties concerned to comply with such provisional measures as it deems necessary or desirable. Such provisional measures shall be without prejudice to the rights, claims, or position of the parties concerned. The Security Council shall duly take account of failure to comply with such provisional measures.

Article 41

The Security Council may decide what measures not involving the use of armed force are to be employed to give effect to its decisions, and it may call upon the Members of the United Nations to apply such measures. These may include complete or partial interruption of economic relations and of rail, sea, air, postal, telegraphic, radio, and other means of communication, and the severance of diplomatic relations.

Article 42

Should the Security Council consider that measures provided for in Article 41 would be inadequate or have proved to be inadequate, it may take such action by air, sea, or land forces as may be necessary to maintain or restore international peace and security. Such action may include demonstrations, blockade, and other operations by air, sea, or land forces of Members of the United Nations.

Article 43

1. All Members of the United Nations, in order to contribute to the maintenance of international peace and security, undertake to make available to the Security Council, on its call and in accordance with a special agreement or agreements, armed forces, assistance, and facilities, including rights of passage, necessary for the purpose of maintaining international peace and security.
2. Such agreement or agreements shall govern the numbers and types of forces, their degree of readiness and general location, and the nature of the facilities and assistance to be provided.
3. The agreement or agreements shall be negotiated as soon as possible on the initiative of the Security Council. They shall be concluded between the Security Council and Members or between the Security Council and groups of Members and shall be subject to ratification by the signatory states in accordance with their respective constitutional processes.

Article 44

When the Security Council has decided to use force it shall, before calling upon a Member not represented on it to provide armed forces in fulfilment of the obligations assumed under Article 43, invite that Member, if the Member so desires, to participate in the decisions of the Security Council concerning the employment of contingents of that Member's armed forces.

Article 45

In order to enable the United Nations to take urgent military measures, Members shall hold immediately available national air-force contingents for combined international enforcement action. The strength and degree of readiness of these contingents and plans for their combined action shall be determined within the limits laid down in the special agreement or agreements referred to in Article 43, by the Security Council with the assistance of the Military Staff Committee.

Article 46

Plans for the application of armed force shall be made by the Security Council with the assistance of the Military Staff Committee.

Article 47

1. There shall be established a Military Staff Committee to advise and assist the Security Council on all questions relating to the Security Council's military requirements for the maintenance of international peace and security, the employment and command of forces placed at its disposal, the regulation of armaments, and possible disarmament.

2. The Military Staff Committee shall consist of the Chiefs of Staff of the permanent members of the Security Council or their representatives. Any Member of the United Nations not permanently represented on the Committee shall be invited by the Committee to be associated with it when the efficient discharge of the Committee's responsibilities requires the participation of that Member in its work.
3. The Military Staff Committee shall be responsible under the Security Council for the strategic direction of any armed forces placed at the disposal of the Security Council. Questions relating to the command of such forces shall be worked out subsequently.
4. The Military Staff Committee, with the authorization of the Security Council and after consultation with appropriate regional agencies, may establish regional subcommittees.

Article 48

1. The action required to carry out the decisions of the Security Council for the maintenance of international peace and security shall be taken by all the Members of the United Nations or by some of them, as the Security Council may determine.
2. Such decisions shall be carried out by the Members of the United Nations directly and through their action in the appropriate international agencies of which they remembers.

Article 49

The Members of the United Nations shall join in affording mutual assistance in carrying out the measures decided upon by the Security Council.

Article 50

If preventive or enforcement measures against any state are taken by the Security Council, any other state, whether a Member of the United Nations or not, which finds itself confronted with special economic problems arising from the carrying out of those measures shall have the right to consult the Security Council with regard to a solution of those problems.

Article 51

Nothing in the present Charter shall impair the inherent right of individual or collective selfdefence if an armed attack occurs against a Member of the United Nations, until the Security Council has taken measures necessary to maintain international peace and security. Measures taken by Members in the exercise of this right of self-defence shall be immediately reported to the Security Council and shall not in any way affect the authority and responsibility of the Security Council under the present Charter to take at any time such action as it deems necessary in order to maintain or restore international peace and security.

CHAPTER VIII. REGIONAL ARRANGEMENTS

Article 52

1. Nothing in the present Charter precludes the existence of regional arrangements or agencies for dealing with such matters relating to the maintenance of international peace and security as are appropriate for regional action provided that such arrangements or agencies and their activities are consistent with the Purposes and Principles of the United Nations.
2. The Members of the United Nations entering into such arrangements or constituting such agencies shall make every effort to achieve pacific settlement of local disputes through such regional arrangements or by such regional agencies before referring them to the Security Council.

3. The Security Council shall encourage the development of pacific settlement of local disputes through such regional arrangements or by such regional agencies either on the initiative of the states concerned or by reference from the Security Council.

4. This Article in no way impairs the application of Articles 34 and 35.

Article 53

1. The Security Council shall, where appropriate, utilize such regional arrangements or agencies for enforcement action under its authority. But no enforcement action shall be taken under regional arrangements or by regional agencies without the authorization of the Security Council, with the exception of measures against any enemy state, as defined in paragraph 2 of this Article, provided for pursuant to Article 107 or in regional arrangements directed against renewal of aggressive policy on the part of any such state, until such time as the Organization may, on request of the Governments concerned, be charged with the responsibility for preventing further aggression by such a state.

2. The term enemy state as used in paragraph 1 of this Article applies to any state which during the Second World War has been an enemy of any signatory of the present Charter.

Article 54

The Security Council shall at all times be kept fully informed of activities undertaken or in contemplation under regional arrangements or by regional agencies for the maintenance of international peace and security.

CHAPTER IX. INTERNATIONAL ECONOMIC AND SOCIAL CO-OPERATION

Article 55

With a view to the creation of conditions of stability and well-being which are necessary for peaceful and friendly relations among nations based on respect for the principle of equal rights and self-determination of peoples, the United Nations shall promote:

a. higher standards of living, full employment, and conditions of economic and social progress and development;

b. solutions of international economic, social, health, and related problems; and international cultural and educational cooperation; and

c. universal respect for, and observance of, human rights and fundamental freedoms for all without distinction as to race, sex, language, or religion.

Article 56

All Members pledge themselves to take joint and separate action in co-operation with the Organization for the achievement of the purposes set forth in Article 55.

Article 57

1. The various specialized agencies, established by intergovernmental agreement and having wide international responsibilities, as defined in their basic instruments, in economic, social, cultural, educational, health, and related fields, shall be brought into relationship with the United Nations in accordance with the provisions of Article 63.

2. Such agencies thus brought into relationship with the United Nations are hereinafter referred to as specialized agencies.</OL>

Article 58

The Organization shall make recommendations for the co-ordination of the policies and activities of the specialized agencies.

Article 59

The Organization shall, where appropriate, initiate negotiations among the states concerned for the creation of any new specialized agencies required for the accomplishment of the purposes set forth in Article 55.

Article 60

Responsibility for the discharge of the functions of the Organization set forth in this Chapter shall be vested in the General Assembly and, under the authority of the General Assembly, in the Economic and Social Council, which shall have for this purpose the powers set forth in Chapter X.

CHAPTER X. THE ECONOMIC AND SOCIAL COUNCIL

Composition

Article 61

1. The Economic and Social Council shall consist of fifty-four Members of the United Nations elected by the General Assembly.
2. Subject to the provisions of paragraph 3, eighteen members of the Economic and Social Council shall be elected each year for a term of three years. A retiring member shall be eligible for immediate re-election.
3. At the first election after the increase in the membership of the Economic and Social Council from twenty-seven to fifty-four members, in addition to the members elected in place of the nine members whose term of office expires at the end of that year, twentyseven additional members shall be elected. Of these twenty-seven additional members, the term of office of nine members so elected shall expire at the end of one year, and of nine other members at the end of two years, in accordance with arrangements made by the General Assembly.
4. Each member of the Economic and Social Council shall have one representative.

Functions and Powers

Article 62

1. The Economic and Social Council may make or initiate studies and reports with respect to international economic, social, cultural, educational, health, and related matters and may make recommendations with respect to any such matters to the General Assembly to the Members of the United Nations, and to the specialized agencies concerned.
2. It may make recommendations for the purpose of promoting respect for, and observance of, human rights and fundamental freedoms for all.
3. It may prepare draft conventions for submission to the General Assembly, with respect to matters falling within its competence.
4. It may call, in accordance with the rules prescribed by the United Nations, international conferences on matters falling within its competence.

Article 63

1. The Economic and Social Council may enter into agreements with any of the agencies referred to in Article 57, defining the terms on which the agency concerned shall be brought into relationship with the United Nations. Such agreements shall be subject to approval by the General Assembly.
2. It may co-ordinate the activities of the specialized agencies through consultation with and recommendations to such agencies and through recommendations to the General Assembly and to the Members of the United Nations.

Article 64

1. The Economic and Social Council may take appropriate steps to obtain regular reports from the specialized agencies. It may make arrangements with the Members of the United Nations and with the specialized agencies to obtain reports on the steps taken to give effect to its own recommendations and to recommendations on matters falling within its competence made by the General Assembly.
2. It may communicate its observations on these reports to the General Assembly.

Article 65

The Economic and Social Council may furnish information to the Security Council and shall assist the Security Council upon its request.

Article 66

1. The Economic and Social Council shall perform such functions as fall within its competence in connexion with the carrying out of the recommendations of the General Assembly.
2. It may, with the approval of the General Assembly, perform services at the request of Members of the United Nations and at the request of specialized agencies.
3. It shall perform such other functions as are specified elsewhere in the present Charter or as may be assigned to it by the General Assembly.

Voting

Article 67

1. Each member of the Economic and Social Council shall have one vote.
2. Decisions of the Economic and Social Council shall be made by a majority of the members present and voting.

Procedure

Article 68

The Economic and Social Council shall set up commissions in economic and social fields and for the promotion of human rights, and such other commissions as may be required for the performance of its functions.

Article 69

The Economic and Social Council shall invite any Member of the United Nations to participate, without vote, in its deliberations on any matter of particular concern to that Member.

Article 70

The Economic and Social Council may make arrangements for representatives of the specialized agencies to participate, without vote, in its deliberations and in those of the commissions established by it, and for its representatives to participate in the deliberations of the specialized agencies.

Article 71

The Economic and Social Council may make suitable arrangements for consultation with non-governmental organizations which are concerned with matters within its competence. Such arrangements may be made with international organizations and, where appropriate, with national organizations after consultation with the Member of the United Nations concerned.

Article 72

1. The Economic and Social Council shall adopt its own rules of procedure, including the method of selecting its President.
2. The Economic and Social Council shall meet as required in accordance with its rules, which shall include provision for the convening of meetings on the request of a majority of its members.

CHAPTER XI. DECLARATION REGARDING NON-SELF-GOVERNING TERRITORIES

Article 73

Members of the United Nations which have or assume responsibilities for the administration of territories whose peoples have not yet attained a full measure of self-government recognize the principle that the interests of the inhabitants of these territories are paramount, and accept as a sacred trust the obligation to promote to the utmost, within the system of international peace and security established by the present Charter, the well-being of the inhabitants of these territories, and, to this end:

a. to ensure, with due respect for the culture of the peoples concerned, their political, economic, social, and educational advancement, their just treatment, and their protection against abuses;
b. to develop self-government, to take due account of the political aspirations of the peoples, and to assist them in the progressive development of their free political institutions, according to the particular circumstances of each territory and its peoples and their varying stages of advancement;
c. to further international peace and security;
d. to promote constructive measures of development, to encourage research, and to cooperate with one another and, when and where appropriate, with specialized international bodies with a view to the practical achievement of the social, economic, and scientific purposes set forth in this Article; and
e. to transmit regularly to the Secretary-General for information purposes, subject to such limitation as security and constitutional considerations may require, statistical and other information of a technical nature relating to economic, social, and educational conditions in the territories for which they are respectively responsible other than those territories to which

CHAPTERS XII AND XIII APPLY.

Article 74
Members of the United Nations also agree that their policy in respect of the territories to which this Chapter applies, no less than in respect of their metropolitan areas, must be based on the general principle of good-neighbourliness, due account being taken of the interests and wellbeing of the rest of the world, in social, economic, and commercial matters.

CHAPTER XII. INTERNATIONAL TRUSTEESHIP SYSTEM

Article 75
The United Nations shall establish under its authority an international trusteeship system for the administration and supervision of such territories as may be placed there under by subsequent individual agreements. These territories are hereinafter referred to as trust territories.

Article 76

The basic objectives of the trusteeship system, in accordance with the Purposes of the United Nations laid down in Article 1 of the present Charter, shall be:

a. to further international peace and security;
b. to promote the political, economic, social, and educational advancement of the inhabitants of the trust territories, and their progressive development towards self-government or independence as may be appropriate to the particular circumstances of each territory and its peoples and the freely expressed wishes of the peoples concerned, and as may be provided by the terms of each trusteeship agreement;
c. to encourage respect for human rights and for fundamental freedoms for all without distinction as to race, sex, language, or religion, and to encourage recognition of the interdependence of the peoples of the world; and
d. to ensure equal treatment in social, economic, and commercial matters for all Members of the United Nations and their nationals, and also equal treatment for the latter in the administration of justice, without prejudice to the attainment of the foregoing objectives and subject to the provisions of Article 80.

Article 77

1. The trusteeship system shall apply to such territories in the following categories as may be placed there under by means of trusteeship agreements:
   a. territories now held under mandate;
   b. territories which may be detached from enemy states as a result of the Second World War; and
   c. territories voluntarily placed under the system by states responsible for their administration.
2. It will be a matter for subsequent agreement as to which territories in the foregoing categories will be brought under the trusteeship system and upon what terms.

Article 78

The trusteeship system shall not apply to territories which have become Members of the United Nations, relationship among which shall be based on respect for the principle of sovereign equality.

Article 79

The terms of trusteeship for each territory to be placed under the trusteeship system, including any alteration or amendment, shall be agreed upon by the states directly concerned, including the mandatory power in the case of territories held under mandate by a Member of the United Nations, and shall be approved as provided for in Articles 83 and 85.

Article 80

1. Except as may be agreed upon in individual trusteeship agreements, made under Articles 77, 79, and 81, placing each territory under the trusteeship system, and until such agreements have been concluded, nothing in this Chapter shall be construed in or of itself to alter in any manner the rights whatsoever of any states or any peoples or the terms of existing international instruments to which Members of the United Nations may respectively be parties.
2. Paragraph 1 of this Article shall not be interpreted as giving grounds for delay or postponement of the negotiation and conclusion of agreements for placing mandated and other territories under the trusteeship system as provided for in Article 77.

Article 81

The trusteeship agreement shall in each case include the terms under which the trust territory will be administered and designate the authority which will exercise the administration of the trust territory. Such authority, hereinafter called the administering authority, may be one or more states or the Organization itself.

Article 82

There may be designated, in any trusteeship agreement, a strategic area or areas which may include part or all of the trust territory to which the agreement applies, without prejudice to any special agreement or agreements made under Article 43.

Article 83

1. All functions of the United Nations relating to strategic areas, including the approval of the terms of the trusteeship agreements and of their alteration or amendment shall be exercised by the Security Council.
2. The basic objectives set forth in Article 76 shall be applicable to the people of each strategic area.
3. The Security Council shall, subject to the provisions of the trusteeship agreements and without prejudice to security considerations, avail itself of the assistance of the Trusteeship Council to perform those functions of the United Nations under the trusteeship system relating to political, economic, social, and educational matters in the strategic areas.

Article 84

It shall be the duty of the administering authority to ensure that the trust territory shall play its part in the maintenance of international peace and security. To this end the administering authority may make use of volunteer forces, facilities, and assistance from the trust territory in carrying out the obligations towards the Security Council undertaken in this regard by the administering authority, as well as for local defence and the maintenance of law and order within the trust territory.

Article 85

4. The functions of the United Nations with regard to trusteeship agreements for all areas not designated as strategic, including the approval of the terms of the trusteeship agreements and of their alteration or amendment, shall be exercised by the General Assembly.
5. The Trusteeship Council, operating under the authority of the General Assembly shall assist the General Assembly in carrying out these functions.

CHAPTER XIII. THE TRUSTEESHIP COUNCIL

Composition

Article 86

1. The Trusteeship Council shall consist of the following Members of the United Nations:
   a. those Members administering trust territories;
   b. such of those Members mentioned by name in Article 23 as are not administering trust territories; and
   c. as many other Members elected for three-year terms by the General Assembly as may be necessary to ensure that the total number of members of the Trusteeship Council is equally divided between those Members of the United Nations which administer trust territories and those which do not.
2. Each member of the Trusteeship Council shall designate one specially qualified person to represent it therein.

Functions and Powers

Article 87

The General Assembly and, under its authority, the Trusteeship Council, in carrying out their functions, may:

a. consider reports submitted by the administering authority;
b. accept petitions and examine them in consultation with the administering authority;
c. provide for periodic visits to the respective trust territories at times agreed upon with the administering authority; and
d. take these and other actions in conformity with the terms of the trusteeship agreements.

Article 88

The Trusteeship Council shall formulate a questionnaire on the political, economic, social, and educational advancement of the inhabitants of each trust territory, and the administering authority for each trust territory within the competence of the General Assembly shall make an annual report to the General Assembly upon the basis of such questionnaire.

Voting

Article 89

1. Each member of the Trusteeship Council shall have one vote.
2. Decisions of the Trusteeship Council shall be made by a majority of the members present and voting.

Procedure

Article 90

1. The Trusteeship Council shall adopt its own rules of procedure, including the method of selecting its President.
2. The Trusteeship Council shall meet as required in accordance with its rules, which shall include provision for the convening of meetings on the request of a majority of its members.

Article 91

The Trusteeship Council shall, when appropriate, avail itself of the assistance of the Economic and Social Council and of the specialized agencies in regard to matters with which they are respectively concerned.

CHAPTER XIV. THE INTERNATIONAL COURT OF JUSTICE

Article 92

The International Court of Justice shall be the principal judicial organ of the United Nations. It shall function in accordance with the annexed Statute, which is based upon the Statute of the Permanent Court of International Justice and forms an integral part of the present Charter.

Article 93

1. All Members of the United Nations are *ipso facto* parties to the Statute of the International Court of Justice.
2. A state which is not a Member of the United Nations may become a party to the Statute of the International Court of Justice on conditions to be determined in each case by the General Assembly upon the recommendation of the Security Council.

Article 94

1. Each Member of the United Nations undertakes to comply with the decision of the International Court of Justice in any case to which it is a party.
2. If any party to a case fails to perform the obligations incumbent upon it under a judgment rendered by the Court, the other party may have recourse to the Security Council, which may, if it deems necessary, make recommendations or decide upon measures to be taken to give effect to the judgment.

Article 95

Nothing in the present Charter shall prevent Members of the United Nations from entrusting the solution of their differences to other tribunals by virtue of agreements already in existence or which may be concluded in the future.

Article 96

1. The General Assembly or the Security Council may request the International Court of Justice to give an advisory opinion on any legal question.
2. Other organs of the United Nations and specialized agencies, which may at any time be so authorized by the General Assembly, may also request advisory opinions of the Court on legal questions arising within the scope of their activities.

CHAPTER XV. THE SECRETARIAT

Article 97
The Secretariat shall comprise a Secretary-General and such staff as the Organization may require. The Secretary-General shall be appointed by the General Assembly upon the recommendation of the Security Council. He shall be the chief administrative officer of the Organization.

Article 98
The Secretary-General shall act in that capacity in all meetings of the General Assembly, of the Security Council, of the Economic and Social Council, and of the Trusteeship Council, and shall perform such other functions as are entrusted to him by these organs. The Secretary- General shall make an annual report to the General Assembly on the work of the Organization.

Article 99
The Secretary-General may bring to the attention of the Security Council any matter which in his opinion may threaten the maintenance of international peace and security.

Article 100
1. In the performance of their duties the Secretary-General and the staff shall not seek or receive instructions from any government or from any other authority external to the Organization. They shall refrain from any action which might reflect on their position as international officials responsible only to the Organization.
2. Each Member of the United Nations undertakes to respect the exclusively international character of the responsibilities of the Secretary-General and the staff and not to seek to influence them in the discharge of their responsibilities.

Article 101
1. The staff shall be appointed by the Secretary-General under regulations established by the General Assembly.
2. Appropriate staffs shall be permanently assigned to the Economic and Social Council, the Trusteeship Council, and, as required, to other organs of the United Nations. These staffs shall form a part of the Secretariat.
3. The paramount consideration in the employment of the staff and in the determination of the conditions of service shall be the necessity of securing the highest standards of efficiency, competence, and integrity. Due regard shall be paid to the importance of recruiting the staff on as wide a geographical basis as possible.

CHAPTER XVI. MISCELLANEOUS PROVISIONS

Article 102
1. Every treaty and every international agreement entered into by any Member of the United Nations after the present Charter comes into force shall as soon as possible be registered with the Secretariat and published by it.
2. No party to any such treaty or international agreement which has not been registered in accordance with the provisions of paragraph 1 of this Article may invoke that treaty or agreement before any organ of the United Nations.

Article 103

In the event of a conflict between the obligations of the Members of the United Nations under the present Charter and their obligations under any other international agreement, their obligations under the present Charter shall prevail.

Article 104

The Organization shall enjoy in the territory of each of its Members such legal capacity as may be necessary for the exercise of its functions and the fulfilment of its purposes.

Article 105

1. The Organization shall enjoy in the territory of each of its Members such privileges and immunities as are necessary for the fulfilment of its purposes.
2. Representatives of the Members of the United Nations and officials of the Organization shall similarly enjoy such privileges and immunities as are necessary for the independent exercise of their functions in connexion with the Organization.
3. The General Assembly may make recommendations with a view to determining the details of the application of paragraphs 1 and 2 of this Article or may propose conventions to the Members of the United Nations for this purpose.

CHAPTER XVII. TRANSITIONAL SECURITY ARRANGEMENTS

Article 106

Pending the coming into force of such special agreements referred to in Article 43 as in the opinion of the Security Council enable it to begin the exercise of its responsibilities under Article 42, the parties to the Four-Nation Declaration, signed at Moscow, 30 October 1943, and France, shall, in accordance with the provisions of paragraph 5 of that Declaration, consult with one another and as occasion requires with other Members of the United Nations with a view to such joint action on behalf of the Organization as may be necessary for the purpose of maintaining international peace and security.

Article 107

Nothing in the present Charter shall invalidate or preclude action, in relation to any state which during the Second World War has been an enemy of any signatory to the present Charter, taken or authorized as a result of that war by the Governments having responsibility for such action.

CHAPTER XVIII. AMENDMENTS

Article 108

Amendments to the present Charter shall come into force for all Members of the United Nations when they have been adopted by a vote of two thirds of the members of the General Assembly and ratified in accordance with their respective constitutional processes by two thirds of the Members of the United Nations, including all the permanent members of the Security Council.

Article 109

1. A General Conference of the Members of the United Nations for the purpose of reviewing the present Charter may be held at a date and place to be fixed by a twothirds vote of the mem-

bers of the General Assembly and by a vote of any nine members of the Security Council. Each Member of the United Nations shall have one vote in the conference.

2. Any alteration of the present Charter recommended by a two-thirds vote of the conference shall take effect when ratified in accordance with their respective constitutional processes by two thirds of the Members of the United Nations including all the permanent members of the Security Council.

3. If such a conference has not been held before the tenth annual session of the General Assembly following the coming into force of the present Charter, the proposal to call such a conference shall be placed on the agenda of that session of the General Assembly, and the conference shall be held if so decided by a majority vote of the members of the General Assembly and by a vote of any seven members of the Security Council.

CHAPTER XIX. RATIFICATION AND SIGNATURE

Article 110

1. The present Charter shall be ratified by the signatory states in accordance with their respective constitutional processes.

2. The ratifications shall be deposited with the Government of the United States of America, which shall notify all the signatory states of each deposit as well as the Secretary-General of the Organization when he has been appointed.

3. The present Charter shall come into force upon the deposit of ratifications by the Republic of China, France, the Union of Soviet Socialist Republics, the United Kingdom of Great Britain and Northern Ireland, and the United States of America, and by a majority of the other signatory states. A protocol of the ratifications deposited shall thereupon be drawn up by the Government of the United States of America which shall communicate copies thereof to all the signatory states.

4. The states signatory to the present Charter which ratify it after it has come into force will become original Members of the United Nations on the date of the deposit of their respective ratifications.

Article 111

The present Charter, of which the Chinese, French, Russian, English, and Spanish texts are equally authentic, shall remain deposited in the archives of the Government of the United States of America. Duly certified copies thereof shall be transmitted by that Government to the Governments of the other signatory states.

IN FAITH WHEREOF the representatives of the Governments of the United Nations have signed the present Charter.

DONE at the city of San Francisco the twenty-sixth day of June, one thousand nine hundred and forty-five.

Statute of the International Court of Justice

Article 1

The International Court of Justice established by the Charter of the United Nations as the principal judicial organ of the United Nations shall be constituted and shall function in accordance with the provisions of the present Statute.

CHAPTER I
ORGANIZATION OF THE COURT

Article 2

The Court shall be composed of a body of independent judges, elected regardless of their nationality from among persons of high moral character, who possess the qualifications required in their respective countries for appointment to the highest judicial offices, or are jurisconsults of recognized competence in international law.

Article 3

1. The Court shall consist of fifteen members, no two of whom may be nationals of the same state.
2. A person who for the purposes of membership in the Court could be regarded as a national of more than one state shall be deemed to be a national of the one in which he ordinarily exercises civil and political rights.

Article 4

1. The members of the Court shall be elected by the General Assembly and by the Security Council from a list of persons nominated by the national groups in the Permanent Court of Arbitration, in accordance with the following provisions.
2. In the case of Members of the United Nations not represented in the Permanent Court of Arbitration, candidates shall be nominated by national groups appointed for this purpose by their governments under the same conditions as those prescribed for members of the Permanent Court of Arbitration by Article 44 of the Convention of The Hague of 1907 for the pacific settlement of international disputes.
3. The conditions under which a state which is a party to the present Statute but is not a Member of the United Nations may participate in electing the members of the Court shall, in the absence of a special agreement, be laid down by the General Assembly upon recommendation of the Security Council.

Article 5

1. At least three months before the date of the election, the Secretary-General of the United Nations shall address a written request to the members of the Permanent Court of Arbitration belonging to the states which are parties to the present Statute, and to the members of the national groups appointed under Article 4, paragraph 2, inviting them to undertake, within a given time, by national groups, the nomination of persons in a position to accept the duties of a member of the Court.
2. No group may nominate more than four persons, not more than two of whom shall be of their own nationality. In no case may the number of candidates nominated by a group be more than double the number of seats to be filled.

Article 6

Before making these nominations, each national group is recommended to consult its highest court of justice, its legal faculties and schools of law, and its national academies and national sections of international academies devoted to the study of law.

Article 7

1. The Secretary-General shall prepare a list in alphabetical order of all the persons thus nominated. Save as provided in Article 12, paragraph 2, these shall be the only persons eligible.
2. The Secretary-General shall submit this list to the General Assembly and to the Security Council.

Article 8

The General Assembly and the Security Council shall proceed independently of one another to elect the members of the Court.

Article 9

At every election, the electors shall bear in mind not only that the persons to be elected should individually possess the qualifications required, but also that in the body as a whole the representation of the main forms of civilization and of the principal legal systems of the world should be assured.

Article 10

1. Those candidates who obtain an absolute majority of votes in the General Assembly and in the Security Council shall be considered as elected.
2. Any vote of the Security Council, whether for the election of judges or for the appointment of members of the conference envisaged in Article 12, shall be taken without any distinction between permanent and non-permanent members of the Security Council.
3. In the event of more than one national of the same state obtaining an absolute majority of the votes both of the General Assembly and of the Security Council, the eldest of these only shall be considered as elected.

Article 11

If, after the first meeting held for the purpose of the election, one or more seats remain to be filled, a second and, if necessary, a third meeting shall take place.

Article 12

1. If, after the third meeting, one or more seats still remain unfilled, a joint conference consisting of six members, three appointed by the General Assembly and three by the Security Council, may be formed at any time at the request of either the General Assembly or the Security Council, for the purpose of choosing by the vote of an absolute majority one name for each seat still vacant, to submit to the General Assembly and the Security Council for their respective acceptance.

2. If the joint conference is unanimously agreed upon any person who fulfills the required conditions, he may be included in its list, even though he was not included in the list of nominations referred to in Article 7.

3. If the joint conference is satisfied that it will not be successful in procuring an election, those members of the Court who have already been elected shall, within a period to be fixed by the Security Council, proceed to fill the vacant seats by selection from among those candidates who have obtained votes either in the General Assembly or in the Security Council.

4. In the event of an equality of votes among the judges, the eldest judge shall have a casting vote.

Article 13

1. The members of the Court shall be elected for nine years and may be re-elected; provided, however, that of the judges elected at the first election, the terms of five judges shall expire at the end of three years and the terms of five more judges shall expire at the end of six years.

2. The judges whose terms are to expire at the end of the above-mentioned initial periods of three and six years shall be chosen by lot to be drawn by the Secretary-General immediately after the first election has been completed.

3. The members of the Court shall continue to discharge their duties until their places have been filled. Though replaced, they shall finish any cases which they may have begun.

4. In the case of the resignation of a member of the Court, the resignation shall be addressed to the President of the Court for transmission to the Secretary-General. This last notification makes the place vacant.

Article 14

Vacancies shall be filled by the same method as that laid down for the first election subject to the following provision: the Secretary-General shall, within one month of the occurrence of the vacancy, proceed to issue the invitations provided for in Article 5, and the date of the election shall be fixed by the Security Council.

Article 15

A member of the Court elected to replace a member whose term of office has not expired shall hold office for the remainder of his predecessor's term.

Article 16

1. No member of the Court may exercise any political or administrative function, or engage in any other occupation of a professional nature.

2. Any doubt on this point shall be settled by the decision of the Court.

Article 17

1. No member of the Court may act as agent, counsel, or advocate in any case.

2. No member may participate in the decision of any case in which he has previously taken part as agent, counsel, or advocate for one of the parties, or as a member of a national or international court, or of a commission of enquiry, or in any other capacity.
3. Any doubt on this point shall be settled by the decision of the Court.

Article 18
1. No member of the Court can be dismissed unless, in the unanimous opinion of the other members, he has ceased to fulfill the required conditions.
2. Formal notification thereof shall be made to the Secretary-General by the Registrar.
3. This notification makes the place vacant.

Article 19
The members of the Court, when engaged on the business of the Court, shall enjoy diplomatic privileges and immunities.

Article 20
Every member of the Court shall, before taking up his duties, make a solemn declaration in open court that he will exercise his powers impartially and conscientiously.

Article 21
1. The Court shall elect its President and Vice-President for three years; they may be re-elected.
2. The Court shall appoint its Registrar and may provide for the appointment of such other officers as may be necessary.

Article 22
1. The seat of the Court shall be established at The Hague. This, however, shall not prevent the Court from sitting and exercising its functions elsewhere whenever the Court considers it desirable.
2. The President and the Registrar shall reside at the seat of the Court.

Article 23
1. The Court shall remain permanently in session, except during the judicial vacations, the dates and duration of which shall be fixed by the Court.
2. Members of the Court are entitled to periodic leave, the dates and duration of which shall be fixed by the Court, having in mind the distance between The Hague and the home of each judge.
3. Members of the Court shall be bound, unless they are on leave or prevented from attending by illness or other serious reasons duly explained to the President, to hold themselves permanently at the disposal of the Court.

Article 24
1. If, for some special reason, a member of the Court considers that he should not take part in the decision of a particular case, he shall so inform the President.
2. If the President considers that for some special reason one of the members of the Court should not sit in a particular case, he shall give him notice accordingly.
3. If in any such case the member Court and the President disagree, the matter shall be settled by the decision of the Court.

Article 25

1. The full Court shall sit except when it is expressly provided otherwise in the present Statute.
2. Subject to the condition that the number of judges available to constitute the Court is not thereby reduced below eleven, the Rules of the Court may provide for allowing one or more judges, according to circumstances and in rotation, to be dispensed from sitting.
3. A quorum of nine judges shall suffice to constitute the Court.

Article 26

1. The Court may from time to time form one or more chambers, composed of three or more judges as the Court may determine, for dealing with particular categories of cases; for example, labour cases and cases relating to transit and communications.
2. The Court may at any time form a chamber for dealing with a particular case. The number of judges to constitute such a chamber shall be determined by the Court with the approval of the parties.
3. Cases shall be heard and determined by the chambers provided for in this article if the parties so request.

Article 27

A judgment given by any of the chambers provided for in Articles 26 and 29 shall be considered as rendered by the Court.

Article 28

The chambers provided for in Articles 26 and 29 may, with the consent of the parties, sit and exercise their functions elsewhere than at The Hague.

Article 29

With a view to the speedy dispatch of business, the Court shall form annually a chamber composed of five judges which, at the request of the parties, may hear and determine cases by summary procedure. In addition, two judges shall be selected for the purpose of replacing judges who find it impossible to sit.

Article 30

1. The Court shall frame rules for carrying out its functions. In particular, it shall lay down rules of procedure.
2. The Rules of the Court may provide for assessors to sit with the Court or with any of its chambers, without the right to vote.

Article 31

1. Judges of the nationality of each of the parties shall retain their right to sit in the case before the Court.
2. If the Court includes upon the Bench a judge of the nationality of one of the parties, any other party may choose a person to sit as judge. Such person shall be chosen preferably from among those persons who have been nominated as candidates as provided in Articles 4 and 5.
3. If the Court includes upon the Bench no judge of the nationality of the parties, each of these parties may proceed to choose a judge as provided in paragraph 2 of this Article.
4. The provisions of this Article shall apply to the case of Articles 26 and 29. In such cases, the President shall request one or, if necessary, two of the members of the Court forming the

chamber to give place to the members of the Court of the nationality of the parties concerned, and, failing such, or if they are unable to be present, to the judges specially chosen by the parties.

5. Should there be several parties in the same interest, they shall, for the purpose of the preceding provisions, be reckoned as one party only. Any doubt upon this point shall be settled by the decision of the Court.

6. Judges chosen as laid down in paragraphs 2, 3, and 4 of this Article shall fulfil the conditions required by Articles 2, 17 (paragraph 2), 20, and 24 of the present Statute. They shall take part in the decision on terms of complete equality with their colleagues.

Article 32

1. Each member of the Court shall receive an annual salary.
2. The President shall receive a special annual allowance.
3. The Vice-President shall receive a special allowance for every day on which he acts as President.
4. The judges chosen under Article 31, other than members of the Court, shall receive compensation for each day on which they exercise their functions.
5. These salaries, allowances, and compensation shall be fixed by the General Assembly. They may not be decreased during the term of office.
6. The salary of the Registrar shall be fixed by the General Assembly on the proposal of the Court.
7. Regulations made by the General Assembly shall fix the conditions under which retirement pensions may be given to members of the Court and to the Registrar, and the conditions under which members of the Court and the Registrar shall have their travelling expenses refunded.
8. The above salaries, allowances, and compensation shall be free of all taxation.

Article 33

The expenses of the Court shall be borne by the United Nations in such a manner as shall be decided by the General Assembly.

CHAPTER II
COMPETENCE OF THE COURT

Article 34

1. Only states may be parties in cases before the Court.
2. The Court, subject to and in conformity with its Rules, may request of public international organizations information relevant to cases before it, and shall receive such information presented by such organizations on their own initiative.
3. Whenever the construction of the constituent instrument of a public international organization or of an international convention adopted thereunder is in question in a case before the Court, the Registrar shall so notify the public international organization concerned and shall communicate to it copies of all the written proceedings.

Article 35

1. The Court shall be open to the states parties to the present Statute.

2. The conditions under which the Court shall be open to other states shall, subject to the special provisions contained in treaties in force, be laid down by the Security Council, but in no case shall such conditions place the parties in a position of inequality before the Court.
3. When a state which is not a Member of the United Nations is a party to a case, the Court shall fix the amount which that party is to contribute towards the expenses of the Court. This provision shall not apply if such state is bearing a share of the expenses of the Court

Article 36

1. The jurisdiction of the Court comprises all cases which the parties refer to it and all matters specially provided for in the Charter of the United Nations or in treaties and conventions in force.
2. The states parties to the present Statute may at any time declare that they recognize as compulsory ipso facto and without special agreement, in relation to any other state accepting the same obligation, the jurisdiction of the Court in all legal disputes concerning:
   a. the interpretation of a treaty;
   b. any question of international law;
   c. the existence of any fact which, if established, would constitute a breach of an international obligation;
   d. the nature or extent of the reparation to be made for the breach of an international obligation.
3. The declarations referred to above may be made unconditionally or on condition of reciprocity on the part of several or certain states, or for a certain time.
4. Such declarations shall be deposited with the Secretary-General of the United Nations, who shall transmit copies thereof to the parties to the Statute and to the Registrar of the Court.
5. Declarations made under Article 36 of the Statute of the Permanent Court of International Justice and which are still in force shall be deemed, as between the parties to the present Statute, to be acceptances of the compulsory jurisdiction of the International Court of Justice for the period which they still have to run and in accordance with their terms.
6. In the event of a dispute as to whether the Court has jurisdiction, the matter shall be settled by the decision of the Court.

Article 37

Whenever a treaty or convention in force provides for reference of a matter to a tribunal to have been instituted by the League of Nations, or to the Permanent Court of International Justice, the matter shall, as between the parties to the present Statute, be referred to the International Court of Justice.

Article 38

1. The Court, whose function is to decide in accordance with international law such disputes as are submitted to it, shall apply:
   a. international conventions, whether general or particular, establishing rules expressly recognized by the contesting states;
   b. international custom, as evidence of a general practice accepted as law;
   c. the general principles of law recognized by civilized nations;
   d. subject to the provisions of Article 59, judicial decisions and the teachings of the most highly qualified publicists of the various nations, as subsidiary means for the determination of rules of law.
2. This provision shall not prejudice the power of the Court to decide a case ex aequo et bono, if the parties agree thereto.

CHAPTER III
PROCEDURE

Article 39

1. The official languages of the Court shall be French and English. If the parties agree that the case shall be conducted in French, the judgment shall be delivered in French. If the parties agree that the case shall be conducted in English, the judgment shall be delivered in English.
2. In the absence of an agreement as to which language shall be employed, each party may, in the pleadings, use the language which it prefers; the decision of the Court shall be given in French and English. In this case the Court shall at the same time determine which of the two texts shall be considered as authoritative.
3. The Court shall, at the request of any party, authorize a language other than French or English to be used by that party.

Article 40

1. Cases are brought before the Court, as the case may be, either by the notification of the special agreement or by a written application addressed to the Registrar. In either case the subject of the dispute and the parties shall be indicated.
2. The Registrar shall forthwith communicate the application to all concerned.
3. He shall also notify the Members of the United Nations through the Secretary-General, and also any other states entitled to appear before the Court.

Article 41

1. The Court shall have the power to indicate, if it considers that circumstances so require, any provisional measures which ought to be taken to preserve the respective rights of either party.
2. Pending the final decision, notice of the measures suggested shall forthwith be given to the parties and to the Security Council

Article 42

1. The parties shall be represented by agents.
2. They may have the assistance of counsel or advocates before the Court.
3. The agents, counsel, and advocates of parties before the Court shall enjoy the privileges and immunities necessary to the independent exercise of their duties.

Article 43

1. The procedure shall consist of two parts: written and oral.
2. The written proceedings shall consist of the communication to the Court and to the parties of memorials, counter-memorials and, if necessary, replies; also all papers and documents in support.
3. These communications shall be made through the Registrar, in the order and within the time fixed by the Court.
4. A certified copy of every document produced by one party shall be communicated to the other party.
5. The oral proceedings shall consist of the hearing by the Court of witnesses, experts, agents, counsel, and advocates.

Article 44

1. For the service of all notices upon persons other than the agents, counsel, and advocates, the Court shall apply direct to the government of the state upon whose territory the notice has to be served.

2. The same provision shall apply whenever steps are to be taken to procure evidence on the spot.

Article 45

The hearing shall be under the control of the President or, if he is unable to preside, of the Vice-President; if neither is able to preside, the senior judge present shall preside.

Article 46

The hearing in Court shall be public, unless the Court shall decide otherwise, or unless the parties demand that the public be not admitted .

Article 47

1. Minutes shall be made at each hearing and signed by the Registrar and the President.
2. These minutes alone shall be authentic.

Article 48

The Court shall make orders for the conduct of the case, shall decide the form and time in which each party must conclude its arguments, and make all arrangements connected with the taking of evidence.

Article 49

The Court may, even before the hearing begins, call upon the agents to produce any document or to supply any explanations. Formal note shall be taken of any refusal.

Article 50

The Court may, at any time, entrust any individual, body, bureau, commission, or other organization that it may select, with the task of carrying out an enquiry or giving an expert opinion.

Article 51

During the hearing any relevant questions are to be put to the witnesses and experts under the conditions laid down by the Court in the rules of procedure referred to in Article 30.

Article 52

After the Court has received the proofs and evidence within the time specified for the purpose, it may refuse to accept any further oral or written evidence that one party may desire to present unless the other side consents.

Article 53

1. Whenever one of the parties does not appear before the Court, or fails to defend its case, the other party may call upon the Court to decide in favour of its claim.
2. The Court must, before doing so, satisfy itself, not only that it has jurisdiction in accordance with Articles 36 and 37, but also that the claim is well founded in fact and law.

Article 54

1. When, subject to the control of the Court, the agents, counsel, and advocates have completed their presentation of the case, the President shall declare the hearing closed.
2. The Court shall withdraw to consider the judgment.
3. The deliberations of the Court shall take place in private and remain secret.

Article 55

1. All questions shall be decided by a majority of the judges present.
2. In the event of an equality of votes, the President or the judge who acts in his place shall have a casting vote.

Article 56

1. The judgment shall state the reasons on which it is based.
2. It shall contain the names of the judges who have taken part in the decision.

Article 57

If the judgment does not represent in whole or in part the unanimous opinion of the judges, any judge shall be entitled to deliver a separate opinion.

Article 58

The judgment shall be signed by the President and by the Registrar. It shall be read in open court, due notice having been given to the agents.

Article 59

The decision of the Court has no binding force except between the parties and in respect of that particular case.

Article 60

The judgment is final and without appeal. In the event of dispute as to the meaning or scope of the judgment, the Court shall construe it upon the request of any party.

Article 61

1. An application for revision of a judgment may be made only when it is based upon the discovery of some fact of such a nature as to be a decisive factor, which fact was, when the judgment was given, unknown to the Court and also to the party claiming revision, always provided that such ignorance was not due to negligence.
2. The proceedings for revision shall be opened by a judgment of the Court expressly recording the existence of the new fact, recognizing that it has such a character as to lay the case open to revision, and declaring the application admissible on this ground.
3. The Court may require previous compliance with the terms of the judgment before it admits proceedings in revision.
4. The application for revision must be made at latest within six months of the discovery of the new fact.
5. No application for revision may be made after the lapse of ten years from the date of the judgment.

Article 62

1. Should a state consider that it has an interest of a legal nature which may be affected by the decision in the case, it may submit a request to the Court to be permitted to intervene.
2. It shall be for the Court to decide upon this request.

Article 63

1. Whenever the construction of a convention to which states other than those concerned in the case are parties is in question, the Registrar shall notify all such states forthwith.

2. Every state so notified has the right to intervene in the proceedings; but if it uses this right, the construction given by the judgment will be equally binding upon it.

Article 64
Unless otherwise decided by the Court, each party shall bear its own costs.

CHAPTER IV
ADVISORY OPINIONS

Article 65
1. The Court may give an advisory opinion on any legal question at the request of whatever body may be authorized by or in accordance with the Charter of the United Nations to make such a request.
2. Questions upon which the advisory opinion of the Court is asked shall be laid before the Court by means of a written request containing an exact statement of the question upon which an opinion is required, and accompanied by all documents likely to throw light upon the question.

Article 66
1. The Registrar shall forthwith give notice of the request for an advisory opinion to all states entitled to appear before the Court.
2. The Registrar shall also, by means of a special and direct communication, notify any state entitled to appear before the Court or international organization considered by the Court, or, should it not be sitting, by the President, as likely to be able to furnish information on the question, that the Court will be prepared to receive, within a time limit to be fixed by the President, written statements, or to hear, at a public sitting to be held for the purpose, oral statements relating to the question.
3. Should any such state entitled to appear before the Court have failed to receive the special communication referred to in paragraph 2 of this Article, such state may express a desire to submit a written statement or to be heard; and the Court will decide.
4. States and organizations having presented written or oral statements or both shall be permitted to comment on the statements made by other states or organizations in the form, to the extent, and within the time limits which the Court, or, should it not be sitting, the President, shall decide in each particular case. Accordingly, the Registrar shall in due time communicate any such written statements to states and organizations having submitted similar statements.

Article 67
The Court shall deliver its advisory opinions in open court, notice having been given to the Secretary-General and to the representatives of Members of the United Nations, of other states and of international organizations immediately concerned.

Article 68
In the exercise of its advisory functions the Court shall further be guided by the provisions of the present Statute which apply in contentious cases to the extent to which it recognizes them to be applicable.

CHAPTER V
AMENDMENT

Article 69
Amendments to the present Statute shall be effected by the same procedure as is provided by the Charter of the United Nations for amendments to that Charter, subject however to any provisions which the General Assembly upon recommendation of the Security Council may adopt concerning the participation of states which are parties to the present Statute but are not Members of the United Nations.

Article 70
The Court shall have power to propose such amendments to the present Statute as it may deem necessary, through written communications to the Secretary-General, for consideration in conformity with the provisions of Article 69.

The North Atlantic Treaty

The Parties to this Treaty reaffirm their faith in the purposes and principles of the Charter of the United Nations and their desire to live in peace with all peoples and all governments. They are determined to safeguard the freedom, common heritage and civilisation of their peoples, founded on the principles of democracy, individual liberty and the rule of law. They seek to promote stability and well-being in the North Atlantic area. They are resolved to unite their efforts for collective defence and for the preservation of peace and security. They therefore agree to this North Atlantic Treaty :

ARTICLE 1

The Parties undertake, as set forth in the Charter of the United Nations, to settle any international dispute in which they may be involved by peaceful means in such a manner that international peace and security and justice are not endangered, and to refrain in their international relations from the threat or use of force in any manner inconsistent with the purposes of the United Nations.

ARTICLE 2

The Parties will contribute toward the further development of peaceful and friendly international relations by strengthening their free institutions, by bringing about a better understanding of the principles upon which these institutions are founded, and by promoting conditions of stability and well-being. They will seek to eliminate conflict in their international economic policies and will encourage economic collaboration between any or all of them.

ARTICLE 3

In order more effectively to achieve the objectives of this Treaty, the Parties, separately and jointly, by means of continuous and effective self-help and mutual aid, will maintain and develop their individual and collective capacity to resist armed attack.

ARTICLE 4

The Parties will consult together whenever, in the opinion of any of them, the territorial integrity, political independence or security of any of the Parties is threatened.

Washington D.C. — 4 April 1949

ARTICLE 5

The Parties agree that an armed attack against one or more of them in Europe or North America shall be considered an attack against them all and consequently they agree that, if such an armed attack occurs, each of them, in exercise of the right of individual or collective self-defence recognised by Article 51 of the Charter of the United Nations, will assist the Party or Parties so attacked by taking forthwith, individually and in concert with the other Parties, such action as it deems necessary, including the use of armed force, to restore and maintain the security of the North Atlantic area.

Any such armed attack and all measures taken as a result thereof shall immediately be reported to the Security Council. Such measures shall be terminated when the Security Council has taken the measures necessary to restore and maintain international peace and security .

ARTICLE 6[1]

For the purpose of Article 5, an armed attack on one or more of the Parties is deemed to include an armed attack:

- on the territory of any of the Parties in Europe or North America, on the Algerian Departments of France[2], on the territory of or on the Islands under the jurisdiction of any of the Parties in the North Atlantic area north of the Tropic of Cancer;
- on the forces, vessels, or aircraft of any of the Parties, when in or over these territories or any other area in Europe in which occupation forces of any of the Parties were stationed on the date when the Treaty entered into force or the Mediterranean Sea or the North Atlantic area north of the Tropic of Cancer.

ARTICLE 7

This Treaty does not affect, and shall not be interpreted as affecting in any way the rights and obligations under the Charter of the Parties which are members of the United Nations, or the primary responsibility of the Security Council for the maintenance of international peace and security.

ARTICLE 8

Each Party declares that none of the international engagements now in force between it and any other of the Parties or any third State is in conflict with the provisions of this Treaty, and undertakes not to enter into any international engagement in conflict with this Treaty.

ARTICLE 9

The Parties hereby establish a Council, on which each of them shall be represented, to consider matters concerning the implementation of this Treaty. The Council shall be so organised as to be able to meet promptly at any time. The Council shall set up such subsidiary bodies as may be necessary; in particular it shall establish immediately a defence committee which shall recommend measures for the implementation of Articles 3 and 5.

ARTICLE 10

The Parties may, by unanimous agreement, invite any other European State in a position to further the principles of this Treaty and to contribute to the security of the North Atlantic area to accede to this Treaty. Any State so invited may become a Party to the Treaty by depositing its instrument of accession with the Government of the United States of America. The Government of the United States of America will inform each of the Parties of the deposit of each such instrument of accession.

ARTICLE 11

This Treaty shall be ratified and its provisions carried out by the Parties in accordance with their respective constitutional processes. The instruments of ratification shall be deposited as soon as possible with the Government of the United States of America, which will notify all the other signatories of each deposit. The Treaty shall enter into force between the States which have ratified it as soon as the ratifications of the majority of the signatories, including the ratifications of Belgium, Canada, France, Luxembourg, the Netherlands, the United Kingdom and the United States, have been deposited and shall come into effect with respect to other States on the date of the deposit of their ratifications.[3]

ARTICLE 12

After the Treaty has been in force for ten years, or at any time thereafter, the Parties shall, if any of them so requests, consult together for the purpose of reviewing the Treaty, having regard for the factors then affecting peace and security in the North Atlantic area, including the development of universal as well as regional arrangements under the Charter of the United Nations for the maintenance of international peace and security.

ARTICLE 13

After the Treaty has been in force for twenty years, any Party may cease to be a Party one year after its notice of denunciation has been given to the Government of the United States of America, which will inform the Governments of the other Parties of the deposit of each notice of denunciation.

ARTICLE 14

This Treaty, of which the English and French texts are equally authentic, shall be deposited in the archives of the Government of the United States of America. Duly certified copies will be transmitted by that Government to the Governments of other signatories.

Notes

1. The definition of the territories to which Article 5 applies was revised by Article 2 of the Protocol to the North Atlantic Treaty on the accession of Greece and Turkey signed on 22 October 1951.

2. On January 16, 1963, the North Atlantic Council noted that insofar as the former Algerian Departments of France were concerned, the relevant clauses of this Treaty had become inapplicable as from July 3, 1962.

3. The Treaty came into force on 24 August 1949, after the deposition of the ratifications of all signatory states.